PRACTICING RELIGION IN THE AGE OF THE MEDIA

PRACTICING RELIGION IN THE AGE OF THE MEDIA

Explorations in Media, Religion, and Culture

Stewart M. Hoover and Lynn Schofield Clark, Editors

COLUMBIA UNIVERSITY PRESS

NEW YORK

Columbia University Press

Publishers Since 1893

New York   Chichester, West Sussex

Copyright © 2002 Columbia University Press

All rights reserved

Library of Congress Cataloging-in-Publication Data

Practicing religion in the age of the media : explorations in media, religion, and culture /
Stewart M. Hoover and Lynn Schofield Clark, editors.

p.   cm.

Includes bibliographical references and index.

ISBN 0-231-12088-5 (alk. paper) — ISBN 0-231-12089-3 (pbk. : alk. paper)

1. Mass media—Religious aspects.   2. Mass media and culture.   I. Hoover, Stewart M.
II. Clark, Lynn Schofield.

P94. P73 2001

291.1'75—dc21   2001042389

Casebound editions of Columbia University Press books
are printed on permanent and durable acid-free paper.

Printed in the United States of America

c 10 9 8 7 6 5 4 3 2 1

p 10 9 8 7 6 5 4 3 2 1

A version of the essay appearing as chapter 7 in this book was published as John
Schmalzbauer, "Between Professional and Religious Worlds: Catholics and Evangelicals in
American Journalism," *Sociology of Religion,* Winter 1999, vol. 60, issue 4, p. 363.
© Association for the Sociology of Religion, Inc. All Rights Reserved.

CONTENTS

ACKNOWLEDGMENTS

This book had its beginnings in the First Public Conference on Media, Religion, and Culture, held in Boulder, Colorado, on a series of unseasonably sunny January days in 1996. Maybe it was the perfect weather that generated vibrant conversations between academics from various disciplines and practicing journalists, television producers, and new media designers. Perhaps it was the coincidence of the conference with the meteoric rise of the Internet that kept those conversations going. Whatever the cause, that conference and subsequent similar occasions have led to a new day in the way scholars, media practitioners, and religious leaders consider the relationships between the media, the various religions, and cultures from around the world.

While this book began with the Boulder event, its final design has been shaped both by developments that have occurred since then and the perceived needs that have arisen in their wake—namely, the need for books that introduce this field to graduate and undergraduate students, social analysts, journalists, leaders of religious organizations, and others with an interest in the subject. In preparing the book, which we see as one more early step in a developing and vibrant area of investigation, the editors have felt privileged to work with such dedicated scholars as those represented here.

We are indebted to several organizations and people whose support has made this book possible. The Lilly Endowment, Inc., and Craig Dykstra, in particular, have pioneered the financing of studies in this area. Ann Miller, our editor at Columbia University Press, was enthusiastic and attentive to this project from its earliest days. Ron Harris ably saw the manuscript through the editorial process. The anonymous reviewers of the manuscript offered timely and helpful advice. We are also grateful to the many faculty members, staff, and graduate students at the University of Colorado at Boulder who assisted us: they helped first in the Boulder conference and later in offering feedback on papers that eventually became chapters in the book. We are especially indebted to Crystal Atkinson, a research and archives associate who tracked down vague footnote references, provided copyediting assistance, and prepared the final manuscript for publication.

Stewart M. Hoover also wishes to thank Garda Meyer, who provided invaluable support during his tenure as interim dean of the School of Journalism and Mass Communication, a period that coincided with critical phases of this project. He also wants to acknowledge here the contribution of the colleagues who have participated in the development of the scholarly discourse represented here, particularly his colleagues in the Uppsala Group: Alf Linderman, Knut Lundby, and Jolyon Mitchell, and David Morgan and Diane Winston. And, as always, he recognizes his wife, Karen, for her advice, consultation, and support.

Lynn Schofield Clark extends her thanks to her husband, Jon Clark, who patiently listened throughout this project's development and execution. His occasional gentle prodding for a bike ride or mountain hike with their son and daughter served as an important reminder of the things that matter most.

PRACTICING RELIGION IN THE AGE OF THE MEDIA

INTRODUCTION:
THE CULTURAL CONSTRUCTION OF
RELIGION IN THE MEDIA AGE

Stewart M. Hoover

The intersection between religion and the media first came to public and scholarly attention in the middle of the twentieth century. At that time, the "presenting problem," as it was called, was the emergence of religious broadcasts not sanctioned by religious and secular authorities. Interest was heightened in the 1970s when another new phenomenon, televangelism, burst onto the scene. Alongside these discussions of religious uses of the media, debates arose about media coverage of religion at a time when religion was playing an ever more important role in domestic and international politics.

These earlier considerations were rooted in a particular way of looking at both media and religion: as separate and separable entities that could be seen as acting independently of one another and as having impacts or effects on one another. In this view, "religion" and "the media" are autonomous, independent realms, and the central questions involve a kind of competition between them.

Today, we can see that the situation is more complex. A good deal of what goes on in the multiple relationships between religion and the media involves layered interconnections between religious symbols, interests, and meanings and the modern media sphere within which much of contemporary culture is made and known. When, for example, icons of popular music openly express their religious faiths, but in ways that are consciously and deeply embedded in contemporary, mediated, musical, visual, and performative genres, the lines between "religion" and "the media" become blurred.

The realms of both "religion" and "the media" are themselves transforming and being transformed. Religion today is much more a public, commodified, therapeutic, and personalized set of practices than it has been in the past. At the same time, the media (movies, radio, television, print and electronic media, and more) are collectively coming to constitute a realm where important projects of "the self" take place—projects that include spiritual, transcendent, and deeply meaningful "work." This means that, rather than being autonomous actors involved in institutionalized projects in relation to each other, religion and media are increasingly converging. They are meeting on a common turf: the everyday world of lived experience.

This book marks the emergence of a scholarly project addressed to the issues and questions that arise with this convergence. It is an effort rooted in a commonality of interests between those who study religion and those who study the media. Among media scholars, attention has begun to focus on culture and questions of culture, opening up scope for consideration of those dimensions of life we traditionally have thought of as "religious." At the same time, scholars of religion have begun investigating ways in which religion is done outside the boundaries of traditional faiths, doctrines, histories, and orders. The approach taken is necessarily cross-disciplinary. The chapters here demonstrate the range of resources available from a variety of fields. There are contributions from cultural studies, material culture, cultural anthropology, religious studies, ritual studies, critical theory, reception studies, performance studies, history, and sociology, among others.

Within this complexity, there are, at the same time, ways of finding a central viewpoint. To say merely that things are complex and evolving and that we need a variety of perspectives and contexts would be trite and unhelpful. Instead, it can be said that what the contributors to this volume agree on is that the most logical scholarly and interpretive standpoint is that of *practice*. This means that instead of focusing on social structure, or institutions, or formal claims about meanings and values, the contributors stand in the middle of these things, where individuals and communities can be seen to be active in the construction of meaning.

This view obviously borrows much from the work of Pierre Bourdieu, who called that realm the habitus: "[This theory] insists . . . that the objects of knowledge are constructed, not passively recorded, and contrary to intellectualist idealism, that the principle of this construction is the system of structured, structuring dispositions, the habitus, which is constituted in practice and is always oriented towards practical functions."[1]

This is an approach that recognizes the various complexities as they converge in real experience, as they are engaged, constructed, reconstructed, made meaning of, and used. Each contributor here focuses on such practices. While some discuss texts at length and others address institutional issues, all share in common the sensibility that we must look at where and how things are actively engaged. How and where are meanings made out of all this?

By extension, we can say some things about what this book is and is not. It focuses on the intersections of social and cultural life. It wants to know how and where people are acting in pursuance of religious, spiritual, and meaning-focused goals. It is not so interested in those goals per se—where they come from or where they are going. That is a task for a different book and a different set of resources. The book thus does not make totalized or global claims or projections. It is about rich and focused moments and contexts.

As it is focused on practice, this book also has less to say about institutions and structures. While a strong case is made by many contributors (directly and by inference) that some forms of institutional religion and its structures are under assault, if not on the wane, the arguments are not so much about that or about the prospects for those institutions and structures. We can, it is true, from what we see here, begin to make some informed speculations about the implications for formal, organized religions. However, that is not the purpose of this book.

Most of the book further recognizes that the compelling perspective is one that *looks at* these convergences, rather than inscribing clear boundaries or distinctions. Too much of the writing and thinking about religion and the media has fallen into discussions of the sacrality or secularity of forms or practices. The editors and authors in this volume believe that both the sacred and secular, as traditionally conceived, can be seen to be active in both religion and the media. It does not help much to assign a given phenomenon to one or the other of these categories when things can be seen to move between them. The practices of meaning-making that are described here (or that are seen to be possible) do not necessarily recognize that there is a clear-cut boundary.

Traditional approaches to media and religion have further suffered from being too *instrumental* in orientation; that is, they have been based on what James Carey has called the "transportation" model of communication, where communication is thought of only in terms of its causes and consequences for known autonomous and independent actors and receivers. Instead, contributors to this book tend to see communication as something that arises out of the interactions between texts, producers, receivers, and the contexts wherein they reside.

These chapters also carry a challenge to the traditional way of understanding ritual. They draw much from the branch of ritual studies that holds that ritual must be understood as it evolves, more than with reference to its original, pure, or prescribed forms. What we see in many of these chapters is the emergence of new forms, contexts, and experiences of ritual, many of which are possible only because we now live at a time when media play such an important role.

These chapters are thus about the experiences and practices that have evolved in the media age (many of them are, in fact, dependent upon it). They are not about "mediated religion" or "religious media." Those categories are too narrow and too constraining to contain the rich range of phenomena that appear in these pages. The point is to describe in some detail moments and locations where we can see active the kind of religious, spiritual, transcendent, or meaning-centered practice that seems to be evolving with reference to, and in the context of, media culture.

As the scholarship around religion and media continues to develop and expand, certain debates and definitions have begun to form. In general, these have emerged along lines of demarcation that are brought into relief when we think about the religion/media intersection—and, more importantly, when we look at actual practices in actual contexts. The chapters in this volume address a number of these dimensions and are organized so as to move progressively through them.

The first of these lines is between the *private* and the *public*. Religion has both private and public faces; at the same time, media, while often consumed privately, are also a dominant feature of the public sphere. Which valence of each should we see as most significant, and under what circumstances?

A second line of demarcation is that between the *popular* and the *legitimated*, or elite, realms of culture. Religion has long entailed both popular and elite forms and discourses, and religious history can be seen as a continuing struggle over the power to establish and legitimate certain forms at the expense of others. Media, while they also work on both sides of this line, have most often been identified with popular forms, and this has led to a good deal of controversy. Religious and secular cultural authorities have seen media religion as benefiting the popular at the expense of the legitimated forms.

A third line of demarcation is related to the elite/popular one: the line between *mainstream* and *marginal* forms and practices. Social and historical forces act to establish certain cultural forms and practices as the dominant, mainstream ones; others as a consequence are marginalized. In this case, the media are significant for their ability to bring marginal voices (both domestic and foreign) into contexts where they have traditionally not been accessible.

A fourth line of demarcation is that between *explicit* and *implicit* religion. What we think of as religion per se involves explicit forms of expression, symbol, practice, and history. At the same time, forms emerge that inhabit similar spaces, serve similar purposes, or are appropriations of formally religious objects or actions. A great deal of what goes on in the popular media can be (and has been) described using religious terms. Sporting events have been called "religious rituals"; advertising has been said to manipulate "sacred" impulses; media figures have been described as evoking religious charisma. Critics have raised concerns about the impact of such "secular" phenomena on authentic, sacred, explicit religion.

A fifth line of demarcation is between *direct* and *mediated* experience. Religion is thought to have a set of "authentic" forms and practices, which can be experienced only directly. Worship, community, revelation, prayer, private piety, and religious instruction are each thought to have special benefits (or indeed to be accessible) only when experienced without mediation. Mediated communication is thought necessarily to intervene in such direct experience and thus detract from it, or even destroy it.

A sixth line of demarcation explored in this book is that between the *North* and the *South*. Both religion and the media take forms specific to national and cultural contexts. Much of the debate about religion and the media, besides being focused around their legitimacy as institutions, has also largely assumed that the only important context for consideration is that of the developed North and West. In fact, there is much to be learned by looking at media and religion as they are coming together in the "two-thirds world" of the Southern Hemisphere.

Chapters 2 through 17 of the book are divided into six parts, and in brief introductions to each part I continue this exploration of the lines of demarcation and debate in the field. Chapter 1, which immediately follows this introduction, is a comprehensive exploration by Lynn Schofield Clark of the subsequent chapters.

Placing these contributions in an expansive and helpful scholarly framework, Clark traces the historical developments that have shaped inquiry into media, religion, and culture. She notes that traditions of freedom of inquiry and an ethic of religious tolerance make it necessary to move the field beyond specific sectarian aims and applications. Clark argues that future research must continue to build interdisciplinary alliances so as to expand our understanding. In this way, the work will become meaningful not only for those within religious organizations but for those who strive for a fuller understanding of contemporary culture.

NOTES

1. Pierre Bourdieu, *The Logic of Practice* (Stanford: Stanford University Press, 1990), 52.

CHAPTER I

OVERVIEW:
THE "PROTESTANTIZATION" OF RESEARCH
INTO MEDIA, RELIGION, AND CULTURE

Lynn Schofield Clark

Research into the intersecting fields of media, religion, and culture has grown exponentially in the past decade. The pages in this volume represent a starting point for the reader new to the field. Yet while the contributions to this book are consistent with an overall trend that will be reviewed in this chapter, they are by no means exhaustive of current approaches. In this overview, I discuss how research in this area has developed, seeking to place current agendas—both those represented here and those taking place in other settings—into social and historical perspective.

By using the term *Protestantization* to describe the contemporary situation, I do not mean to assert that American Protestantism has at some level defeated Roman Catholicism, or for that matter any other denomination or religion.[1] I wish, rather, to point to what N. Jay Demerath III has described as a paradox of cultural victory and organizational decline for liberal Protestantism in the United States.[2] Most of us are familiar with the statistics regarding the atrophy of membership in the liberal Protestant church, but, as Demerath points out, we must not overlook the fact that a set of culturally dominant values—a set that includes individualism, freedom, pluralism, tolerance, democracy, and intellectual inquiry—has its roots in the Protestant Reformation and its challenges to the authority of religious institutions.

Demerath's assertion follows related arguments made a century earlier by social observers Alexis de Tocqueville and Max Weber, both of whom identified the interrelation of religious foundations and the emergent cultural values of collectivity, individualism, and capitalism.[3] I use the term *Protestantization* in this sense, referring not to certain theological positions or the specific workings of the denominations that bear that name, but to the values emergent with the Reformation.[4] Those values specific to my argument include the rise of intellectual inquiry as an endeavor separated from religious aims and the cultural norm of religious tolerance and relativism in the context of a U.S. society that is increasingly pluralistic.

I will illustrate what I mean by relating two occurrences that reveal what I believe is an inherent tension for research into media, religion, and culture today. Each of the events took place during the Second Public Conference on Media, Religion, and Culture in Edinburgh, Scotland, in the summer of 1999. In the first happening, a longtime researcher in media, religion, and culture was ruminating about subjects he felt younger scholars should pursue. Among other things, he bemoaned the contemporary religious "crisis" in a European country that, like many locations around the world, has in the last decade seen a significant upswing in Muslim converts. The wording of his description caught the attention of several of those seated around me. "*Crisis?*" someone gasped. It struck many that those in the room who were Muslim certainly would not describe the phenomenon in that way; the words spoke of a time when it was possible to assume that people interested in this interdisciplinary research topic came primarily from Christian traditions. The discomfort obvious in the audience illustrated the extent to which pluralism and tolerance, rather than an assumed common starting point of Christian confessions, has become the norm.

The second event involved me more directly. In an amiable conversation, a fellow researcher asked rather pointedly, "Why conduct this research if you can't directly apply the research to solving the church's problems?" As I attempted to argue for the "practical" applicability of my research, others around us immediately responded to his question by raising the benefits of knowledge for its own sake. I admit that sometimes when confronted with this issue, I, like the journalists interviewed by John Schmalzbauer in chapter 7, am struck by a tension between the norms of religious organizations that *en*courage the disclosure of religious beliefs and the norms of professional life that *dis*courage them. No one asks what personal journey brought someone to the study of the media and its political economic system, so why should the study of religion and media be different? Yet of course, it *is* different, both because of the specific history of the field of inquiry and its earlier, uneasy relationship to the presumed "objective" scholarship of the social sciences. Appeals to inquiry for the sake of knowledge itself have not always applied to studies of religion as comfortably as they do today. As evidenced by my interlocutor, many people are still uncomfortable with the idea that one might conduct a neutral, or even critical, analysis of religion and its role in society.

Those seasoned analysts who have conducted research in religion and media over recent decades may be dismayed by the developments signaled in these and other examples of the shifting sands of scholarship. In another session during the same conference, one veteran railed against those he perceived as less committed or even indifferent to work that he passionately described as a "mission." How is it that we have come to a point in history when a subject as personally important (to some) as religion can be thought to be studied impartially? Moreover, is it not strange that this should occur just as the rising epistemological tides encourage greater, not less, attention to self-reflexivity in research? Like Demerath, I see the roots of this development in the cultural success of Protestantism, and therefore we turn first to a discussion of contemporary values in the historical context in which they emerged.

KNOWLEDGE AND RELIGION FROM THE REFORMATION ONWARD

In the sixteenth century, Protestantism was first and foremost a movement that signaled a new independence from the institutions of religion. Divine authority was no longer solely and completely anchored in the church, and this initiated a long process of increased privatization of religion. This privatization is related to what Philip Hammond has termed a rise in "personal autonomy," or the sense in which the individual is the ultimate authority over his or her understanding of religion; it also provides an important context for the individualism that Bellah and his colleagues have described as culturally dominant in the United States.[5] Of course, the Reformation not only changed relationships between individuals and religious institutions but also reordered society as a whole, fostering a

movement toward greater protection of individual rights relative to the
state and displacing notions of truth from religious institutions into the
realm of scientific inquiry and human understanding.

At first, the weakening of papal authority led to increased power for
the monarchies of Europe. However, the religious and political debates of
the time, coupled with the rise of a mercantilist middle class and the
wider distribution of ideas (the latter being fostered by both increased
travel and the printing press) provided the necessary context for the emergence of democratic forms of government emphasizing freedoms from
imposed or "established" religion as well as protection for the pursuit of
intellectual inquiry. The era of the Reformation, with its increased scientific experimentation and geographic exploration, fundamentally called
into question the notion that the church was the only and final source of
truth, thus fostering a position of pluralism and tolerance toward other
religions. Eventually, the pursuit of knowledge came to be understood in
relation to the greater good of society rather than specifically related to
the fostering of religious faith.

Scientific methods and rationalist views supplanted the religious community's explanatory powers regarding the natural world. Eventually,
Western theology itself took on the methods of hermeneutical philosophy, in many cases complementing learnings of the natural world with explorations of the relationship between humans and the divine. Increasingly, however, scientific exploration and the thought of religious leaders
were seen to occupy different spheres and to serve different purposes.

Philosophers of the French Enlightenment era, and later the German
idealists, viewed religion as at best a retrogressive aspect of a society yearning for greater economic and political freedoms. Yet while divisions between these influential political philosophers and religious institutions reinforced a separation in intellectual traditions, the deep commitment to
religious institutions among a large part of the population preserved an
important role for religion in social change.

During the era of the industrial revolution in Europe and the United
States, as many Christian organizations sought to relieve urban poverty,
philosophers and sociologists developed tools to explore the changing social relationships wrought by immigration and urbanization. While religion was accepted by some as important in the private realm, it remained
problematic in intellectual circles. James Turner, in fact, has dated the
roots of intellectual agnosticism in the United States to the post–Civil

War period—a time when Christianity, perhaps ironically, continued to serve as the primary content and hence driving force behind the spread of magazines, almanacs, and other printed materials throughout the settled East and the Western frontier.[6] An interesting intellectual history has yet to be done on this verdant period for the intersection of media, religion, and culture.[7]

Not coincidentally, it was during the era of the industrial revolution that the mass media became an object of study in a significant way. Prior to this, published accounts tended to debate the worth of ideas put forth in printed form rather than the political and social issues raised by the emergent industries themselves. By the mid-nineteenth century, newspapers had come to be widely accepted as a key instrument for an informed democracy, and as such they were studied both in Europe and in the United States. Writers of this period such as Weber, Tonnies, and Simmel bemoaned the workings of capitalism and urbanization, nostalgically longing for a past that sometimes included religion's presumed peaceful and moral influence. At the turn of the century, John Dewey, Robert Park, and others in what is known as the Chicago school embraced the Progressive's views of technology and social life articulated by Tocqueville nearly a century earlier, arguing that newspapers could provide a basis for consensual understandings that would foster a "great community" and thus counter the negative results of urbanization and immigration.

While religion was favorably linked with the domestic sphere in these and other writings, Freud, following Marx and Feuerbach a century and more earlier, related religion to unproductive illusions created in the mind of needy individuals. Darwin's theory of evolution, which in the mid-nineteenth century had further called into question basic tenets of Christianity, culminated in the 1925 conviction of a teacher who taught evolution in a biology class, a case known as the Scopes trial. Meanwhile, revolutions in Russia and World War I had provided further means for reflecting on religion's role in preserving the social order.

The lack of consensus regarding religion's role in social life, coupled with the rise at the beginning of the twentieth century of the social sciences, may have fostered even greater resistance to religion in intellectual circles. The social sciences were a nascent discipline, and the presumed "biased" views associated with religion (particularly as it was understood as a private and personal affair) could be seen as a threat to the field's bid for recognition and status as a legitimate science within higher education. This concern carried over to several related disciplines and still rears its head today.

PROTESTANTISM AND THE PROBLEM OF TELEVISION

By the middle of the twentieth century, the study of religion had been limited to subfields of the social sciences such as sociology, history, and anthropology in addition to the study of theology. At that time, as Michele Rosenthal outlines in chapter 6, liberal Protestants increasingly had come to identify themselves with high culture, and this made the emergence and success of television particularly problematic for them. Several critics perceived television as being responsible for widespread moral decadence, superficiality, and commercialization, and ultimately linked the rise of the new medium to the decline of religious faith.[8] Writing with a tone of urgency, these critics echoed concerns voiced more generally in what has been called the "mass culture" debate.[9]

Others, however—notably those of the emergent Protestant evangelical persuasion and the more conservative Roman Catholic tradition—embraced television's and radio's presumed potential to speak to current and prospective adherents.[10] Diane Winston's chapter 5 presents as a case in point the Salvation Army's initially optimistic approach to theater and mass media. When religious leaders such as Billy Graham and Charles Fuller sought to harness television, they were part of an already existing tradition of religious broadcasters—Aimee Semple McPherson, the Moody Bible Institute, Father Charles Coughlin, and others—who had pioneered radio for religious purposes.

Yet this approach to media, particularly television, was problematic. As Willard Rowland has pointed out, "Political, educational, and religious institutions were all paralyzed by the conflict between their apprehensions about television and their various interests in harnessing and exploiting it for themselves."[11] Rosenthal argues in chapter 6 that these approaches to television echoed the utopic-dystopic discourse that had arisen around the introduction of each new form of communication technology since the nineteenth century. Moreover, she notes that both perspectives adopt a utilitarian approach to communication media, assuming a passive audience while attributing to television a powerful means of influence.

Studies into the effects of media at the time, however, were moving in the opposite direction, countering presumed "magic bullet" approaches to communication's persuasive effects on individuals with a limited-effects model.[12] The development of radio and its presumed role in relation to Hitler's rise to power, coupled with a commitment on the part of the U.S. government to mitigate the effects of industrialization through social research and policy formation, led to large-scale research efforts that explored the role of the mass media in persuasion in the 1930s.[13]

One of the central figures in this research was Harold Lasswell, a political scientist who explored the role of symbols in political campaigns. He argued that propaganda did not create facts, but reinterpreted existing ideas. Others following his line of research during World War II and after affirmed the importance of interpersonal relationships in persuasion, noting the limited effects of media messages alone. At the same time, the commercialization of radio and the evolution of advertising agencies sparked a need in those industries for research into the habits of media consumption. Thus other research, notably led by Paul Lazarsfeld, delineated relationships between personal attributes and such behaviors as voting and product purchasing. Within the positivist model of survey-based research that predominated in the social sciences of the 1950s and beyond (and provided important legitimacy and funding for mass-media research), religion was viewed as one such personal attribute or "variable." Some contemporary research approaches religion in this way, examining how religious affiliations affect viewing selections,[14] and how religious symbols appear in conjunction with other images in mass-mediated contexts.[15]

By the mid-1950s, the economy was enjoying a peacetime expansion and young people pursued higher education in greater numbers than ever before, providing new opportunities for the expansion of university research programs. Communication had begun as a vocational or skills-oriented curriculum, but by midcentury its study had been institutionalized in such forms as Lazarsfeld's Princeton Office of Radio Research and the Office of War Information. These forums consolidated the interests and funds of government and industry into "practical" research (not coincidentally, "limited effects" conclusions tended to serve the interests of the nascent television industry). Television's role in society continued to be debated, however, and even celebrated, as in the case of the popular writings of Marshall McLuhan in the 1960s and 1970s. Still, problems of an increasingly complex society, such as pervasive violence and perceived changes in mainstream values, seemed to many to be linked to the emergence of television. Thus, studies of the effects of television were funded by organizations—including U.S. government agencies—that were charged with addressing social problems, and such projects continue today.[16]

MEDIA, CULTURAL STUDIES, AND RELIGION

By the 1970s, however, a long-dormant tradition of employing historical, critical, and anthropological methods in the exploration of the media's role in U.S. society was beginning to reemerge. In large part this was the result of increased interaction between researchers in the United States and Europe, as European scholars, working in what has come to be known as cultural studies, had experienced a revived interest in Marxism. The tradition challenged the scientific commitments of U.S.-based mass-communication research, while also rejecting the moralist and elitist tone of the mass-culture debates on both continents. This approach to mass communication—in particular to its popular-culture forms—may have been particularly appealing to younger scholars at the time, as they were members of that same large population of young people who, fifteen or so years earlier, had fostered the development of a "youth culture" and provided the economic basis for the development of popular culture in the United States and Europe.

In a highly influential work, Raymond Williams redefined the term *culture*, replacing its earlier implicit references to taste and refinement with what he called the "anthropological" definition of culture as "a particular way of life."[17] In subsequent studies at the Birmingham Center for Contemporary Cultural Studies at the University of Birmingham, England, popular culture came to be viewed not so much as a threat to a perceived "better" culture, but as an expression of ideology that was found to be meaningful in the everyday life of citizens.[18] Building upon Gramsci, Althusser, and other neo-Marxists, cultural studies came to see within popular culture possible seeds for social change, a topic of great interest in the wake of the turbulent era of the 1960s.[19]

Research in the tradition of cultural studies has come to be defined by several traits: (1) as noted earlier, a foregrounding of popular culture forms and their reception in everyday life; (2) a commitment to social, historical, and political-economic contextualization of analyses, with particular attention to the examination of power relations and their maintenance through codes and symbols; (3) an embrace of critical and humanistic research methods; and perhaps most importantly, (4) a commitment to interdisciplinary inquiry and exploration. In this volume, chapters by Erika Doss, David Morgan, Shawn Landres, Diane Winston, Michele Rosenthal and Jan Fernback exemplify cultural studies approaches, and other chapters also in some ways build upon this tradition. Cultural historians such as Jürgen Habermas, who explored the emergence of the public sphere and public opinion, and Elizabeth Eisenstein, who traced the emergence of the printing press in the era of the Reformation,[20] have provided models for the historical explorations of religious communication industries such as radio.[21] Interest has also turned to the interconnections between significant historical events, religious identity, and the media, such as in Jeffrey Shandler's study of television and the Holocaust[22] and studies by Frank Walsh and by Gregory Black of the Roman Catholic Church and its censorship efforts in Hollywood earlier in the century.[23] In this volume (chap. 15) Michael Berkowitz examines emergent Jewish leadership in the early twentieth century. Elsewhere, numerous scholars of cultural studies are exploring the interplay between entertainment media representations and reception practices within (and at the margins of) various faith traditions. These include Rubina Ramji's analysis of representations of Islam in popular culture and Hamid Naficy's study of television and its reception among recent Iranian immigrants;[24] Marie Gillespie's work on interpretations of televised versions of the Mahabharat among diasporic communities in the United Kingdom;[25] Rebecca Sullivan's analysis of Catholic sisters as represented in popular culture and in their own promotional materials;[26] Ann Hardy's work on interpretations of Christian films in New Zealand;[27] Gregory Stephens's exploration of Rastafarianism and liberatory ideals within reggae music;[28] Jane Iwamura's analysis of the oriental monk in popular culture;[29] and my own work on representations of the supernatural and interpretations among U.S. teens.[30] Following in the cultural studies tradition, these researchers call into question earlier observations about the lack of religion in popular media by exploring connections between certain religious representations and hegemonic ideas.[31]

The emergent field of ritual studies has also made an important contribution to cultural studies questions of media and religion. An influential article by media theorist James Carey introduced what he termed a "ritual" view of communication, creating an alternative metaphor to the "transmission" model that had dominated lay theories of mass communication.[32] Carey argued that "a ritual view of communication is directed not toward the extension of messages in space but toward the maintenance of society in time; not the act of imparting information but the representation of shared beliefs."[33] Scholars in media studies following in Carey's path have explored the ritualistic role of media events in providing coherence to society.[34] In this volume's chapter 9, Carolyn Marvin highlights the rituals of the U.S. legal system in her analysis of the importance of sacrifice in national cohesion.[35] Ronald Grimes has made important contributions to ritual theory, bringing together cultural anthropological concerns for everyday life and the emphasis in religious studies upon performance of celebratory rituals;[36] in this volume's chapter 10, he reviews both the developments in ritual theory and the use of this theory (whether explicitly or not) among media theorists.

Another important and recent contribution to interdisciplinary work has come from the emergent field of material culture studies, itself an inquiry that explores the study of both popular and commodified religious artifacts and mass-mediated representations.[37] A few studies have focused specifically on holiday celebrations and the interplay between these events and commercial culture.[38] Studies in this approach look at the home as the center for religious activities and thus foreground negotiations between tradition, the commercialized media, and the environment of domestic space. As such, they provide an important foundation for current ethnographic investigations into media use and religion in the home at the Center for Mass Media Research in Boulder, Colorado,[39] and also for parallel work being conducted at the Gregorian University in Rome.[40] Also influential in this work is the emergent generational studies, explored in both the United States and Canada.[41]

Research into media, religion, and culture, however, has also taken specific trajectories due to the historical conditions of recent decades. As noted elsewhere, beginning in the 1980s with the emergence of the Religious Right in the political realm, televangelism became a topic of interest to researchers.[42] Studies of televangelism contributed to analyses of the emergence of evangelicalism within mainstream U.S. culture.[43] Current research examines the role of televangelism's reception in other parts of the world, as seen in part 6 of this volume in the chapters by Knut Lundby, Alf Linderman, and Keyan Tomaselli and Arnold Shepperson. These and other studies extend analyses of the global rise of conservative

Christian views, exploring how these may be intertwined with U.S. values associated with capitalism and individualism.[44] Conservative Christian subcultures and their relation to entertainment media continue to be an area of interest; examples of such work are Hillary Warren's analysis of the Southern Baptist boycott of Disney[45] and Michael Roth's study of constraints and creativity within the contemporary Christian music industry.[46]

Another important area in research on media, religion, and culture has addressed the representation of religion in the news. This area of research is perhaps the one most specifically lodged within the traditional scope of media studies. John Dart and Jimmy Allen attributed a dearth of religion coverage to ignorance rather than hostility on the part of reporters and editors;[47] Stewart M. Hoover traced the increasing attention to religion and its relation to religion's role in the broader culture;[48] and Judith Buddenbaum offered a useful textbook for those pursuing careers in religion journalism.[49]

Mark Silk and his colleagues at the Pew Program on Religion and the News Media provide ongoing analyses of the coverage of religion,[50] and a new interest group in the Association for Education in Journalism and Mass Communication has provided an important venue for research in (and not limited to) this area. The Public Religion Project,[51] led by Martin Marty, links scholars of religion with journalists, while a number of activist groups (e.g., the Muslim Media Watch group)[52] monitor and alert constituents of problematic media coverage. In this volume, John Schmalzbauer (chap. 7) and Mark Borchert (chap. 8) explore negotiations between the media and religious institutions at both institutional and individual levels.[53] Others are extending this trajectory, such as Eric Gormly's argument for the teaching of religion in journalism higher education,[54] Andrew Weltch's exploration of the use of newspapers for religious purposes,[55] Joyce Smith's analysis of how readers may learn about religion from news stories beyond the religion page,[56] and the examination of specific news events such as Dane Claussen's work on the Promise Keepers movement.[57] Additionally, increased attention is being given to the representation of non-Christian, non-Western groups in the news media.[58]

Other new areas of interest are also emerging. The Internet has introduced a host of new questions for the field, and chapters by Jan Fernback, David S. Nash, and Bruce Lawrence in part 5 of this volume represent the beginning of work there. Research in this area is being undertaken in both Europe[59] and the United States.[60] Recent literature has dealt with issues of the relationship between new communication technologies and sacred space[61] and that between technology, cognition, and humanity more generally.[62]

It is important to note that the many research approaches outlined here have roots in academic disciplines other than religious studies or theology. While findings from this research are of interest to religious institutions, their intent is lodged in intellectual inquiry, rather than toward addressing the problems of religious institutions or general theological concerns. Thus while, as I have argued, they stem from Protestantization, these research efforts are intended to draw connections between the interests of religious institutions and scholarly work—efforts notably led by the International Study Commission on Media, Religion, and Culture.[63]

Promising work in this area is being done by Mary E. Hess, who has studied the application of media-literacy programs employing popular culture in religious education,[64] and by Mark Johns, who has focused on Protestant congregations' media uses. Johns's work led to the design of resources to assist in these efforts.[65] Students at Gregorian University and in the University of Edinburgh's Theology and Ethics of Communication Project are exploring issues such as John Joshva's study of the communication theories underlying official religious documents.[66] Some religious leaders have also written about the mass media specifically for audiences involved in religious organizations.[67]

Unfortunately, for some time the study of mass media has been on the margins of theological and religious studies, leaving it to scholars from other fields to ruminate on the relationships between theology and the forms of mass media.[68] This, however, seems to be changing. Film has been of particular interest for theologians.[69] Recent works have moved away from earlier studies of "art" films[70] to include examination of popular music,[71] advertising,[72] and television.[73] There is emergent interest in the relationship of youth culture and religion: several studies on music videos and their interpretation have been done by scholars in both religious studies and media studies,[74] and research is under way on young people, popular culture, and religious identity.[75]

This brief overview makes clear that research into media, religion, and culture has increased tremendously in the last decade. I have attempted to explain this increase in part by demonstrating the extent to which the centrifugal forces of Protestantization have opened a space for inquiry that only gradually gained critical mass, following developments of interdisciplinary exploration more generally. As scholars have built upon various academic traditions lodged in intellectual inquiry rather than in practical applications for religious bodies, this research can no longer be dismissed as of value to sectarian interests only. In fact, its very interdisciplinarity makes the field particularly appealing for those currently in graduate school who are interested in cultural studies.

The indications are that such explorations will only grow richer. Annual academic conferences such as the Association for Education in Journalism and Mass Communication, the National Communication Association, the International Association for Mass Communication Research, the Society for the Scientific Study of Religion, the American Academy of Religion, and the International Communication Association now regularly devote panels to the discussion of these issues. There were public conferences on media, religion, and culture in 1996 and 1999, with another planned for 2002 in Los Angeles, and thereafter every three years. Institutionalization of the study is occurring: there are now the Theology and Ethics of Communication Project at the University of Edinburgh; the Anthropology of Media program in the Religious Studies Department at the University of London; and the Media, Culture, and Religion consortium made up of the University of California at Santa Barbara, the University of Colorado at Boulder, New York University, Trinity College at Hartford, Connecticut, Uppsala University in Sweden, the University of Edinburgh, the Gregorian University in Italy, and Helsinki University. These all promise increased attention to such studies, as does the start-up announcement of a journal to be devoted specifically to the field and the launching, in 2002, of a doctoral dissertation fellowship program in media, religion, and culture.[76]

In academia generally, there are norms of pluralism and relativism, and therefore scholars who situate their work solely within the sectarian concerns of religious organizations will still encounter wariness on the part of the larger scholarly community. In the emergent tradition of interdisciplinary research into media, religion, and culture, however, scholars are finding ways to engage in dialogues (scholarly, sectarian, or both), sometimes using completely different frames of reference to suit various audiences. There are those who wish we could return to a common agenda in the field of media, religion, and culture, but today such a position appears imperialistic. This in fact has been an argument for flexibility and openness. The contemporary situation demands a willingness to approach research with a self-awareness of religion's problematic past with reference to the traditions of free intellectual inquiry and of tolerance for a plurality of religious expression.

Paradoxically, perhaps, the tolerant and somewhat relativistic stance toward religion demonstrated in this volume, rather than documenting a declining interest in religion, actually opens up new avenues for understanding the interactions between media, religion, and culture. It is the editors' hope that the work represented here will continue to nourish this verdant field of inquiry.

NOTES

1. While in this overview I relate certain cultural themes to the Protestant Reformation, I am convinced of the problems inherent in elevating values associated with Puritanism to a privileged status relative to the unfolding of U.S. history. Jonathan Butler convincingly argues for the plurality of experiences and views that ground contemporary U.S. experience; it is, however, also clear that certain values may be best understood in relation to the hegemony of Protestantism in the United States. Butler, *Awash in a Sea of Faith: Christianizing the American People* (Cambridge: Harvard University Press, 1990).

2. N. Jay Demerath III, "Cultural Victory and Organizational Defeat in the Paradoxical Decline of Liberal Protestantism," *Journal for the Scientific Study of Religion* 34, no. 4 (1995): 458–69.

3. Alexis de Tocqueville, *Democracy in America,* ed. J. P. Mayer, trans. George Lawrence (Garden City, N.Y.: Doubleday, 1969; orig. ed., 1835); Max Weber, *The Protestant Ethic and the Spirit of Capitalism* (New York: Scribner's, 1928).

4. The term was coined by Demerath and Williams in their description of the democratizing forces at work in the Roman Catholic parishes they observed in Springfield, Mass. See N. Jay Demerath III and Rhys H. Williams, *A Bridging of Faiths* (Princeton: Princeton University Press, 1992).

5. Philip Hammond, *Religion and Personal Autonomy: The Third Disestablishment in America* (Columbia: University of South Carolina Press, 1994); Robert N. Bellah, *Habits of the Heart: Individualism and Commitment in America* (Berkeley: University of California Press, 1985).

6. James Turner, *Without God: Without Creed* (Baltimore: Johns Hopkins University Press, 1985).

7. Important works from historians that explore the relationship between religion and the role of almanacs, magazines, and other media during the earlier eras

of U.S. history include Butler, *Awash in a Sea of Faith;* Charles Lippy, *Being Religious, American Style* (Westport, Conn.: Greenwood Press, 1994); David Hall, *Worlds of Wonder, Days of Judgment: Popular Religious Belief in Early New England* (New York: Knopf, 1989; and Lawrence Moore, *Selling God* (New York: Oxford University Press, 1994). See also Leonard I. Sweet, ed., *Communication and Change in American Religious History* (Grand Rapids, Mich.: Eerdmans, 1993).

8. See, for example, Tom F. Driver, "The Arts and the Christian Evangel," *Christian Scholar* 40, no. 4 (1957): 334, cited in Sally Promey, "Interchangeable Art: Warner Sallman and the Critics of Mass Culture," in *Icons of American Protestantism: The Art of Warner Sallman,* ed. David Morgan (New Haven: Yale University Press, 1996), 149–80. Promey also highlights the importance of Paul Tillich's critiques of "non-authentic" art and religion, thus further cementing religion's alignment with the "mass society" taste-based critiques of the era. Later critiques within Protestantism that speak from similar positions include William Fore, *Television and Religion* (Minneapolis: Augsburg, 1987), and Malcolm Muggeridge, *Christ and the Media* (London: Hodder & Stoughton, 1977).

9. Bernard Rosenberg and David Manning White, *Mass Culture: The Popular Arts in America* (New York: Macmillan, 1957).

10. Ben Armstrong, *The Electric Church* (Nashville: Thomas Nelson, 1979).

11. Willard Rowland, *The Politics of TV Violence: Policy Uses of Communication Research* (Beverly Hills: Sage, 1983), 24.

12. Jesse Delia has pointed out that the influential presumption of a "magic bullet" theory against which wartime communication researchers defined themselves was first articulated in Katz and Larzarsfeld. See Elihu Katz and Paul Lazarsfeld, *Personal Influence* (Glencoe, Ill.: Free Press, 1955). Delia also notes that while communication research became institutionalized during the war years, the work of the Chicago school at the turn of the century marks the beginnings of communication research as we know it today. Delia speculates that this earlier school of research found increasingly less support as it was grounded in European theories less amenable to the developing empirical models of research increasingly accepted in the pragmatic U.S. tradition. In Jesse Delia, "Communication Research: A History," in *Handbook of Communication Science,* ed. Charles Berger and Stephen Chaffee (Newbury Park, Calif.: Sage, 1987).

13. Rowland, *Politics of TV Violence.*

14. Judith Buddenbaum and Daniel A. Stout, *Religion and Mass Media: Audiences and Adaptations* (Thousand Oaks, Calif.: Sage, 1996); Neal Hamilton and Alan Rubin, "The Influence of Religiosity on Television Viewing," *Journalism Quarterly* 69, no. 3 (1992): 667–78.

15. Carol J. Pardun and Kathy B. McKee, "Strange Bedfellows: Symbols of Religion and Sexuality on MTV," *Youth and Society* 26, no. 4 (1995): 438–49.

16. See, for example, Surgeon General's Scientific Advisory Committee on Television and Social Behavior, *Television and Growing Up: The Impact of Televised Violence* (Washington, D.C.: GPO, 1972); David Pearl, Lorraine Bouthilet, and Joyce Lazar, eds., *Television and Behavior: Ten Years of Scientific Progress and Implications for the Eighties* (Rockville, Md.: National Institute of Mental Health, 1982); Russell Green and Edward Donnerstein, eds., *Human Aggression: Theories, Research, and Implications for Social Policy* (San Diego: Academic, 1998); Dale Kunkel, "Policy Battles over Defining Children's Educational Television," *Annals of the American Academy of Political and Social Sciences* 557 (1998): 39–53.

17. Raymond Williams, *The Long Revolution* (Harmondsworth, U.K.: Penguin, 1965), 57.

18. See, for example, Stuart Hall and Tony Jefferson, eds., *Resistance through Rituals: Youth Subcultures in Post-War Britain* (London: Center for Contemporary Cultural Studies, 1976).

19. See, for example, John Fiske, *Television Culture* (London: Methuen, 1987); Jesus Martin-Barbero, *Communication, Culture, and Hegemony: From the Media to Mediations,* trans. E. Fox and R. White (London: Sage, 1993).

20. Jürgen Habermas, *The Structural Transformation of the Public Sphere,* trans. Thomas Burger (Cambridge: MIT Press, 1992); Elizabeth L. Eisenstein, *The Printing Press an an Agent of Change: Communications and Cultural Transformations in Early Modern Europe* (New York: Cambridge University Press, 1979).

21. Jolyon Mitchell, *Visually Speaking: Radio and the Renaissance of Preaching* (Edinburgh: Presbyterian and Reformed Publishers, 2000); Tona Hangen, "Redeeming the Radio Dial: Evangelical Radio and Religious Culture, 1920–1960" (Ph.D. diss., Brandeis University, 1999).

22. Jeffrey Shandler, *While America Watches: Televising the Holocaust* (New York: Oxford University Press, 1999).

23. Frank Walsh, *Sin and Censorship: The Catholic Church and the Motion Picture Industry* (New Haven: Yale University Press, 1996); Gregory Black, *Hollywood Censored: Morality Codes, Catholics, and the Movies* (Cambridge: Cambridge University Press, 1994).

24. Rubina Ramji, "Representation of Islam in North American Mass Media: Becoming the 'Other' " (paper at the Conference on Media, Religion, and Culture, Edinburgh, 1999); Hamid Naficy, *The Making of Exile Subcultures: Iranian Television in Los Angeles* (Minneapolis: University of Minnesota Press, 1993).

25. Marie Gillespie, "The Mahabharata: From Sanskrit to Sacred Soap," in *Reading Audiences: Young People and the Media,* ed. David Buckingham (Manchester: Manchester University Press, 1993), 48–73.

26. Rebecca Sullivan, "Revolution in the Convent: Women Religious and American Popular Culture, 1950–1971" (Ph.D. diss., McGill University, 1999).

27. Ann Hardy, "Sites of Value: The Construction and Reception of Religion in Contemporary New Zealand Film and Television" (Ph.D. diss. in progress, University of Waikato).

28. Gregory Stephens, *On Racial Frontiers: The New Culture of Frederick Douglass, Ralph Ellison, and Bob Marley* (Cambridge: Cambridge University Press, 1999).

29. Jane Iwamura, "The Oriental Monk in Popular Culture," in *Religion and Popular Culture in America,* ed., Bruce Forbes and Jeffrey Mahan (Berkeley: University of California Press, 1999).

30. Lynn Schofield Clark, "From Angels to Aliens: Teens, the Media, and Beliefs in the Supernatural," forthcoming.

31. See also Mark Hulsether, "Sorting out the Relationships among Christian Values, U.S. Popular Religion, and Hollywood Films," *Religious Studies Review* 25 (1999): 3–12.

32. James Carey, "Communication and Culture," *Communication Research* 2 (1975): 173–91. Reprinted in James Carey, *Communication as Culture: Essays on Media and Society* (Boston: Unwin Hyman, 1989).

33. Ibid., 18.

34. See, for example, Eric W. Rothenbuhler, *Ritual Communication: From Everyday Conversation to Mediated Ceremony* (Thousand Oaks, Calif.: Sage, 1998); Daniel Dayan and Elihu Katz, *Media Events: The Live Broadcasting of History* (Cambridge: Harvard University Press, 1992).

35. Carolyn Marvin and David W. Ingle, *Blood Sacrifice and the Nation: Totem Rituals and the American Flag* (New York: Cambridge University Press, 1999).

36. Ronald Grimes, *Beginnings in Ritual Studies* (Columbia: University of South Carolina Press, 1995).

37. David Morgan, *Protestants and Pictures* (New York: Oxford University Press, 1999); David Morgan, *Visual Piety: A History and Theory of Popular Religious Images* (Berkeley: University of California Press, 1998); David Morgan, ed., *Icons of American Protestantism: The Art of Warner Sallman* (New Haven: Yale University Press, 1996); Lawrence Moore, *Selling God: American Religion in the Marketplace of Culture* (New York: Oxford University Press, 1994); Colleen McDannell, *Material Christianity: Religion and Popular Culture in America* (New Haven: Yale University Press, 1995).

38. Leigh E. Schmidt, *Consumer Rites: The Buying and Selling of American Holidays* (Princeton: Princeton University Press, 1995); Rex A. E. Hunt, "Carols, Cards, and Claus: The Australian Experience of Christmas in a Culture of Mediation" (Sydney: University of Western Sydney, forthcoming).

39. For information, contact http://www.colorado.edu/Journalism/MEDIALYF.

40. For information, contact Robert White, director, Center for the Interdisciplinary Study of Communications, the Pontifical Gregorian University, Piazza della Pilotta, 4 Rome, Italy 00187.

41. W. Clark Roof, *A Generation of Seekers: The Spiritual Journey of the Baby Boom Generation* (San Francisco: HarperSanFrancisco, 1993); W. Clark Roof, *Spiritual Marketplace* (Princeton: Princeton University Press, 1999); Jacques Grand'Maison and Solange Lefebvre, *Une generation bouc emissaire: Enquete sure la baby boomers* (Montreal: Fides, 1993); Thomas Beaudoin, *Virtual Faith: The Irreverent Spiritual Quest of Generation X* (New York: Jossey Bass, 1999).

42. Lynn Schofield Clark and Stewart M. Hoover, "At the Intersection of Media, Culture, and Religion: A Bibliographic Essay,"in *Rethinking Media, Religion, and Culture,* ed. Stewart M. Hoover and Knut Lundby (Thousand Oaks, Calif.: Sage, 1997), 15–36.

43. Stewart M. Hoover, *Mass Media Religion: The Social Sources of the Electronic Church* (Newbury Park, Calif.: Sage, 1988); Quentin Schultze, *Televangelism and American Culture: The Business of Popular Religion* (Grand Rapids, Mich.: Baker, 1991); Janice Peck, *The Gods of Televangelism* (Cresskill, N.J.: Hampton Press, 1993); Jeffrey K. Hadden and Anson Shupe, *Televangelism, Power, and Politics or God's Frontier* (New York: Holt, 1988).

44. See also Rosalind Hackett, "Charismatic/Pentecostal Appropriations of Media Technologies in Nigeria and Ghana," *Journal of Religion in Africa* 24, no. 4 (1998).

45. Hillary Warren, "Standing against the Tide: Conservative Protestant Families, Mainstream and Christian Media" (Ph.D. diss., University of Texas at Austin, 1998); Hillary Warren, "Southern Baptists as Audience and Public: A Cultural Analysis of the Disney Boycott," in *Religion and Popular Culture: Studies on the Interaction of Worldviews.* ed. Daniel A. Stout and Judith M. Buddenbaum (Ames: Iowa State University Press, 2000).

46. Michael Roth, "That's Where the Power Is: Identification and Ideology in the Construction of Contemporary Christian Music," (master's thesis, University of New Mexico, 1999).

47. John Dart and Jimmy Allen, "Bridging the Gap: Religion and the News Media (report of the Freedom Forum First Amendment Center, Vanderbilt University, Nashville, 1993).

48. Stewart M. Hoover, *Religion in the News: Faith and Journalism in American Public Discourse* (Thousand Oaks, Calif.: Sage, 1998).

49. Judith Buddenbaum, *Reporting News about Religion* (Ames: Iowa State University Press, 1998).

50. For information, contact the Center for the Study of Religion in Public Life, Trinity College, 300 Summit Street, Hartford, Conn. 06106. http://frontpage.trincoll.edu/csrpl.

51. The Public Religion Project, 919 N. Michigan Avenue, Ste. 540, Chicago, Ill. 60611-1601.

52. Muslim Media Watch, Council on American-Muslim Relations, 1050 Seventeenth Street NW, Ste. 490, Washington, D.C. 20036. URL: www.cair-net.org.

53. For an extended historical analysis of journalists and religious identification similar to Schmalzbauer's, see Sean McCloud, "Constructing an American Religious Fringe: Religious Taxonomies, Representational Logic, and Print Media, 1955–1993" (Ph.D. diss. in progress, University of North Carolina at Chapel Hill).

54. Eric K. Gormly, "The Study of Religion and the Education of Journalists," *Journalism and Mass Communication Educator* 54, no. 2 (1999): 24–39.

55. Andrew Weltch, "Spirituality in the Headlines? A Critical Examination of Media, Spiritual, and Religious Values" (master's thesis, University of Wales College, Newport, 1999).

56. Joyce Smith, "In through the Out Door: Learning about Religion via Analogy in the News Media" (paper at the annual meeting, the Society for the Scientific Study of Religion, Boston, 1999).

57. Dane Claussen, ed., *Standing on the Promises: Promise Keepers and the Revival of Manhood* (Cleveland, Ohio: Pilgrim Press, 1999); Dane Claussen, ed., *The Promise Keepers: Essays on Masculinity and Christianity* (Jefferson, N.C.: McFarland, 1999).

58. Edward Said, *Covering Islam* (New York: Pantheon, 1981); Melissa Wall, "More Barney than Buddhist: How the Media Framed the Story of the Little Lama" (paper at the annual meeting, the Association of Educators in Journalism and Mass Communication, New Orleans, 1999); Hamid Mowlana, "Media, Islam, and Culture" (keynote presentation at the Conference on Media, Religion, and Culture, Edinburgh, 1999).

59. Alf Linderman and I. T. Lovheim, *Gemenskap och identitet. En forskningsansats med religion som typfall* (Uppsala: Teologiska Institutionen, 1997).

60. Charles Ess, ed., *Philosophical Perspectives on Computer-Mediated Communication* (Albany: State University of New York Press, 1996); Brenda Brasher, "Thoughts on the Status of the Cyborg: On Technological Socialization and Its Link to the Religious Function of Popular Culture," *Journal of the American Academy of Religion* 64, no. 4 (1996): 809; idem, *Give Me That Online Religion* (San Francisco: Jossey-Bass, 2001); Jeffrey Zaleski, *The Soul of Cyberspace: How New Technology Is Changing Our Spiritual Lives* (San Francisco: HarperEdge, 1997); Gary Bunt, *Virtually Islamic Computer-mediated Communication and Cyber Islamic Environments* (Cardiff: University of Wales Press, 2000); Margaret Wertheim, *The Pearly Gates of Cyberspace: A History of Space from Dante to the Internet* (New York: Norton, 1999).

61. Stephen O'Leary, "Cyberspace as Sacred Space: Communicating Religion on Computer Networks," *Journal of the American Academy of Religion* 64, no. 4 (1996).

62. Anne Foerst, "Cog, a Humanoid Robot, and the Question of the Image of God," *Zygon* 33, no. 1 (1998): 91.

63. http: jmcommunications.com.

64. Mary E. Hess, "Media Literacy in Religious Education: Engaging Popular Culture to Enhance Religious Experience" (Ph.D. diss., Boston College, 1998).

65. Mark Johns, *Go Public! Developing Your Plan for Communication Evangelism* (Minneapolis: Augsburg Press, 1998).

66. John Joshva, "The Parable of the Good Samaritan and the Principles of Christian Communication" (Ph.D. diss., University of Edinburgh, Theology and Ethics of Communication Project, 2000).

67. Michael Slaughter, *Out on the Edge: A Wake-up Call for Church Leaders on the Edge of the Media Reformation* (Nashville, Tenn.: Abingdon, 1998); Leonard Sweet, *Faithquakes* (Nashville, Tenn.: Abingdon, 1995); Dennis Benson, *The Visible Church* (Nashville, Tenn.: Abingdon, 1988); William Romanowski, *Pop Culture Wars: Religion and the Role of Entertainment in American Life* (Downers Grove, Ill.: InterVarsity Press, 1996); Tex Sample, *The Spectacle of Worship in a Wired World* (Nashville, Tenn.: Abingdon, 1998); Len Wilson, *The Wired Church: Making Media Ministry CD-ROM* (Nashville, Tenn.: Abingdon, 1999).

68. See, for example, Horace Newcomb, "Religion on Television," in *Channels of Belief: Religion and American Commercial Television*, ed. J. Ferre (Ames: University of Iowa Press, 1990), 29–44. Some attention to these areas has been paid by prominent scholars of religion; see, for example, Andrew Greeley, *God in Popular Culture* (Chicago: Thomas More Press, 1988).

69. Margaret Miles, *Seeing and Believing: Religion and Values in the Movies* (Boston: Beacon Press, 1996); Bruce Forbes and Jeffrey Mahan, eds., *Religion and Popular Culture in America* (Berkeley: University of California Press, 1999); Joel Martin and Conrad Ostwalt Jr., *Screening the Sacred: Religion, Myth and Ideology in Popular American Film* (Boulder, Colo.: Westview Press, 1995).

70. John May and Michael Bird, eds., *Religion in Film* (Knoxville: University of Tennessee Press, 1982).

71. Theodore Trost, "The Transient and the Permanent: Evaluating U2's 'Pop' " (paper at the Conference on Media, Religion, and Culture, Edinburgh, 1999).

72. Catherine Roach, "Fantasies of Aseity: Religion and Nature Imagery in North American Advertising" (paper at the Conference on Media, Religion, and Culture, Edinburgh, 1999).

73. Gunter Thomas, "Liturgy and Cosmology: Religious Forms in the Context of Television" (paper at the Symposium on Religion and Television, Heidelberg, 1999); Jennifer Porter and Darcee McLaren, eds., *Star Trek and Sacred Ground: Explorations of Star Trek, Religion, and American Culture* (Albany: State University of New York Press, 1999).

74. Beaudoin, *Virtual Faith;* Anders Sjvborg, "Religion and Youth Culture (paper at the Thirteenth Nordic Conference in the Sociology of Religion, Lund, 1996); Pardun and McKee, "Strange Bedfellows."

75. Lynn Schofield Clark, "Identity, Discourse, and Media Audiences: A Critical Ethnography of the Role of Visual Media in Religious Identity-Construction among U.S. Teens" (Ph.D. diss., University of Colorado, 1998); and at the University of Uppsala, Mia Lovheim is at work on a dissertation on teens, religious identity, and the Internet.

76. For information on the Media, Religion, and Culture Fellowship, see http://www.Colorado.EDU/Journalism/MEDIALYF.

BIBLIOGRAPHY

Armstrong, Ben. *The Electric Church.* Nashville: Thomas Nelson, 1979.

Beaudoin, Thomas. *Virtual Faith: The Irreverent Spiritual Quest of Generation X.* New York: Jossey Bass, 1999.

Benson, Dennis. *The Visible Church.* Nashville: Abingdon, 1988.

Bellah, Robert N. *Habits of the Heart: Individualism and Commitment in America.* Berkeley: University of California Press, 1985.

Black, Gregory. *Hollywood Censored: Morality Codes, Catholics, and the Movies.* Cambridge: Cambridge University Press, 1994.

Brasher, Brenda. "Thoughts on the Status of the Cyborg: On Technological Socialization and its Link to the Religious Function of Popular Culture." *Journal of the American Academy of Religion* 64, no. 4 (1996): 809.

Buddenbaum, Judith. *Reporting News about Religion.* Ames: Iowa State University Press, 1998.

Buddenbaum, Judith, and Daniel A. Stout. *Religion and Mass Media: Audiences and Adaptations.* Thousand Oaks, Calif.: Sage, 1996. Bunt, Gary. *Virtually Islamic Computer-mediated Communication and Cyber Islamic Environments.* Cardiff: University of Wales Press, 2000.

Butler, Jonathan. *Awash in a Sea of Faith: Christianizing the American People.* Cambridge: Harvard University Press, 1990.

Carey, James W. *Communication as Culture: Essays on Media and Society.* New York: Routledge, 1992.

Clark, Lynn Schofield. *From Angels to Aliens: Teens, the Supernatural, and the Popular Imagination.* Forthcoming.

——. "Identity, Discourse, and Media Audiences: A Critical Ethnography of the Role of Visual Media in Religious Identity-Construction among U.S. Teens." Ph.D. diss., University of Colorado at Boulder, 1998.

Clark, Lynn Schofield, and Stewart M. Hoover. "At the Intersection of Media, Culture, and Religion: A Bibliographic Essay." In *Rethinking Media, Religion, and Culture,* ed. Stewart M. Hoover and Knut Lundby. Thousand Oaks, Calif.: Sage, 1997.

Claussen, Dane, ed. *Standing on the Promises: Promise Keepers and the Revival of Manhood.* Cleveland, Ohio: Pilgrim Press, 1999.

———. *The Promise Keepers: Essays on Masculinity and Christianity.* Jefferson, N.C.: McFarland, 1999.

Dart, John, and Jimmy Allen. "Bridging the Gap: Religion and the News Media." Report of the Freedom Forum First Amendment Center, Vanderbilt University, Nashville, 1993.

Dayan, Daniel, and Elihu Katz. *Media Events: The Live Broadcasting of History.* Cambridge: Harvard University Press, 1992.

Delia, Jesse. "Communication Research: A History." In *Handbook of Communication Research,* ed. Charles Berger and Stephen Chaffee. Newbury Park, Calif.: Sage, 1988.

Demerath, N. Jay, III. "Cultural Victory and Organizational Defeat in the Paradoxical Decline of Liberal Protestantism." *Journal for the Scientific Study of Religion* 34, no. 4 (1995): 458–69.

Demerath, N. Jay, III, and Rhys H. Williams. *A Bridging of Faiths.* Princeton: Princeton University Press, 1992.

Dewey, John. *The Public and Its Problems.* New York: Henry Holt, 1927.

Driver, Tom F. "The Arts and the Christian Evangel." *Christian Scholar* 40, no. 4 (1957): 334. Cited in Sally Promey, "Interchangeable Art: Warner Sallman and the Critics of Mass Culture," in *Icons of American Protestantism: The Art of Warner Sallman.* ed. David Morgan. New Haven: Yale University Press, 1996.

Eisenstein, Elizabeth L. *The Printing Press as an Agent of Change: Communications and Cultural Transformations in Early Modern Europe.* New York: Cambridge University Press, 1979.

Ess, Charles, ed. Philosophical Perspectives on Computer-Mediated Communication. Albany: State University of New York Press, 1996.

Fiske, John. *Television Culture.* London: Methuen, 1987.

Foerst, Anne. "Cog, a Humanoid Robot, and the Question of the Image of God." *Zygon* 33, no. 1 (1998): 91.

Forbes, Bruce, and Jeffrey Mahan, eds. *Religion and Popular Culture in America.* Berkeley: University of California Press, 1999.

Fore, William. *Television and Religion.* Minneapolis: Augsburg Press, 1987.

Gillespie, Marie. "The Mahabharata: From Sanskrit to Sacred Soap." In *Reading Audiences: Young People and the Media.* ed. David Buckingham. Manchester: Manchester University Press, 1993.

Gormly, Eric K. "The Study of Religion and the Education of Journalists." *Journalism and Mass Communication Educator* 54, no. 2 (1999): 24–39.

Grand'Maison, Jacques, and Solange Lefebvre. *Une generation bouc emissaire: En-quete sure la baby boomers.* Montreal: Fides, 1993.

Greeley, Andrew. *God in Popular Culture.* Chicago: Thomas More Press, 1988.

Green, Russell, and Edward Donnerstein, eds. *Human Aggression: Theories, Re-search, and Implications for Social Policy.* San Diego: Academic, 1998.

Grimes, Ronald. *Beginnings in Ritual Studies.* Columbia: University of South Caro-lina Press, 1995.

Habermas, Jürgen. *The Structural Transformation of the Public Sphere.* Trans. Thomas Burger. Cambridge: MIT Press, 1992.

Hackett, Rosalind. "Charismatic/Pentecostal Appropriations of Media Tech-nologies in Nigeria and Ghana." *Journal of Religion in Africa* 28, no. 3 (1998): 258–77.

Hadden. Jeffrey K., and Anson Shupe. *Televangelism, Power, and Politics or God's Frontier.* New York: Holt, 1988.

Hangen, Tona. "Redeeming the Radio Dial: Evangelical Radio and Religious Cul-ture, 1920–1960." Ph.D. diss., Brandeis University, 1999.

Hall, David. *Worlds of Wonder, Days of Judgment: Popular Religious Belief in Early New England.* New York: Knopf, 1989.

Hall, Stuart, and Tony Jefferson, eds. *Resistance through Rituals: Youth Subcultures in Post-War Britain.* London: Centre for Contemporary Cultural Studies, 1976.

Hamilton, Neal, and Alan Rubin. "The Influence of Religiosity on Television Viewing." *Journalism Quarterly* 69, no. 3 (1992): 667–78.

Hammond, Philip. *Religion and Personal Autonomy: The Third Disestablishment in America.* Columbia: University of South Carolina Press, 1994.

Hardy, Ann. "Sites of Value: The Construction and Reception of Religion in Con-temporary New Zealand Film and Television." Ph.D. diss. in progress, Univer-sity of Waikato.

Hess, Mary E. "Media Literacy in Religious Education: Engaging Popular Culture to Enhance Religious Experience." Ph.D. diss., Boston College, 1998.

Hoover, Stewart M. *Religion in the News: Faith and Journalism in American Public Discourse.* Thousand Oaks, Calif.: Sage, 1998.

——. *Mass Media Religion: The Social Sources of the Electronic Church.* Newbury Park, Calif.: Sage, 1988.

Hulsether, Mark. "Sorting out the Relationships among Christian Values, U.S. Popular Religion, and Hollywood Films." *Religious Studies Review* 25, no. 1 (1999): 3–12.

Hunt, Rex A. E. "Carols, Cards, and Claus: The Australian Experience of Christ-mas in a Culture of Mediation." Sydney: University of Western Sydney, forth-coming.

Iwamura, Jane. "The Oriental Monk in Popular Culture." In *Religion and Popular*

Culture in America, ed. Bruce Forbes and Jeffrey Mahan. Berkeley: University of California Press, 1999.

Johns, Mark. *Go Public! Developing Your Plan for Communication Evangelism.* Minneapolis: Augsburg Press, 1998.

Joshva, John. "The Parable of the Good Samaritan and the Principles of Christian Communication." Ph.D. diss. University of Edinburgh, Theology and Ethics of Communication Project, 2000.

Katz, Elihu, and Paul Lazarsfeld. *Personal Influence.* Glencoe, Ill.: Free Press, 1955.

Kunkel, Dale. "Policy Battles over Defining Children's Educational Television." *Annals of the American Academy of Political and Social Sciences* 557 (1998): 39–53.

Linderman, Alf, and I. T. Lovheim. *Gemenskap och identitet: En forskningsansats med religion som typfall.* Uppsala: Teologiska Institutionen, 1997.

Lippy, Charles. *Being Religious, American Style.* Westport, Conn.: Greenwood Press, 1994.

Martin, Joel, and Conrad Ostwalt Jr. *Screening the Sacred: Religion, Myth, and Ideology in Popular American Film.* Boulder, Colo.: Westview Press, 1995.

Martin-Barbero, Jesus. *Communication, Culture, and Hegemony: From the Media to Mediations.* Trans. E. Fox and R. White. London: Sage, 1993.

Marvin, Carolyn, and David W. Ingle. *Blood Sacrifice and the Nation: Totem Rituals and the American Flag.* New York: Cambridge University Press, 1999.

May, John, and Michael Bird, eds. *Religion in Film.* Knoxville: University of Tennessee Press, 1982.

McCloud, Sean. "Constructing an American Religious Fringe: Religious Taxonomies, Representational Logic, and Print Media, 1955–1993." Ph.D. diss. in progress, University of North Carolina at Chapel Hill.

McDannell, Colleen. *Material Christianity: Religion and Popular Culture in America.* New Haven: Yale University Press, 1995.

Miles, Margaret. *Seeing and Believing: Religion and Values in the Movies.* Boston: Beacon Press, 1996.

Mitchell, Jolyon. *Visually Speaking: Radio and the Renaissance of Preaching.* Edinburgh: Presbyterian and Reformed Publishers, 2000.

Moore, Lawrence. *Selling God: American Religion in the Marketplace of Culture.* New York: Oxford University Press, 1994.

Morgan, David. *Protestants and Pictures.* New York: Oxford University Press, 1999.

——. *Visual Piety: A History and Theory of Popular Religious Images.* Berkeley: University of California Press, 1998.

Morgan, David, ed. *Icons of American Protestantism: The Art of Warner Sallman.* New Haven: Yale University Press, 1996.

Mowlana, Hamid. *Media, Islam, and Culture.* Keynote presentation at the Conference on Media, Religion, and Culture, Edinburgh, 1999.

Muggeridge, Malcolm. *Christ and the Media*. London: Hodder & Stoughton, 1977.

Naficy, Hamid. *The Making of Exile Subcultures: Iranian Television in Los Angeles*. Minneapolis: University of Minnesota Press, 1993.

Newcomb, Horace. "Religion on Television." In *Channels of Belief: Religion and American Commercial Television*, ed. J. Ferre. Ames: University of Iowa Press, 1990.

O'Leary, Stephen. "Cyberspace as Sacred Space: Communicating Religion on Computer Networks." *Journal of the American Academy of Religion* 64 (1996): 781–808.

Pardun, Carol J., and Kathy B. McKee. "Strange Bedfellows: Symbols of Religion and Sexuality on MTV." *Youth and Society* 26 (1995): 438–49.

Pearl, David, Lorraine Bouthilet, and Joyce Lazar, eds. *Television and Behavior: Ten Years of Scientific Progress and Implications for the Eighties*. Rockville, Md.: National Institute of Mental Health, 1982.

Peck, Janice. *The Gods of Televangelism*. Cresskill, N.J.: Hampton Press, 1993.

Porter, Jennifer, and Darcee McLaren, eds. *Star Trek and Sacred Ground: Explorations of Star Trek, Religion, and American Culture*. Albany: State University of New York Press, 1999.

Ramji, Rubina. "Representation of Islam in North American Mass Media: Becoming the 'Other.' " Paper at the Conference on Media, Religion, and Culture, Edinburgh, 1999.

Roach, Catherine. "Fantasies of Aseity: Religion and Nature Imagery in North American Advertising." Paper at the Conference on Media, Religion, and Culture, Edinburgh, 1999.

Romanowski, William. *Pop Culture Wars: Religion and the Role of Entertainment in American Life*. Downers Grove, Ill.: InterVarsity Press, 1996.

Roof, W. Clark. *Spiritual Marketplace*. Princeton, N.J.: Princeton University Press, 1999.

Roof, W. Clark. *A Generation of Seekers: The Spiritual Journey of the Baby Boom Generation*. San Francisco: HarperSanFrancisco, 1993.

Rosenberg, Bernard, and David Manning White, *Mass Culture: The Popular Arts in America*. New York: Macmillan, 1957.

Roth, Michael. "That's Where the Power Is: Identification and Ideology in the Construction of Contemporary Christian Music." Master's thesis, University of New Mexico, 1999.

Rothenbuhler, Eric W. *Ritual Communication: From Everyday Conversation to Mediated Ceremony*. Thousand Oaks, Calif.: Sage, 1998.

Rowland, Willard. *The Politics of TV Violence: Policy Uses of Communications Research*. Beverly Hills: Sage, 1983.

Said, Edward. *Covering Islam*. New York: Pantheon, 1981.

Sample, Tex. *The Spectacle of Worship in a Wired World*. Nashville, Tenn.: Abingdon, 1998.

Schmidt, Leigh E. *Consumer Rites: The Buying and Selling of American Holidays*. Princeton: Princeton University Press, 1995.

Schultze, Quentin. *Televangelism and American Culture: The Business of Popular Religion*. Grand Rapids, Mich.: Baker, 1991.

Shandler, Jeffrey. *While America Watches: Televising the Holocaust*. New York: Oxford University Press, 1999.

Sjvborg, Anders. "Religion and Youth Culture." Paper at the Thirteenth Nordic Conference in the Sociology of Religion, Lund, 1996.

Slaughter, Michael. *Out on the Edge: A Wake-up Call for Church Leaders on the Edge of the Media Reformation*. Nashville, Tenn.: Abingdon, 1998.

Smith, Joyce. "In through the Out Door: Learning about Religion via Analogy in the News Media." Paper at the annual meeting of the Society for the Scientific Study of Religion, Boston, 1999.

Stephens, Gregory. *On Racial Frontiers: The New Culture of Frederick Douglass, Ralph Ellison, and Bob Marley*. Cambridge: Cambridge University Press, 1999.

Sullivan, Rebecca. "Revolution in the Convent: Women Religious and American Popular Culture, 1950–1971." Ph.D. diss., McGill University, 1999.

Surgeon General's Scientific Advisory Committee on Television and Social Behavior. *Television and Growing Up: The Impact of Televised Violence*. Washington, D.C.: GPO, 1972.

Sweet, Leonard. *Faithquakes*. Nashville, Tenn.: Abingdon, 1995.

Sweet, Leonard I. *Communication and Change in American Religious History*. Grand Rapids, Mich.: Eerdmans, 1993.

Thomas, Günter. "Liturgy and Cosmology: Religious Forms in the Context of Television." Paper at the Symposium on Religion and Television, Heidelberg, 1999.

Tocqueville, Alexis de. *Democracy in America*. Ed. J. P. Mayer, trans. George Lawrence. Garden City, N.Y.: Doubleday, 1969; orig. ed., 1835).

Trost, Theodore. "The Transient and the Permanent: Evaluating U2's 'Pop.'" Paper at the Conference on Media, Religion, and Culture, Edinburgh, 1999.

Turner, James. *Without God: Without Creed*. Baltimore: Johns Hopkins University Press, 1985.

Wall, Melissa. "More Barney than Buddhist: How the Media Framed the Story of the Little Lama." Paper at the annual meeting of the Association of Educators in Journalism and Mass Communication, New Orleans, 1999.

Walsh, Frank. *Sin and Censorship: The Catholic Church and the Motion Picture Industry*. New Haven: Yale University Press, 1996.

Warren, Hillary. "Standing against the Tide: Conservative Protestant Families,

Mainstream and Christian Media." Ph.D. diss., University of Texas at Austin, 1998.

Warren, Hillary. "Southern Baptists and Disney." In *Religion and Popular Culture: Studies on the Interaction of Worldviews,* ed. Daniel A. Stout and Judith M. Buddenbaum. Ames: Iowa State University Press, 2000.

Weber, Max. *The Protestant Ethic and the Spirit of Capitalism.* New York: Scribner's, 1928.

Weltch, Andrew. "Spirituality in the Headlines? A Citical Examination of Media, Spiritual, and Religious Values." Master's thesis, University of Wales College, Newport, 1999.

Wertheim, Margaret. *The Pearly Gates of Cyberspace: A History of Space from Dante to the Internet.* New York: Norton, 1999.

Williams, Raymond. *The Long Revolution.* Harmondsworth: Penguin, 1965.

Wilson, Len. *The Wired Church: Making Media Ministry CD-ROM.* Nashville, Tenn.: Abingdon, 1999.

Zaleski, Jeffrey. *The Soul of Cyberspace: How New Technology Is Changing Our Spiritual Lives.* San Francisco: HarperEdge, 1997.

PART I

MEDIATION IN POPULAR RELIGIOUS PRACTICE

We continue in a provocative way, right at the intersection of several of our lines of demarcation. David Morgan's work has ably demonstrated that one of the reasons for our lack of serious or summative accounts of contemporary religious practice has been our inability to account for its visual nature. Morgan argues that popular Protestant piety has been visual, in spite of the tendency for those in authority in religious institutions to resist certain forms of visual religion as mundane or banal. Thus, he invites us in chapter 2 to think about how objects once dismissed as "trivial" because they are popular rather than legitimated, and marginalized rather than mainstream, might need to be seen in a different way. These private objects of devotion exercise important roles in piety.

Erika Doss's chapter 3, on the material culture of the Elvis phenomenon, is also about popular and marginalized practice, but it considers another of our lines of demarcation. Her work addresses a case that in some ways does not present itself as "religious" in any formal sense at all. Unlike the subjects of Morgan's work, many of her informants in fact resist the notion that their activities are in any way religious. Doss does not let the matter rest there, however: she provokes us to look beyond the surface toward the possibility that these activities may be more authentic and meaningful than even those involved might wish to admit—in fact be authentic, though implicit, practice that taps deep levels of meaning for its participants. Also, unlike the practices described by Morgan, the activities carried out by Doss's informants are done very much with an eye to the public and to the public sphere.

CHAPTER 2

PROTESTANT VISUAL PRACTICE AND AMERICAN MASS CULTURE

David Morgan

It is becoming increasingly obvious today that religious images are a part of the study of media, religion, and culture. Indeed, images are and always have been a principal source of information about the world, and religionists in modern American history, contrary to the old Protestant saw about sparseness, have bowed to no one in applying the power of visual display to the transmission of information and to the character formation of youth, the unconverted, and neophytes. Hence, today, the religious uses of imagery and the visual practices of instruction and devotion are being studied to great effect by scholars of art, religion, and popular culture.[1] We are only now beginning to realize that evangelical Protestants two hundred years ago were in no doubt about the rhetorical effectiveness of images at the very moment when modern mass culture was coming into being.

IMAGES AS RELIGIOUS MEDIA

American Protestants manifest a persistent inclination to experience media as an untrammeled representation of "the truth." Images are a medium that has contributed to this Protestant propensity by helping to naturalize what believers have wanted to assume about the world and their

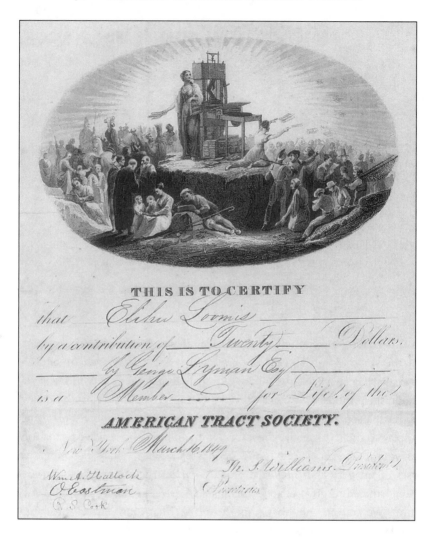

FIGURE 2.1

Printing press, American Tract Society Certificate of Contribution, New York, signed March 16, 1849. Wood engraving on paper, 10.5 × 7.75 inches. (Courtesy of the Billy Graham Center Museum.)

pressing mission within it. This is clear when examining an emblem of the evangelical desire to spread the gospel to all parts of the globe—the printing press shown in figure 2.1. The American Tract Society—founded in New York City in 1825 with the express goal of universal evangelization—gathered the optimistic energies of the new republic toward the millennial task of national renewal, and it placed the image of the printing press on a certificate of contributions to the society.

The press in the figure sits atop an earthy platform around which a diverse crowd of people gathers for a kind of Gutenbergian Sermon on the Mount. The biblical allusion was not accidental: antebellum evangelicals regarded the printing and distribution of the Bible and tracts as the appropriately modern instrument for universal evangelization. The preacher and orator have been replaced by the tract and colportage, just as Jesus has been transmogrified into a mechanical printing press. Instead of listening to a sermonic discourse, the people gather to read tracts distributed by the press's allegorical attendants. Rich and poor, young and old, foreign and domestic, ancient and modern—over the ages, all respond alike to the inexpensive, ephemeral transcription of the Word of God. The image conflates inspiration, production, and dissemination into a single moment that defies time and tradition in order to place in the hands of everyone the changeless divine truth.

It would be difficult to point to a more Protestant image. Derived from personifications of liberty and truth, the female figure standing beside the press holds the Bible in one arm and extends a tract to the multitude with the other, all the while looking heavenward in the image's single gesture acknowledging the source of what the American Tract Society (ATS) fondly called its production of "printed truth." By refusing to visualize more explicit connections to the divine, the image trained the society's efforts on the physical means of production and distribution, suggesting that the enterprise was indeed the result of human initiative, a voluntary act, one that depended on human choice and determination. It is impossible to overstate the optimism of benevolent organizations in the antebellum United States and the important role they played in promoting belief in the social efficacy of philanthropy and religious benevolence.[2]

The press was for many U.S. and British evangelicals the preeminent emblem of the modern age of church history. In the day of canal transportation, steam-powered transport, the telegraph, and the improvement of the national postal system, evangelicals framed their cause in terms of technology and communication. They believed that the new American republic exhibited unique and progressive features that were more than accidental. Many nineteenth-century U.S. Protestants believed that they were the special beneficiaries of a providentially designed confluence of changes in modern civilization. The age was filled with prospects for the spiritual transformation of the nation and progress toward the millennium.

An article in the 1834 *Christian Almanac* included among the "characteristics of the age" the "liberty of the people," the proliferation of voluntary associations, the practical benefits of technological innovations, enhanced commerce and transportation, the universal dissemination of knowledge, and the power of the printing press. "The churches . . . are beginning to survey the field and map it out. Commerce is opening the roads and bridging the seas. The [printing] press is felling the dark forests of ignorance. The way is clear."[3] Commerce, technology, republicanism, and nationhood combined to promise an unprecedented revival in the United States that would usher in the glorious thousand-year reign of Christ. What remains significant in all of this triumphalist rhetoric for historians today is not only the early formation of American nationalism, the reformulation of American exceptionalism, and a noteworthy manifestation of America's perennial crusade for national homogeneity and purpose, but also a clear view of the religious grounding of modern mass culture and its roots in industrialization.

Mass culture emerged in the antebellum period in rapid step with the territorial gains of the United States and the migration of pioneers, industrialists, and entrepreneurs. Mail order, uniform currency, and dependable transportation via an ever-expanding infrastructure of roads, railroads, canals, and steam-powered river vessels provided the material base on which mass-produced publishing enterprises could flourish. Furthermore, antebellum religious benevolence defined itself in terms of its goal of universal evangelization—a goal it did not propose to achieve merely by the traditional means of oral culture such as sermons, revivals, and face-to-face evangelism, but through the new mass culture of printed material (fig. 2.2). In fact, in a widely cited essay, historian of journalism David Nord has rightly attributed to the evangelical Christians of the American Tract and Bible Societies the invention of the mass media in America.[4]

The origins of mass culture were commercial and technological and grounded in modern urbanization, but in the case of nineteenth-century Protestantism, the production and circulation of massive amounts of printed matter was fueled by the need to compensate for the physical limitations of face-to-face communication in a rapidly expanding nation and

No. 1.

THE ADDRESS

OF THE

EXECUTIVE COMMITTEE

OF THE

AMERICAN TRACT SOCIETY,

TO THE

CHRISTIAN PUBLIC.

FIGURE 2.2
Distribution of tracts, ca. 1825; Wood engraving by
Alexander Anderson American Tract Society, New York.

a world that was increasingly connected in networks of commerce and tourism. Oral culture simply was not equal to the evangelical imperative of converting a world that was overwhelmingly non-Christian and a nation with a burgeoning population of Roman Catholic immigrants in the East and West and Asians in the Far West. Thus, the American Tract Society hoped that the evangelical press could make up for the lack of pastors and missionaries in a world where Christians were a minority. The press was so efficacious that one account from India, "that land of idols," reported the power of two tracts alone to convert an entire village of "the heathen." The story related that a missionary entered a remote village and inquired about why no signs of Hindu or Muslim worship were apparent. "We believe in Jesus," was the answer. The villagers told the missionary that one of their number had returned from a "distant fair" one day with two religious tracts, which the village members read and determined "to give up the worship of idols, and serve the living and true God."[5]

The power of the evangelical press was the autonomous power of the written word to convince the reader of the religious truths of evangelical Christianity. Faith in the Word made flesh was convertible into the word made of ink and paper; or, as one ATS document put it, print holds "the same relation to the word of God, in addressing the mind through *the eye,* that the living ministry does in addressing it through *the ear.*"[6] The advantage, of course, was that the tract was not limited to the oral medium of local culture, but was based on mechanical reproduction in mass culture, a fundamentally *visual* culture. The tract societies conflated oral communication with manual and mechanical forms in order to package mass culture as local culture. Thus, the tracts often incorporated first-person forms of address in order to fit face-to-face encounter to mass-culture practices of communication. The intention was to enhance the printed text's persuasive effect by discerning in it the persistent presence of the author as speaker, a trace of oral culture's face-to-face construction of authority.

A great deal of Protestant visual culture was prepared for children, to be used in religious instruction or as gifts for attendance at Sunday school and membership or participation in benevolent enterprises. In fact, the rise of the Sunday school in the United States as well as initiatives like tract distribution were in part a result of the widespread discovery that the church could begin the formal socialization process into religion much earlier than adolescence or adulthood. In her superb study of the U.S. Sunday school in the nineteenth century, Anne Boylan has argued that one of the reasons behind the phenomenal growth of Sunday school attendance and the robust national and local organizations that sponsored

SABBATH SCHOOL MEETING.

" *Behold he prayeth.*"—Acts, ix. 11.

FIGURE 2.3

Sunday school meeting card, reproduced in *American Sunday School Teacher's Magazine and Journal of Education* 1, no. 8 (1824): 257. Wood engraving, 4 × 3.5 inches.

religious instruction was the new idea that children were susceptible to religious conversion.[7]

One of these organizations, the American Sunday School Union (ASSU), printed in the first volume of its *American Sunday School Teacher's Magazine* (1824) a report from its New York branch that noted the success of an illustrated gift card (fig. 2.3); the branch urged use of the card by other members. On its reverse side, the card invited parents to send their children to Sunday school. The illustrated cards formally announced the meeting, secured parental permission, acted as tokens of admission, and enhanced instruction. The report made the point that because the cards were collected at the door, children felt privileged to enter and participate. The cards were thus embedded in the social practices of Sunday school attendance, membership, and learning.[8] Given the importance of the Sunday school as the first step toward the formation of adult congregations, the cards were also subtle contributions to evangelical mission work.

In 1859, a missionary for the ASSU observed that "most, if not all, the Churches of the [Mississippi and Ohio River valleys] of recent formation, have grown out of Sunday-schools previously existing."[9] Children, evangelicals came to learn, were a most effective avenue toward reaching adults and establishing the traditional form of institutional religion—the congregation. Such a strategy was logical: in 1820, more than half of the white population in the United States was sixteen years old or younger, and in 1840 the ratio was little changed (the number of white persons aged twenty or older was equal (.99%) to that of white children under sixteen).[10] There were proportionately more young people to convert and, because they were still susceptible to authority and control, they were easier to convert than adults. This activation of youth via the mass media—evident in children's literature and religious magazines in the nineteenth century—helped usher in mass culture as we know it today; indeed, sociologist Edward Shils once remarked that the unprecedented modern-day production and massive consumption of popular culture for youth lies at the heart of the "revolution of mass culture."[11]

RELIGIOUS INSTRUCTION AND THE DIDACTIC IMAGE

The purpose of the image was to attract children to evangelical learning, to install them in Sunday schools and other benevolent activities, to appeal to their parents, and to facilitate the memorization of information. Children like pictures—and so do Protestants, especially pictures that act like texts, presumably because that makes the image a more reliable vessel of scriptural truth, or one that at least draws less attention to itself than does a work of art.

It may be that when two sets of signs corroborate one another, as words and images were made to do in evangelicalism, the result is a higher semiotic security—one that would have been particularly reassuring when deployed among children and immigrants, both of whom represented uncivilized "others" not fluent in the literacy of the status quo. Moreover, when left to themselves, images are able to do alarming things such as bleed, speak, heal, move, weep, and incite popular pilgrimages. This is because iconic images are portraits that return our gaze or interact in some other way with viewers, even performing miracles of one sort or another in response to a local need or petition. A characteristic feature of

FIGURE 2.4

Heathen mother, from *Dr. Scudder's Tales for Little Readers: About the Heathen,* by Rev. John Scudder (New York, American Tract Society, 1853).

the religious icon is that it seems to possess a life of its own, a vitality and presence that can exceed even the restraints of liturgy, text, or biblical narrative. This quality is particularly manifest if the image responds directly to the viewer—for example, through the gaze of a portrait's eyes or in miraculous manifestation of blood or tears. Images anchored to words are much more easily controlled.

The miraculous and mysterious aside, any reflective teacher will recognize that, when keyed to images, certain emotional sensations assist dramatically in memory retention. The history of images of religious education indicates the importance of affective associations. Fear, revulsion, pity, shame, comfort, humor, and surprise appear to tag memories in a way that makes them indelible, forceful, easily retrieved, and formative. Each of these feelings has accompanied the use of certain images in the religious training of American children. Below I look at three: fear, humor, and comfort.

Fear was an especially powerful emotional sheath in which to place images. By fear I mean not only the obvious terror of hellfire and brimstone, but also the much subtler but no less shocking use of fear that adults relied on to lodge in the minds of children cultural and racial distinctions between Christian and non-Christian and between Protestant and Roman Catholic. Consider an image that appeared in *Dr. Scudder's Tales for Little Readers,* published by the Tract Society in 1853 (fig. 2.4). The text contrasts the tenderness of American mothers with the cruel indifference of this "heathen mother," a Hindu woman who is throwing her child to a crocodile. The image reverses the story of Moses being retrieved from the Nile by a servant girl and plays on any child's fear of maternal indifference. Whatever else the image suggested, it certainly reinforced the belief that American domesticity, rooted in Christianity, was superior to non-Christian family practices.[12]

Closer to home were uses of imagery that monitored relations between Protestant and Catholic. Fear operated powerfully in instructional imagery among nineteenth-century Adventists, who following the demise of Millerism in the 1840s for a time were concerned with inculcating a distinct sense of group identity among their young. In a dialogue between a father and son published in 1846 in the *Children's Advent Herald,* a father displays on a wall of the family home a "Bible chart" that provokes in the boy "the highest expression of interest and delight."[13] The father carefully describes paradise, the fall into sin, and the entry into the heavenly Jerusalem, then turns to the prophetic symbols of Daniel 7, which appear as illustrations with the article. When the child asks where such horrible monsters as the "Roman beast" were kept, the father replies: "There are some of them in Boston, some in Charlestown, and some of them almost all over the world. Wherever there is a Roman Catholic priest, there that great ugly monster is."[14]

Comfort was an emotional value that became increasingly popular among evangelicals as the cult of domesticity developed during the nineteenth century. The iconography of comfort was promoted in advice books and literature directed to parents—particularly to young mothers. Not infrequently, identical images were shared among evangelical publications, as was the one shown in figure 2.5, which marks a clear contrast to *Heathen Mother* by depicting a cozy, comforting maternal ideal. The text accompanying this image in a Massachusetts children's newspaper in 1861 noted that the editor was "always delighted to meet those [children] who are gentle and kind to each other, and obedient and affectionate to their parents."[15]

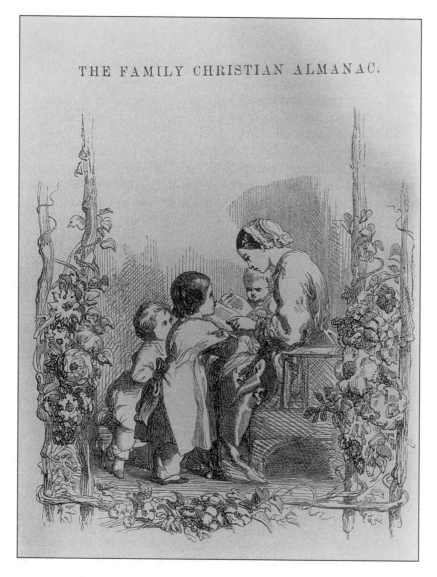

FIGURE 2.5

Mother reading to children, from *Christian Almanac* (New York: American Tract Society, 1869).

The same image, cropped differently for use in the *Christian Almanac* of 1869, appeared with the words: "Consider what picture-books are to a child; not only culture, nutriment, play, but medicine, comfort, rest; nothing enters so completely and entirely into child-life. They are repeated, quoted, dramatized, remembered. What sense and sensibility, spice and

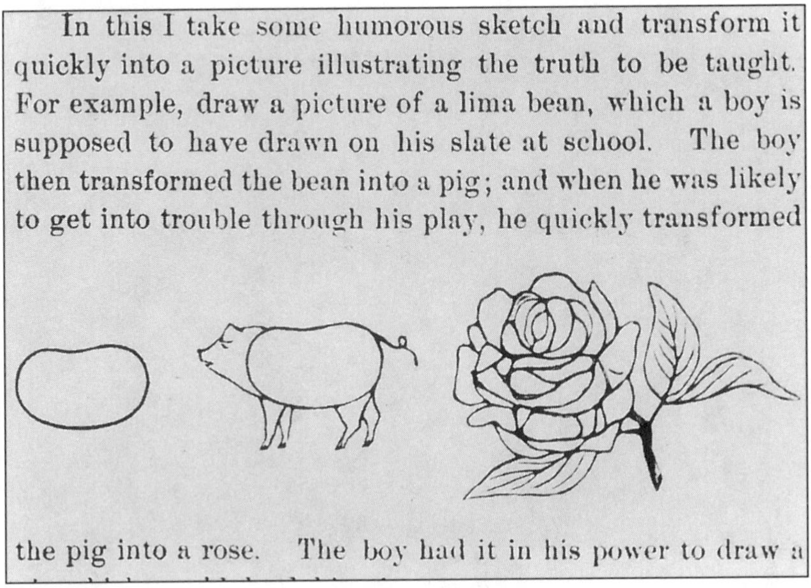

In this I take some humorous sketch and transform it quickly into a picture illustrating the truth to be taught. For example, draw a picture of a lima bean, which a boy is supposed to have drawn on his slate at school. The boy then transformed the bean into a pig; and when he was likely to get into trouble through his play, he quickly transformed

the pig into a rose. The boy had it in his power to draw a

FIGURE 2.6

Lima bean/pig/rose, from *Pictured Truth: A Hand-Book of Blackboard and Object Lessons,* by Rev. Robert F. Y. Pierce (New York: Fleming H. Revell, 1895).

shortness are required to write one! I had rather be the author of a lively and wholesome picture-book, than to be Hume or Smollet. Let not picture-book makers undervalue their mission."[16] The text pitted the highbrow culture of philosopher and novelist against the culture of child rearing, echoing the widespread belief that the influence exerted over children lasted a lifetime and exceeded in importance the impact that adults— even learned and artistic authorities—could extend over one another.

Humor and surprise were used effectively to aid instruction. For instance, surprise was an important factor in deciphering the rebus puzzles in illustrated primers and hieroglyphic Bibles, a popular form of Protestant visual culture for children in the eighteenth and nineteenth centuries. Finding hidden or coded meanings aroused the young person's curiosity and served to direct and fix the child's attention on biblical themes and passages.[17]

Another amusing genre of performative Protestant image making was the chalk talk, a didactic application of the image to learning biblical truths and church doctrines. Used in the Sunday school movement in the 1860s, and perhaps even earlier, the chalk talk, or blackboard talk, gathered students to watch the word preached with the supplement of active illustration. Surprise and humor were interlaced in the presentation, and timing became an important aspect of performing images. Chalk talkers were aware that the simpler the mark, the greater the freedom allowed to the viewer in having his or her imagination engaged.

Most manuals on chalk talk included examples of metamorphosis as a favorite device for amusing an audience and keeping its attention. The artist illustrated the transformation of one thing into another in a series of drawings. An image in an 1895 manual on biblical chalk talks (fig. 2.6) illustrated the transformation of a lima bean into a pig, which in turn became a rose—a series of metamorphoses that visually demonstrated the capacity of young people to turn something objectionable in their behavior—the pig—into something commendable, the rose.[18]

FROM CONVERSION TO CHARACTER FORMATION

In the use of comfort as a value we find an important shift in the application of images to instruction, for the task of comforting, particularly the tenderness of maternal instruction, was geared not necessarily to the memorization of information—indeed, what could an infant memorize?—but to the formation of character. Protestants of many stripes warmly commended the influence of mothers and the early effects of domestic life.

An item in the *Christian Almanac* commented on an image of the mother of the future evangelist Philip Doddridge (fig. 2.7). In the illustration, she is teaching her son from images of biblical episodes, and the caption reads: "The impressions of childhood are proverbially deep and lasting. Some of the best, and also some of the worst characters the world has ever known, have been formed for their future career by the lessons of their earliest days."[19] Learning was rooted in the domestic sphere of a mother's teaching, but by midcentury shaping character had become the deeper concern.

The idea of character formation entered theological discourse most notably in Horace Bushnell's widely read book *Christian Nurture*, first published in 1840 and followed by a longer, revised edition in 1861. While many Sunday school organizations focused on conversion and the classroom, the move toward the domestic nurture of children stressed the or-

FIGURE 2.7

Mother of Doddridge, *Christian Almanac* (New York: American Tract Society, 1857).

ganic evolution of character and the preeminence of the home in this gradual development. Bushnell considered the home the true seat of the church and envisioned the congregation seated before the hearth as the ideal emblem of home religion. In a passage that evokes any one of numerous illustrations of family scenes beside the hearth used in Protestant and Catholic publications to promote the importance of the domestic altar (fig. 2.8), Bushnell wrote:

> We look in upon the Christian family, where every thing is on a footing of religion, and we see them around their own quiet hearth and table,

FIGURE 2.8
Family reading Bible at hearth from, *Christian Almanac*
(New York: American Tract Society, 1863).

away from the great public world and its strifes, with a priest of their own to lead them. They are knit together in ties of love that make them one; even as they are fed and clothed out of the same fund, interested in the same possessions, partakers in the same successes and losses, suffering together in the same sorrows, animated each by hopes that respect the future benefit of all.[20]

Bushnell described a utopian retrieval of the ancient Christian fellowship, now realized in the family, a refuge from the outer world, a self-contained community with a priest of its own. The task, according to Bushnell, was no longer to fill the memory with religious information, but to plant seeds, to nurture the growth of the individual's character, to shape the whole person in the organic body of the family long before intellectual development even began.

The priest of the family was nominally the father, but in practice, particularly for younger children, religious instruction was dominated in the home by the mother, or by other women in Sunday school instruction. One of the most basic tools in Christian formation was the illustrated book. As we saw in the case of this mother reading a picture book to her eager children, the *Christian Almanac* urged the importance of illustrated literature for children (see fig. 2.5). This image visualized what the experience of picture books meant to youth: three children listen transfixed, as their mother reads to them. The small company is snugly framed in a trellis of vines and festoons, a secure nest of visual storytelling that, the caption tells us, removes the children from the ordinary world of "toothache, earache, finger-ache . . . fretfulness, moping, pouts."[21] This domestic world suspended pain and misbehavior and was freighted with moral purpose. It opened an affective avenue to the child's heart and constituted an aesthetic committed to the formation of character. The "picture story" that the children requested of their mother became the occasion for domestic bonding and intimacy, which imprinted deeply on the child's memory and became a powerful vehicle of the evangelical message of Jesus.

The image, in other words, was about more than memorizing information: it became the site for the child's relationship to siblings and parents—the focus for the experience of domestic life. Furthermore, with the commercial production of lithographs intended for domestic display and the rise of portrait photography as a popular visual culture, the portrait format began to service the domestic piety of the nineteenth-century Christian home. Images were displayed in both Catholic and Protestant homes in order to shape character in tandem with such practices as prayer and family devotion. The gaze of Mary or Jesus that followed family members about the domestic interior provided a constant sense of presence and made the heavenly person portrayed accessible to petition and prayer. The devotional sensibility allowed Protestants to practice a visual piety that Roman Catholics had long enjoyed: one that visualized a personal relationship with the sacred other.

THE ORIGIN OF A DEVOTONAL ICONOGRAPHY

The first signs of the development of a devotional visual piety, a use for images that accorded to them the power to shape an individual's relationship with the divine, appeared in the mid-nineteenth century. It is helpful to draw a distinction between the *didactic* function of images in providing the memory with affective devices for recalling information and the *devotional* use of images, which I believe, was aimed at shaping character.

In the United States before the Civil War, devotional images were largely restricted to Roman Catholicism, hundreds having been produced as lithographs by firms such as Currier & Ives. The lithographs depicted a variety of saints and carried captions in Italian, French, Spanish, and German. They were intended for immigrants in this country and also for export to Canada, Mexico, and Europe. But with the new use of images described above—to form the person by nurturing the relationships the child was to enjoy with Jesus and with family members—the image in Protestant homes became, in addition to being a bearer of propositional information, a conveyer of personality and such affections as tenderness, sympathy, and sentiment. Portraiture thus acquired new significance in the iconography of American Protestantism. Portraits of Luther and fellow reformers or the Puritan author John Bunyan had long populated frontispieces and mantels in evangelical homes, but now the portraiture of Jesus and the disciples was added to the arsenal of Protestant pedagogy as a fundamental element in Christian nurture.[22]

Whereas didactic images were powerful by virtue of informing the child's religious identity as the repository of concepts that characterized a group or tradition, devotional images offered a direct, visual access to the person portrayed, an icon by which the child could enjoy an affective relationship with that person. Nurture, according to the theologically liberal Bushnell but also the conservative evangelicals who applied his theories to their religious sphere, consisted of immersing the child in an organic, evolving matrix and genetic pedigree, the effects of which were communicated not as discursive knowledge but as feeling and sensibility. Influence over time rather than abrupt conversion was considered the avenue of grace and the truly decisive articulation of faith in the individual's life.

The devotional image of Jesus became especially important among two broad groups of American Protestants. While the devotional portrait had often been employed in Roman Catholic devotion, American evangelicals and liberal Protestants came to see in the portrait of Christ christological aspects central to their pieties. For instance, when the christology of friendship emerged as one of the most popular ways of understanding one's relationship to God—that is, as the hymn put it, "What a friend we have in Jesus, all our sins and griefs to bear"—we begin to find a popular consumption of portraits of Jesus that was not about information to be memorized but about looking hopefully into the human visage of one's personal savior. In the new age of photography, when families, friends, and lovers collected photographs of one another, it seemed only natural to treasure a portrait of one's best, most intimate Friend.

The task of portraying Jesus for a Protestant market, which was increasingly shaped by the visual rhetoric of photography, found textual support in a medieval manuscript that purported to be (and was long respected as) a description of Jesus by a contemporary. Attributed to Publius Lentulus, a Roman official said to be a contemporary of Pontius Pilate, working in Palestine, the letter was addressed to the Roman senate. As late as 1871, Henry Ward Beecher believed the letter to have originated in the fourth century. The document, therefore, offered "a clear view of the countenance which [early Christian] art had already adopted, and which afterward served virtually as the type of all the heads of Christ by the great Italian masters, and by almost all modern artists."[23]

The letter had acquired sufficient interest to warrant a lithograph from the ambitiously entrepreneurial firm of Currier & Ives. *The True Portrait of Our Blessed Savior, Sent by Publius Lentullus to the Roman Senate* (fig. 2.9) was produced sometime between 1857 and 1872 (the dating is based on the address of the firm recorded at the foot of the print). Currier & Ives may have released the print in the hope of capitalizing on the growing popularity of such illustrated lives of Jesus as Beecher's biography.[24] While many Currier & Ives images were intended for a Roman Catholic market, and therefore included Spanish, French, or German text, the caption of this image is limited to English, suggesting perhaps that this was a commodity aimed at both Protestant and Catholic customers. Other than the trinimbus, the image is shorn of iconography. It is a pictorial rendering of

THE TRUE PORTRAIT OF
OUR BLESSED SAVIOUR.
Sent by Publius Lentullus to the Roman Senate.

FIGURE 2.9
The True Portrait of Our Blessed Saviour (Currier & Ives, ca. 1857–72). Lithograph, 13 × 8.5 inches. Courtesy of the Billy Graham Center Museum.

FIGURE 2.10

Head of Christ, by Warner Sallman, 1940. Oil on canvas, 28.25 × 22.125 inches. (Courtesy of the Jessie C. Wilson Galleries, Anderson University.)

the medieval description. Christ looks directly into the viewer's eyes and bears the features described by Publius: a short, forked beard, shoulder-length brown hair parted in the center, a smooth, large forehead, and bright, clear eyes.[25]

The idea of the "true portrait" was indebted to the Latin tradition of Veronica, the legendary woman who acquired the "true icon" of Christ when the Savior's features were mysteriously transferred to the cloth Veronica handed him as he paused on the way to Calvary.[26] But the Currier & Ives print translates the icon into a portrait with a claim to first-hand authority. The simplicity and directness of the image exhibits aspects of contemporary photographic portraiture. Christ turns from a three-quarters view to face the viewer. Background detail is eliminated in favor of a plain backdrop. The close focus on head and shoulders is reminiscent both of ancient icons and modern portraiture.

How viewers were meant to encounter this person was paramount. There is no text other than the brief caption assuring viewers of the image's authenticity. This autonomy from a narrative or textual reference is what made the image new for American Protestants. Christ is seen here as a visual description of himself—that and that alone. His features are encoded with his character as a benevolent, solemn, tranquil savior. We do not see him in a particular narrative moment, but abstracted from the events of his life and placed against the plain screen of a commercial studio. The image presents itself as a journalistic, eyewitness rendition of Christ's appearance as a human being, God in the flesh (as the halo reminds us). By focusing on what Jesus looked like rather than what he did, the image meant to visualize his character and to address it to the devout viewer with the directness of Christ's gaze. It was important that the Currier & Ives image eliminated everything but the person. The resulting portrait was intended and likely received as an accurate, untrammeled, historical, literal—a truthful—portrayal, and even a visual record of the historical Jesus.

There is no indication that the Currier & Ives image was used among Protestants in the way that Roman Catholic piety invested images with an iconic power. Protestant devotional practice would not use the image in this way until the twentieth century (fig. 2.10).[27] But the newfound power of portraits of Jesus as a visual medium of Christian nurture fueled the development toward Protestant icons. Mass culture contributed in important ways to this by offering an inexpensive imagery whose mechanical reproduction hardly eliminated the aura, as Walter Benjamin would have it, but in fact made aura graphically transmissible. If the irony of Protestant visual piety sliding almost imperceptibly into Roman Catholic practice was complete by the mid-twentieth century, it was thanks in no small way to mass culture and the commodification of nurture.

NOTES

This chapter is drawn from the author's *Protestants and Pictures: Religion, Visual Culture, and the Age of American Mass Culture*. New York: Oxford University Press, 1999.

1. James R. Curtis, "Miami's Little Havana: Yard Shrines, Cult Religion and Landscape," in *Rituals and Ceremonies in Popular Culture*, ed. Ray B. Browne (Bowling Green: Bowling Green University Popular Press, 1980), 105–19; John Davis, *Landscape of Belief: Encountering the Holy Land in Nineteenth-Century American Art and Culture* (Princeton: Princeton University Press, 1996); Erika Doss, *Elvis Culture: Fans, Faith, and Image in Contemporary America* (Lawrence: University of Kansas Press, 1999); David Freedberg, *The Power of Images: Studies in the History and Theory of Response* (Chicago: University of Chicago Press, 1989); Gregor T. Goethals, *The Electronic Golden Calf: Images, Religion, and the Making of Meaning* (Cambridge, Mass.: Cowley, 1990); David Halle, *Inside Culture: Art and Class in the American Home* (Chicago: University of Chicago Press, 1993), 171–92; Colleen McDannell, *Material Christianity: Religion and Popular Culture in America* (New Haven: Yale University Press, 1995); Margaret Miles, *Image as Insight: Visual Understanding in Western Christianity and Secular Culture* (Boston: Beacon, 1985); David Morgan, *Visual Piety: A History and Theory of Popular Religious Images* (Berkeley: University of California Press, 1998); David Morgan, ed., *Icons of American Protestantism: The Art of Warner Sallman* (New Haven: Yale University Press, 1996); Sally M. Promey, *Spiritual Spectacles: Vision and Image in Mid-Nineteenth-Century Shakerism* (Bloomington: Indiana University Press, 1993); Leigh Eric Schmidt, *Consumer Rites: The Buying and Selling of American Holidays* (Princeton: Princeton University Press, 1995); and Thomas Tweed, *Our Lady of Exile: Diasporic Religion at a Cuban Catholic Shrine in Miami* (New York: Oxford University Press, 1997).

2. For a thorough study of the American Tract Society, see Karl Eric Valois, "To Revolutionize the World: The American Tract Society and the Regeneration of the Republic, 1825–1877" (Ph.D. diss., University of Connecticut, 1994). On the ATS and mass-communication, see David Paul Nord, "The Evangelical Origins of Mass Media in America, 1815–1835," *Journalism Monographs* (1984): 1–30; see also

Nord, "Systematic Benevolence: Religious Publishing and the Marketplace in Early Nineteenth-Century America," in *Communication and Change in American Religious History*, ed. Leonard I. Sweet (Grand Rapids, Mich.: Eerdmans, 1993), 239–69.

3. "Characteristics of the Age," *Christian Almanac* (New York: American Tract Society, 1834), 36.

4. Nord, "Evangelical Origins," 24.

5. "The Unknown Christians of India," *Christian Almanac* (New York: American Tract Society, 1858), 40. The full title for this issue was *The Illustrated Family Christian Almanac of 1858*. The title of the almanac changed several times over the course of its publication; for consistency, throughout this chapter it is referred to as *Christian Almanac*.

6. *American Colporteur System* (New York: American Tract Society, 1843), 4. Emphasis in original.

7. Anne M. Boylan, *Sunday School: The Formation of an American Institution, 1790–1880* (New Haven: Yale University Press, 1988), 15–16; Anne M. Boylan, "The Role of Conversion in Nineteenth-Century Sunday Schools," *American Studies* 20 (1979): 35–48; see also Joseph Kett, *Rites of Passage. Adolescence in America 1790 to the Present* (New York: Basic Books, 1977), 118–20.

8. "Improvements in Sunday Schools: Extract from the Report of Sunday School No. 23," *The American Sunday School Teacher's Magazine and Journal of Education* 1, no. 8 (1824): 258. Boylan, *Sunday School*, 48, has discussed how gift cards proved to be a very popular inducement among children to attend Sunday school.

9. Quoted in Boylan, *Sunday School*, 34.

10. U.S. Bureau of the Census, *A Century of Population Growth from the First Census of the United States to the Twelfth, 1790–1900* (Washington, D.C.: GPO, 1909), 103.

11. Edward Shils, "Mass Society and Its Culture," in *Culture and Mass Culture*, ed. Peter Davison, Rolf Meyersohn, and Edward Shils, vol. 1 of Literary Taste, Culture, and Mass Communication (Cambridge, England: Chadwyck-Healy, 1978), 214. Early nineteenth-century schoolbooks were one of the early examples of mass-produced imagery occasioned by the need to educate children. Noah Webster was one of the most important authors of such schoolbooks, publishing the most successful speller. Although his spellers were not illustrated until the 1820s, thereafter they and competing spellers were often densely illustrated. On significant pedagogical reforms, see R. Freeman Butts, *Public Education in the United States: From Revolution to Reform* (New York: Holt, Rinehart, & Winston, 1978), 31–33. Webster's speller was variously titled: first called *A Grammatical Institute of the English Language*, it became *The American Spelling Book* and later *The Elementary Spelling Book* and *The Blue-Back Speller*. The combined impact of Webster's dictionary and his speller can hardly be overstated on the formation of American English during the early national period. Between 1783 and 1804, the spelling book passed through eighty-eight numbered

editions; from 1804 to 1818, an additional 3.3 million copies were printed; and from 1818 to 1832, more than 4.5 million. Monaghan estimates the total number from 1783 to 1847 to have been 17 million: E. Jennifer Monaghan, *A Common Heritage: Noah Webster's Blue-Back Speller* (Hamden, Conn.: Archon Books, 1983), 215–28.

12. For some viewers there were limits to what was visually acceptable. Several readers of the children's newspaper *Well-Spring* wrote to the editor in the spring of 1861 to object to the horror and vulgarity of graphic depictions of a dead horse in one issue and a crocodile devouring a black child in another; see *Well-Spring* 18, no. 15 (1861): 60, and vol. 18, no. 22 (May 31, 1861), 86.

13. "Conversation between a Father and Son, on the 7th Chapter of Daniel," *Children's Advent Herald* 1, no. 4 (1846): 14.

14. Ibid.: 15.

15. "Mama's Story," *Well-Spring* 18, no. 25 (1861): 96. In this instance, a common link between the *Well-Spring* and the *Christian Almanac* was *Well-Spring* editor Helen Cross Knight. She edited the almanac in the 1860s and published religious books through the Massachusetts Sabbath School Society.

16. *Christian Almanac* (1869): 41–42.

17. Popular responses to Sallman's *Head of Christ* have claimed that hidden imagery is in the portrait (fig. 2.10). Reports indicate as many as eleven embedded hidden images; see Morgan, *Visual Piety,* 124–51.

18. Robert F. Y. Pierce, *Pictured Truth. A Hand-Book of Blackboard and Object Lessons* (New York: Fleming H. Revell, 1895), 20.

19. "The Mother of Doddridge," *Christian Almanac* (1857): 23.

20. Horace Bushnell, *Christian Nurture* (Grand Rapids, Mich.: Baker Book House, 1979), 405.

21. *Christian Almanac* (1869): 41. For further discussion of the role of mother and father in the domestic altar, see Colleen McDannell, *The Christian Home in Victorian America, 1840–1900* (Bloomington: Indiana University Press, 1986), esp. chaps. 5 and 6.

22. For a discussion of portrait busts of Wesley, see Colleen McDannell, *Material Christianity: Religion and Popular Culture in America* (New Haven: Yale University Press, 1995), 43–45.

23. Henry Ward Beecher, *The Life of Jesus, the Christ* (New York: J. B. Ford, 1871), 141.

24. *Currier & Ives: A Catalogue Raisonn,,* 2 vols. (Detroit: Gale Research, 1984), 1: xvi. A black-and-white version of the print is listed with a slightly different title in vol. 2 of the catalog (#5026).

25. For the text of the letter of Publius, see Beecher, *Life of Christ,* 140–41, n. 2.

26. A fine study of Veronica is Ewa Kuryluk, *Veronica and Her Cloth: History, Symbolism, and Structure of a "True" Image* (Cambridge, Mass.: Basil Blackwell, 1991).

27. On the imagery by Sallman and its reception, see Morgan, *Icons.*

BIBLIOGRAPHY

American Colporteur System. New York: American Tract Society, 1843.

Beecher, Henry Ward. *The Life of Jesus, the Christ.* New York: J. B. Ford, 1871.

Boylan, Anne M. *Sunday School: The Formation of an American Institution, 1790–1880.* New Haven: Yale University Press, 1988, 15–16.

Boyland, Anne M. "The Role of Conversion in Nineteenth-Century Sunday Schools." *American Studies* 20 (1979): 35–48.

Bushnell, Horace. *Christian Nurture.* Grand Rapids, Mich.: Baker Book House, 1979, 405.

Butts, R. Freeman. *Public Education in the United States: From Revolution to Reform.* New York: Holt, Rinehart, & Winston, 1978, 31–33.

"Characteristics of the Age." *Christian Almanac.* New York: American Tract Society, (1834): 36. Ibid. (1869): 41.

"Conversation between a Father and Son, on the 7th Chapter of Daniel." *Children's Advent Herald* 1, no. 4 (1846): 14.

Currier & Ives: A Catalogue Raisonn, 2 vols. Detroit: Gale Research, 1984.

Curtis, James R. "Miami's Little Havana: Yard Shrines, Cult Religion, and Landscape." In *Rituals and Ceremonies in Popular Culture,* ed. Ray B. Browne. Bowling Green: Bowling Green University Popular Press, 1980.

Davis, John. *Landscape of Belief: Encountering the Holy Land in Nineteenth-Century American Art and Culture.* Princeton: Princeton University Press, 1996.

Doss, Erika. *Elvis Culture: Fans, Faith, and Image in Contemporary America.* Lawrence: University of Kansas Press, 1999.

Freedberg, David. *The Power of Images: Studies in the History and Theory of Response.* Chicago: University of Chicago Press, 1989.

Goethals, Gregor T. *The Electronic Golden Calf: Images, Religion, and the Making of Meaning.* Cambridge, Mass.: Cowley, 1990.

Halle, David. *Inside Culture: Art and Class in the American Home.* Chicago: University of Chicago Press, 1993.

"Improvements in Sunday Schools: Extract from the Report of Sunday School No. 23." *American Sunday School Teacher's Magazine and Journal of Education* 1, no. 8 (1824): 258.

Kuryluk, Ewa. *Veronica and Her Cloth: History, Symbolism, and Structure of a "True" Image.* Cambridge, Mass.: Basil Blackwell, 1991.

Kett, Joseph. *Rites of Passage: Adolescence in America 1790 to the Present.* New York: Basic Books, 1977.

"Mama's Story," *Well-Spring* 18, no. 25 (1861): 96.

McDannell, Colleen. *The Christian Home in Victorian America, 1840–1900.* Bloomington: Indiana University Press, 1986.

McDannell, Colleen. *Material Christianity: Religion and Popular Culture in America*. New Haven: Yale University Press, 1995.

Miles, Margaret. *Image as Insight: Visual Understanding in Western Christianity and Secular Culture*. Boston: Beacon Press, 1985.

Monaghan, E. Jennifer. *A Common Heritage: Noah Webster's Blue-Back Speller*. Hamden, Conn.: Archon Books, 1983.

Morgan, David, ed., *Icons of American Protestantism: The Art of Warner Sallman*. New Haven: Yale University Press, 1996.

Morgan, David. *Visual Piety: A History and Theory of Popular Religious Images*. Berkeley: University of California Press, 1998.

"The Mother of Doddridge." *Christian Almanac* (1857): 23.

Nord, David Paul. "The Evangelical Origins of Mass Media in America, 1815–1835." *Journalism Monographs* (1984): 1–30.

Nord, David Paul. "Systematic Benevolence: Religious Publishing and the Marketplace in Early Nineteenth-Century America." In *Communication and Change in American Religious History*, ed. Leonard I. Sweet. Grand Rapids, Mich.: Eerdmans, 1993.

Pierce, Robert F. Y. *Pictured Truth: A Hand-Book of Blackboard and Object Lessons*. New York: Fleming H. Revell, 1895.

Promey, Sally M. *Spiritual Spectacles: Vision and Image in Mid-Nineteenth-Century Shakerism*. Bloomington: Indiana University Press, 1993.

Schmidt, Leigh Eric. *Consumer Rites: The Buying and Selling of American Holidays*. Princeton: Princeton University Press, 1995.

Shils, Edward. "Mass Society and Its Culture." In *Culture and Mass Culture*, ed. Peter Davison, Rolf Meyersohn, and Edward Shils Vol. 1 of Literary Taste, Culture, and Mass Communication. Cambridge, England: Chadwyck-Healy, 1978.

Tweed, Thomas. *Our Lady of Exile: Diasporic Religion at a Cuban Catholic Shrine in Miami*. New York: Oxford University Press, 1997.

U.S. Bureau of the Census, *A Century of Population Growth from the First Census of the United States to the Twelfth, 1790–1900*. Washington, D.C.: GPO, 1909.

"The Unknown Christians of India." *Christian Almanac*. New York: American Tract Society, (1858): 40.

Valois, Karl Eric. "To Revolutionize the World: The American Tract Society and the Regeneration of the Republic, 1825–1877." Ph.D. diss., University of Connecticut, 1994.

Well-Spring. Vol. 18, no. 15 (1861): 60; and vol. 18, no. 22 (1861): 86.

CHAPTER 3

BELIEVING IN ELVIS:
POPULAR PIETY IN
MATERIAL CULTURE

Erika Doss

In 1985, Kiki Apostolakos, a language and psychology teacher in Athens, married a Greek American and emigrated to Memphis in order to "be closer" to Elvis Presley; she now lives near Graceland, Elvis's home and his burial site. "The day he passed away, it hit me like lightning," she remembers. "That very day I started making my arrangements, using the gold foil from cigarette packages, and decorating Elvis pictures. I feel so blessed that I can live in Memphis and do this. Elvis, his image, is so alive inside me."[1] Apostolakos, whose Memphis apartment is covered with images of Elvis, spends every spare moment she can at Elvis's grave, honoring him with votive offerings—angels, hearts, tokens, small portable shrines—all handmade and all featuring his image (fig. 3.1).

Her image making and grave-site rituals symbolize her deeply spiritual relationship with Elvis. A devout Roman Catholic (raised Greek Orthodox), Apostolakos does not worship Elvis but sees him as a man sent by God "to wake us up, to shake us, to ask us, what are we doing, where are we going?" Elvis is a mediator, an intercessor, between herself and other fans and God. As she says, "There is a distance between human beings and God. That is why we are close to Elvis. He is like a bridge between us and God."[2] If, along with other fans, Apostolakos imagines Elvis as a saint, she also sees him as a redemptive figure. "I believe in Jesus Christ and I believe in God," she remarks, "but Elvis was special. Elvis

FIGURE 3.1
Elvis shrine made by Kiki Apostolakos, at Graceland's
Meditation Gardens during Elvis Week 1993.

was in our times, he was given to us to remind us to be good." Servant of God and Christ-like savior, Elvis brings Apostolakos joy, intensity, pleasure, and purpose. "I don't go to church much now. I don't ask for anything else from God, my prayers have been answered," she says, acknowledging that her personal relationship with Elvis—as well as the works of art she makes and the rituals she performs that express that relationship—is the most meaningful cultural and social practice in her life.

Although Elvis died on August 16, 1977, he remains everywhere—his image seen on almost every conceivable mass-produced consumer item, his music honored in multiple tribute concerts and greatest-hits rereleases, his life dissected in endless biographies, art exhibitions, and documentaries. Contemporary folklore has it that the three most recognized words in the world are *Jesus, Coca-Cola,* and *Elvis.* Elvis fans are everywhere, too. Some belong to the five hundred or so official Elvis Presley fan clubs that exist around the globe. Others habitually visit Graceland, making it the second most popular house tour in the United States (after the White House). During Elvis International Tribute Week, a Memphis phenomenon that occurs each August on the anniversary of his death, the city swells as thousands of fans gather in grief and celebration around Elvis's grave at Graceland's Meditation Gardens, displaying a kind of emotional intensity and reverence that clearly intimates Elvis's popular-culture canonization.

THE RELIGION OF ELVIS

Eager to explain, and especially to debunk, the preponderance of Elvis imagery and the emotional and collective behavior of his fans, many journalists and critics relate how "culture" has become "cult." Some point out that Elvis's rags-to-riches life story and his tragic death neatly parallel the secular/sacred narrative of Jesus Christ, and hint at the contemporary possibility of Elvis's own eponymous cult foundation. Several hilarious spoofs of these Elvis-as-Messiah analogies have emerged in recent years, including *The Two Kings,* which contrasts "the bizarre parallels and strange similarities" between Jesus and Elvis ("Jesus was baptized in the River Jordan," "Elvis's backup group was the Jordanaires"), and the piously tongue-in-cheek *Gospel of Elvis,* which tells how "a boy from the poorest village of the land of Plenty became the Priest-King of the Whole World."[3]

Others cite a long list of quasi-religious factors that seem to confirm Elvis's contemporary deification: how in the years since his death, a veritable Elvis religion has emerged, replete with prophets (Elvis impersonators), sacred texts (Elvis records), disciples (Elvis fans), relics (the scarves, Cadillacs, and diamond rings that Elvis lavished on fans and friends), pilgrimages (to Tupelo, where Elvis was born, and Graceland), shrines (his grave site), churches (such as the Twenty-four-Hour Church of Elvis in Portland, Oregon), and all the appearances of a resurrection (with reported Elvis sightings at, among other places, a Burger King in Kalamazoo, Michigan). Ritual activities that occur during Elvis Week are cited as further evidence of Elvis's cult status.

"The worship, adoration and the perpetuation of the memory of Elvis today, closely resembles a religious cult," baldly states Ted Harrison, a former religious-affairs correspondent with the British Broadcasting Corporation. It is, he proclaims, "nothing less than a religion in embryo." Writer Ron Rosenbaum agrees, arguing in a 1995 *New York Times* article that Elvis's popularity has "transcended the familiar contours of a dead celebrity cult and has begun to assume the dimensions of a redemptive faith." A host of scholars have probed the Celtic, Gnostic, Hindi, and vodun derivations of Elvis culture, contemplated Graceland's status as "sacred space," and considered how and why some fans insist that Elvis, like Jesus, defeated death. Less charitable writers cynically attribute the entire phenomenon to the fierce mass-marketing techniques of his estate, Elvis Presley Enterprises, Inc. "Explicit manifestations of 'Elvis Christ' did not exactly evolve," carps British journalist John Windsor. "They were cunningly contrived for a mass market."[4]

Easy explanations that Elvis's omnipresence and the devotion of his fans embodies a cult or religion bring up all sorts of questions, including the issue of religious essentialism. What is it about the revered images, ritual practices, and devotional behaviors within Elvis culture that is essentially religious? And do these images and practices constitute the making of a discrete and legitimate religion? Why is it that *images* of Elvis seem to have taken on the dimensions of faith and devotion, viewed by many Elvis fans as links between themselves and God, votive offerings for expressing and giving thanks, as empowered objects that can fulfill wishes and desires?

ELVIS: NOT A RELIGION

These questions are complicated by the fact that most Elvis fans quickly dismiss intimations that Elvis is a religious figure or that Elvis images and Elvis-centered practices constitute any sort of Elvis religion. "Elvis did not die for our sins, nor is he Jesus Christ and it is very wrong to even try and draw comparisons," writes one fan. "It's only the media who seem to be obsessed with turning Elvis into a religion, you don't hear normal fans discuss it," says another, who adds: "You only have to see the number of books published on the topic in recent years to see it's yet another way to make yet more money out of Elvis. This topic makes Elvis fans look foolish and I'm sure Elvis would be deeply offended."

Such protestations may confuse Elvis's cult status: What does it mean when adherents deny the religiosity of something that looks so much like a religion? Yet their resistance begs consideration. Some fans object in order to avoid charges of heresy or iconoclasm, because their religion forbids sacred status for secular figures. But most do so to avoid being ridiculed as religious fanatics. If religion was "respectable and respected" at the close of the 1950s, today it is often spoofed by a popular press that is generally uneasy with displays of religious emotionalism and obsessed more with religious misconduct than with genuine, deeply felt human needs for intimations of the divine.[5] Fringe religions, moreover, are almost always held up against the standards and values of mainstream religions, so most media accounts of Elvis's "cult" status frame his fans as abnormal outsiders whose faith does not follow institutionalized spiritual practices. Canny to their media marginalization, it is not surprising that many fans deny fidelity to any sort of Elvis cult or religion, suspicious of facile analyses that come close to equating them with the Branch Davidians or the Japanese followers of Aum Supreme Truth.

Without discounting their objections, however, it is important to recognize that from its "city on the hill" creation myth to the present-day proliferation of New Age spirituality and the growth of fundamentalism, religiosity—mainstream and fringe—remains central to American identity and experience. As a religious people, Americans tend to treat things on religious terms, apply religious categories, and generally make a religion out of much of what is touched and understood. According to a 1980 Gallup Poll, Americans "value religion" and maintain "strong religious beliefs" to far greater degrees than the citizens of any other Western industrial nation.[6] Yet Americans tend to be predominantly private and diverse in their religious beliefs and practices. Indeed, much of America's "ongoing religious vitality" can be attributed to the long-standing democratic, or populist, orientation of U.S. Christianity: as "custodians of their own beliefs," Americans have traditionally shaped and accommodated their religious practices to mesh with individual, rather than strictly institutional, desires. Contemporary Americans continue to mix and match religious beliefs and practices, creating their own spiritual convictions out of that amalgamation.[7] It may be that when Elvis fans protest that their devotion to Elvis is not "religious," they are really objecting to an institutional definition of the term. In fact, their privatizing veneration of Elvis is one strong historical form of American religiosity.

My references here to "religion" are not meant as metaphorical flourishes; nor do I want to mitigate the reverence that many fans have for Elvis as a "kind of" religion. Religion constitutes those practices and attitudes that imbue a person's life with meaning by linking him or her to a transcendent reality: that which is beyond purely immanent, or secular, experience and understanding. Assertions of affinity between religion and the generally privatized spiritual beliefs and practices of Elvis fans stem from their similarly supernatural, and inexplicable, character and authority. Collecting Elvis stuff, creating Elvis shrines, and going to Graceland are not, in and of themselves, religious acts and practices. But they can become religious if they affect a transcendent and all-powerful order that can influence human affairs and is not inherently apprehensible.

THE ICON OF ELVIS

The issue of Elvis's place in America's democratic, diverse, and individually synthesized religious realm may best be considered by asking why so many Americans have come to place their faith in an image of Elvis. Why is Elvis an icon, and what does this reveal about how contemporary Americans visualize faith? Examining how and why his fans have made him a figure of popular-culture canonization, and how his iconic dominance is actually embedded in and extended from their specific religious feelings and practices, may provide some answers.

Elvis was, of course—and remains—a profoundly charismatic figure, which clearly contributes to his popular, and perhaps religious, status. Mainstream religions tend to be fronted by charismatic types (Jesus, Confucius, Gautama Buddha, Muhammad, Joseph Smith), as do their cult counterparts (most recently, Jim Jones, David Koresh, Shoko Ashahara). And the diversity of Elvis's extraordinarily magnetic image, whether sexually provocative teen idol or jumpsuited superstar, has certainly generated his appeal on many different levels for many different fans. But being charismatic does not automatically translate into reverential status; plenty of contemporary rock stars and sports heroes are objects of adoration, but few sustain religious veneration. Contrary to presumptions about "the religion of the stars," the cult of celebrity and the religious beliefs and practices cultivated by Elvis fans are not exactly the same. Elvis's religious import hinges on his multifaceted image, which is for many fans imbued with a certain mystical greatness and looked on for access to a transcendent reality. It is long-standing, too—as early as 1957, some fans were trying to start an Elvis Presley Church, and as recently as 1995 a Saint Louis group (the Congregation for Causes of Saints) sought his canonization.[8] Most fans, however, prefer to commune with Elvis privately, in their homes.

ELVIS IN THE DOMESTIC SPHERE

The domestic sphere can be a safe haven far and away from an unfriendly outside world, a sanctuary where fans can be with Elvis without drawing attention. Many fans have special rooms or areas in their homes especially dedicated to Elvis, which they describe as "quiet places" where they can think about and "be really close to Elvis." Some spend hours each day in their Elvis Rooms, listening to Elvis's music, watching his movies, looking at pictures of him in books and magazines. "I like to go to my Elvis Room, down in the basement, after supper," remarks one fan in Roanoke. "It's a quiet space and time for me." Filled with Elvis stuff that she has collected since the 1950s, the room "helps to keep memories of Elvis alive." As places where secular thoughts and tasks are suspended, Elvis Rooms allow personal and private moments of contemplation and solitude. As places where fans spotlight their collections of Elvis stuff, they also speak to the ways in which material culture plays a major role in sanctifying and legitimizing Elvis as a special, important entity.

This combination of religious and commercial sensibilities in the American home is not new: in the nineteenth-century, as we saw in the preceding chapter, Protestants and Catholics alike linked religiosity with domesticity, creating a more sanctified home with parlor organs, Bibles, and religious pictures and sculptures.[9] Filling special rooms, and sometimes whole houses, with Elvis paintings, plates, trading cards, limited-edition lithographs, watches, dolls, and many other mass-produced and handmade items, Elvis fans similarly sacralize their homes, using images and objects to declare their deep-felt devotion to Elvis.

The ways they organize their Elvis Rooms reveal how they freely appropriate the look and feel of domestic religiosity in order to cultivate a reverential atmosphere in a secular realm. Whatever their religious affiliation, or lack thereof, Elvis fans tend to choose patterns of visual piety that closely correspond to the home shrines that have long been a "vital part of domestic Christianity" for Americans of African, Irish, Italian, Latino, Polish, Portuguese, and many other backgrounds.[10] From the modest grouping of a framed religious motto and family photographs on top of a living room piano or television set to more elaborate assemblages of holy cards, votive candles, and school photos, home shrines sacralize domestic interiors. Uniquely coded by their creators, who are primarily female, home altars integrate personal and sentimental items with more purely devotional offerings, thus blurring distinctions between the domestic and the divine.

The circulation of these Judeo-Christian visual and material traditions within Elvis culture is clearly evident in the homes of particularly dedicated fans. Stepping into Mary Cartaya's Florida home, for example, is like walking into a private Roman Catholic chapel, but in place of crucifixes, religious pictures, and reliquaries there are dense, neat rows of Elvis posters, decanters, pennants, spoons, and plates (fig. 3.2). This fan calls her home a "memorial to Elvis" and calls Elvis her "guardian angel." She is a practicing Catholic and has special allegiance to Our Lady of the Miraculous Medal,[11] but there are few Catholic religious items displayed in her home.

Born in 1942, Cartaya describes her father as an "abuser" who beat his wife and three children and kicked Mary out of their South Miami home at the age of fifteen. "All I had was my record player and my Elvis records," she recalls, "and I listened to them over and over." In 1967, Cartaya married; her only child died at birth in the early 1970s. Her second marriage, in 1982, lasted only six months. "I was alone and Elvis was there for me," she remarks. "Elvis has brought so much to me, and when he died I wanted to make sure his image wasn't mutilated. He gives me the boost to overcome the hurdles. Through him I know that things can be done."

For such fans, Elvis Rooms are creative means to help them cope with the difficulties and needs in their lives, refuges where they experience their feelings for Elvis privately, on their own terms. Judeo-Christian home shrines are similarly powerful forms of domestic piety, especially for women. Generally excluded from public forms of religious leadership and expression, Christian women often use the domestic sphere to communicate their personal spiritual needs and desires. Home altars are one of these manifestations—both private religious endeavors and visibly conscious expressions of family relationships, traditions, and memories. By making them, women strengthen those relationships and traditions, their religious beliefs, and their own identities.[12] By blending the domestic and the divine, home altars nurture female and family spirituality and

FIGURE 3.2
Elvis images in the home of Mary Cartaya, Florida, 1995.

transform the private sphere into a powerful locus of religiosity. The look and feel of many Elvis Rooms suggests that various Judeo-Christian traditions of domestic religiosity that allow believers to decorate their homes and venerate their chosen deities or holy figures in highly personalized ways appear to have been absorbed by many Elvis fans.

ELVIS AND PUBLIC DEVOTION

Many of the images, effects, and rituals that fans use in their homes to articulate their devotion to Elvis are repeated in the public sphere, especially at Graceland during Elvis Week. Religious terms like *pilgrimage* and *shrine* are not part of the average Graceland visitor's vocabulary, and many might be offended at the use of such words. Still, Graceland—set back on a hill and completely surrounded by fieldstone walls and white fences—is conceptualized by thousands of Elvis fans as an especially hallowed place whose every surface is charged with Elvis's spirit. Fans go to Graceland to walk in his mansion, gaze at his things, mourn at his grave site, and be

FIGURE 3.3
Elvis fans in the Graceland Meditation Gardens, Elvis Week 1996.

that much closer to the man they adore (fig. 3.3). Some leave notes: slips of paper tucked under vases or hidden behind curtains with messages like "Elvis, we miss you. Love, Bob and Marge." Others are unable to resist the temptation to take a little of piece of Graceland home with them, pocketing leaves, pebbles, sticks, and pinches of dirt as tokens of their pilgrimage and their brush with Elvis. It is the stuff of material culture—which in this case is Graceland and its relics—that is pivotal to the devotional practices and beliefs of Elvis's fans.

Graceland's shrine-like sensibility is particularly evident during Elvis Week, when fans engage in specific rituals. They tour Graceland, attend fan festivals and memorial services, watch Elvis-impersonator contests, visit Sun Studios near downtown Memphis, eat at local restaurants, and tag their names on the walls in front of Graceland. They spend a lot of time buying Elvis stuff at the gift shops that surround Graceland. Fans at area motels participate in elaborate window-decorating competitions; others submit pictures and crafts to the annual Elvis Art Exhibit held at the Graceland Plaza Visitor Center. Ordinary spaces—motels and restaurants, for example—become sacred spaces during Elvis Week, because Elvis fans occupy them and fill them with images and objects that they deem to have special significance. Simultaneously a shrine and a shopping mall, Graceland's multi-acre complex is no different than other pilgrimage sites: at Lourdes, at the Basilica of the Virgin of Guadalupe, and at Graceland, devotional practices, material culture, and commercialism are typically mixed.

Elvis Week culminates in the all-night Candlelight Vigil on the anniversary of Elvis's death, when fans gather at the gates of Graceland and walk up the mansion's steep pathway to the Meditation Gardens for a brief, private tribute. Each solemnly bears a glowing candle, lit from a torch at the start of the procession. Once back down the driveway and outside Graceland's gates, the celebrant snuffs the candle out. The tone of this ritual is clearly borrowed from traditional religious practices, from the ceremonial ambiance of a Christmas midnight mass to the precise vigils at the Shrine of Saint Jude in Chicago, where the lighting of candles marks the beginning and the end of each pilgrim's devotional encounter.[13] It also resembles secular rituals such as Bic flicking at rock concerts (an encore summons) to the lighting of the Olympic Torch. For those who are not familiar with ceremonial behavior, sacred or secular, Elvis Inc. provides some "special guidelines": "Please avoid loud talking or laughter or any behavior that might be offensive to, or unappreciated by those who take this tribute seriously. The Candlelight Vigil is intended to be a solemn, respectful tribute."

For most Elvis fans, the Candlelight Vigil is a hushed, somber ceremony, the cathartic moment of an emotional week. Rituals often have special meaning because of a tangible sensual quality, and this one is particularly sensational: there are the sounds of cicadas, low murmurs, hushed cries, and Elvis's music, broadcast over strategically placed loudspeakers; there is the visual spectacle of Graceland lit up at night, and of flickering candles and a seemingly endless line of fans slowly parading along Graceland's serpentine driveway; and then there are the smells of wax, perfume, flowering magnolias, mounds of roses, and sweat—and, of course, the damp and steamy heat, made even more oppressive from standing in line with tens of thousands of other fans, pressed together, for hours on end. Combined, these make the Candlelight Vigil an especially spectacular ritual.

The event's special character is further enhanced by the offerings that fans leave at Elvis's tomb: flowers, photographs, pictures, dolls, toys, teddy bears, and records (see fig. 3.4). A fan from Missouri often leaves

FIGURE 3.4
Gifts left by fans at Elvis's grave during Elvis Week 1996.

one or more tableaux that incorporate letters or mementos from fans who have not been able to make the trip to Graceland. One, a sculpture of of tinfoil, gift wrap, and plastic flowers, included a pledge of devotion from Ralf, a disabled fifteen-year-old fan from Germany; another combined Elvis images with pages from Kahlil Gibran's poem *The Prophet,* one of Elvis's favorite books (fig. 3.5). Some of these gifts, especially those featuring images of Elvis, are offered much as are ex-votos, or *milagros,* at Catholic shrines. Made of tin and shaped like body parts (hearts, hands, feet), ex-votos are commonly left as petitions or to thank a saint for a cure or healing;[14] an ex-voto of a leg might be left at Lourdes, for example, to thank the Virgin Mary for the mending of a broken bone. Offerings representing Elvis—dolls and pictures that simulate his body or face and that are placed on or near the spot where he is buried—seem to have similarly powerful connotations for Elvis fans.

These gifts are a way of saying thank you—expressions of gratitude to Elvis from his fans. In a culture where mourning often takes material form (the placing of flowers on graves; the leaving of dog tags at the Vietnam Veterans Memorial; the making of panels for the AIDS NAMES Quilt) the offerings left at Graceland, especially during Elvis Week, help fans

FIGURE 3.5
Elvis gift made by Ilse Oullette, featuring Kahlil Gibran's *The Prophet*,
left, at Graceland Meditation Gardens, Elvis Week 1993.

express their grief at Elvis's death. The images and objects they place on Elvis's grave are the physically expressive focal points of their tributes to both his greatness and his absence; they help atone for the pleasure he gives them, for the pain of his death, and for the sorrow of their loss.

THE CHURCH OF ELVIS

There are also other quasi-religious manifestations of Elvis Culture. Elvis "churches" that have sprouted in recent years include the First Church of Elvis ("pastored" by Doug Isaacks, of Austin, Texas, since 1991) and the First Presleyterian Church of Elvis the Divine. In 1996, the latter staged a widely publicized, two-day "Elvis Revival" that was bent on "E-vangelizing" students at Lehigh University, Bethlehem, Pennsylvania. The First Presleyterian, like most of these manifestations of Elvis divine, is mostly realized on-line—a click-in church of the cyberspace, says Lotus software founder Mitch Kapor, that is the "great new spiritual frontier."[15] Primarily the products of Gen X fans who have cottoned on to Elvis's vast spiritual appeal, these Elvis churches are certainly more cynical than the home shrines and Graceland rituals of "authentic" Elvis fans.

Distinctions such as authentic and inauthentic don't really work, however, since the tricksters who organize the campy parodies of an institutionalized Elvis faith say that they are Elvis fans, too. Silly and sardonic, to be sure, they aim to debunk the "secret" religious underpinnings of Elvis Culture and generally to demystify Elvis's iconic status. A lot of time and energy is invested in producing "sacred" cyberspace Elvis texts and shrines, such as the First Presleyterian's on-line "sermons"; these have weekly topics like "How to be Spiritually Correct" and "The Contract with Elvis." "Although I see all this as satire," says Isaacks, "Elvis may actually evolve into a major religion some day. Let's face it, it's no sillier than any other religion." Or as Norm Girardot, a professor of religious studies, comments, "The Presleyterians remind us [that] the seriousness of religion can only be rediscovered in relation to all of its glorious absurdity." Humor and jokes and derision, after all, are all forms of participation, ways of mocking and celebrating at the same time.[16] Embedded in all of the quasi-religious revelations of Elvis along the electronic highway, there lurks a real contemporary yearning for spiritual intensity and belonging.

People build shrines and make pilgrimages for religious reasons because of deeply felt needs for meaning and enlightenment, in hopes of salvation or expectations of spiritual satisfaction and as tributes to special, sacred figures, things, or places. The burgeoning of Elvis home shrines, Elvis Week rituals, and Elvis cyberspace temples and texts suggests that Elvis culture has taken on the dimensions of religious faith and belief. The central component in this quasi-religious construction is, of course, Elvis himself and the ways he is increasingly imagined as a special, wondrous, virtuous, transcendent, and even miraculous figure. "Elvis was no god," his fans say again and again, but the ways they revere him suggest that he is often perceived as a saint and a savior, an intercessor and a redeemer. Infiltrated by evangelical and New Age manifestations of spirituality and therapy, of metaphysics, healing, miracles, and meditation, today's Judeo-Christian religions are awash in a blend of mysticism and millennialism, and today's faith in Christian redemption is often accompanied by dabblings in a variety of other spiritual strains. Devotion to Elvis dovetails with this contemporary religious blending, particularly among Americans who have long made a habit of spiritual synthesis and reconfiguration. As Mary Cartaya remarks, "I've got Elvis sitting on my left shoulder and God on my right and with that combination, I cannot fail."

Not surprisingly, fans' understanding of Elvis's religiosity generally correspond to their own particular religious persuasions. Fundamentalist Christians say Elvis was "very religious" and cite his Pentecostal upbringing, his religious faith ("All good things come from God," said Elvis in 1956), and his various gospel albums (including *How Great Thou Art* of 1967).[17] Other fans see Elvis as a New Age spiritualist, recounting his interest in alternative religions, mysticism, and the occult, pointing out that the book he was reading when he died was *A Scientific Search for the Face of Jesus* (about the Shroud of Turin). Recently, many fans have imaged Elvis as an angel—not a teen angel but a radiant personality appointed for spiritual service. He was the cherub of the month for a 1995 issue of *Angel Times*, a glossy magazine with the publishing philosophy that "God's angels appear to all peoples of the world regardless of religion, race, culture."[18] Whether as Southern fundamentalist, supernatural New Ager, or rock-and-roll angel, fans make of Elvis the religious icon they want him to be.

FAITH IN ELVIS

Understanding the faith that fans have in Elvis does not lend itself easily to deterministic models of cultural analysis. Fans talk about the "wonder" and "mystique" of Elvis and repeatedly describe him as a "miracle." As one writes, "Elvis is an emotion that entails everything we are capable of feeling. It cannot be captured. It cannot be bought. You cannot draw it. You cannot write it. You cannot take a photograph of it. You can't even explain it. YOU HAVE TO FEEL IT—IT MUST BE FELT BECAUSE IT COMES STRAIGHT FROM THE HEART!!" There are "popular ways of knowing" that are emotive, irrational, superstitious, and revelatory, and these are the ways that fans feel about Elvis and how they see him as a special and transcendent figure in their lives.[19] Their faith in him is made "real" through the tangible stuff of material culture, through Elvis's image.

Some argue that these materialist forms of Elvis's "deification" are only a facet of the American obsession with transformative consumerism. Elvis is indeed an intercessor in this scenario, but his mediation is between his fans and their faith in consumption; in other words, collecting Elvis stuff and making Elvis shrines may help fans construct meaning in their everyday lives, but it mainly keeps them addicted to an ideology of buying things to feel better. Obviously, Elvis culture is thoroughly drenched in the world of consumerism, and fans readily admit that they "need" Elvis stuff in order to "take care" of Elvis and participate in his fandom. But such a view fails to take into consideration the ways in which fans rely on Elvis's image as an all-powerful, nonreferential, and largely incomprehensible transcendence. As such, Elvis's image does not simply prop up fundamental beliefs in consumerism but raises the issue, as art historian David Freedberg writes, of the "deep cognitive potential that arises from the relations between looking—looking hard—and figured material object[s]."[20]

Looking plays a large role in the formation and practice of religious belief: there is the "identification of the *seen* with what is to be *believed*," Michel de Certeau argues. There is a plurality of visual pieties, as well, and different fans see Elvis in different religious roles.[21] Some see him as an especially integrative spiritual figure. One remarks: "Although I am a Christian, I have never experienced such unity in any form of worship. Elvis bonds us between nations, religions, and across all age ranges." Others see Elvis as a loving, intimate, and merciful figure, imagining him in much the same way that antebellum American Christian women imagined Jesus as a warmer and more affectionate spiritual authority.[22] He was a "gentle man," writes Cartaya; he "never hurt us, but instead, left so much for us to enjoy." Still other see Elvis as a healer. In an especially poignant memoir, a fan from Duluth writes that her mother's long and painful bout with cancer was eased by her vast collection of Elvis memorabilia: "The velvet Elvis was in her bedroom. The bronze plaque was hanging above the stove in the kitchen. The 26 inch statue that could play Elvis songs on mini cassettes was on the TV set. There was even a painting in the bathroom. In the final stages of illness, when she was heavily medicated on morphine, she often commented that the various Elvises around the house were talking to her, comforting her."

Most religions make distinctions between a higher god (or gods) and lesser divines. In the Christian world, saints are seen as advocates, as mediators between believers and the divine. Only Christ is viewed as a figure of salvation. Based on their comments and behaviors and the way they look at Elvis, it appears that many Christian Elvis fans, and even those who are not Christian but whose sense of what is religious stems from living in America's overwhelmingly Judeo-Christian milieu, see Elvis as both a saintly mediator and a redemptive, Christ-like figure. Blending religious archetypes, or simply mixing them up, fans liken Elvis as a spiritual intercessor whom they produce and personalize—in art and in ritual practices—as an instrument of therapeutic relief.

Some fans say Elvis "was no saint," but these are often Roman Catholic fans for whom the term *saint* strictly connotes a canonized figure who performed miracles and lived in an especially virtuous manner—which Elvis, most fans agree, did not. Others argue that there are differences between religious beings and contemporary celebrities, but they tend to ignore the way secular figures and heroes (from Eva Peron to Che Guevara) can become saints by way of shrines, pilgrimages, and popular veneration. The fact that so many Elvis fans look upon his image as a source of protection and relief and think of him as a special man who was "beyond human" and "bigger than life" certainly suggests that they have extended sanctity to Elvis.

Whether he is viewed as Saint Elvis or "alter Christus," fan understandings of Elvis's religiosity follow from their imaging of him as a legendary entertainer, a down-home Southern gentleman, a patriot, a philanthropist, and a sad man who died alone—each image an amalgamation of

Elvis fact and Elvis apocrypha. Some suggest Elvis is especially seen as a "permissive savior" who encourages his followers to indulge and consume and enjoy themselves. But as much as fans find pleasure in Elvis's image and his music, it is pain, and the sense that through their devotion to him they can somehow ease that pain, that is most evident in their ritualistic behaviors during Elvis Week. Aside from assassinated political figures (Lincoln, J.F.K., Martin Luther King Jr.), Americans have historically embraced few secular-realm martyrs. Elvis's pain and suffering, his drug-addict death in a gilded bathroom, his failure to find happiness despite achieving stardom and wealth, may be what attracts so many of his fans, likewise caught up in pursuing the myth of the American dream. They identify Elvis as a fellow sufferer, which may explain that the image of Elvis most loved by contemporary American fans, and most frequently evoked by his impersonators, is that of the Vegas Elvis, the "Late, Fat, Pain-Racked, Self-Destructive Elvis."[23] That image of Elvis embodies the pleasure *and* the pain of his many fans.

Elvis Rooms and Elvis Week rituals reveal how Elvis is understood by his fans as a revered figure of enormous capacity who mediates between themselves and their particular theological constructs. Images of Elvis, by extension, are understood by fans as icons with the explicit power to intercede between themselves and a higher power (god). This works because images of Elvis are multifaceted and mercurial and because American religiosity is essentially flexible and democratic. On one level, then, fans place their faith in images of Elvis because they correspond to the personal mores and ecclesiastical self-image they desire. On another level, fans place their faith in images of Elvis because he provides a kind of "secular spiritual succor," because he both shares and can minister to their pleasure and their pain.[24]

For many fans, the authority of Elvis's image lies in its iconic ability to satisfy spiritual needs and respond to *personal* notions of contemporary piety. Many critics lump these private constellations of belief and practice all together, eager to construct cultish apparitions of an Elvis religion. But there is no totalizing institutional religious paradigm at work in Elvis culture. Instead, Elvis fans independently construct a series of cultural and social practices that both foster a sense of belonging (to Elvis fan clubs, for example), and allow room for individual beliefs. Faith in Elvis neatly corresponds to abiding American needs for spiritual community and spiritual solitude, which makes Elvis a profoundly democratic American icon.

NOTES

This is a shortened version of the chapter "Saint Elvis," in Erika Doss, *Elvis Culture: Fans, Faith, and Image* (Lawrence: University Press of Kansas, 1999), 69–113, 266–70. Reprinted with permission of Erika Doss.

1. Kiki Apostolakos, quoted in author interview, August 14, 1995. Unless otherwise noted, all quotes from fans in this chapter stem from author interviews conducted in Memphis and elsewhere between 1993 and 1996 or from surveys of Elvis fans during 1996.

2. Apostolakos, quoted in Ted Harrison, *Elvis People: The Cult of the King* (London: Fount Paperbacks, 1992), 68, 53.

3. A. J. Jacobs, *The Two Kings* (New York: Bantam, 1994); Louie Ludwig, *The Gospel of Elvis* (New Orleans: Summit, 1996).

4. Harrison, *Elvis People*, 9; Ron Rosenbaum, "Among the Believers," *New York Times Sunday Magazine*, New York, September 24, 1995, 50–57, 62, 64; John Windsor, "Faith and the State of Graceland Enterprises," *Independent* (London), August 15, 1992, 33. See also Lucinda Ebersole, "The God and Goddess of the Written Word," and Gary Vikan, "Graceland as *Locus Santos*," in *Elvis + Marilyn: 2 x Immortal* (New York: Rizzoli, 1994), 136–45, 150–66; John H. Lardas, "Graceland: An Analysis of Sacred Space on the American Religious Landscape," (paper given at the 1995 American Academy of Religion annual conference); Sue Bridwell Beckham, "Death, Resurrection and Transfiguration: The Religious Folklore in Elvis Presley Shrines and Souvenirs," *International Folklore Review* 5 (1987): 88–95; and John Fiske, *Power Plays Power Works* (New York: Verso, 1993), 181–205.

5. James Wall raised these points at the conference "The Expression of American Religion in the Popular Media," held in Indianapolis, April 1993. See also Stewart M. Hoover, *Mass Media Religion: The Social Sources of the Electronic Church* (Newbury Park, Calif.: Sage, 1988), and Stewart M. Hoover and Knut Lundby, eds., *Rethinking Media, Religion, and Culture* (Thousand Oaks, Calif.: Sage, 1997).

6. Poll noted in Nathan O. Hatch, *The Democratization of American Christianity* (New Haven: Yale University Press, 1989), 210.

7. Robert N. Bellah et al., *Habits of the Heart: Individualism and Commitment in American Life* (Berkeley: University of California Press, 1985), 220–21 and passim; Hatch, *The Democratization of American Christianity*, 212, 218; Wade Clark Roof, *A Generation of Seekers: The Spiritual Journeys of the Baby Boom Generation* (New York: Harper, 1993). Ideas of personal religious pluralism in complex industrial societies were first advanced in the works of Peter L. Berger and Thomas Luckman; see, for example, Berger's *The Sacred Canopy* (New York: Doubleday, 1967) and Luckman's *The Invisible Religion* (New York: Macmillan, 1967).

8. Edgar Morin, *The Stars*, trans. Richard Howard (New York: Grove Press, 1960), 71–108. The 1957 Elvis "church" is noted in Patricia Jobe Pierce, *The Ultimate Elvis: Elvis Presley Day by Day* (New York: Simon & Schuster, 1994), 136.

9. Colleen McDannell, *The Christian Home in Victorian America, 1840–1900* (Bloomington: Indiana University Press, 1986), and McDannell, *Material Christianity: Religion and Popular Culture in America* (New Haven: Yale University Press, 1995); David Morgan, ed., *Icons of American Protestantism: The Art of Warner Sallman, 1892–1968* (New Haven: Yale University Press, 1996), and David Morgan, *Visual Piety: A History and Theory of Popular Religious Images* (Berkeley: University of California Press, 1998). See also David Halle's analysis of religious iconography in contemporary Catholic homes in *Inside Culture: Art and Class in the American Home* (Chicago: University of Chicago Press, 1993), 171–92.

10. McDannell, *Material Christianity*, 275.

11. This group was founded in 1830 after the Virgin Mary was said to have appeared to a Parisian nun, instructing her to make a special medal in her honor.

12. See, for example, Kay Turner, "Mexican-American Women's Home Altars: The Art of Relationship" (Ph.D. diss., University of Texas, Austin, 1990), and Turner, "Home Altars and the Art of Devotion," in *Chicano Expressions: A New View in American Art*, ed. Inverna Lockpez (New York: Intar Latin American Gallery, 1986), 40–48.

13. Robert Orsi, "The Center Out There, In here, and Everywhere Else: The Nature of Pilgrimage to the Shrine of Saint Jude, 1929–1965," *Journal of Social History* 25, no. 2 (1991): 222.

14. See also Christine King, "His Truth Goes Marching On: Elvis Presley and the Pilgrimage to Graceland," in *Pilgrimage in Popular Culture*, ed. Ian Reader and Tony Walter (New York: Macmillan, 1992), 103. On votive offerings, see Stephen Wilson, introduction to *Saints and Their Cults: Studies in Religious Sociology, Folklore, and History*, ed. Stephen Wilson (Cambridge: Cambridge University Press, 1983), 21.

15. For the home page of the First Presleyterian Church of Elvis the Divine, see http://chelsea.ios.com/hkarlini.welcome.html. On the revival at Lehigh University, which was organized by Professor Norman J. Girardot for his course "Jesus, Buddha, Confucius, and Elvis," see Girardot's essay "But Seriously: Taking the Elvis Phenomenon Seriously," *Religious Studies News* 11, no. 4 (1996): 11–12. Mitch Kapor is quoted in Eugene Taylor, "Desperately Seeking Spirituality," *Psychology Today* 27, no. 6 (1994): 54–62, 64, 66, 68.

16. Norman Girardot, "What Really Happened in Bethlehem? The Religious Power and Apocalyptic Pathos of the Religious Phenomenon" (paper at the Third Annual Conference on Elvis Presley, Memphis, August 15, 1997). On similar forms of derision, see Nathalie Heinich, *The Glory of Van Gogh: An Anthropology of Admiration*, trans. Paul Leduc Browne (Princeton: Princeton University Press, 1996), 129–30, and

Celeste Olalquiaga, *Megalopolis: Contemporary Cultural Sensibilities* (Minneapolis: University of Minnesota Press, 1992), 45–46. See also Greil Marcus, *Dead Elvis: A Chronicle of a Cultural Obsession* (New York: Doubleday, 1991), 74–85.

17. Elvis, quoted in William Steif, "What Makes Elvis Presley Tick—No. 3: The Pelvis Explains That 'Vulgar' Style," *San Francisco News*, October 17, 1956, 3.

18. Maia C. M. Shamayyim, "Elvis and His Angelic Connection," *Angel Times* 1, no. 4 (1995): 20–25. See also Raymond Moody Jr., *Elvis After Life: Unusual Psychic Experiences Surrounding the Death of a Superstar* (Atlanta: Peachtree, 1987); Jack D. Mallay and Warren Vaughn, *Elvis: The Messiah?* (Mount Horeb, Wisc.: TCB, 1992); Isabelle Tanner, *Elvis—A Guide to My Soul* (Dobbs Ferry, N.Y.: Elisabelle International, 1995); and Catherine L. Albanese's analysis of Elvis's religiosity in *America: Religions and Religion* (Belmont, Calif.: Wadsworth, 1981), 318–20.

19. Fiske, *Power Plays*, p. 181.

20. P. Stromberg, "Elvis Alive? The Ideology of American Consumerism," *Journal of American Culture* 24, no. 3 (1990): 11–19; David Freedberg, *The Power of Images: Studies in the History and Theory of Response* (Chicago: University of Chicago Press, 1989), 432.

21. Michel de Certeau, *The Practice of Everyday Life*, trans. Steven Randall (Berkeley: University of California Press, 1984), 187; see also David Morgan, *Visual Piety*.

22. Fan quoted in Adrienne Young, "Taking Care of Business: Elvis Fans and Moral Community" (master's thesis, George Washington University, 1994), 123. On women and affectionate religion in the nineteenth century, see Ann Douglas, *The Feminization of American Culture* (New York: Knopf, 1977).

23. Mark Gottdiener, "Dead Elvis as Other Jesus," in *In Search of Elvis: Music, Race, Art, Religion*, ed. Vernon Chadwick (Boulder: Westview Press, 1997), 189–200; Rosenbaum, "Among the Believers," 62, 64.

24. Rosenbaum, "Among the Believers," 52.

BIBLIOGRAPHY

Albanese, Catherine L. *America: Religions and Religion*. Belmont, Calif.: Wadsworth, 1981.

Apostolakos, Kiki. Interview by author. August 14, 1995.

——. Quoted in Ted Harrison, *Elvis People: The Cult of the King*. London: Fount Paperbacks, 1992.

Beckham, Sue Bridwell. "Death, Resurrection and Transfiguration: The Religious Folklore in Elvis Presley Shrines and Souvenirs." *International Folklore Review* 5 (1987): 88–95.

Bellah, Robert N., Richard Madsen, William M. Sullivan, Ann Swidler, and Steven M. Tipton. *Habits of the Heart: Individualism and Commitment in American Life.* Berkeley: University of California Press, 1985.

Berger, Peter L. *The Sacred Canopy.* New York: Doubleday, 1967.

de Certeau, Michel. *The Practice of Everyday Life.* Trans. Steven Randall. Berkeley: University of California Press, 1984.

Doss, Erika. *Elvis Culture: Fans, Faith, and Image.* Lawrence: University Press of Kansas, 1999.

Douglas, Ann. *The Feminization of American Culture.* New York: Knopf, 1977.

Ebersole, Lucinda. "The God and Goddess of the Written Word." In *Elvis + Marilyn 2 x Immortal,* ed. Geri DePaoili. New York: Rizzoli, 1994.

First Presleyterian Church of Elvis the Divine home page http://chelsea.ios .com/hkarlin1.welcome.html.

Fiske, John. *Power Plays Power Works.* New York: Verso, 1993.

Freedberg, David. *The Power of Images: Studies in the History and Theory of Response.* Chicago: University of Chicago Press, 1989.

Girardot, Norman J. "But Seriously: Taking the Elvis Phenomenon Seriously." *Religious Studies News* 11, no. 4 (1996): 11–12.

——. "What Really Happened in Bethlehem? The Religious Power and Apocalyptic Pathos of the Religious Phenomenon." Paper at the Third Annual Conference on Elvis Presley, Memphis, August 15, 1997.

Gottdiener, Mark. "Dead Elvis as Other Jesus." In *In Search of Elvis: Music, Race, Art, Religion,* ed. Vernon Chadwick. Boulder, Colo.: Westview Press, 1997.

Halle, David. *Inside Culture: Art and Class in the American Home.* Chicago: University of Chicago Press, 1993.

Hatch, Nathan O. *The Democratization of American Christianity.* New Haven: Yale University Press, 1989.

Heinich, Nathalie. *The Glory of Van Gogh: An Anthropology of Admiration.* Trans. Paul Leduc Browne. Princeton: Princeton University Press, 1996.

Hoover, Stewart M. *Mass Media Religion: The Social Sources of the Electronic Church.* Newbury Park, Calif.: Sage, 1988.

Hoover Stewart M., and Knut Lundby, eds. *Rethinking Media, Religion, and Culture.* Thousand Oaks, Calif.: Sage, 1997.

Jacobs, A. J. *The Two Kings.* New York: Bantam, 1994.

Kapor, Mitch. Quoted in Eugene Taylor, "Desperately Seeking Spirituality." *Psychology Today* 27, no. 6 (1994): 54–62, 64, 66, 68.

King, Christine. "His Truth Goes Marching On: Elvis Presley and the Pilgrimage to Graceland." In *Pilgrimage in Popular Culture,* ed. Ian Reader and Tony Walter. New York: Macmillan, 1992.

Lardas, John H. "Graceland: An Analysis of Sacred Space on the American Religious Landscape." Paper at the annual conference of the American Academy of Religion, 1995.

Luckman, Thomas, *The Invisible Religion*. New York: Macmillan, 1967.

Ludwig, Louie. *The Gospel of Elvis*. New Orleans: Summit, 1996.

Mallay, Jack D., and Warren Vaughn. *Elvis: The Messiah?* Mount Horeb, Wisc.: TCB, 1992.

Marcus, Greil. *Dead Elvis: A Chronicle of a Cultural Obsession*. New York: Doubleday, 1991.

McDannell, Colleen. *The Christian Home in Victorian America, 1840–1900*. Bloomington: Indiana University Press, 1986.

——. *Material Christianity: Religion and Popular Culture in America*. New Haven: Yale University Press, 1995.

Moody, Raymond, Jr. *Elvis After Life: Unusual Psychic Experiences Surrounding the Death of a Superstar*. Atlanta: Peachtree, 1987.

Morin, Edgar. *The Stars*. Trans. Richard Howard. New York: Grove Press, 1960.

Morgan, David. *Visual Piety: A History and Theory of Popular Religious Images*. Berkeley: University of California Press, 1998.

Morgan, David, ed. *Icons of American Protestantism: The Art of Warner Sallman, 1892–1968*. New Haven: Yale University Press, 1996.

Olalquiaga, Celeste. *Megalopolis: Contemporary Cultural Sensibilities*. Minneapolis: University of Minnesota Press, 1992.

Orsi, Robert. "The Center Out There, In here, and Everywhere Else: The Nature of Pilgrimage to the Shrine of Saint Jude, 1929–1965." *Journal of Social History* 25, no. 2 (1991): 222.

Pierce, Patricia Jobe. *The Ultimate Elvis: Elvis Presley Day by Day*. New York: Simon & Schuster, 1994.

Roof, Wade Clark. *A Generation of Seekers: The Spiritual Journeys of the Baby Boom Generation*. New York: Harper, 1993.

Rosenbaum, Ron. "Among the Believers," *New York Times Sunday Magazine*, September 24, 1995, 50–57, 62, 64.

Shamayyim, Maia C. M. "Elvis and His Angelic Connection." *Angel Times* 1, no. 4 (1995): 20–25.

Steif, William "What Makes Elvis Presley Tick—No. 3, The Pelvis Explains That 'Vulgar' Style." *San Francisco News*, October 17, 1956, 3.

Stromberg, P. "Elvis Alive? The Ideology of American Consumerism." *Journal of American Culture* 24, no. 3 (1990): 11–19.

Tanner, Isabelle. *Elvis—A Guide to My Soul*. Dobbs Ferry, N.Y.: Elisabelle International, 1995.

Turner, Kay. "Mexican-American Women's Home Altars: The Art of Relationship." Ph.D. diss., University of Texas, Austin, 1990.

——. "Home Altars and the Art of Devotion." In *Chicano Expressions: A New View in American Art,* ed. Inverna Lockpez. New York: Intar Latin American Gallery, 1986.

Vikan, Gary. "Graceland as *Locus Santos.*" In *Elvis + Marilyn 2 x Immortal,* ed. Geri DePaoili. New York: Rizzoli, 1994.

Wall, James. Points raised at conference, "The Expression of American Religion in the Popular Media," Indianapolis, April 1993.

Wilson, Stephen. Introduction to *Saints and Their Cults: Studies in Religious Sociology, Folklore, and History,* ed. Stephen Wilson. Cambridge: Cambridge University Press, 1983.

Windsor, John. "Faith and the State of Graceland Enterprises." *Independent* (London), August 15, 1992, 33.

Young, Adrienne. "Taking Care of Business: Elvis Fans and Moral Community." Master's thesis, George Washington University, 1994.

THE MEDIATION OF RELIGION IN THE PUBLIC SPHERE

The kind of public action we saw in chapter 3 focused on the participation in and reception of meaningful materials that are publicly available. The chapters in part 2 will address the dimension of the public and public-ness from a different perspective—that of public display and production in and for the public sphere. There is no doubt that the religion we see in these chapters is explicit, but these cases continue our contemplation of questions of popular and marginalized expression.

Shawn Landres (chap. 4) takes us to a context of practice that problematizes both our definition of religion and our definition of media. Far from the world of "legitimate" art and far from the rarified realms of the commercial public media, mural artists in Los Angeles work to craft a kind of visual and iconic expression that speaks radically to the needs, wants, and aspirations of specific cultural communities. These murals are public expressions that provide valuable insights into what, in their contexts, is meaningful and valuable. Within those contexts, the murals are topical and public at the same time: they combine elements of high art, folk art, and media symbols in ways that, while creative and unexpected, are nevertheless meaningful in the communities where they are sited. They reaffirm the notion that religion as it is expressed is often quite different from religion as we see it when it is associated with formal institutions. Thus they serve to raise in another way the question of the popular and popular expression, and to affirm their legitimacy.

The public mural is a specific kind of medium. While it has its own peculiar limitations, its role as a place of public expression operates with a measure of autonomy when compared with the more mechanized and industrial mass media of print and electronic communication. The media age presents religious movements with a set of unique challenges. Diane Winston (chap. 5) shows that religious movements and organizations have always had to struggle between their motivation to "use" the media and their fear of losing control over how they will be represented therein. The explanatory power of disciplined historical scholarship is demonstrated as Winston details the collision that occurred in the late nineteenth century between the Salvation Army, the emergent concerns of new immigrant communities, and the New York of those days. Far from being a time "before media," as we often think of it, the turn from the nineteenth century to the twentieth was a time of great foment and change in the means and practices of publicity and publication.

Like some other religious groups of the period (one thinks of Christian Science and its publishing activities, as well as of the Protestant fundamentalism that, a decade or so later, rather quickly found its way into the new medium of radio) the Army took the historical moment seriously. Winston shows how this recognition led to a change in the movement itself. Further, she shows that this was not only to do with one particular medium of communication but the whole context of *public*—of the public sphere that was emerging that constituted the challenge to which the Army felt it must respond.

In chapter 6, we see that formal, mainstream, organized religion responded to the challenge posed by the emergence of the media age in ways very different than those used by the Salvation Army. The marginal religious groups were searching for legitimacy and purpose in the public sphere; the mainstream groups, already established, found the emergence of the electronic media to be a challenge to religious authority. Michele Rosenthal describes a mainstream reaction (that of the Protestant establishment) to television. As she shows, the relationship between the Protestants and television has never been smooth or easy. Interest in televangelism as employed by conservative Protestants eclipsed the more basic (and in some ways more important) story of how the majority of Protestants—

particularly the liberal or progressive leadership—reacted to the new medium.

Rosenthal's account of this period is fascinating both for what it reveals about the conflict between the two sides and for what it tells us about Protestantism at midcentury. The exact nature of the challenge to authority is itself fascinating, but even more interesting is the way Protestant leaders interpreted matters for themselves and their constituents. One comes away from Rosenthal's chapter with the sense that the intellectual centers of the movement simply lacked the conceptual frameworks and discourses necessary to the task, and some suspicion that this situation still holds today (and not only for Protestantism). The issue is a central question for Protestantism, the dominant religious movement of the twentieth-century United States, and it is not reassuring to realize that Rosenthal's is the first real scholarship ever done on the topic.

PUBLIC ART AS SACRED SPACE: ASIAN AMERICAN COMMUNITY MURALS IN LOS ANGELES

J. Shawn Landres

Public mural art has become an important mode for expressing community self-identity, especially among Asian Americans in Los Angeles.[1] Like other art forms, public mural art incorporates sacred images and concepts; I suggest that "the sacred" often plays a significant role in public mural art, not simply by expressing these sacred images and articulating sacred or religious concepts, but also by turning public murals into "sacred places." Public murals transform untamed and profane spaces into socially constituted sacred places.

Sacred places are highly charged sites for contested negotiations over the ownership of the symbolic capital (or symbolic real estate) that signifies power relations. Although spearheaded by specific cultural entrepreneurs, cultural brokers, or cultural workers, struggles over the ownership of sacred space inevitably draw upon the commitment of larger constituencies that hold an investment in the contest.[2]

Moreover, in the absence of symbols provided by a unifying established religion, the symbol systems of neighborhood public art may be far more "meaningful as a cultural expression" than those of institutional monuments.[3]

The purpose of this chapter is to show, through a discussion of three murals created by Asian American artists, how public murals in Los Angeles are just such "highly charged sites" and thus may be interpreted as

FIGURE 4.1
Vibul Wonprasat, *East Meets West* (1991).

instances of sacred space. The chapter does not seek to prove that the sacred is inherently related to all forms of public art per se. Although there are many ways to discuss "sacred art," the question here is neither, "What is sacred art?" nor even, "What makes sacred art public?" Rather this study asks, "In what ways can public art be sacred space, or create a sacred place?" I explore the extent to which the sacred—imagery, messages, and motifs (including the ways in which the viewer relates to the work) within the form and structure of specific public artworks—is represented, communicated, and produced *in* public artwork.[4]

The public mural is an integrated "event"; the work of art should not be separated from the process by which it was created. Truly "public" art is primarily concerned with process, which involves at least four elements: (1) the involvement of the local community in the conceptualization, siting, and production of the work; (2) the transformation of a nonpublic "space" into a socially constituted "place"; (3) the ongoing relationship—interaction—between the completed work and the viewing public; and (4) the continuing activity of "meaning making" shared by the artist and the observer. To study public art is to attend to issues of "audience, context, and meaning."[5] Moreover, "the question of context distinguishes mural [public] art from easel [studio] painting."[6] Whereas in so-called private art these contexts are important but not central, public art is driven by the self-conscious, explicit consideration of the relationship between the work and its contexts.[7]

FIGURE 4.2
Hitoshi Yoshida, *Flight to the Angel* (1989).

PRIDE OF THE NEIGHBORHOOD: THE MURALS

In Los Angeles, the "Great Walls Unlimited: Neighborhood Pride Program" of the Social and Public Art Resource Center (SPARC) every year commissions the painting of public murals in different neighborhoods across the city.[8] One of the Neighborhood Pride Program's primary tasks is community building; as Lindsey Haley, SPARC's manager of the program, observed, the meetings to develop the murals' concepts are often "the first time that various people have gotten a chance to get together and dialogue. . . . It becomes a problem-solving meeting . . . networking."[9] The artists who are candidates for the commission attend at least two meetings, and often more, and incorporate community concerns and ideas into their final proposals; according to Jennifer Easton, the curator of the City of Los Angeles Public Arts Division, many artists appreciate this critical part of the process and "actively seek [those] opinion[s]." A reason for this is that the "gallery system, and museums, take art away from the cultural context, or put it in a very rarefied cultural context. [Public art] is hopefully a way to bring in artists, [often] important artists, and re-attach them with the community so they are a part of it."[10]

The three community-sponsored public murals discussed here are all located in the City of Los Angeles, in or near downtown. They are among the first to have been produced by and for Asian Americans in that city.[11] Vibul Wonprasat's *East Meets West* (1991) is located at 4757 Melrose Avenue in Hollywood. Part of the 1990–91 Neighborhood Pride Program, it was painted on the wall of the Bangkok Market, which opened in 1931, the oldest Thai-owned business in Los Angeles. Wonprasat, a devout Buddhist, is president of the Thai Community Arts and Cultural Center and a leading figure in the Los Angeles Wat Thai, the city's Thai temple complex at Coldwater and Roscoe in the San Fernando Valley. The mural, which covers two sides of the market, moves from abstract imagery on its left side to highly specific representations on the right. A montage of images from Asian and Western cultures surround the central motif: an inverted heart that contains six students of various ethnic backgrounds. Two students are seated at computer terminals, a third stands next to one of the computers, and the other three, shaking hands, stand behind them.

Hitoshi Yoshida's *Flight to the Angel* (1989) was the Neighborhood Pride Program's first mural commission to an Asian American artist. Yoshida, a Japanese immigrant, painted the mural on a wall at 407 East Third Street, on the outskirts of Little Tokyo. The mural depicts the threshold between a traditional Japanese room, with tatami mats and painted rice-paper sliding doors, and a fantasy cosmo-scape. Two small, black-haired children stand in the room, behind two women in traditional Japanese dress standing on either side of the doorway. Just beyond the threshold, three boys walk with their arms around each other's shoulders toward a likeness of Los Angeles City Hall.

Hui-Xiang Xiao's *Golden Phoenix Is Flying* (1992) is painted on the wall of the Quon Yick Noodle Factory, at 2730 North Main Street in Boyle Heights. Xiao, a Chinese-born artist living in Alhambra, was commissioned by the Neighborhood Pride Program for the 1991–92 cycle. The mural is sited in a neighborhood populated by Chinese-owned businesses and Hispanic residences. The mural combines Mesoamerican artistic forms and Chinese images to depict three young women and two young men, dressed in flowing robes, following a large winged phoenix. The youths and the phoenix are depicted in highly stylized profile poses.

FIGURE 4.3

Hui-Xiang Xiao, *Golden Phoenix Is Flying* (1992).

SIGNIFICANT CONTESTS: REPRESENTATION, COMMUNICATION, AND PRODUCTION

David Chidester and Edward T. Linenthal define "sacred space" in three distinct but interrelated ways: first, it is "ritual space, a location for formalized, repeatable symbolic performances"; second, it is "significant space, a site, orientation, or set of relations subject to interpretation because it focuses crucial questions about what it means to be a human being in a meaningful world"; and third, it is often "contested space, a site of negotiated contests over the legitimate ownership of sacred symbols."[12] Chidester's and Linenthal's definition is useful for several reasons. First, their term *significant space* is broad enough to include public art. Second, *negotiated contests* allows us both to consider the communicative use of the "significant space[s]" and to inquire, *who* is negotiating *what,* and with *whom?* The notion of negotiation implies ongoing interaction and allows us to follow the sacred from artistic intent to audience consciousness, and from viewer perception to community interpretation. Third, the definition posits a quest for understanding in a "meaningful world" that is both larger than and wholly other than (though probably not unrelated to) the individual. And fourth, while the term *set of relations* acknowledges the potential for shared understandings, it does not assume them to be present; although there is much to be said about the multivalence of symbols, it cannot be denied that often what makes a place "sacred" is its dependence on a set of signs that mark that place as fundamentally different from the surrounding territory and whose core meanings are collectively produced and commonly understood by the community in which it is located.

With respect to public art, the seminal ethnography of the "contemporary mural movement" is *Toward a People's Art,* published in 1977, by Eva Cockcroft, John Weber, and Jim Cockcroft. Their study remains the only sustained investigation of the origins of the mural movement in the late 1960s and of the continuing processes by which muralists and communities collaborate to produce public art. Their reports on the first Asian American murals in New York and Chicago suggest that many of the themes to be addressed in the present study—especially those of representation, communication, community identity, and social criticism—have their roots in these early projects of the 1960s. Thus, to the extent that it documents the mural movement in Los Angeles, and that it contributes to the ongoing conversation about the mural movement, this project continues the ethnographic effort initiated by Cockcroft, Weber, and Cockcroft. However, I also aim to expand upon their limited discussion of aesthetics and to explore the relationship between aesthetics—in particular, considerations of space and place—and the mural-production process.[13]

The elements of public mural art that relate most directly to issues of sacred space and place are threefold: representation, communication, and process (for the purposes of this study, limited to production). Two of the three have been rendered as a "literary compass" by literary theorist Paul Hernadi so as to facilitate the systematic organization of literary ideas.[14] I draw upon Hernadi's classifications in order to create a "public art compass." Hernadi's map has two axes—the mimetic (representation) and the rhetorical (communication). I add a third axis: the formal (production), which addresses the process by which mimetic and rhetorical ideas proceed from intention to implementation. Hernadi's map distinguishes between issues of mimesis and representation, on the one hand, and issues of rhetoric and communication, on the other. My revised "compass" adds the elements of form and production.

Representation in public art involves the sacred insofar as the artwork includes images, both concrete and abstract, that refer to sacred symbols and ideas. This raises questions of paradigm: within what frame of reference has this artwork been created, and what vision or visions does it express? The viewer's perspective on and understanding of the images depicted also merit consideration: do they fall into an existing framework of meaning or do they create a new framework? Do the images depict reality as it is lived by the viewer or do they depict a vision somehow different from lived reality? Are the images understood by the viewer as representing that which the artist intended them to represent?

To attend to the communicative elements of a public artwork involves considering the messages expressed by and through the work, particularly in works that are sacred or religious. Here the intent of the artist is examined: what does he or she want to say, and why? A similar examination of the sociology of the organizations sponsoring the artwork would inquire as to *their* intentions and motivations. The examination of communication therefore involves assessing the extent to which the artist and sponsors intend to address either the ethical situation of the individual viewer or the sociopolitical situation of the collective audience, or both. If mimetic representation is about what is and what could be, then rhetorical communication is about what is not and what should be.

Production involves the question of the kind of art, be it dance, music, visual art, sculpture, or literature. Is it meant to be seen, heard, or read? Is it static or performative, temporary or enduring? The form of the public artwork might at first appear to have the least to do with the sacred, insofar as questions of process and product are more matters of tactics and style than of content. However, there are at least two ways, both of which consider the *publicness* of public art, in which certain formal classifications are indicators of sacred space. First, the collective process by which the artist works together with the community to conceptualize, site, and actually make the artwork reflects the ongoing production of the sacred in everyday life. There is an important link between the sacred and "the sense of power that derives from doing things with others—being in their presence and doing things collectively with them."[15] The "publicness" of "public art" depends on precisely this kind of social practice. Second, the radical incongruity of public mural art in Los Angeles—its unexpected presence in the mundane urban setting—implies a conscious interpolation of the sacred into the profane world. "Public art" is a communicative endeavor driven by the self-conscious, explicit consideration of the relationship between the work and its contexts, and aimed at the transformation of a "space" into a "place."[16]

MIMESIS AND RHETORIC: THE SUBSTANCE OF SACRED SPACE

What is the relationship between the images and the ideas? Does the presence of sacred imagery translate into a religious message? Simply put, this is the field in which to analyze the artwork as if it were a literary *text*, independent of the manner of its creation. This is an important level of analysis precisely because it is the only one where "publicness" and "process" do not enter into the interpretive model: that is to say, it is on this level that the sacred is functionally refracted and reflected into the artwork, and it is here that one can most clearly speak of the extent to which the sacred is present in a public artwork. Such analysis reveals the ways in which the artwork manages the tensions between its expressions of community identification and representations of ideal possibilities, on the one hand, and its communicative critiques of the existing situation, on the other.

How are the sacred or religious images organized? At the center or on the periphery? As a central source for societal values or as a diffuse variety of community expressions? Is the sacred even important to the understanding of a particular artwork? In *East Meets West,* Vibul Wonprasat places religious images on the upper-left of the mural because, as he put it, "in Asia, [in] our culture, we have to put religion mostly on the top of anything in the picture. So I put it in the right place. Not under."[17] Similarly, in *Flight to the Angel,* Hitoshi Yoshida arranges images of Japanese Buddhist angels and Tibetan *mandu,* representations of the universe, around the mural's single-point perspective, so as to convey "life's possibilities, expressed with human and divine imagery," as the mural's main theme.[18]

If sacred space is determined to be an important element, then the way in which sacred or religious images are juxtaposed against one another also merits consideration. Here I am following sociologist Anthony Giddens's understanding of "displacement," "disembedding," and "reembedding": "The disembedding mechanisms lift social relations and the exchange of information out of specific time-space contexts, but at the same time provide new opportunities for their reinsertion."[19] Vibul Wonprasat intentionally combines different forms of Buddhism and other Asian religions, from the image of the Thai Theravadan Eastern Temple of the Dawn in Bangkok to that of a woman wearing a costume affiliated with Korean Confucianism, from a Japanese Shinto banner and the Great Buddha of Kamakura to a Western-oriented interpretation of the Mahayana Heart of Understanding (which might just as easily be read as the Sacred Heart of Jesus). He told me that he did this because there are "not just Thais living in Los Angeles. [There are] so many Asian, Cambodian, Thai, Japanese, Chinese. So if I do Thai, it's small, narrow." The mural, he said, is designed "for contact" between the general categories of "East" and "West," because that is how Asians and Westerners perceive each other.[20]

In *Flight to the Angel*, Hitoshi Yoshida creates a "synthesis of Eastern Buddhist mandala symbolism with primal pictorial Western landscapes."[21] He combines the Tibetan *mandu*, a form that represents the universe, with the Japanese *hibo-kannon*, the Meiji-era androgynous angel who protects childbirth.[22] Finally, Hui-Xiang Xiao, in *Golden Phoenix Is Flying*, unites, in a single picture, Chinese imagery and content (a phoenix leading youths, all of them bearing Taoist yin-yang symbols, in the traditional colors of orange, gold, and black) reflecting the Chinese-owned businesses in the neighborhood, with forms and structures derived from the pre-Colombian heritage of the area's Latino residents.

These three examples show how "religion" and "sacred space" may be disembedded from their traditional web of relations, out of traditional modes of time and location, and then reinserted into a wholly new context. At the same time, however, the replacement of religious imagery and the juxtaposition of previously unrelated icons, indexes, and symbols opens up the possibility of reembedding in a new web of relations. The reembedded sacred and religious images thus create new visions and new worlds—in other words, new forms of sacred space, and new sacred places.

Although Giddens suggests that reembedding leads to the creation of new contexts, this need not be the case; reembedding may lead to the *re-creation of fundamental* contexts.[23] The difference is between envisioning a new world and revisioning the existing world. Vibul Wonprasat and Hitoshi Yoshida's uses of imagery reflect such envisioning and revisioning. In both murals, an image of Los Angeles City Hall occupies a central position—in *East Meets West* it is atop the central inverted heart, while in *Flight to the Angel* it is the single point from which all perspectives are drawn out, and both murals focus on images of young boys with their arms around one another. The City Hall imagery suggests a revisioning of the existing civic fabric, while the representation of the children offers a vision for an ideal future.

How are religious and other messages presented to the mural's audience? In many respects, this process begins to occur as early as the community meetings designed to conceptualize the mural. According to Lindsey Haley, "the mural is . . . already being used as a vehicle of communication." SPARC's "Cultural Explainers Koreatown" project, involving a Korean American public monument covered with photographs, draws explicitly on the communicative power of public art. The project is designed to "build bridges, open doors, and literally *'explain'* cultures between ethnic groups."[24] Clearly a message has a better chance of being understood if it is presented in a manner intelligible to the viewing public.[25]

It is not sufficient to ask if the images suggest a new way of seeing the existing world (identification), or if they actually create a new world (utopia); it is also necessary to understand how the public participates in the creation and recreation of the new vision and the new world.

Public art can serve as a vehicle by which the community expresses a sense of collective identity in the face of global and civic homogenization. This may often serve as an attempt to "resist global planning. Global production of space seeks to homogenize spaces; locales seek to humanize (and naturalize) places. Interventions are necessarily local and may be undertaken by many communities on behalf of their own survival."[26] As Cockcroft, Weber, and Cockcroft observe, "people identify with the murals because murals tell the story of the people themselves. They see their lives reflected in the murals on a heroic scale. . . . The basis for identification is not primarily figure resemblances but theme and its expression in a vocabulary of 'vernacular' images, which are embedded in the common visual culture of an area—images that are immediately recognizable and charged with evocative power."[27]

Golden Phoenix Is Flying combines elements from Chinese traditions with pre-Columbian figurative themes in order to evoke an image with which the entire neighborhood—both the Chinese business-owners and the Latino residents—might identify. Similarly, *East Meets West* and *Flight to the Angel* contain images of people in traditional native clothing alongside people in Western dress, perhaps to suggest that identification as a member of the community is possible through either traditional Asian or contemporary Western modes, or a combination of both.

The mural may also serve to express an ideal to which the community aspires but has not yet achieved. Public artworks often represent utopias in a Foucauldian sense: they are "sites with no real place. They are sites that have a general relation of direct or inverted analogy with the real space of Society. They present society itself in a perfected form, or else society turned upside down [inversée]."[28] In East Meets West, Wonprasat centers his principal image, that of "people living together peacefully in Los Angeles," inside a large, inverted heart; the peaceful society, society "in perfected form," is figuratively and literally "society turned upside down."[29] Yoshida's Flight to the Angel is a "dramatic dreamscape" containing a "fantastic panorama."[30] On either side of the mural, Yoshida places a small image of the memorial to Japanese Americans interned at Manzanar during World War II. This is in some sense an inversion of the memorial's function in reality. Whereas at Manzanar it is located at the camp's gates, serving as a boundary marker for the internment camp and thus implying a boundary between the ideal world of freedom and the "real" world of historical memory, in Flight to the Angel, the double image of the memorial encompasses Yoshida's entire vision of a utopian future, perhaps suggesting that the achievement of true freedom depends on maintaining the memory of one's past while taking responsibility for the present and future of one's community. The message of the Manzanar memorial is thus inverted from one of separation to one of incorporation.

This process of expressing identity and creating and recreating utopias is a kind of ritual, the enactment and reenactment of a "religious" vision. Very often, ritual practices serve as identity-creating activities that mark and make the community and separate it from other groups around and beyond it. This has analogies in the differentiation between the sacred (us) and the profane (them).[31] Anthony Giddens, for instance, posits that the reembedding process "provid[es] encounters and rituals which sustain collegial trustworthiness."[32] East Meets West, sited on a wall of the Bangkok Market, a central meeting point for many Thais, makes explicit the ritual reenactment (and reembedding) of social practices that in Thailand traditionally took place at the local temple. "Thai culture uses the Thai temple as a center of community," Wonprasat said. "Everybody [comes] to the Thai temple, offering food to the monks, and talking about everybody's business. Even gossip. . . . Thai people [in Los Angeles] shop mostly at the Thai grocery. Here they use it as a community center, [to meet] and make appointments." The placement of Thai religious imagery—particularly the representation of the Eastern Temple of the Dawn—might therefore signify an attempt by the artist to remind his community of the ritual aspects of their activities at the market: what in Los Angeles they do at the Bangkok Market, in Thailand they did at a temple.

Messages in public—art works, as seen earlier, address what is not and what ought to be. They reveal how a work of art "disrupts the image of a pacified, utopian public sphere, . . . exposes contradictions, and adopts an ironic, subversive relation to *the public it addresses, and the public space where it appears.*"[33] The messages (again, religious, political, or otherwise) are embedded in the place and time of the artwork's site, thus creating what Foucault has called a heterotopia, "a kind of effectively enacted utopia in which the real sites, all the other real sites that can be found within the culture, are simultaneously represented, contested, and inverted. . . . Places of this kind are outside of all places, even though it may be possible to indicate their location in reality."[34] If the mural production process is read into the mural "event" as a whole, *Flight to the Angel* may be seen to contain traces of a heterotopia. Not only did the process "allow each young person as a member of the group to confront through the creative process their own individual artistic sense and to see its actual realization in the finished mural,"[35] but that process was enacted just up the street from skid row and the Los Angeles Mission, where the "creative process" has been stunted, where senses are dulled by drink and by despair, and where "realization" means the shattering of illusions, not the creation of dreams.

The heterotopia, then, provides a kind of commentary criticism of reality—parallel, in many ways, to prophecy. Prophecy, as it is defined by philosopher Cornel West, may involve "discernment . . . connection . . . tracking hypocrisy . . . [and] hope."[36] Like heterotopia, *discernment* and *tracking hypocrisy* involve "a broad and deep analytical grasp of the present in light of the past, . . . [the] ability to keep track, to remain attuned to the ambiguous legacies and hybrid cultures in history; . . . [and] accenting boldly, and defiantly, the gap between principles and practice, between promise and performance, *between rhetoric and reality.*"[37] Similarly, *connection* shares with heterotopia (and with utopia) "empathy, . . . the capacity to get in contact with the anxieties and frustrations of others; . . . [and] the notion that history is incomplete, that the world is unfinished, that the future is open-ended and that what we think and what we do can make a difference."[38] The link between *hope* and heterotopia is tenuous, perhaps, except insofar as a heterotopia is a site of potential, a "reserve of imagination . . . without which dreams dry up,"[39] and it is from such a reserve that hope may emerge.

I have reproduced West's definitions at length because they eloquently illuminate that aspect of public art which shares with religion the search for social transformation. Public art, as Suzanne Lacy puts it, is "connected both to a broad public and to action."[40] Prophecy can be spatial as well as temporal: in Los Angeles, it "now involves a geographical rather than historical projection: it is space not time that hides consequences from us. To prophesize today it is only necessary to know men [and women] as they are throughout the whole world in all their inequality."[41] The prophetic, heterotopic power of public art, so frequently sited in visibly unequal, marginalized communities, is in the representation and communication of the difference between the idealized utopia on the wall and the lived dystopia in the street.

Public art mediates the tension and the struggle for power between mimesis-as-identification/utopia and rhetoric-as-critique. Just as manifestations of the sacred can incorporate both rituals and prophecies, so does public art incorporate mimetic identifications and utopias, on the one hand, and rhetorical critiques, on the other. The prophetic aspect of public art—that which seeks social transformation—cannot be satisfied by a dialogue that does not propose significant change. So on the other side of the dialogic fulcrum from Foucault's heterotopia, where the vision is in tension with and mocks reality, one might observe Giddens's "utopian realism," where the vision enacts reality in that the identification of the community *creates* the community and the expression of utopia becomes a goal to be achieved by the community. Utopian realism, for Giddens, outlines "heavily counterfactual . . . future-oriented thought . . . [which] envisage[s] alternative futures whose very propagation might help them be realized."[42] In other words, utopian realism does not simply envision a new world; rather, it tries to make the real world resemble the ideal world as closely as possible. This point parallels Jonathan Z. Smith's suggestion that ritual has a strongly prophetic aspect: "Ritual is a means of performing the way things ought to be in conscious tension to the ways things are."[43] For Giddens, though, the continued ritual articulation of these "utopias"—the ongoing creation of public artworks—is "antithetical to both the reflexivity and the temporality of modernity. Utopian prescriptions or anticipations set a baseline for future states of affairs which blocks off modernity's endlessly open character."[44] "Utopian realism," then, is a vision that is rooted in an understanding of the contemporary situation. As SPARC's Lindsey Haley commented, "It's good to have murals that reflect a better and happier and hopeful [situation]. You want to instill hope in the people, of course, but in order to accomplish that you really need to grab hold of your own reality. Because if you are constantly looking there, you can't see here and what needs to be done here."

One way to understand this is to think of a mirror: it tells us what we are and what we are not, and it often suggests what we should be. Haley's visual metaphor suggests a parallel between the mural "event" and Foucault's image of the mirror as "a sort of mixed, joint experience" mediating between utopia and heterotopia. The mirror is a utopia in that "I see myself there where I am not, in an unreal, virtual space that opens up behind the surface"; so, too, is the mural, insofar as the viewer is intended to project himself or herself into the vision expressed through the mural, to imagine oneself there without actually being there. The mirror is a heterotopia in that "it makes this place that I occupy at the moment when I look at myself in the glass at once absolutely real, connected with all the space that surrounds it, and absolutely unreal, since in order to be perceived it has to pass through this virtual point which is over there."[45]

Similarly, the mural is a heterotopia: first, the collective enterprise by which it is created is an ideal space effectively enacted, if only temporarily, as a real place; and second, the mural, once created, stands in a critical posture over and against the reality on the street, pointing up that the ideals on the wall are as yet unrealized. This idea of the mural as mirror is well expressed in the depiction of multiethnic harmony in *East Meets West* (the children shaking hands) and in *Flight to the Angel* (the young boys with arms across each other's shoulders). Both projects involved the cooperative participation of neighborhood youth apprentices from different ethnic communities, but the created mural stands as a reminder that interethnic cooperation in Los Angeles is not yet a part of everyday reality.

BETWEEN THE ARTIST AND THE PROPHETIC: EMPLACING SACRED SPACE

How, then, to begin mapping a public mural as a sacred place? How to account for the complex set of relationships that mark and make the work? One way to do so is through the examination of power relations, which lie at the heart both of prophetic engagement and of ritual;[46] ritualization "produces relationships of power, . . . characterized by acceptance and resistance, negotiated appropriation, and redemptive reinterpretation of the hegemonic order."[47] The problem of power relations incorporates prophecy, ritual, and space: just as "space is fundamental in any form of communal life," so "space is fundamental in any exercise of power."[48] This is especially so in sacred space, insofar as the "contest" in (to return to Chidester's and Linenthal's terminology) "contested sacred space" is the ongoing struggle for the power to construct, define, and possess sacred space.[49] This struggle manifests itself in two ways: (1) the use of power to assert identity and maintain control, and (2) the critique of that power. The struggle parallels the tension between the ritual/mimetic—Giddens's "utopian realism"—and the prophetic/rhetorical—Foucault's "heterotopia."

This tension reveals that the meaning of public art is never stable. From one perspective, the ritual act of envisioning a utopia implies a dissatisfaction with reality, and thus a heterotopic tension. From another perspective, the prophetic criticism of power suggests a desire for change, and the sense of hope implicit in this desire indicates the possibility for a utopian vision. In coproducing community murals with the city and with extensive community commitment, SPARC, perhaps, mediates between the two approaches and plays on the inherent instability of the dynamic dialogue.

In the postmodern world of Los Angeles, sacred places may be generated through the production of dynamic and unstable meanings in public murals. This study began with the assumption that sacred space is alive and well in the urban environment, and that it may be found in the aesthetic meaning-making activity of community-based public mural art. I asked, "In what ways can public art be sacred space, or create a sacred place?" Using the cases of Asian American murals in Los Angeles commissioned by SPARC, I have attempted to provide some answers to that question; however, as I cautioned at the outset, this contribution to production of culture theory is intended to initiate conversation, not comprise the entire discussion. More research is needed on murals produced by and for other groups—African Americans, Chicanos, and Native Americans, for example. Additional ethnographic and survey evidence drawn from neighborhoods where murals are located, perhaps at yearly intervals, might better gauge the impact of murals on their environments. And theoretical discussions would profit from an examination of the difference between the more abstract notion of sacred space and more localized, embedded conceptions of "sacred *places*": future studies could compare murals as sacred places with other urban sacred places, or might consider cross-cultural comparisons of the production, use, and interpretation of murals as sacred places. It remains that public art is transformative, irrupting into the profane present the possibility for a sacred future.

NOTES

An expanded version of this chapter, which originated as the author's master's thesis in the Department of Religious Studies at the University of California, Santa Barbara, under the direction of Wade Clark Roof, appeared in *Religion and the Arts* 1, no. 3 (1997): 6–26. It is reprinted with permission.

1. The Social and Public Art Resource Center, sponsor of the murals considered in this chapter, uses the term *Asian American* to refer to murals produced by and for Chinese, Japanese, Korean, Pilipino, and Thai Americans. The term is problematic, however, insofar as it conflates the disparate identities of a wide range of peoples. Nonetheless, a number of artists of Asian heritage have tentatively accepted the Asian American label because "it designates a collective experience; it points to shared problems, questions, and goals that go beyond the confines of any one Asian ethnic group." See David Mura, "A Shift in Power, a Sea Change in the Arts: Asian American Constructions," in *The State of Asian America: Activism and Resistance in the 1990s*, ed. Karin Aguilar—San Juan (Boston: South End Press, 1994), 194.

2. David Chidester and Edward Tabor Linenthal, eds., *American Sacred Space* (Bloomington: Indiana University Press, 1995), 16.

3. Stephen Carr et al., *Public Space* (Cambridge: Cambridge University Press, 1992), 269–70.

4. It is important to make clear the distinction between "the replacement of religion *by* art" (for which this chapter does not make a claim) and the filtering of the sacred *through* art, which is the object of this investigation. See Mike Featherstone, *Consumer Culture and Postmodernism* (London: Sage, 1991), 118 (italics mine). This is neither to argue that *all* social symbols are sacred or religious nor to suggest that *no* social symbols are sacred or religious. Art and the sacred share important parallels, and it is possible to "take a wider definition of culture which will focus not only on formal religious institutions and movements but also on those social processes and practices which generate and regenerate sacred symbols": Featherstone, *Consumer Culture*, 121–22. In this case, these processes and practices center around community-

sponsored public mural art, which is explicitly aimed at addressing social conflicts and attempts to encourage community cohesion.

5. Suzanne Lacy, ed., *Mapping the Terrain: New Genre Public Art.* (Seattle, Wash.: Bay Press, 1995), 291, 296–99.

6. Eva Cockcroft, John Weber, and Jim Cockcroft, *Toward a People's Art: The Contemporary Mural Movement* (New York: Dutton, 1977), 238.

7. Cockcroft, Weber, and Cockcroft distinguish between two different types of murals: "urban-environmental" murals, conceived as "personalistic or nonobjective decoration," and "community-based" murals, conceived as "social communication." This chapter concerns the latter type, which "while also concerned with the environment, has a rationale of working for the local audience around issues that concern the immediate community, using art as a medium of expression of, for, and with the local audience. [These murals] involve artists with community issues, community organizing, and community response to their artwork." See Cockcroft, Weber, and Cockcroft, *Toward a People's Art,* 29–30.

8. The projects are done under contract from the city's Cultural Affairs Commission. City of Los Angeles, Cultural Affairs Commission, *Minutes,* April 13, 1989; March 28, 1991; June 11, 1992.

9. Interview with Lindsey Haley, manager, Neighborhood Pride Program, Social and Public Arts Resource Center, April 10, 1995. Unless otherwise indicated, all Haley statements are drawn from interview transcripts.

10. Interview with Easton in Los Angeles, March 6, 1995. Unless otherwise indicated, all Easton statements are from interview transcripts.

11. The murals are virtually the only places identified as Asian that are officially recognized as important by the city's cultural establishment; for instance, of the 588 "historic-cultural monuments" designated by the city's Cultural Heritage Commission between 1962 and 1994, only two acknowledge the Asian American presence and contribution to the life of the city. The two are the Japanese Union Church (No. 312, designated in 1986) and a "19th Century Los Angeles Chinese Cemetery Shrine" (No. 486, designated in 1990). See City of Los Angeles, *Historic-Cultural Monuments 1–588,* May 1994.

12. Chidester and Linenthal, *American Sacred Space,* 9, 12, 15.

13. Absent from this study, however, is a comprehensive assessment of the impact of the murals on their communities; as the titles of the interview subjects indicate, this study is primarily concerned with mural *production.* The study of the "reception of culture" remains an important part of any future agenda for public-art research.

14. Paul Hernadi, "Literary Theory: A Compass for Critics," *Critical Inquiry* 3, no. 2 (1976): 369–86.

15. Robert Wuthnow, *Producing the Sacred: An Essay on Public Religion* (Urbana: University of Illinois Press, 1994), 57.

16. "Abstract space, lacking significance other than strangeness, becomes concrete place (only when it is) filled with meaning." Yi-Fu Tuan, quoted in Jonathan Z. Smith, *To Take Place: Toward Theory in Ritual* (Chicago: University of Chicago Press, 1987), 28. Also Yi-Fu Tuan, *Space and Place: The Perspectives of Experience* (Minneapolis: n.p., 1977).

17. Interview with Vibul Wonprasat, Marina Del Rey, February 11, 1995. Unless otherwise indicated, all Wonprasat statements are drawn from interview transcripts.

18. Michael Several, *Little Tokyo: The Public Art of Los Angeles,* part 2 (Los Angeles: Los Angeles Cultural Affairs Department, 1994), 18.

19. Anthony Giddens, *The Consequences of Modernity* (Stanford: Stanford University Press, 1990), 141.

20. It must be acknowledged that the representation of images here based on what is "commonly perceived" also tends to reinforce existing stereotypes. For example, in *East Meets West,* the chrysanthemum emblem on the Shinto banner represents the Japanese imperium, while the Great Buddha of Kamakura was built by the shogunate as an expression of military might. Although this might simply reflect a projection onto Japan of the Thai understanding of religion and political power (see Stanley J. Tambiah, "Sangha and Polity in Modern Thailand: An Overview," in *Religion and Legitimation of Power in Thailand, Laos, and Burma,* ed. Bardwell L. Smith [Chambersburg, Pa.: ANIMA Books, 1978], 111–33), it remains that many Japanese Americans might be uncomfortable with this *puissantist* representation of Japanese religiocultural traditions; it also raises serious questions about the authority of symbol development in public art. Similarly, the image of the woman wearing a Korean Confucian costume suggests the unquestioning acceptance of Confucian notions about the subordinate role of the woman, a stance with which many Korean Americans might take issue. David Mura addresses the multiplicity of centers and margins in Asian American identity in "Shift in Power"; see 200–201.

21. Hitoshi Yoshida, "Neighborhood Pride Mural Project Proposal," October 28, 1988.

22. Michael Several, interview with Hitoshi Yoshida, Los Angeles, January 30, 1990. The idea of "Tibet" and the esoteric nature of Tibetan Buddhism have become a kind of Orient for many young Japanese. If this was the case for Yoshida, then his use of the *mandu* is more an act of appropriation than of synthesis; in either case, it is a form of "embedding." Furthermore, the *hibo-kannon* is not necessarily representative of contemporary Japanese religious identity; it was developed during the Meiji Restoration as part of the imperial project of massive population growth for military purposes; more recently, it has reappeared on the fringe of

mainstream practices as an object of devotion during postabortion propitiation rites, again referring to an older, conservative, imperial order.

23. Diane Apostolos-Cappadona, "Picasso's *Guernica* as Mythic Iconoclasm: An Eliadean Reading of the Myth of Modern Art," in *Myth and Method: Perspectives on Sacred Narratives,* ed. Laurie L. Patton and Wendy Doniger O'Flaherty (Charlottesville: University of Virginia Press, 1996). This "re-visioning" may involve the artistic resuscitation of beneficent social forms: "In the public place par excellence, art is faced with its greatest civil responsibility. In places . . . where the sense of common good has evaporated, it is the duty of art to denounce that evaporation. Moreover, it is duty-bound to present itself as the bearer and representative of new collective values." See Vittorio Magnago Lampugnani, "Public Art and Civil Art," *Domus* 751 (July / August 1993): 65–66.

24. Social and Public Art Resource Center, *Cultural Explainers Koreatown* (Los Angeles: SPARC, 1994), 2.

25. One of the reasons that public artworks may communicate a wide range of religious, political, and other messages is that many city ordinances governing public art guarantee freedom of expression. For example, the City of Los Angeles has outlined its policy as follows: "Ideological and Political Signs. No provision of this chapter shall prohibit an ideological, political or other noncommercial message on a sign otherwise permitted by this chapter" (*1991 Uniform Building Code,* chap. 62, section 6201[d]). Other cities seek free expression without writing it into law; see, for example, "Metro-Dade [County, Florida] Art in Public Places Master Plan," in Jeffrey L. Cruikshank and Pam Korza, *Going Public: A Field Guide to Developments in Art in Public Places* (Amherst, Mass.: Arts Extension Service in cooperation with Visual Arts Program, National Endowment for the Arts, 1988), 203.

26. Richard Carp, ed., *Saber es Poder/Interventions* (Los Angeles: ADOBE LA, 1994).

27. Cockroft, Weber, and Cockcroft, *Toward a People's Art,* 83–84.

28. Michel Foucault, "Of Other Spaces," trans. Jay Miskoviec, *Diacritics* 16 no. 1 (1986 [1967]): 22–27; esp. 24.

29. To be sure, the paradoxical nature of the inverted heart could imply that this utopian vision is impossible to achieve. This image, and others like it, could be read as envisioning a utopia that displaces the sociocultural conflicts of the real world onto an inaccessible, imaginary, metaphysical plane.

30. Yoshida, "Mural Project Proposal."

31. Catherine Bell, *Ritual Theory, Ritual Practice* (New York: Oxford University Press, 1992), 91.

32. Giddens, *Consequences of Modernity,* 87.

33. W. J. T. Mitchell, ed. *Art and the Public Sphere* (Chicago: University of Chicago Press, 1990), 3 (emphasis added).

34. Foucault, "Of Other Spaces," 24. In a later interview, Foucault described heterotopias as "those singular spaces whose functions are different or even the opposite of others." See Michel Foucault, "Space, Power, and Knowledge," in *The Cultural Studies Reader*, ed. Simon During (London: Routledge, 1993), 168.

35. Yoshida, "Mural Project Proposal."

36. Cornel West, *Prophetic Thought in Postmodern Times* (Monroe, Maine: Common Courage Press, 1993), 3–6.

37. Ibid. (italics mine).

38. Ibid., 5–6.

39. Foucault, "Of Other Spaces," 27.

40. Lacy, *Mapping the Terrain*, 27.

41. John Berger, quoted in Edward W. Soja, "Postmodern Geographies: Taking Los Angeles Apart," in *NowHere: Space, Time, and Modernity*, ed. Roger Friedland and Deidre Boden (Berkeley: University of California Press, 1994), 137. See also John Berger, *Ways of Seeing* (London: British Broadcasting Corporation and Penguin Books, 1972).

42. Giddens, *Consequences of Modernity*, 154.

43. Smith, *To Take Place*, 109.

44. Giddens, *Consequences of Modernity*, 178.

45. Foucault, "Space, Power, and Knowledge," 24.

46. The phrase *prophetic engagement* is West's. See West, *Prophetic Thought*, 59–83.

47. Bell, *Ritual Theory*, 196.

48. Foucault, "Space, Power, and Knowledge," 166.

49. It would take a separate study to discern how much control different groups—in particular, the Los Angeles Cultural Affairs Commission and SPARC—actually have over mural sacred space. SPARC blurs the lines between establishment "public art" and insurgent "guerrilla art," insofar as it redirects establishment sponsorship to community needs and reinscribes indigenous community expression into the social fabric. See Rebecca Solnit, "Active Art: Political Art Reclaims Public Space," *New Art Examiner* 19 (January 1992): 24–27, esp. 26. See also Denis Cosgrove's distinction between "dominant" spaces and "emergent" or "excluded" spaces (Cosgrove, "Geography Is Everywhere: Culture and Symbolism in Human Landscapes," in *Horizons in Human Geography*, ed. Derek Gregory and Rex Walford (London: Macmillan, 1985), 124, 130–33. In this reading, SPARC's mural production activity subverts the establishment by projecting emergent and excluded landscapes onto the established, dominant one. See also Michael Dear, "Public Art in the Postmodern City" (paper at conference, "Public Art: Realities, Theories, and Issues," Los Angeles, 1994).

BIBLIOGRAPHY

Apostolos-Cappadona, Diane. "Picasso's *Guernica* as Mythic Iconoclasm: An Eliadean Reading of the Myth of Modern Art." In *Myth and Method: Perspectives on Sacred Narratives*, ed. Laurie L. Patton and Wendy Doniger O'Flaherty. Charlottesville: University of Virginia Press, 1996.

Bell, Catherine. *Ritual Theory, Ritual Practice*. New York: Oxford University Press, 1992.

Berger, John. *Ways of Seeing*. London: British Broadcasting Corporation and Penguin Books, 1972.

Carp, Richard, ed. *Saber es Poder/Interventions*. Los Angeles: ADOBE LA, 1994.

Carr, Stephen, Mark Francis, Leanne G. Rivlin, and Andrew M. Stone. *Public Space*. Cambridge: Cambridge University Press, 1992.

Chidester, David, and Edward Tabor Linenthal, eds. *American Sacred Space*. Bloomington: Indiana University Press, 1995.

City of Los Angeles, Cultural Affairs Department, Cultural Affairs Commission. *Minutes*. April 13, 1989; March 28, 1991; June 11, 1992.

——. *Historic-Cultural Monuments 1–588*. May 1994.

Cockcroft, Eva, John Weber, and Jim Cockcroft. *Toward a People's Art: The Contemporary Mural Movement*. New York: Dutton, 1977.

Cosgrove, Denis. "Geography Is Everywhere: Culture and Symbolism in Human Landscapes." In *Horizons in Human Geography*, ed. Derek Gregory and Rex Walford. London: Macmillan, 1985.

Cruikshank, Jeffrey L., and Pam Korza. *Going Public: A Field Guide to Developments in Art in Public Places*. Amherst, Mass.: Arts Extension Service in cooperation with Visual Arts Program, National Endowment for the Arts, 1988.

Dear, Michael. "Public Art in the Postmodern City." Paper at conference, "Public Art: Realities, Theories, and Issues," Los Angeles, 1994.

Featherstone, Mike. *Consumer Culture and Postmodernism*. London: Sage, 1991.

Foucault, Michel. "Of Other Spaces." Trans. Jay Miskoviec. *Diacritics* 16, no. 1 (1986 [1967]): 22–27.

Foucault, Michel. "Space, Power, and Knowledge." In *The Cultural Studies Reader*, ed. Simon During. London: Routledge, 1993.

Giddens, Anthony. *The Consequences of Modernity*. Stanford: Stanford University Press, 1990.

Hernadi, Paul. "Literary Theory: A Compass for Critics." *Critical Inquiry* 3, no. 2 (1976): 369–86.

Lacy, Suzanne, ed. *Mapping the Terrain: New Genre Public Art*. Seattle: Bay Press, 1995.

Lampugnani, Vittorio Magnago. "Public Art and Civil Art." *Domus* 751 (July/August 1993): 65–66.

Mitchell, W. J. T., ed. *Art and the Public Sphere*. Chicago: University of Chicago Press, 1990.

Mura, David. "A Shift in Power, a Sea Change in the Arts: Asian American Constructions." In *The State of Asian America: Activism and Resistance in the 1990s*, ed. Karin Aguilar—San Juan. Boston: South End Press, 1994.

Several, Michael. Interview with Hitoshi Yoshida. Los Angeles, January 30, 1990.

——. *Little Tokyo: The Public Art of Los Angeles*, part 2. Los Angeles: Los Angeles Cultural Affairs Department, 1994.

Smith, Jonathan Z. *To Take Place: Toward Theory in Ritual*. Chicago: University of Chicago Press, 1987.

Social and Public Art Resource Center. *Cultural Explainers Koreatown*. Los Angeles: SPARC, 1994.

Soja, Edward W. "Postmodern Geographies: Taking Los Angeles Apart." In *NowHere: Space, Time, and Modernity*, ed. Roger Friedland and Deidre Boden. Berkeley: University of California Press, 1994.

Solnit, Rebecca. "Active Art: Political Art Reclaims Public Space." *New Art Examiner* 19 (January 1992): 24–27.

Tambiah, Stanley J. "Sangha and Polity in Modern Thailand: An Overview." In *Religion and Legitimation of Power in Thailand, Laos, and Burma*, ed. Bardwell L. Smith. Chambersburg, Pa.: ANIMA Books, 1978.

Tuan, Yi-Fu. *Space and Place: The Perspectives of Experience*. Minneapolis, Minn.: [n.p.], 1977.

West, Cornel. *Prophetic Thought in Postmodern Times*. Monroe, Maine: Common Courage Press, 1993.

Wuthnow, Robert. *Producing the Sacred: An Essay on Public Religion*. Champaign: University of Illinois Press, 1994.

Yoshida, Hitoshi. "Neighborhood Pride Mural Project Proposal," October 28, 1988.

CHAPTER 5

ALL THE WORLD'S A STAGE: THE PERFORMED RELIGION OF THE SALVATION ARMY, 1880–1920

Diane Winston

The glittering crowd at the Metropolitan Opera House included many of New York City's elite. Now, as rousing music stirred their souls, they sat expectantly. In the darkened auditorium, singers clad in hooded robes of red and white mounted the stage and formed a huge crimson cross. The audience was ready, more than ready—but for what? Were they waiting to hear the next Caruso? Or perhaps Puccini's latest opera? As the anticipation mounted, a single shaft of blue light caught a solitary figure heading down the center aisle. Dressed in tatters and rags, the homely female form picked a tune on her concertina.

The costumed waif was Commander Evangeline Booth, head of the U.S. branch of the Salvation Army and one of the few female denominational leaders in the 1920s. On this night, Booth was using New York's premier stage to present one of her acclaimed pageant-sermons. This presentation, *The Commander in Rags,* was a tale of love, service, and salvation. Booth described her experience as a teenager in London's East End where, working among the poor, she was dubbed "The White Angel of the Slums." Massed bands, songsters, soloists, and fifty simply dressed "slum sisters" were key to the recitation, along with lighting effects and props of all kinds—including lambs, sheep, and, at least on one occasion, a horse (fig. 5.1).[1]

Evangeline Booth hoped her performance would turn the Metropoli-

FIGURE 5.1
Evangeline Booth in her role as the commander in *Rags*.
Salvation Army Archives.

tan Opera House into sacred space. The climax came when she won converts for Christ—or failing that, new contributors to her cause. But the
evening's spectacle was just the culmination of forty years of Salvation
Army stratagems aimed at spiritualizing the profane. Since arriving in
New York in 1881, Salvationists had waged a stealth campaign, seeking to
adapt popular media for religious purposes. By spiritualizing media—
whether parades, pageants, or dramatic presentations—the Army engaged
in a bold crusade to transform an advanced industrialized society into the
kingdom of God.

Salvationists initially mounted their crusade in the streets. Eager to
"purify the moral atmosphere,"[2] they paraded down the avenues and up
the boulevards, crisscrossing New York's east/west and north/south axes.
When they finished marching, officers conducted services dubbed "the
cathedral of the open-air." Their self-described campaign to "sanctify
commonplaces"[3] was described in an editorial that appeared in the *War
Cry,* the Army's weekly newspaper:

> The genius of the Army has been from the first that it has secularized
> religion, or rather that it has religionized secular things. . . . On the one
> hand it has brought religion out of the clouds into everyday life, and
> has taught the world that we may and ought to be as religious about
> our eatings and drinkings and dressing as we are about our prayings.
> On other hand it has taught that there is no religion in a place or in an
> attitude. A house or a store or factory can be just as holy a place as a
> church; hence we have commonly preferred to engage a secular place
> for our meetings . . . our greatest triumphs have been witnessed in the-
> atres, music halls, rinks, breweries, saloons, stores and similar places.[4]

Whether marching through the alleys of Little Italy or testifying on well-
traversed boulevards, Salvationist soldiers aimed their open-airs at spectators who normally eschewed religion. In order to attract the unchurched,
they copied the era's popular entertainments. The brass bands, colorful
flags, and lively singing could have been advertisements for the latest minstrel or variety show.[5] Only when bystanders stopped to listen did they
discover that the familiar forms had a different content. The Army's parades and popular music initially conveyed a straightforward evangelical
message: a call to repentance and salvation. But over time the forms grew
more sophisticated, and the content did likewise. Pageants proceeded

from parades and lectures turned into dramatic presentations with slides and living tableaux. The call to salvation was muted, and financial solicitations became an important part of the mix. The Army's appeal as an evangelical movement was limited, and its work was sustained through aid for humanitarian outreach. The Army's skillful use of popular media generated significant support. But by the end of World War I, Salvationists realized that their use of popular media had affected their message and that the secular media's depictions of their work would alter it even more.

EARLY OUTREACH EFFORTS

The Salvation Army began in London in 1865 as the Christian Mission, a religious outreach run by William Booth, an independent evangelist determined to reach the unchurched masses. Booth, supported by his wife Catherine—an early proponent of women's right to preach—delivered the gospel message to poor and working-class people wherever they were found. In 1878, when Booth changed the name of his organization to the Salvation Army, he was already called "the General," and thereafter his new "army" rapidly adopted a military look and language. The Army's newspaper was titled the *War Cry,* ministers were "officers," and members were "soldiers." Salvationists wore plain, dark clothes that varied from soldier to soldier until Booth standardized a simple blue uniform.[6]

To capture the attention of the "heathen masses," early Salvationists adopted flamboyant tactics. Reaching the unchurched public on its own territory seven days a week meant that the secular market place and its entertainments—rather than the churches—were the main competition. Thus, Salvationists developed a self-consciously dramatic flair. When the official landing party disembarked in New York City, George Scott Railton, the commanding officer, and seven "Hallelujah lassies" knelt in prayer, planted the Blood-and-Fire flag, and claimed America for God. Reporters ballyhooed the "sensation" that the Army made marching through lower Manhattan.[7] The press was also on hand when the plucky band appeared at Harry Hill's Variety, a popular concert saloon where, preceding a panorama of Uncle Tom's Cabin, they prayed and pleaded to a hostile crowd.[8] The Army did not win any converts that night, but it did provide a religious experience unfamiliar to most saloon customers.

Challenging the enemy on its own ground, Salvationists offered an alternative—not just to liquor but also to what they perceived as dry, "churchy" religion.

In 1887, when William Booth sent Maud and Ballington Booth, his son and daughter-in-law, to lead the American Army, the young couple built on the outreach strategies of their predecessors. Two of Maud Booth's preferred modes of presenting her message were by-invitation-only parlor meeting and the Chautauqua-style lecture, both popular with the era's well-to-do. Chautauqua, an upstate New York retreat, provided Protestant laity with a comfortable compromise between religion and commercial entertainment. For the Salvation Army, seeking to widen its outreach to the middle and upper classes, the Chautauqua format was an opportunity to speak in a cultural vernacular that mitigated its use of the streets. Army critics deemed its outdoor evangelizing vulgar and sensational, and Army women—who preached publicly and fraternized with their male counterparts—were considered coarse and morally lax. Accordingly, Maud Booth's use of a class-identified mode of communication was as significant as her message. Her persona was significant, too. The seemingly wayward daughter of a proper Anglican rector, Booth's "angelic" face and dignified mien surprised the movement's detractors.

When Maud Booth announced a lecture on "The New Woman," the auditorium at the Army's national headquarters attracted a standing-room-only crowd. The audience, assembled for a religious critique of this controversial creature, was greeted by an all-female platform of officers, band members, cadets, and soldiers. Booth's plummy tones may have blunted the edge of an arguably feminist thrust, but for those with ears to hear, the message was straightforward. "This is a woman's meeting," she began. "The women are going to do everything here tonight." She proceeded to explicate a model of womanhood that, while explicitly condemning the media caricature of the "mannish" female, implicitly affirmed many of the New Woman's aims. Booth enthusiastically supported women's right to education, athletic exercise, and work—but she called her ideal the "advanced woman" and affirmed her devotion to family, home, and religion.

Booth helped change popular notions of Salvationist womanhood through her lectures and parlor meetings. By projecting a refined demeanor in her public appearances, she modeled behavior that was simultaneously feminine and feminist, religious and secular. A few years later,

FIGURE 5.2

The drawing on this *War Cry* cover depicts the Salvation Army's parallels with medieval Crusaders. The Red Crusade, led by Emma and Frederick Booth-Tucker, was both a pageant and an evangelical campaign. Salvation Army Archives..

Emma Booth-Tucker, Maud's sister-in-law and successor, blended religion and popular entertainment to express her vision of a spiritual crusade. On Easter morning 1900, Booth-Tucker led a column of marching soldiers down the Bowery. A white Maltese cross, the medieval insignia on her red scarf and dress, marked her as a latter-day crusader. Booth-Tucker, known as "the Consul," steered the procession straight to the London Theatre. In their wake, a large crowd scrambled for the vaudeville house's atypically free seats. The Salvation Army's Red Crusade, an evangelistic campaign that used medieval imagery to dramatize its mission, was about to begin (fig. 5.2).

BORROWING FROM VAUDEVILLE

Emma Booth-Tucker, who commanded the Salvation Army in the United States with her husband Frederick from 1896 to 1904, led the packed house in prayer and song. But she did not hold the stage alone: the Red Crusade had a touch of vaudeville about it, religious "acts" performing a Christian version of the theater's regular proceedings. The staff band played a medley of tunes and two of the Army's soldiers—"saved variety actors"—sang duets; "the converted whiskey bottles leapt into the affection of the crowd." "Say," said a boy in the top gallery with a strong odor of garlic about him and not overdressed, "this 'ere is a cinch. It beats the theatre holler—and all seats free! You people must be awful good!"[9]

The Army was good—particularly at adopting the vernacular of the audience they wished to reach. When the Booth-Tuckers began appearing in venues such as the London Theatre, the American stage was booming. New York's theater-seating capacity doubled between 1890 and 1900, and between 1880 and 1900 the number of shows extending New York runs to national tours increased tenfold, from about fifty to more than five hundred.[10] For most of the century, New York audiences had been segregated by class and gender. The wealthy attended opera, lectures, and concerts; men from the lower and working classes went to concert saloons and variety theaters, and the middle classes stayed home. But as women increasingly ventured into public spaces and the pursuit of leisure became a respectable pastime, savvy entrepreneurs redesigned theatrical performances to suit the tastes of women, families, and the middle class. Vaudeville was key. Promoters gathered a wide variety of acts that appealed across class and gender lines. Prices were lowered, theaters cleaned up (besides refurbishing, owners ejected prostitutes who catered to clientele in the upper tiers), and newspaper advertisements promoted special acts. Army productions like the Red Crusade and *Love and Sorrow* took out ads in newspapers' entertainment sections that targeted the same audience.

By the turn of the century, the Salvation Army was not the only religious group using popular forms of entertainment to impart a religious message, but it was noteworthy for the scale, diversity, and sophistication of its productions. The Red Crusade exemplified each of these facets. This production, signifying the saving blood of Jesus (the Army organized and named its evangelistic campaigns thematically), had a medieval flair. During the five years that Red Crusade toured the country, it was usually preceded by *Love and Sorrow,* an illustrated lecture on the Army's rapidly growing social program. Accompanied by a series of stereopticon views of Salvationist social work at home and abroad, the two-hour lecture was punctuated with living tableaux and choral numbers from the Army's Yankee Songsters and the American Staff Cowboy Band. In advance of the lecture, in addition to the articles and advertisements in local newspapers, a brass band marched through the streets tootling loud, military music. Frequently several thousand people sought admission.[11]

The very success of such publicity stunts encouraged Army supporters who sought alternatives to commercial entertainments. As one *War Cry* correspondent noted: "As a Christian and as a lover of my country my heart had often ached as I had watched the dense crowds pouring in and out of the theatres, the music halls and saloons. When I had compared their nightly thousands to the meager audiences that gathered once a week for the purpose of worship, I had been tempted to wonder whether something more could not be done to turn this ever-increasing tide of humanity in an opposite direction."[12]

Love and Sorrow continued the Army practice of suffusing theatrical performances with spiritual meaning. But it was noteworthy because it separated the purely evangelical side of the work from the social mission. Ideally, the lecture laid the foundation for the revival work of the Red Crusade, but even those who chose not to attend the second meeting had been exposed to the Army's work with the poor. For those who questioned whether charitable service was the correct course for a religious group—social workers and charity societies claimed to have a better understanding of the realities and remedies for poverty—*Love and Sorrow* dramatized the Army's vision of the problem.

The Army, in general, and the Booth-Tuckers, in particular, believed in helping anyone who was willing to work. At a time when scientific philanthropists and charity organization workers tried to distinguish between the deserving and the undeserving poor, Salvationists scoffed at the time and expense involved in such calculations. William Booth's 1890 opus *In Darkest England and the Way Out* laid out the movement's social scheme: Help those willing to work and encourage families to stay together. Once reformed, the poor would be shipped from overcrowded, urban slums to farm colonies where they could lead good, Christian lives. Salvationists believed the presence of steady work, an intact family, and food and shelter would enable the power of God's love to bring about spiritual regeneration.

While the Booth-Tuckers expressed this message in their religious vaudeville, Salvationists added other popular attractions to their arsenal. Parades grew more spectacular as floats and costumed battalions became more extravagant. Likewise, evangelical street workers invented ever more dramatic ploys to attract spectators. Loud bands remained the first line of attack, but Salvationists also circulated handbills advertising staged "trials" against the devil, "John Barleycorn," and even Robert Ingersoll, the most famous atheist of the day.[13] Army officers preached in coffins, held marathon hymn-singing contests, and appeared as "specialty" acts with monikers such the Golden Minstrel, the Saved Cowboy, and the Converted Pugilist.

EVANGELINE BOOTH TAKES CENTER STAGE

Performances became even more elaborate when Evangeline Booth took command of the American Army in 1904. Booth's signature piece, *The Commander in Rags* (alternatively referred to as *The Four Keys* and *The Tale of a Broken Heart*) was, like *Love and Sorrow,* a dramatic performance staged in a commercial theater. But Evangeline's lecture was much more of an extravaganza than was her sister Emma's; moreover, it put her, not the Army, at the center of the narrative. "In *Rags,* she recalled her experience as a teenager in London's East End ("The White Angel of the

Slums"). When she performed the lecture on stages across the country, promotional materials announced that the "Commander Miss Booth" would "tell the tale of a broken heart and sing the song of love." But her real message was the need for action. Love was vital, sacrifice necessary, but action was preeminent. As the *War Cry* declared: "It is not even enough that we sacrifice. We must do—do with our hands, do with our lives, do with our money, do with our influence. Action, action! Religion in action, this is what the world needs—religion alive, religion living among the people, religion going about doing good as well as singing hymns."[14]

The Commander in Rags was Booth's tour de force, elaborating on her work in the London slums as a trope for the Army. In the dramatic light cast by her role as a tattered angel, Booth hoped to make audiences see the Salvation Army with new eyes—as the embodiment of love, sympathy, sacrifice, and action. Although the first three were fundamental Christian virtues, action was the Army's special contribution. Through repeated performances around the nation, Booth's emphasis on action-oriented Christianity became the hallmark of the Army's identity during the Progressive Era, a time when Americans sought active solutions for society's ills. Her performances—augmented by the public relations savvy learned from her father and honed by experts who included publicist Bruce Barton and businessman John Wanamaker—helped consolidate the Army's reputation while propelling Booth to celebrity status. Historian Charles L. Ponce de Leon has described "celebrity discourse" as the product of media professionals transforming individuals into "symbols of larger developments and trends" who also bridge the distance between the "masses" and the "classes."[15] Evangeline's performances demonstrated both.

At five feet eight inches, with long, auburn hair, luminous eyes, and an aquiline nose, Evangeline Booth was a commanding presence. Colleagues described her as handsome and well groomed, with silk-lined uniforms handmade by a French seamstress.[16] Evangeline was a talented musician, and her oratory skills were renowned: her dramatic style was compared with Sarah Bernhardt's. Throughout her life, she cultivated a theatrical persona. In a 1947 interview, Evangeline noted that her parents worried she might leave the Army and go on stage because "I had a bit of good looks and a gift for speaking."[17]

From the time she arrived in New York in 1904, Booth sought to strengthen and institutionalize the Army. Working on two fronts, she built up the Army's infrastructure while bolstering its external image. To accomplish the former, she utilized the regnant business principles of organization, efficiency, and systemization in a process parallel to historian Ben Primer's description of denominational rationalization.[18] Yet Booth diverged from the leaders of most other Protestant groups: rather than create a faceless bureaucracy, she gave the Army a persona—her own. The Army, like "The Commander in Rags" herself, embodied love, sympathy, sacrifice, and action. Booth projected that image through the *War Cry*, her public performances, and her interviews in the secular media.

For this reason, the impact of the Army's institutionalization is tied to the language and performances that cast the movement, like Booth herself, as active and action-oriented. Since these characteristics were central to the Progressive temper of the times, the Army garnered popular and financial support that, in turn, fed expanding social programs, new building projects, a growing bureaucracy, and a vigorous public relations campaign. In this light, Army descriptions of Booth's lectures as "representations" rather than theatrical performances are significant. Protestants had long been wary of the thin line between artifice and authenticity. Historian Jackson Lears observes that the tension between the two "was at the heart of Anglo-American Protestant culture."[19] Salvationists prized plain speech, but they also were heirs to the theatrical techniques of antebellum revivalists. Their desire to spiritualize the secular world, as much as their need to finance their work, caused them to commingle the sacred and profane in a complex web of images, entertainment, and market relations.

The tension between artifice and authenticity also permeated the Army's view of its "performances." As R. Laurence Moore notes, the similarities between theater and religious revivals had haunted evangelists ever since George Whitefield turned "preaching into a performance."[20] Although Whitefield eschewed references to the theater when discussing his work, later revivalists made the connection explicit. The "practiced spontaneity" advocated by Charles Finney was modeled on stage acting, although the great revivalist did distinguish between acting and evangelizing. In his view, actors perverted their nature by assuming a variety of roles, corrupting their audiences by presenting fictions that aroused base passions. Evangelists were different: they projected only themselves, and they presented truths aimed at inspiring a change of heart.

While liberal Protestants in the postbellum era accepted secular theatricals as long as they offered wholesome entertainment, evangelical Christians still opposed them. But in its attempts to provide viable alternatives to commercial entertainments, the Salvation Army employed the very idioms and instruments of popular culture and, in the process, often blurred the line between secular performance and religious iteration. That Evangeline, for example, succeeded in entertaining secular audiences on their own terms can be inferred by the defensive tone in *War Cry* reports of her performances. Since Booth's recitation stirred emotions just as a satisfying drama would, one correspondent felt compelled to differentiate between a theatrical performance and Booth's "representation," which derived its power from reality: "The audience applauded and wept, laughed and cried as they beheld that child of God in tatters before them, as delicate almost as the flowers she carried in the basket on her arm; and this was not a performance, it was a representation of real life—of a life lived by the one who was portraying it."[21] That this "representation" was a performance of an earlier performance did not trouble Salvationists familiar with the idea of masquerading to gain access to the lower classes.

Yet the distance from Evangeline's initial impersonation in Piccadilly Circus to her performance in *The Commander in Rags* encompassed significant changes in both the actor and the evangelical mission. Evangeline was no longer a teenager seeking souls in London's East End slums. As head of a large religious and philanthropic organization, she was trying, by sentimentalizing poverty, to win over wealthy audiences. Similarly, the Army itself had evolved from a local evangelical mission to a worldwide movement requiring thousands of dollars to fund its operations. Although Salvationists seemed to ignore the implications of such changes, they were not entirely lost on their contemporaries. An early admirer of the Army's band music, George Bernard Shaw, wrote several anonymous reviews praising the music's "precision and snap."[22] When he learned that William Booth had cited these reviews publicly, Shaw approached Army leaders and suggested they develop their dramatic skills, too. Offering to write a play for their use, Shaw was told that unless every incident had actually occurred, the play would be a lie—and therefore objectionable. (He was asked, instead, for a donation.) Noted Shaw, "To my mind, of course, this was a very curious misapprehension of the difference between truth and mere actuality."[23]

THE ARMY ON BROADWAY

Initially supportive of Booth's attempts at social reform, Shaw grew critical because he believed such efforts were undermined by accepting money from the very people—capitalists, liquor interests, and entrepreneurs—responsible for poverty. While William Booth insisted he would take money from the devil if it could be used for good purposes, Shaw wondered whether such money was simply fuel for maintaining the Army bureaucracy. Shaw's speculations on "tainted money" took dramatic form in his 1905 play *Major Barbara*, the story of a wealthy girl who joins the Army and whose father, a munitions dealer, subsequently offers to fund Salvationist work. The British *War Cry* noted the play's opening with a brief summary of the plot and a quote from the (unnamed) playwright noting that he "greatly admire[d]" the Army's rescue work.[24]

Major Barbara, which debuted on Broadway in 1915, was not the only play to use the Army to highlight larger themes.[25] The power of a good woman's love was the subtext of several plays about the Army. The rehabilitation of the lassies' image—begun by Maud Booth in the 1880s—was complete two decades later. No longer ruined by their association with the Army, lassies were considered virtuous Christian women who could save the most wicked men. In the 1897 musical *The Belle of Broadway,* a young wastrel is redeemed when he falls for a Salvationist lass.[26] The play, which did moderately well on Broadway, was a popular hit in London, where it ran for almost seven hundred performances.[27] Although one critic dismissed *The Belle of Broadway* for having neither "a fertile or suggestive topic," the musical enjoyed several more incarnations on stage and film.[28] A 1919 movie provided a vehicle for Marion Davies, and in 1952 a new screen adaptation starred Vera-Ellen and Fred Astaire as the romantic leads.

A decade after *Belle's* debut, Broadway audiences embraced *Salvation Nell.* A melodrama by an Edward Sheldon, a fledgling playwright who went on to achieve critical and commercial success, *Salvation Nell* thrived despite mixed reviews. A scrubwoman whose lover is sent to jail for murder, Nell considers prostitution to support herself. At the last moment, she decides instead to join the Salvation Army. When her sweetheart is freed, he wants her to return to their old, immoral ways. Refusing, she prays for his conversion. He reforms, becomes a Salvationist, and they wed. While some critics loved *Nell,* others were unimpressed.[29] Opined

FIGURE 5.3
A scene from the 1921 film version of Edward Sheldon's play *Salvation Nell*.
The play was adapted for film three times. (Museum of Modern Art Stills Archive.)

the *New York Times*, "Such an exhibition of sordid and vulgar depravity as Mr. Sheldon presents in *Salvation Nell* will accomplish no good purpose."[30] Like several other plays that season, *Nell* sought to give audiences a vivid picture of slum life, in this case typified by a Cherry Hill street scene complete with tenements, colorful crowds, and the Salvation Army slum post (fig. 5.3).

HOLLYWOOD'S REPRESENTATIONS

The very simplicity of the Army's religion combined with the potency of its symbols made it an ideal vehicle for Hollywood. In years past, Salvationists borrowed from commercial culture to attract new audiences to the gospel message; now commercial culture was ready to borrow back. The lassie, renown for her war service, was a modern heroine. She was courageous, virtuous, and immediately recognizable. Unlike Roman Catholic nuns, who were also religious and easy to spot, the lassie stood

FIGURE 5.4
A baker, standing beside a soldier, testifies to the work of the Salvation Army at the front
during World War I—a scene from the 1919 film *Fires of Faith*.
(Museum of Modern Art Stills Archive.)

for a faith that reached out to everybody. Most crucial for Hollywood's purposes, she could have a romantic life. From D. W. Griffith's *The Salvation Army Lass* (1908) to postwar movies such as *Salvation Nell* (1919) and *Hell's Oasis* (1920), the Army woman saved (and got) her man.[31]

Though the Army's message relied on the icons of American evangelical Christianity, its modes of presentation were more subtle and up-to-date. Having previously appropriated aspects of commercial culture, evidenced in Army advertising, pageants, "vaudeville," and tableaux vivants, Salvationists now turned to the movies. When Paramount approached Evangeline Booth for help in telling the Army's story, she readily complied.[32] The result was *Fires of Faith*, a melodramatic World War I love story with the Army's war work as its centerpiece.

Before *Fires of Faith*, more than a dozen movies had featured Salvationist characters. But this was the first time the Army participated in making and promoting a film. Paramount publicists said Jesse Lasky made the picture as a "tribute" to the Army rather than a commercial feature, but the film's marketing campaign belied that premise.[33] For the Army's part, the movie provided a way to expand its audiences and to raise money for its 1919 Home Service Appeal fund-raising campaign. Yet the Army's participation in the film was rarely publicized among the Salvationist rank-and-file. The *War Cry* did not report on the movie itself, the Army's role in making it, or the money raised by the preview (fig. 5.4).

Most likely, Evangeline Booth did not want to draw the attention of her brother, General Bramwell Booth, to her involvement in such a worldly activity. The Army used forms of popular entertainment for its own purposes, but it definitely opposed patronizing the secular versions. As an item in the movie publicity kit makes clear, Salvationists differentiated between their own representations of reality and the fictional sort. This disclaimer explained that the Salvationists' American leader was being, as opposed to playing, herself: "Miss Booth does not appear as an actress in the development of the story but incidentally as the executive head of The Salvation Army, in the performance of her usual duties."[34]

Fires of Faith was standard melodramatic fare. The complicated story revolves around Elizabeth Blake, a beautiful young woman who, after being seduced by a cad, is rescued by the Army. Following her redemption, she becomes a Salvationist and sails off to serve American troops fighting in France. Serendipitously, she meets several former friends at the front. Agnes Traverse, the daughter of Elizabeth's wealthy patron, has also become a Salvation lassie, or Sallie. Agnes's fiancé, Harry Hammond, who was shanghaied and taken to France, has escaped and joined the Air Service. When Harry's plane is shot down, he ends up in Elizabeth's care. Half-blinded in battle, he does not recognize her. Meanwhile, Luke Barlow, a farm boy who loves Elizabeth, enlists in the U.S. Army because he knows his sweetheart is in France. After many twists and turns, the two couples celebrate a double wedding. In the course of the story, the film recounts Salvation Army history and depicts its religious and humanitarian efforts. Publicists, aware that such potentially didactic material could doom the film's marketability, stressed the movie's drama, star power, and authenticity.

The movie's premier, occurring at the height of the Salvation Army's prestige, set the stage for the Army's role as one of the new century's most popular expressions of public religion. It also illustrates the give-and-take between a spiritual mission and a commercial venture; that is, the Army's work and Hollywood's bottom line. While there are no known extant prints of the film, still photographs, reviews, and the press book suggest that the collaboration on *Fires of Faith* was the closest Salvationists came to faithfully representing themselves for a mass audience. Yet even this effort required compromise: the movie was a commercial melodrama not a religious tract. Once again the Army's saturation strategy, explicit sectarian warfare that sought to Christianize society, gave way to stealth and diffusion. By the end of World War I, the Army's militant evangelism had evolved into a silent model of service and sacrifice. With the peace came a new guise for the heroic lassie, as Hollywood, too, fell for "the doughboy's goddess."

PAGEANTS AS PUBLIC RITUAL

While moviemakers busily projected new images of the Army, Salvationist leaders were spinning their own. During Evangeline's tenure, Army pageantry and filmmaking were both on the rise. Beginning in the late 1880s, the Army mounted pageants to celebrate its ethnic diversity and humanitarian activities. Staged primarily as in-house events for territorial gatherings, these rallies featured Salvationists in native dress of their homelands and performing living tableaux of their efforts to aid the needy. Under Evangeline Booth's aegis, these pageants became spectacles designed not only to inform fellow Salvationists of ongoing activities but also to educate the public at large. Salvationists' pageants borrowed from an already eclectic tradition of public amusements, which drew on church rituals, carnival parades, and theatrical tableaux. Historian David Glassberg argues that during the Progressive Era pageantry was a form of public ritual designed to spur political and social change. Army pageants had a similar rationale and aim. They, too, were public rituals that drew a community together as spectator/participants in the Army's transformative activities.

Spiritual Wonderland mounted at the Carnegie Music Hall in 1909 to celebrate General William Booth's eightieth birthday, was illustrative. To create a festive mood, Salvationists trimmed the auditorium with flags, electric lights, and decorations. For more than four hours, a succession of living tableaux and performances occupied center stage. From a throng of white-garbed children whose presence launched an evening of appearances by bands, choruses, and soldiers swathed in foreign dress, the activity never faltered. Officers pantomimed programs in prisons, slums, and shelters, while the commander elaborated on each one. Toward midnight, a squad of parading youngsters was joined in countermarches by representatives of various brigades to form "a bewildering but fascinating sea of color and motion."[35]

Two years later another pageant, similarly titled *Salvation Wonderland*, was held at the same venue. This time the show included six homeless men "as they were": after telling their stories, the men reappeared, rehabilitated as welders, painters, and furniture-movers in a scene about the Army's Industrial Homes. In another enactment of Army work, white-gowned nurses holding babies marched around a semicircle of swinging cradles. If anyone in the audience doubted whether the blanketed bundles were the real thing, piercing squalls assured them that indeed they were.[36]

While Army pageants strove to impress spectators with the scope and vibrancy of its activities, they also sought to use entertainment for uplift and education. Much like the organizers of historical pageants, Salvationists "plac[ed] their faith in new techniques of mass persuasion to inform public opinion, evoke public sentiment, and spur public action on a variety of issues."[37] By using pageantry to dramatize the Army's civic contributions, Evangeline Booth projected her organization on the public arena. Yet to attract as broad a public as possible, Salvationists played down their particularities, especially their brand of revivalist evangelicalism, and emphasized a vision of service rooted in a nonsectarian humanitarianism. The movement's financial success was based on its leaders' familiarity with worldly trends and techniques; the former's religious goals were achieved by subverting the latter.

> Why it is an age of demonstration! Merchant princes demonstrate their goods: musicians demonstrate their harmonies: druggists demonstrate their remedies: Not a "copper" pounding the pavement, a pill mixer in the apothecary's shop, a broker's clerk at the tape, a jockey on the courts, an actor on the stage, a ball-player at the bat, an artist with his brush or a writer with his pencil, but what is anxious to show rightly or wrongly that he is prepared to "deliver the goods." Good men demonstrate their goodness and alas! bad men their badness. Yea, and even the devil himself is a great demonstrator—the greatest of all, in many ways.

Why then to change the nature of the question, should we not be at the forefront with a demonstration of God's miraculous power in the regeneration of humanity?[38]

Sharing Evangeline Booth's penchant for demonstration and spectacle was Lt. Colonel Edward Parker, who in the 1910s headed the Army's division for social programs, stage-managed its pageants, and directed much of its media work. Parker's enthusiasm for technology dated back to the early 1890s. As a corps commander in Hartford, Connecticut, he had rigged up a large outdoor screen by stretching a twelve-foot muslin sheet from the second-story window of his office to a building across the street. With the aid of a magic lantern, Parker projected scriptural texts and announcements onto the screen. He also developed Limelight Services, similar to the subsequent series of popular Limelight Lectures that used a magic lantern to project stereopticon slides. While his wife sang familiar Army hymns, Parker showed vivid illustrations.[39]

The Limelight Services led to the Limelight Lectures; Parker charged admission for illustrated talks on topics such as "The Rise and Progress of the Salvation Army." In addition to creating slide shows for his own use, Parker assisted Emma Booth-Tucker in developing a pictorial accompaniment for *Love and Sorrow,* her presentation on the Army's social work, and for Evangeline Booth's dramatic monologue, *My Father.* Parker was not alone in finding religious uses for the magic lantern: city missions, Sunday schools, and temperance societies were engaged in similar work. Salvationists around the world were, however, leaders in advancing the medium's potential.[40]

In the late 1890s, Australian Salvationists, directed by Commandant Herbert Booth, began combining magic-lantern slides with motion-picture film. Among their earliest efforts was an illustrated lecture with two hundred slides and two thousand feet of film titled *Our Social Triumphs.* Middle- and upper-class Australians, like their counterparts in the United States and Britain, considered moviegoing a working-class pastime. But Australian Salvationists, recognizing a significant tool for spiritual conversion and moral reform, quickly expanded their Limelight Department into a leader of the country's burgeoning film industry. Perceiving that "story" films were more successful than documentaries, the new department produced several shorts on its rescue work that depicted lassies saving unwed mothers and delivering innocent girls from wicked seducers. The department's next project was a series of short films about the life of Jesus culminating with *The Soldiers of the Cross,* a full-length movie. A saga of the early Christian martyrs, *Soldiers* was first shown in 1900 and ran for more than two hours. In between hymns and classical music, the commandant's resonant tones recounted tales of Christian martyrs that accompanied graphic scenes of crucifixions, beheadings, stonings, torchings, and believers being fed to lions.[41]

In 1901 Parker became head of the American Army's Trade Department. Aware of the Australian Army's success, he added cameras, photographic slides, lantern slides, stereopticons, and motion-picture equipment to the product list. He also set up a dark room at headquarters and directed several officers to prepare photographs to meet the increased demand for slides.[42] His enthusiasm was boundless: Parker designed and manufactured photographic equipment that included a stereopticon called the Optic Lantern and a camera called the Warrior. During World War I, he took hundreds of photographs illustrating the Army's work at the front. He authored a monograph explaining the workings of the magic lantern and for his contributions to the *War Cry* adopted Optic as his nom de plume.

Unlike his Australian counterparts, however, Parker did not begin using the motion-picture camera until the 1900s. His first film was of Emma Booth-Tucker's funeral in 1903.[43] A subsequent project, *Problems of the Poor,* integrated lantern slides and motion pictures. Disguised as a tramp, Parker rented rooms in lower Manhattan so that he could live among the poor and photograph their suffering. Parker presented the subsequent multimedia *Problems of the Poor* to churches, YMCAs, and fellowship clubs across the nation.[44]

NO LONGER CONTROLLING THE IMAGE

The Army's spectacles, pageants, films, and slide shows were vehicles for explaining its brand of religion and social service both to donors and spiritual seekers. The effort succeeded—especially with the former, members of the middle and upper classes, who saw the Army providing a vital public service. Yet the Army's success at commodifying itself through performances began to blunt the efficacy of its evangelical work. The representation had superseded the reality. The resulting confusion between what Army missionaries thought they were doing and what the public perceived can be glimpsed in a 1914 *War Cry* story. When Salvationists "invaded" several Broadway dance palaces, they asked "tango enthusiasts" to reflect on life's serious side. To the soldiers' surprise, the crowds listened respectfully, "apparently enjoying the novelty." At one club, the maitre d' himself led the "picturesque little group" to the center of the dance floor, where they sang and prayed. Afterwards, the crowd applauded loudly and threw coins. The Salvationists accepted the money and were invited to call again.[45]

The gap between the Salvationists' understanding of their actions and the dancers' response to it illustrates the confusion between reality and representation that characterized some of the Army's efforts. To nightclubbers in the mid-1910s, aware of the Army's own pageantry as well as its portrayal in Hollywood movies, invading the dance hall looked like another form of entertainment. The evangelical thrust was blunted by the familiarity of the image juxtaposed with the novelty of an actual encounter. The Army's power to shock and offend had ebbed as its performances moved from evangelical street theater to philanthropic fundraising. Whereas, thirty-four years earlier, the patrons at Harry Hill's—annoyed by the Army's exhortations—hooted and booed their appearance, in 1914, members of the city's demimonde were amused by a similar performance and contributed to Army coffers.

At a time when political and social upheavals, from the Gilded Age to World War I, provided favorable settings for the Army's active brand of religiosity, Salvationists used popular media—both their own and secular society's—to attract attention. Their message, however, was transformed in the process. While the Army thrived institutionally, its mission changed from one of militant evangelism to a humanitarian social service with an underlying Christian witness. The old message could not work with secular audiences made uncomfortable by sectarian expressions of faith. Using popular media to reach this audience compelled the Salvation Army to hold up a common denominator of belief and behavior—a public religion whose message of love and service transcended doctrinal difference.

Salvationists had a part in this transformation, but they were unable to affect all the ways in which their image was appropriated by the secular media. Even the most sympathetic of such representations did not always match their self-perception. For example, lassies in the secular media were vibrant and appealing, while their religion was less so—just the opposite to the emphasis the Army would haven chosen. The concomitant process of cultural negotiation, as the Army tried to exert control over its image yet also sought media attention to further its goals, illuminates the problems faced by a religious group that is both responsible to a higher power and dependent on the public's goodwill. That the Army was adept at using popular media to gain and sustain public support only further complicated the predicament.

NOTES

1. Sallie Chesham, *Born to Battle: The Salvation Army in America* (Chicago: Rand McNally, 1965), 170–71.

2. *American War Cry*, January 28, 1893, 1.

3. *American War Cry*, July 31, 1909, 2.

4. *American War Cry*, September 23, 1896, 8.

5. The Army's loud music and comic antics were aspects of a charivari. Some spectators, familiar with the English tradition of "rough music," may have intuited the subversive quality of the Army's performances. See Natalie Davis, "Charivari, Honor, and Community in Seventeenth-Century Lyon and Geneva," in *Rite, Drama, Festival, Spectacle,* ed. John MacAloon (Philadelphia: Institute for the Study of Human Issues, 1984), 42–57. For charivari and New York, also see Paul A. Gilje, *The Road to Mobocracy: Popular Disorder in New York City, 1763–1834* (Chapel Hill: University of North Carolina Press, 1987) 20–21.

6. For histories of the Salvation Army: Frederick Lee Coutts, *The Better Fight: The History of the Salvation Army* (London: Salvationist Publishing and Supplies, 1977); Edward McKinley, *Marching to Glory: The History of the Salvation Army in the United States, 1880–1980* (San Francisco: Harper & Row, 1980); Robert Sandall, *A History of the Salvation Army* (London: Nelson and Sons, 1947–1986). On William Booth: St. John Ervine, *God's Soldier: Next to God: The Story of William Booth and the Salvation Army* (New York: Macmillan, 1965).

7. *New York Times,* March 11, 1880, 5.

8. McKinley, *Marching to Glory,* 14.

9. *American War Cry,* April 28, 1900, 9.

10. David Nasaw, *Going Out: The Rise and Fall of Public Amusements* (New York: Basic Books, 1993), 34.

11. *American War Cry,* February 11, 1899, 4; *American War Cry,* February 25, 1899, 4.

12. *American War Cry,* February 11, 1899, 4.

13. *American War Cry,* February 24, 1894, 4; *American War Cry,* November 2, 1895, 12; *New York Times,* January 29, 1895, 7.

14. *American War Cry,* April 25, 1908, 13.

15. Charles L. Ponce de Leon, "Idols and Icons: Representations of Celebrity in American Culture, 1850–1940" (Ph.D. diss., Rutgers University, 1992), iii.

16. Margaret Troutt, *The General Was a Lady: The Story of Evangeline Booth* (Nashville: Holman, 1980), 136–37.

17.
Dorothy Walworth, "General of the Army: Evangeline Booth," *Readers Digest,* August 1947, 36.

18. Ben Primer, *Protestants and American Business Methods* (Ann Arbor, Mich.: UMI Research Press, 1979).

19. T. Jackson Lears, *Fables of Abundance: A Cultural History of Advertising in America* (New York: Basic Books, 1994), 53.

20. R. Laurence Moore, *Selling God: American Religion in the Marketplace of Culture* (New York: Oxford University Press, 1994), 42.

21. *American War Cry,* April 25, 1908, 13.

22. Stanley Weintraub, "Bernard Shaw in Darkest England: GBS and the Salvation Army's General Booth," in *Shaw: The Annual of Bernard Shaw Studies,* ed. Stanley Weintraub and Fred D. Crawford, vol. 10 (University Park: Pennsylvania State University Press, 1990), 45–59.

23. Weintraub, "The Salvation Army's General Booth," 50.

24. Arch R. Wiggins, *The History of the Salvation Army,* vol. 5, 1904–14 (London: Nelson & Sons, 1968), 251–52.

25. *New York Times,* December 10, 1915, 13; *New York Times,* December 19, 1915, IV, 8.

26. Gerald Bordman, *The Oxford Companion to American Theatre* (New York: Oxford University Press, 1984), 69–70. The Broadway version played fifty-six performances and starred the popular actress Edna May.

27. *New York Times,* September 29, 1897, 7; *New York Times,* April 14, 1898, 9; *New York Times,* January 23, 1900, 7; *New York Times,* January 24, 1900, 11.

28. *New York Times,* January 24, 1900, 11.

29. Bordman, *The Oxford Companion to American Theatre,* 595; *New York Times* November 15, 1908, VI, 1; *New York Times,* November 18, 1908, 5.

30. *New York Times,* November 22, 1908, VI, 7.

31. Other movies with Salvation Army characters released between 1920 and 1929 include *The Big Punch* (1921), *Salvation Nell* (1921), Human Wreckage (1923), *The Spirit of the USA* (1924), *Satan Town* (1926), *For Heaven's Sake* (1926), *Salvation Jane* (1927), *The Angel of Broadway* (1927), *His Last Haul* (1928), *The Good-bye Kiss* (1928), and *The Street of Sin* (1928).

32. Scrapbooks on *Fires of Faith* offer two accounts of the movie's inception. Several references say Jesse Lasky went to Evangeline Booth with the suggestion and "she was quick to grasp the idea." Another clip says the Army proposed the collabo-

ration to Lasky. New York Library for the Performing Arts, Zan T213 reel 37. Clips undated.

33. New York Library for the Performing Arts, Zan T213 reel 37, "Fires of Faith Worth Seeing," by Louella Parsons (clip without name of paper or date).

34. *Fires of Faith* press packet, p. 7.

35. *American War Cry*, May 8, 1909, 12.

36. *American War Cry*, November 4, 1911, 7; *American War Cry*, December 2, 1911, 8–9, 12.

37. David Glassberg, *American Historical Pageantry: The Uses of Tradition in the Early Twentieth Century* (Chapel Hill: University of North Carolina Press, 1990), 285.

38. *American War Cry*, May 8, 1909, 8–9.

39. Edward Justus Parker, *My Fifty-eight Years* (New York: Salvation Army Headquarters, 1943), 107–8.

40. W. T. Stead, "The Magic Lantern Mission," in *Review of Reviews*, Dec. 1890, 562.

41. Ina Bertrand, ed., *Cinema in Australia: A Documentary History* (Kensington, N.S.W.: New South Wales University Press, 1989), 21–23; Eric Reade, *History and Heartburn: The Saga of Australian Film, 1896–1978* (Rutherford, N.J.: Fairleigh Dickinson University Press, 1989), 3–4; Graham Shirley and Brian Adams, *Australian Cinema: The First Eighty Years* (North Ride, N.S.W.: Angus Robertson, 1983), 10–14.

42. Parker, *My Fifty-eight Years*, 126.

43. The cinematograph was first used by British Salvationists in 1903. Wiggins, *History*, 4: 394.

44. Parker, *My Fifty-eight Years*, 168–170; *American War Cry*, April 23, 1910, 1, 6; *American War Cry*, December 28, 1912, 25.

45. *New York Times*, March 22, 1914, 1.

BIBLIOGRAPHY

Bertrand, Ina, ed. *Cinema in Australia: A Documentary History*. Kensington, N.S.W.: New South Wales University Press, 1989.

Bordman, Gerald. *The Oxford Companion to American Theatre*. New York: Oxford University Press, 1984.

Chesham, Sallie. *Born to Battle: The Salvation Army in America*. Chicago: Rand McNally, 1965.

Coutts, Frederick Lee. *The Better Fight: The History of the Salvation Army*. London: Salvationist Publishing and Supplies, 1977.

Davis, Natalie. "Charivari, Honor, and Community in Seventeenth-Century Lyon and Geneva." In *Rite, Drama, Festival, Spectacle,* ed. John MacAloon. Philadelphia: Institute for the Study of Human Issues, 1984.

Ervine, St. John. *God's Soldier: Next to God: The Story of William Booth and the Salvation Army.* New York: Macmillan, 1935.

Gilje, Paul A. *The Road to Mobocracy: Popular Disorder in New York City, 1763–1834.* Chapel Hill: University of North Carolina Press, 1987.

Glassberg, David. *American Historical Pageantry: The Uses of Tradition in the Early Twentieth Century.* Chapel Hill: University of North Carolina Press, 1990.

Lears, T. Jackson. *Fables of Abundance: A Cultural History of Advertising in America.* New York: Basic Books, 1994.

McKinley, Edward. *Marching to Glory: The History of the Salvation Army in the United States, 1880–1980.* San Francisco: Harper & Row, 1980.

Moore, R. Laurence. *Selling God: American Religion in the Marketplace of Culture.* New York: Oxford University Press, 1994.

Nasaw, David. *Going Out: The Rise and Fall of Public Amusements.* New York: Basic Books, 1993.

Parker, Edward Justus. *My Fifty-eight Years.* New York: Salvation Army Headquarters, 1943.

Ponce de Leon, Charles L. "Idols and Icons: Representations of Celebrity in American Culture, 1850–1940." Ph.D. diss., Rutgers University, 1992.

Primer, Ben. *Protestants and American Business Methods.* Ann Arbor, Mich.: UMI Research Press, 1979.

Reade, Eric. *History and Heartburn: The Saga of Australian Film, 1896–1978.* Rutherford, N.J.: Fairleigh Dickinson University Press, 1989.

Sandall, Robert. *A History of the Salvation Army.* London: Nelson & Sons, 1947–86.

Shirley, Graham, and Brian Adams. *Australian Cinema: The First Eighty Years.* North Ride, N.S.W.: Angus Robertson, 1983.

Stead, W. T. "The Magic Lantern Mission." In *Review of Reviews,* Dec. 1890, 562.

Troutt, Margaret. *The General Was a Lady: The Story of Evangeline Booth.* Nashville: Holman, 1980.

Walworth, Dorothy. "General of the Army: Evangeline Booth." *Readers Digest,* August 1947, 36.

Weintraub, Stanley. "Bernard Shaw in Darkest England: GBS and the Salvation Army's General Booth," In *Shaw: The Annual of Bernard Shaw Studies,* ed. Stanley Weintraub and Fred D. Crawford, vol. 10. University Park: Pennsylvania State University Press, 1990.

Wiggins, Arch R. *The History of the Salvation Army, 1904–14.* London: Nelson & Sons, 1968.

"TURN IT OFF!": TV CRITICISM IN THE CHRISTIAN CENTURY MAGAZINE, 1946–1960

Michele Rosenthal

In May 1960, Elvis Presley, newly released from the army, appeared on television. His performance was "pernicious," declared an editorial in the widely read *Christian Century,* a liberal Protestant weekly; Elvis's wiggling pelvis was a sign of the "depth of decadence into which our scale of values has sunk." The spectacle, dismissed as "revolting exhibitionism," was—most unfortunately in the *Christian Century's* opinion—accessible "at the twist of the youngest wrist." Even worse, this performance had earned Elvis a whopping $125,000, a sum that could have been spent on a year's salaries for twenty-five teachers, forty-two ministers, or sixty-three farmhands. If Americans were willing to allow such "distasteful" programs into their homes, they could expect nothing more than the "ruin which awaits such a people."[1]

Exorbitance was Presley's main crime. The idea that Americans would not only spend leisure time passively watching a wriggling pelvis but pay, indirectly, large sums to do so, conflicted with older ideals—namely, the Protestant work ethic and the correlative understanding of leisure (mostly Victorian in origin). For the *Christian Century* editors, television viewing was, at best, a waste of time, and, at worst, a direct assault on the American (that is, Protestant) way of life. Subsequently, television never received much attention in the magazine's pages.

During the early years of commercial television, a few articles by guest writers had argued that the church (i.e., liberal Protestantism) must confront and harness this new medium for missionary and educational purposes. These pleas for practical involvement in television, however, were largely overshadowed by negative evaluations of programming content. For the editors, little on television warranted positive praise or even critical evaluation. Even religious television was largely ignored by the *Christian Century*. True to its rather highbrow, intellectual character, the magazine was reluctant to cede to this new medium its due cultural weight. For the most part, readers were counseled simply to "turn it off!"[2]

Despite their relative scarcity, the articles and editorials that do mention television provide an opportunity to understand the ways in which this new medium was received and acculturated by a segment of the liberal Protestant leadership.[3] Throughout the nineteenth century, liberal Protestant leaders played an active role in creating and defining acceptably wholesome forms of commercial culture. By the post–World War II era, however, Laurence Moore has argued that this "ambition receded and ended in the tasteful packaging of a commercial product that still sold but did not arouse much consumer enthusiasm."[4] Notably, this so-called liberal Protestant lack of "inventiveness" is dated (more or less) to the era that coincides with the rise of broadcasting. While the theater, fiction, and sports were eventually "reformed" enough to be considered moral forms of entertainment, the movies, the radio, and television proved to be far more problematic.[5] This critical approach toward broadcasting shares something in common with the secular post–World War II critique of mass culture and fear of technology's (mis)uses. At the same time, it indicates a broader shift in the liberal Protestant leadership's approach to commercial culture.[6]

Why at that particular moment in history were liberal Protestant leaders incapable of reinventing the wheel? The new medium of broadcasting may have made that task more difficult or less inviting. Perhaps the social meanings attributed to the radio or television were somehow different than those attributed to nineteenth-century forms of commercial culture. It is, I would argue, not enough to claim that liberal Protestantism was "worn out" or that it had become theologically bankrupt and therefore incapable of effectively transforming yet another form of commercial culture.[7] Some accounts emphasize structural developments in broadcasting and innovations in computer technologies that eventually favored conservative Protestant approaches to media, but, I would again argue, they do not adequately explain why mainline Protestants refused to adapt to those changes.[8]

Ann Swidler has held that to explain a particular cultural outcome (in this case the rise of televangelism and the decline of mainline broadcasting) one must not only understand the relationship between a particular ideology and the action under study, but also suggest why that ideology and not another succeeded under those circumstances.[9] Why did liberal Protestants give up the cultural battle, leaving the task to their more conservative counterparts?[10] Why did conservative Protestants, who heretofore had remained largely critical of such adaptive strategies, pick up these techniques and apply them to contemporary media?[11] The reasons for this transition are far from self-evident. By understanding how the liberal Protestant leadership responded to the introduction of these new media, and by placing these responses in their theological, historical, social, and cultural contexts, we can perhaps begin to unravel the relationships between the decline of liberal Protestant interest in the creation and production of acceptable forms of culture and the subsequent rise of interest among their more conservative counterparts.

In this chapter, I focus on understanding and describing, to use Swidler's words, the "cultural repertoire" that shaped the television strategies pursued by mainline leaders.[12] I argue that in the changing social context of the post–World War II United States, mainline Protestant hegemony was increasingly called into question, both by its own leaders and by the voices of a more pluralist America that had heretofore been mute. In this context, the strategy of Christianization (by which I mean the efforts to reform and shape cultural life according to mainline Protestant norms), which had been so effective in the nineteenth century, could no longer be maintained. The new strategy was one of (almost calculated) disregard. Below I point to the sources of this strategy and show how disregard was constructed and legitimated as a viable approach to this new medium of communications.

I describe how the *Christian Century*'s response to television was shaped by older cultural and theological assumptions—like iconoclasm, anti-Catholicism, asceticism—and by fears of changes in the cultural status quo (e.g., increasing pluralism, the transformation of the American Victorian home and domestic piety, the rise of the leisure society, and decline of the work ethic). In the post-1945 period, as hegemony became harder to maintain, thicker cultural boundaries would need to be drawn. If the culture at large could no longer be assumed to be reflective of Protestant values, mainline Protestant leaders would have to delineate what did reflect Protestant values. In doing so, they would reconfigure the relationship between mainline Protestantism and American culture. Practically speaking, this meant that high culture would increasingly be identified as the sole bearer of mainline Protestant values.

Below I examine some of the different ways television was portrayed, described, and discussed in the *Christian Century* during the first fifteen years or so of commercial broadcasting (approximately 1946–60). By drawing out some of the cultural and theological assumptions that shaped this discourse, I suggest why television was rarely considered worthy of serious consideration by the *Christian Century*. I then take a closer look at the ways in which television is described on the pages of the *Christian Century* and show how the editors understood the effect of television on the audience, the role of government in the regulation of this new medium, and the ethical dilemmas posed by television for liberal Protestants. I conclude by discussing the broader ramifications of this case for our understanding of the relationship between American Protestantism and the mass media, particularly television.

"CAN PROTESTANTISM WIN AMERICA?"

Founded in 1884 as the *Christian Oracle*, the *Christian Century* was optimistically renamed in 1900. Then in 1908 it was purchased by Charles Clayton Morrison. For forty years, Morrison served as editor, turning what had been previously a magazine affiliated to the Disciples of Christ into the nation's preeminent, ecumenical mainline religious weekly. As such, the influence of the *Christian Century* is measured more accurately by the nature of its readership, many of whom would count themselves among the religious and lay leaders of mainline or liberal Protestantism, rather than by its fairly small circulation of 40,000.[13]

Early references to television in the *Christian Century* can be characterized by their moralistic tone, a tone born of an assumption of cultural hegemony. Despite its relatively small circulation, the editors wrote with an assurance that they were the rightful and historical guardians of American culture.[14] For the first ten years of commercial television, this self-perception seemed well warranted. Church attendance and church construction reached their peak just as television became accessible to most of the population.[15] For a brief moment, Protestantism (or "religion in general" as it was called by those who came to oppose the superficial nature of the revival) seemed to be (re)winning America.[16] While there was some reason to worry that the faith of Protestant America was being challenged by Roman Catholicism and secularism, overall the mood was one of triumphalism, tempered only by the fear of imminent cultural change.

In 1946, the first year that RCA and DuMont offered their black-and-white sets for sale to the public, Charles Clayton Morrison, the founder and editor of the *Christian Century,* published his thirteen-part series of articles entitled "Can Protestantism Win America?"[17] This series—written as a follow-up to Harold Fey's controversial set of articles "Can Catholicism Win America?" that was published in the *Christian Century* a year before—was both a lament on the state of Protestantism in America and a strategy to preserve Protestant cultural prominence.[18] In the fifth article "Protestantism and Commercialized Entertainment," Morrison argued that along with a "secularized educational system and the widespread acceptance of the messianic pretensions of science" (subjects of earlier articles), overexposure to commercialized entertainment was making the "culture . . . removed farther out of reach of the appeal of Protestant Christianity."[19] Commercialized entertainment was not just morally deplorable (that was too obvious to deserve comment), but had affected the content and balance of the American mind: "This incessant bombardment of the mind with sensuous stimuli has subtly, but profoundly, changed the quality of the mentality of our generation."[20] While the Puritans may have overemphasized the mind over the senses, the contemporary generation had tipped the scale toward sensations to the point where all standards had been undermined, and tastes corrupted (554–55). For Morrison, the new emphasis on technique over subject matter illustrated the "complete inversion of aesthetic values and moral standards," a process that testified to the high degree of "cultural decadence."[21] To save America from the fate of Rome, the church needed to actively intervene: "The task of saving America from the enervating influence of the commercial exploitation of the people's leisure, rests uniquely upon the shoulders of Protestantism. It must assume this responsibility if it is to save itself and win America" (556).

In this article, Morrison explicitly links the decline of Protestant influence to the rise of commercial entertainment. Although television has yet to appear on his mental horizon, it is clear that Morrison would judge it to be irredeemable. Television, as another example of a sensuous medium that stresses technique over content and image over idea, could not play a positive role in American culture (at least not in a Protestant America). No number of sustaining or public-service hours for religious programming on radio or television could offset the destructive influence of everyday commercial entertainment. For Morrison, the aesthetic resulted from his ascetic, inner-worldly Protestantism. The post–World War II leisure society, as it was coming to be known, was at odds with the work ethic. There was no "elective affinity" between this new America and ascetic Protestantism. If Protestantism (as Morrison understood it) was to survive these cultural shifts, it would need to convince Americans to reject the hedonistic comforts of the armchair for the austerity of the pew on Sunday. Only a united Protestantism could "win America" from the Catholics and Secularists and prevent America from sliding down a decadent and slippery slope.

Morrison's critique of commercial entertainment rested on an older discourse, which rejected play as "the devil's work."[22] Despite the efforts of nineteenth-century liberal Protestant leaders like Frederick Sawyer, Horace Bushnell, and James Leonard Corning to elevate and control play, there were those who continued to condemn all forms of leisure and to oppose Protestantism's entrance into the marketplace of culture.[23] As Moore notes, "A prejudice of this strength does not simply disappear. What happens first is a shift in its terms and tone."[24] Shying away from a blanket condemnation of play, Morrison focused his attention on its twentieth-century incarnation: commercialized entertainment. A new cultural boundary was in the process of being drawn. The enemy was not play but its commodified cousins, leisure and entertainment, whose main crime was their contribution to the secularization of society. In the end, however, Morrison avoided positively defining moral leisure, entertainment, or art.

Unlike the nineteenth-century leaders who strategized how to Christianize and reform new forms of culture, struggling with areas of the fine arts (like painting), twentieth-century liberal Protestant leaders largely rejected or ignored the newer forms of commercial culture. As the fear of losing Protestant America to the Catholics and Secularists grew, the cultural confidence of liberal Protestant leaders declined. In such a climate, it was increasingly difficult not to see commercial culture as a threat, rather than a potential ally in the fight to maintain hegemony.[25] Echoing their secular contemporaries who were increasingly critical and fearful of mass culture, liberal Protestant leaders increasingly looked toward the sacralized world of high art to provide religious culture.[26]

This general approach to culture provides a context for viewing the early reception of television in the *Christian Century*. While Morrison's traditionally triumphalist (but pacifist) liberal Protestantism was being challenged by a younger generation of Christian realists who were more accepting of (maybe even embracing of) pluralist America, they remained equally suspicious of commercial entertainment and the new leisure society.[27] These suspicions often came to be vocalized as a fear of depersonalization in an age of conformity. If the older generation of liberals (represented here by Morrison) and the younger generation of realists (H. Richard Niebuhr et al.) found little to agree about the role of the church in society (or the depravity of man), they could find common ground in their rejection of commercial entertainment, albeit for different reasons. By the early 1960s, television was still a rare item on the pages of the *Christian Century*, and when it was mentioned the content of the criticism had shifted away from personal moral considerations (alcohol, gambling, etc.) to larger public concerns, particularly the civil rights movement. Here, however, I will limit my comments to the early years of television, 1946 through 1960—a particularly transitional era for TV and for the *Christian Century*—as first Paul Hutchison (1947–56) and then Harold Fey (1956–64) took over the editorship from Morrison.

"TV—A GIANT FOR GOOD OR ILL"

Understanding the rejection or lukewarm reception of broadcasting media by the liberal Protestants' leadership also gives us an opportunity to explore the ambivalent side of American popular discursive conventions concerning communications technologies.[28] Scholars have documented the double-sided, utopic/dystopic discourse that seems to accompany the introduction of new technologies from the nineteenth century until today. Religious leaders have tended to speak this mixed language as well. Electricity, for example, was both celebrated (as the best way to reach the savages with the gospel) and feared (for its social effects on the local church body).[29] The radio church service was promoted as the ideal substitute for those physically unable to go to their local churches, but it was considered to have a potentially detrimental affect on church attendance.[30] In both its optimistic and pessimistic variations, this discourse notably shares an assumption of audience passivity, as well as a didactic understanding of broadcasting.[31]

In addition to editorials, the *Christian Century* also published articles by guest writers about television, particularly religious television. Both the editorials and articles by guest writers concerning television were equally ambivalent about the potential affects of this new medium on the audience. If television really was as effective in convincing its viewers as advertisers seemed to think, then the church had "a miraculous opportunity for witnessing."[32] Advertising strategies were considered to provide a potential model for religious broadcasting. "Television missionaries," argued J. Edward Carothers, "must profit by the discovery of the beer manufacturers; namely, that a regularly appearing personality is the best way to hold a regularly listening audience."[33] Other guest writers, however, were more cautious: television could be an effective minister/salesman, but left in the wrong hands it could be lethal. A. Gordon Nasby in a 1949 article warned that "Hitler did his job in Germany in the space of a few years because he had modern techniques and methods of communication at his disposal. Today with television at hand, the time in which men's minds can be molded has been frightfully shortened."[34] Two years later, Alton M. Motter reiterated this fear: "This constant flood of words, sounds and pictures is doing something to the American mind."[35]

Notably, the fear of mass propaganda and its political effects seems to have been far greater than the fear of television's effects on liberal Protestantism itself. Motter was one of the few contemporary critics who understood that the television was transforming the American home and, right along with it, domestic piety: "Grace at the table or family devotions must compete with Charlie McCarthy. And in many homes Charlie wins out!"[36] If the television set replaced the hearth, symbolically and physically, then television rituals might also came to replace what Colleen Mc-Dannell has labeled "rituals of the hearth."[37] Throughout the nineteenth century, the Protestant home had been the center of a domestic religion that had been promoted and accepted as a legitimate and effective means for preserving the Christian nature of the nation.[38] Centered around the Bible, both physically and verbally, family worship marked both the beginning and end of the day.[39] The physical home itself, both in terms of its layout (the parlor) and the articles displayed within it, likewise reflected the central role of domestic religion. What happened to domestic religion in the twentieth century? How was it transformed in the transition to Levitown and the hundreds of other new suburbs that popped up in post–World War II America? While the history of twentieth-century domestic religion has yet to be written, it is clear that the television must be seen as one of the important additions to the post–World War II household. As Cecilia Tichi and Lynn Spigel have documented, the advent of the television set required Americans to reconfigure many aspects of domestic life—the structure of the living room, the way in which women's work was perceived, and so on. Clearly, domestic religion was transformed in the process as well. In this respect, the advent of television would prove to be far more threatening to Protestant hegemony than most liberal Protestant leaders could foresee.

In contrast to the guest writers, the editors tended to be even more critical of television as a medium, and largely uninterested in the compensatory potential of religious television. Television first made its appearance on the *Christian Century*'s editorial pages while there was still some public discussion over what might be the medium's format. Two of the earliest columns that mention TV refer to the possibility of an "advertising-free" version of the medium. Listening to radio advertisements had been annoying, but the visual dimension of television made advertising seem almost obscene: "Will we have to stop in the midst of one news commentary to see the commentator rub tonic into his hair, or another down a fizzy hangover pill, or another lather his face with brushless cream?"[40] Iconoclastic Protestants had largely come to accept painting as morally permissible, but visual images used for commercial ends were far more problematic.[41] Reaching into the heart of the Christian home, television advertisements promised daily exposure to a wide variety of random and potentially problematic images. Thinking in a futuristic manner, the editors asked if a "pay per view" system could be installed that would bill individuals for programs much like a telephone bill, and thus bypass commercial advertising.[42]

Once the format of commercial TV had been established, editorials refocused the cause on public-interest television, backing suggestions that the Federal Communications Commission (FCC) set aside a channel in each community[43] and that each channel be forced to provide public-service time, part of which should be devoted to religious programming.[44] The hope was that the sustaining-time system, which had been established in radio and gave the mainline Federal (and then National) Council of Churches almost complete control over public-service Protestant programming, would be duplicated in the new medium.[45] Despite this stated editorial position, however, on-air efforts by mainline religious broadcasters were largely ignored by the *Christian Century*. Until 1960, mainline Protestants continued to receive free time on television as a public service by the broadcasters, but the programs co-produced by the National Council of Churches Broadcast and Film Commission with the networks during this time are generally not reviewed in the *Christian Century*. With the exception of one 1952 editorial that enthusiastically praised *This Is the Life*, a program produced by the Missouri Synod Lutherans (notably, a denomination outside the National Council of Churches), no endorsement was given by the *Christian Century* to any religious television program during these years.[46]

In the eyes of the *Christian Century* editors, TV's potential contribution (however limited) lay in the realms of politics and education—notably, not that of entertainment. Observing Gov. Thomas E. Dewey's 1950 political campaign, the editors were hopeful that television could bring the "town-meeting" to America's living rooms. These fleeting hopes that television could create a new public sphere or act as an alternative educator in remote areas were soon dashed. The editors soon questioned whether any public-service programming would or could have much effect on viewers. A campaign encouraging parents to use the Salk vaccine was considered to be a failure: "Could we have overestimated people's responsiveness to propaganda?"[47] If the audience was not really paying attention, television's potential both for good and evil was far more limited than previously thought. Despite this growing awareness of the limitations of television, the editors nonetheless remained committed to challenging the networks to use television in as productive and as responsible a manner as possible. This included broadcasting political campaigns, debates in Congress, speeches by the president, and educational courses.[48]

THE CATHOLIC THREAT

Overall, the editors paid far more attention to what they perceived as the misuse of television by the Roman Catholic Church and those outsider, old-time Protestants such as Billy Graham and Oral Roberts. Faith healing made good television, and the editors noted that no mainline programming was on the air "to offset this travesty on Christian teaching."[49] Even Graham's evangelical crusades were considered to embody a particularistic theology and tactic from which "official Protestantism" should keep a distance.[50]

The Roman Catholic use of television provoked even greater controversy in the pages of the *Christian Century*. There was a general fear that the opulent ritual of Catholicism was far more televisable than ascetic Protestantism;[51] it was thought that Catholics would use this advantage to sway America to their cause. Catholics were also not afraid to be doctrinally specific on television, and the editors were afraid that Protestant viewers would be exposed to heresies such as the doctrine of the Virgin Mary, especially on TV holiday specials at Easter and Christmas.[52] Bishop Fulton Sheen, the most recognized and popular religious television celebrity in the 1950s, received a full-blown condemnation, especially for his implication that the miracle of television was equivalent to the incarnation of Christ. This "blasphemy" shocked the editors: how could the Roman Catholic hierarchy with their elaborate system of censorship let this pass into public discourse?[53] But for the most part, while the Roman Catholic Church was considered to be a grave threat to Protestant America, the would-be televangelists were not taken very seriously by the *Christian Century*.

To the magazine's editors, more disturbing than the Roman Catholics' broadcasting efforts was the Catholic hierarchy's censorial approach to commercial culture. While Protestant clergy in the 1850s had blamed Catholics for "introducing permissiveness into American society," in the 1950s they blamed them for introducing repressiveness.[54] Throughout the 1940s, the Catholic association with fascism brought sharp rebuke on the pages of the *Christian Century*.[55] Viewing the terms *American, Protestant,* and *Democratic* as largely interchangeable, the *Christian Century* found great fault with the Roman Catholic efforts to monitor and affect the culture at large. A conflict with the Roman Catholic Church over a film about Martin Luther exemplifies this position.

Outraged that a local Chicago channel had canceled the Martin Luther film under pressure from the archbishop, the *Christian Century* commented, "This is the beginning of tyranny. Sectarian censorship is based on fear of the truth and fear of the uses people will make of their democratic freedom."[56] Yet in the same article, the writer evokes the privilege and rights of the Protestant majority: "While Protestantism is the faith of the majority of people in the Chicago area, it has never previously spoken with one voice. So the illusion has easily been kept alive that the largest Catholic archdiocese in the country must be granted everything it asks, whether or not what it asks is consistent with American principles."[57] The author implicitly assumes that mainline Protestantism, in its very nature, exemplified American principles, while the Roman Catholic Church with its hierarchical structures was in direct contradiction with them. In another article titled "Censorship: A Case History," Robert E. A. Lee seriously questioned the Roman Catholic Church's right to influence the public agenda at all: "Is one religious group really attempting to dictate what the public can see and hear through mass consumption media? Is the Roman Catholic Church becoming more aggressive in extending its censorship program beyond its own sphere?"[58]

Censorship, however, was not the real issue at hand. After all, the mainliners themselves had pressed the networks for "self-restraint," in broadcasting liquor ads and quiz shows. What was disturbing about the Martin Luther case was not that a particular group had lobbied the TV station and won, but the fact that a Protestant television show had been censored by the Roman Catholic Church. The mainliners' attempts to ban particular uses of television were justified because they represented the "right kind . . . of religion," which reflected the popular sentiment of most Americans. In other words, the Roman Catholic Church's actions violated the implicit rules of acceptable censorship. Censorship was acceptable when enacted on behalf of the (perceived) Protestant majority; censorship that appeared to be motivated by the Roman Catholic Church's hierarchy was not. Censorship that protected little children from viewing too much violence was acceptable; censorship of the great Protestant reformer was not. Thus, the *Christian Century* could suggest that the FCC regulate quiz shows because they violated the work ethic and were therefore essentially anti-American. In hindsight, these positions seem clearly to reflect Protestant theology, but in the 1950s the mainliners found it difficult to distinguish American from Protestant.

THE SECULAR THREAT

After Roman Catholicism, the next enemy was secularism. The commercialization of the sacred holidays was a disturbing phenomenon to the *Christian Century,* and the editors were quick to blame television for its part in this process. Programming on Easter of 1952, for example, was condemned by the *Christian Century* as deceiving and nonrepresentative: "Last year as our readers will recall, they prostituted this day supposedly sacred to the most important triumphant festival of the Christian year to commercial and theatrical exploitation so crass that it revolted every decent viewer. They employed their technological resources to make the world believe that this country, though it may pretend to keep the Christian feast, is a pagan wilderness."[59] While the commercialization of Easter had been a long process (Leigh E. Schmidt dates its beginnings to the period between 1860 and 1890), the 1952 televised version of the New York Easter Parade brought special protest, with television held partly responsible for the new heights of holiday commercialism.[60] The national image of Protestantism had been irredeemably tarnished and TV was to blame.

If Easter on Fifth Avenue wasn't bad enough, the great success of the weekly quiz shows, such as *The $64,000 Question,* seemed to indicate that a great percentage of the American public did not at all object to gambling and that they were foolish enough to believe "that at last the magic has been found that will lead them to a pot of gold at the rainbow's foot."[61] Long before the quiz show scandal of 1958-59, the editors questioned the ethical integrity of such shows: "Any device which encourages gambling and leads people to put their faith in 'getting something for nothing' mars the integrity of the individual personality for which the churches have a particular concern."[62] The Protestant work ethic was being publicly chipped away. Worse than promoting cheating, the quiz show "offered opium to broad-bottomed viewers, it drugged those who might have been ambitious. It dangled the illusion of easy money before people who work for a living but spite the necessity."[63] When the scandal broke, it gave the editors momentary hope that America would once and for all reject the "get-rich-quick pabulum" and give "the moral leadership of the country its chance."[64] Even as the younger generation of *Christian Century* writers such as Martin E. Marty were beginning to plea for Protestants to come to terms with their new minority status, they still held hope that in a moment of crisis, like that of the quiz show scandal, Americans would turn back, embrace their religious roots, and recognize their true moral leaders.[65]

While quiz shows offered ethically problematic entertainment, Westerns were violent and sadistic: "It cannot even be said of the sadist [TV] 'on the seventh day he rested.' Sunday proposes *Maverick*, Alfred Hitchcock, *Colt 45*, *The Lawman* and *Northwest Passage* for its offering."[66] Variety Shows were not much better, offering vulgar and base entertainment: "Since the popularity of the Paar show presumably reflects the mental climate and entertainment tastes of a considerable share of the American public, it provides occasion for serious concern."[67]

"YAWN AND FLIP"

In the end, TV was worthy only of protest. If TV couldn't be redeemed as an educator, or as a political tool for democratization, then the editors could see little reason to spend time viewing the television. Abstention was the only answer: "Neither the Western or the shocker can outlive a yawn, or a flip of the knob. Turn it off."[68] The TV, like any other vice (including the consumption of alcohol and cigarettes, commodities it advertised), provided an opportunity to exhibit self-control.[69]

Indeed, the *Christian Century* editors really seemed to believe that Americans would just get tired of the base forms of entertainment offered: "The fact is that TV is now censoring itself. As the novelty of television sets wears off, the lure of the sexy and the macabre wears thin. In regions where TV has been in operation for a year or more there are already hundreds, probably thousands, of sets which are hardly turned on from one week to the next."[70]

For the most part, television was viewed as a moral problem rather than a new form of entertainment. Television watching was a vice that needed to be personally regulated by each individual viewer. Strict government regulation was not an option for these great believers in the free, self-regulating market system. The editors could only advocate self-restraint. In their eyes, American Protestantism's self-definition rested upon its advocacy of cultural and political democracy. As a 1945 editorial, "Protestantism and Tolerance," stated:

Protestantism, by virtue of its history and its own principles, is under a mandate to preserve this cultural democracy. It does not preserve it by suppressing its own convictions in sentimental deference to others. Protestantism is the spiritual guarantor of cultural and religious freedom. In contrast with Catholicism, it guarantees—to the limit of its power—the very freedom Catholicism enjoys in this nation. It asks no favor of the state, nor any privileged position in relation to the state. Nor does it ask that any political disfavor be shown toward other religious faiths. It did not do so when it was in the clear ascendancy in numbers and influence in American life, and it does not do so now that its ascendancy—not yet in numbers but in power—is open to challenge.[71]

State intervention could be advocated only when it was clearly to protect the public interest, an interest that was implicitly defined as synonymous with the liberal Protestant leadership's interest. Even moderate forms of censorship (e.g., concerning violence on children's shows) were considered to be dangerous in the long run, and too Roman Catholic in the short-run.[72]

For the *Christian Century* editors, turning off the TV was the only form of resistance to mass culture they felt comfortable advocating. While there were occasional editorials urging the church to be involved in FCC policy making, for the most part television was just ignored. The editors, like many others in the secular elite, could not see beyond their own print culture.

Ann Swidler has suggested that in times of social transformation "ideologies—explicit, articulated, highly organized meaning systems (both political and religious)—establish new styles or strategies of action."[73] In the post–World War II period, mainline Protestant hegemony was challenged like never before. Within a very short period of time, the once dominant leaders quickly had to come to terms with an existent (if previously ignored) pluralist America. Part of this shift from hegemony to pluralism required a different approach to culture. The strategy of Christianization, by which I mean the efforts to reform and shape cultural life according to mainline Protestant norms, no longer worked in such a context. Torn between coming to terms with this new pluralist reality and maintaining the old ways, liberal Protestant leaders approached the new medium of television with great ambivalence.

In the *Christian Century*, this ambivalence was largely translated into a strategy of disregard. For the liberal Protestant editors, television was often dismissed as a passing phase, a discountable threat. But despite this rhetoric, television also served as a focal point for expressing fears of cultural change. Older and more familiar theological and cultural assumptions about play and leisure rhetorically justified these fears. Articles and editorials about television in the *Christian Century* reveal not only the weakness of mainline Protestantism but also Protestant anxieties about the strengths of postwar Catholicism and the threats of secularism and pluralism. This discourse coexisted alongside essays that promoted tolerance and suggested that Protestants come to terms with the end of their cultural reign. Through the rejection of television, the editors channeled their fear of these changes in familiar terms. Television, the most prominent sign of the new leisure society, was categorized as a vice, and Protestant America was called upon to operate with self-restraint. Censorship was avoided, for although it may have aided short-term goals, it clashed with the editors understanding of the Protestant ethos.

As liberal Protestant leaders came slowly to recognize their decline of influence in the public sphere, they only reluctantly admitted its erosion in the private sphere.[74] In the case of the *Christian Century* editors, part of their reluctance to address television must be attributed to a general lack of interest in the domestic sphere or domestic piety; the magazine's main concern was American public life.[75] In the 1950s, that public was conceived in masculine terms.[76] Occasionally one reads a letter from a woman reader or an article by a woman guest writer, but the overall impression is of a magazine written by men for a largely male readership. It is perhaps not surprising then that given the feminine hue of mass culture in general and television in particular, the *Christian Century* showed little interest in this new medium.[77]

By 1960 the presuppositions underlying the Elvis editorial discussed at the opening of this chapter were becoming less and less tenable. In the next decade, this kind of cultural criticism and its founding principles were largely abandoned by the *Christian Century* as other issues, most prominently the civil rights movement, came to occupy the foreground.[78] The television set had replaced the hearth in most American living rooms, and with that transition (as Lynn Spigel argues) the Victorian domestic sphere, which had been shaped so fundamentally by ascetic Protestantism, had been transformed.[79] The younger generation at the *Christian Century* no longer hoped to keep the United States Protestant. The new model was the church as sanctuary, or respite from the culture.

By 1969, the editors self-consciously announced that they had changed the print of the masthead (the paper's name) in order to reflect that "transition from a triumphalist model of Christendom to the witness of a servant church, given to serving humanity in its time."[80] The editors reconceived the mainline Protestant church as an escape from the homogenized, mechanized world that was increasingly the norm in the age of TV culture. In this redefined landscape, television would remain problematic, but for different reasons. Conceived of less as a potential personal vice and more as an important shaper of social values, television would remain suspect for promoting violence (particularly on children's programs), social inequality, and generally offering a worldview that was in direct conflict and competition with mainline Protestantism.

NOTES

1. "What a Twisted Scale of Values!" *Christian Century* 77 (May 25, 1960): 630.

2. The chapter title "Turn It Off!" comes from "Yawn and Flip the TV Knob," *Christian Century* 75 (October 22, 1958): 1198.

3. In the magazine's pages, television was given far less space than either book reviews or film reviews—this despite its being a new medium. Overall, cultural matters came second to church politics and politics in general.

4. R. Laurence Moore, *Selling God: American Religion in the Marketplace of Culture* (New York: Oxford, 1994), 236.

5. For Moore's account of liberal Protestant responses to the moving pictures in *Selling God*, see 159, 222–30; on radio, see 232–35; on television, see 244–54.

6. On liberal Protestant responses to mass culture in the 1950s, see Sally M. Promey, "Interchangeable Art: Warner Sallman and the Critics of Mass Culture," in *Icons of American Protestantism: The Art of Warner Sallman*, ed. David Morgan (New Haven: Yale University Press, 1996), 167–73.

7. Moore, *Selling God*, 236. Leonard Sweet has suggested that, generally, the decline of liberal Protestantism was largely due to "theological dry rot": see "The 1960s: The Crises of Liberal Christianity," in *Evangelicalism and Modern America*, ed. George Marsden (Grand Rapids, Mich.: Eerdmans, 1984), 32.

8. Horsfield has described several interactive elements that produced an environment conducive to the televangelists' success: changes in government regulations, the growth of conservative churches and the decline of mainline churches, the advent of new computer technologies, the adaptability of evangelical theology to television, and the changing economic considerations of television stations in the 1960s and 1970s; see Peter Horsfield, *Religious Television: The American Experience* (New York: Longman, 1984), 15–23. Several others offer similar explanations: see Steve Bruce, *Pray TV: Televangelism in America* (London: Routledge, 1990); William F. Fore, *Television and Religion: The Shaping of Faith, Values, and Culture* (Minneapolis, Minn.: Augsburg, 1987); Razelle Frankl, *Televangelism: The Marketing of Popular Religion* (Carbondale, Ill.: Southern Illinois University Press, 1987); Jeffrey Hadden and A. Shupe, *Televangelism: Power and Politics on God's Frontier* (New York: Holt, 1988); Stewart M. Hoover, *Mass Media Religion: The Social Sources of the Electronic Church* (Newbury Park, Calif.: Sage, 1988).

9. Ann Swidler, "Culture in Action: Symbols and Strategies," *American Sociological Review* 51 (1986): 280.

10. Bruce briefly (and perhaps a bit too simply) defines the theological and sociological differences between liberal and conservative Protestants that would explain their different approaches to the media; see Bruce, *Pray TV,* 44–48.

11. Schultze has identified three basic elements in evangelicalism that promote an affinity with the media culture: "a disinterest in tradition, a faith in technology, a drive to popularize and a spirit of individualism"; see Quentin J. Schultze "Keeping the Faith: American Evangelicals and the Media," in *American Evangelicals and the Mass Media,* ed. Quentin J. Schultze (Grand Rapids, Mich.: Zondervan, 1990), 41.

12. "Thus culture appears to shape action only in that the cultural repertoire limits the available strategies of action"—Swidler, "Culture in Action," 284.

13. Charles H. Lippy, ed., *Religious Periodicals of the United States: Academic and Scholarly Journals* (Westport, Conn.: Greenwood Press, 1986), 112; Martin E. Marty, "Peace and Pluralism: *The Century,* 1946–1952," *Christian Century* 101 (October 24, 1984): 979–83; Mark G. Toulouse, "The *Christian Century* and American Public Life," in *New Dimensions in American Religious History,* ed. Jay P. Dolan and James P. Wind, (Grand Rapids, Mich.: Eerdmans, 1993), 44–82.

14. Lippy, *Religious Periodicals,* 112; Marty, "Peace and Pluralism," 979–83; Toulouse, "The *Christian Century* and American Public Life," 44–82.

15. Lynn Spigel, *Make Room for TV: Television and the Family Ideal in Postwar America* (Chicago: University of Chicago Press, 1992), 32.

16. For the heading of this section I have used the title of Charles Clayton Morrison's 1946 series in the *Christian Century* "Can Protestantism Win America?" The series was also published as a book, *Can Protestantism Win America?* (New York: Harper & Bros., 1948). For an example of the debate on the revival in the 1950s, see

Seymour M. Lipset, "Religion in America: What Religious Revival?" in *Review of Religious Research* 1 (summer 1959): 17–24, and Will Herberg's response, "There Is a Religious Revival!" *Review of Religious Research* 1 (fall 1959): 45–51. On religion in the 1950s, see James Hudnut-Beumler, *Looking for God in the Suburbs: The Religion of the American Dream and Its Critics, 1945–1965* (New Brunswick, N.J.: Rutgers University Press, 1994); Martin E. Marty, *Under God, Indivisible, 1941–1960*, vol. 3 of *Modern American Religion* (Chicago: University of Chicago Press, 1996); Robert Wuthnow, *The Restructuring of American Religion* (Princeton: Princeton University Press, 1988).

17. Morrison, "Can Protestantism Win America?"

18. Harold Fey, "Can Catholicism Win America?" *Christian Century* 61 (November 29, 1944): 1378–80; Morrison, "Can Protestantism Win America?" For an account of the significance of this series, see Marty, *Under God, Indivisible*, 144–49.

19. Charles Clayton Morrison, "Protestantism and Commercialized Entertainment," *Christian Century* 63 (May 1, 1946): 553.

20. Ibid.

21. Ibid., 554. On the development of aesthetic theory in the *Christian Century* see Linda-Marie Delloff, " 'God as Artist': Aesthetic Theory in the *Christian Century*, 1908–1955" (Ph.D. diss., University of Chicago, 1985).

22. Moore, *Selling God*, 97.

23. Ibid., 98.

24. Ibid., 100.

25. Gans has argued that intellectuals are more likely to criticize popular culture when their own status and power is in question or in decline: see Herbert J. Gans, *Popular Culture and High Culture: An Analysis and Evaluation of Taste* (New York: Basic Books, 1974), 7.

26. For an overview of secular critiques of mass culture in the 1950s, see Andrew Ross, *No Respect: Intellectuals and Popular Culture* (New York: Routledge, 1989), 42–64. On high art as Protestant art, see, for example, Tillich's essay on "Protestantism and Artistic Style," in Paul Tillich, *Theology of Culture* (New York: Oxford University Press, 1959), where he calls Picasso's Guernica "a great Protestant painting" (68). On liberal Protestant responses to mass culture, see Promey, "Interchangeable Art," 167–73. Notably, Morrison did not embrace all high art as sacred art, but remained committed to realistic and therefore didactic art. On art criticism in the *Christian Century*, see Linda-Marie Delloff, "God as Artist." On the sacralization of high culture, see Laurence W. Levine, *Highbrow/Lowbrow: The Emergence of Cultural Hierarchy in America* (Cambridge: Harvard University Press, 1988).

27. Tillich, *Theology of Culture*; H. Richard Niebuhr, *Christ and Culture* (New York: Harper & Row, 1951).

28. My section heading is taken from "TV—a Giant for Good or Ill," *Christian Century* 72 (February 2, 1955): 131.

29. Carolyn Marvin, *When Old Technologies Were New: Thinking about Electric Communication in the Late Nineteenth Century* (New York: Oxford University Press, 1988), 124–28.

30. Susan Douglas, *Inventing American Broadcasting, 1899–1922* (Baltimore: Johns Hopkins University Press, 1987), 311–12; Moore, *Selling God*, 232.

31. This assumption of audience passivity is shared by secular mass-culture critics of this era as well. On the educational model of religious broadcasting, see J. Harold Ellens, *Models of Religious Broadcasting* (Grand Rapids, Mich.: Eerdmans, 1974), 95–123.

32. A. Gordon Nasby, "Television and the Church," *Christian Century* 66 (February 2, 1949): 143.

33. J. Edward Carothers, "A Television Ministry," *Christian Century* 66 (May 11, 1949): 591–92.

34. Nasby, "Television and the Church," 142–43.

35. Alton M. Motter, "Back to the Kefauver TV Show," *Christian Century* 68 (May 9, 1951): 584.

36. Ibid.

37. On the evolution of the domestic hearth into the electronic hearth, see Cecilia Tichi, *The Electronic Hearth: Creating an American Television Culture* (New York: Oxford University Press, 1991), 42–61. Tichi convincingly argues that the preexistent image of the hearth was used by television networks and advertisers to sell television to the U.S. public. Although she traces the historical origins of the hearth, Tichi unfortunately ignores their religious dimension. Lynn Spigel argues in *Make Room for TV* that television transformed Victorian domestic ideology, but she ignores domestic religion. On Victorian domestic religion, see Colleen McDannell, *The Christian Home in Victorian America, 1840–1900* (Bloomington: Indiana University Press, 1986), 77–107. On the ritual use of television today, see Gregor Goethals, *The TV Ritual: Worship at the Video Altar* (Boston: Beacon Press, 1981).

38. McDannell, *Christian Home*, 106.

39. Ibid., 79.

40. "Will Television Depend on Advertising?" *Christian Century* 61 (October 25, 1944): 1221. Emphasis mine.

41. See Moore, *Selling God*, 109, on the gradual erosion of liberal Protestant prejudice against painting over the nineteenth century. On the visual culture of Protestantism, see David Morgan, introduction to *Icons of American Protestantism: The Art of Warner Sallman*, ed. David Morgan (New Haven, Conn.: Yale University Press, 1996), 4–18. On the liberal rejection of mass-cultural images, see Promey, "Interchangeable Art," 150–80.

42. "Can't It Be Applied to Television?" *Christian Century* 61 (November 1, 1944): 1245–46; "One More Argument for Subscription TV," *Christian Century* 72 (May 18,

1955): 589. In a similar vein, TV manufacturers' advertisements were condemned for their explicit manipulation of children; see "TV Manufacturers Stir up a Storm," *Christian Century* 67 (December 6, 1950): 1444.

43. "TV Opportunity Is Fleeing," *Christian Century* 67 (November 29, 1950): 1414.

44. Nasby, "Television and the Church," 142; Charles M. Crowe, "Television Needs Religion," *Christian Century* 66 (August 10, 1949): 938; "TV Opportunity Is Fleeing"; "Insist Religion Merit[s] Public Service Time," *Christian Century* 75 (March 19, 1958): 333–34.

45. On the sustaining-time system, see Fore, *Television and Religion*, 77–81; Dennis N. Voskuil, "The Power of the Air: Evangelicals and the Rise of Broadcasting," *in American Evangelicals and the Mass Media,* ed. Quentin J. Schultze (Grand Rapids, Mich.: Academic Books, 1990), 69–95; esp. 83–84.

46. "Missouri Lutherans Produce TV Series," *Christian Century* 69 (August 13, 1952): 916.

47. "How Effective Are the Mass Media?" *Christian Century* 73 (August 29, 1956): 988.

48. "TV—a Giant for Good or Ill," *Christian Century* 72 (February 2, 1955): 131; "Is Television Making a Nation of Hypochondriacs?" *Christian Century* 72 (October 19, 1955): 1198; "Is Television a Fiasco?" *Christian Century* 73 (October 17, 1956): 1188; "Television Arrives in Education," *Christian Century* 75 (October 1, 1958): 1102; "Networks Miss a Good Bet," *Christian Century* 75 (March 12, 1958): 301.

49. "Oklahoma Faith-Healer Draws a Following," *Christian Century* 71 (June 29, 1955): 750. See also "TV—a Giant for Good or Ill"; "What about Oral Roberts?" *Christian Century* 73 (September 5, 1956): 1018–21.

50. "Graham Clarifies the Issue," *Christian Century* 75 (July 30, 1958): 870.

51. "What about Religious Doctrine on Television?" *Christian Century* 68 (February 14, 1951): 196. See also guest writer Nasby, "Television and the Church," 143.

52. "What about Religious Doctrine on Television?" 196. Part of the agreement of sustaining-time religious programming included the avoidance of creedal specificity. See Voskuil, "Power of the Air," 83–84.

53. "Bishop Cloys as Critic," *Christian Century* 73 (December 5, 1956): 1413.

54. Moore, *Selling God*, 112. Roman Catholic (Irish, German, and Italian) immigrants were held responsible for the rise of permissiveness, while the Catholic elite was held responsible for the rise of repressiveness. On the *Christian Century's* attitude to the Roman Catholic role in the censorship of moving pictures, see Moore, *Selling God*, 227–31.

55. For the years 1943 to 1946, see, for example: "Notre Dame Would Censor Professor's Speeches," *Christian Century* 60 (October 6, 1943): 1325–26; "Radio Used to Attack Protestant Missions," *Christian Century* 60 (October 6, 1943): 1123; "Where Can the Pope Go?" *Christian Century* 60 (December 22, 1943): 1496–97; Harry F.

Ward, "Vatican Fascism," 61 (7 June 1944): 693–95; "Public Money Diverted for Catholic Schools," *Christian Century* 62 (January 24, 1945): 101; "Oppose Conscription on Moral Grounds," *Christian Century* 62 (January 31, 1945): 131–32; "How the Catholic Church Supervised Movies," *Christian Century* 62 (February 7, 1945); "Protestantism and Tolerance," *Christian Century* 62 (February 14, 1945): 198–200; "Roman Catholic Church Never Sells Spiritual Blessings," *Christian Century* 62 (March 7, 1945): 292; Charles M. Crowe, "So This Is Good Will!" *Christian Century* 62 (April 4, 1945): 427–29; Ralph W. Sockman, "Catholics and Protestants," *Christian Century* 63 (May 15, 1945): 545–47; "Can the Home be Saved?" *Christian Century* 62 (February 21, 1945): 231; "Prelate Sees Catholicism Winning Japan," *Christian Century* 63 (August 21, 1946): 1004–5; "Denies Civil Power over Marriage," *Christian Century* 63 (July 17, 1946): 883–84; "Roman Catholicism and Religious Liberty," *Christian Century* 63 (September 4, 1946): 1052; "Protestantism Coming Alive," *Christian Century* 63 (October 23, 1946): 1267. For a more charitable view of the *Christian Century*'s anti-Catholicism, see Tolouse, *Christian Century,* 61–65.

56. "Censorship in Chicago," *Christian Century* 74 (January 23, 1957): 102.

57. "Censorship in Chicago," ibid.

58. Robert E. A. Lee, "Censorship: A Case History," *Christian Century* 74 (February 6, 1957): 163.

59. "Easter on TV," *Christian Century* 70 (March 25, 1953): 339. On critiques of the commercialization of Easter, see Leigh Schmidt, *Consumer Rites: The Buying and Selling of American Holidays* (Princeton: Princeton University Press, 1995): 234–43. According to Schmidt, the "televised antics" in 1952 were enough to put in motion reform efforts to rid Easter of commercialization (239).

60. Schmidt, *Consumer Rites,* 239.

61. "All Aboard for Rainbow Land!" *Christian Century* 72 (September 14, 1955): 1045.

62. "Give-Away Shows Raise Ethical Questions," *Christian Century* 71 (February 24, 1954): 227.

63. "Turn the Dial," *Christian Century* 75 (September 10, 1958): 1011.

64. "CBS Ousts Source of TV Corruption," *Christian Century,* 76 (October 28, 1959): 1238.

65. Martin E. Marty, "Second-Chance Protestantism," *Christian Century* 78 (June 21, 1961): 770–72.

66. "Yawn and Flip the TV Knob," 1198. Violence continued to be a problem for the editors even after 1960. See, for example, "Murder by TV," *Christian Century* 79 (April 18, 1962): 482, on the televised death of boxer Benny Paret, the world welterweight champion.

67. "Paar Show a Measure of American Culture," *Christian Century* 76 (September 23, 1959): 1076–77.

68. "Yawn and Flip the TV Knob," 1198.

69. On alcohol advertising, see "Ban Liquor Drinking on Michigan TV?" *Christian Century* 71 (March 24, 1954): 356; "Beer Consumption Declining," *Christian Century* 72 (August 24, 1955): 964–65.

70. "What Should Be Done about TV Programs?" *Christian Century* 69 (May 28, 1952): 637.

71. "Protestantism and Tolerance," *Christian Century* 62 (February 14, 1945): 198.

72. On a television code, see "How Far from Code to Control?" *Christian Century* 73 (June 13, 1956): 716. On the need for network self-censorship, see "Responsible Broadcasting in Racial Disturbances," *Christian Century* 72 (August 17, 1955): 941. On the Roman Catholic use of censorship, see "TV Station Yields to Catholic Pressure," *Christian Century* 74 (January 2, 1957): 4; "Censorship in Chicago," *Christian Century* 74 (January 23, 1957): 102–3; Lee, "Censorship: A Case History," 163–65; "Demand License Hearing on Chicago TV Station," *Christian Century* 74 (February 20, 1957): 220; "Luther Film Makes Belated Television Debut," *Christian Century* 74 (March 13, 1957): 317; "TV Censorship Case Enters New Phase," *Christian Century* 74 (March 27, 1957): 379–80.

73. Swidler, *Culture in Action,* 278.

74. McDannell, *Christian Home,* 49, argues that domestic piety was the private side of the "Righteous Empire."

75. See Tolouse, *"Christian Century and American Public Life,* 44–82.

76. See Marty, *Under God, Indivisible,* 5–6, on the lack of "public women" in mid-century.

77. Andreas Huyssen in "Mass Culture as Woman: Modernism's Other" in his *After the Great Divide: Modernism, Mass Culture, Postmodernism* (Bloomington: Indiana University Press, 1986), 44–62, has argued that mass culture was gendered as feminine and inferior in the late nineteenth century. On the gendering of the television audience see Spigel, *Make Room for TV,* particularly "Women's Work," 73–98.

78. On the civil rights movement and the National Council of Churches see James Findlay, *Church People in the Struggle: The National Council of Churches and the Black Freedom Movement, 1950–1970* (New York: Oxford University Press, 1993).

79. Spigel, *Make Room for TV.*

80. Quoted in Toulouse, *"Christian Century* and American Public Life," 77 (original source, "Good-by to Gothic," *Christian Century* (January 1, 1969): 4).

BIBLIOGRAPHY

Bruce, Steve. *Pray TV: Televangelism in America.* London: Routledge, 1990.

Christian Century, selected editorials and articles, 1946–60.

Delloff, Linda-Marie. " 'God as Artist': Aesthetic Theory in the *Christian Century,* 1908–1955." Ph.D. diss., University of Chicago, 1985.

Douglas, Susan. *Inventing American Broadcasting, 1899–1922.* Baltimore: Johns Hopkins University Press, 1987.

Ellens, J. Harold. *Models of Religious Broadcasting.* Grand Rapids, Mich.: Eerdmans, 1974.

Findlay, James. *Church People in the Struggle: The National Council of Churches and the Black Freedom Movement, 1950–1970.* New York: Oxford University Press, 1993.

Fore, William F. *Television and Religion: The Shaping of Faith, Values, and Culture.* Minneapolis: Augsburg, 1987.

Frankl, Razelle. *Televangelism: The Marketing of Popular Religion.* Carbondale: Southern Illinois University Press, 1987.

Gans, Herbert J. *Popular Culture and High Culture: An Analysis and Evaluation of Taste.* New York: Basic Books, 1974.

Goethals, Gregor. *The TV Ritual: Worship at the Video Altar.* Boston: Beacon Press, 1981.

Hadden, Jeffrey, and A. Shupe. *Televangelism: Power and Politics on God's Frontier.* New York: Holt, 1988.

Herberg, Will. "There Is a Religious Revival!" *Review of Religious Research* 1 (fall 1959): 45–51.

Hoover, Stewart M. *Mass Media Religion: The Social Sources of the Electronic Church.* Newbury Park, Calif.: Sage, 1988.

Horsfield, Peter. *Religious Television: The American Experience.* New York: Longman, 1984.

Hudnut-Beumler, James. *Looking for God in the Suburbs: The Religion of the American Dream and Its Critics, 1945–1965.* New Brunswick, N.J.: Rutgers University Press, 1994.

Huyssen, Andreas. "Mass Culture as Woman: Modernism's Other." In *After the Great Divide: Modernism, Mass Culture, Postmodernism,* ed. Andreas Huyssen. Bloomington: Indiana University Press, 1986.

Levine, Lawrence W. *Highbrow/Lowbrow: The Emergence of Cultural Hierarchy in America.* Cambridge: Harvard University Press, 1988.

Lippy. Charles H., ed. *Religious Periodicals of the United States: Academic and Scholarly Journals.* Westport, Conn.: Greenwood Press, 1986.

Lipset, Seymour M. "Religion in America: What Religious Revival?" *Review of Religious Research* 1 (summer 1959): 17–24.

Marty, Martin E. *Under God, Indivisible, 1941–1960.* Vol. 3 of *Modern American Religion.* Chicago: University of Chicago Press, 1996.

——. Selected editorials and articles in the *Christian Century.*

Marvin, Carolyn. *When Old Technologies Were New: Thinking About Electric Communication in the Late Nineteenth Century.* New York: Oxford University Press, 1988.

McDannell, Colleen. *The Christian Home in Victorian America, 1840–1900.* Bloomington: Indiana University Press, 1986.

Moore, R. Laurence. *Selling God: American Religion in the Marketplace of Culture.* New York: Oxford University Press, 1994.

Morgan, David. Introduction to *Icons of American Protestantism: The Art of Warner Sallman,* ed. David Morgan, 4–18. New Haven, Conn.: Yale University Press, 1996.

Niebuhr, H. Richard. *Christ and Culture.* New York: Harper & Row, 1951.

Promey, Sally M. "Interchangeable Art: Warner Sallman and the Critics of Mass Culture." In *Icons of American Protestantism: The Art of Warner Sallman,* ed. David Morgan. New Haven, Conn.: Yale University Press, 1996.

Ross, Andrew. *No Respect: Intellectuals and Popular Culture.* New York: Routledge, 1989.

Schmidt, Leigh. *Consumer Rites: The Buying and Selling of American Holidays.* Princeton, N.J.: Princeton University Press, 1995.

Schultze, Quentin J. "Keeping the Faith: American Evangelicals and the Media." In *American Evangelicals and the Mass Media,* ed. Quentin J. Schultze. Grand Rapids, Mich.: Zondervan, 1990.

Spigel, Lynn. *Make Room for TV: Television and the Family Ideal in Postwar America.* Chicago: University of Chicago Press, 1992.

Sweet, Leonard. "The 1960s: The Crises of Liberal Christianity." In *Evangelicalism and Modern America,* ed. George Marsden. Grand Rapids, Mich.: Eerdmans, 1984.

Swidler, Ann. "Culture in Action: Symbols and Strategies." *American Sociological Review* 51 (1986): 280.

Tichi, Cecilia. *The Electronic Hearth: Creating an American Television Culture.* New York: Oxford University Press, 1991.

Tillich, Paul. *Theology of Culture.* New York: Oxford University Press, 1959.

Toulouse, Mark G. "The *Christian Century* and American Public Life." In *New Dimensions in American Religious History,* ed. Jay P. Dolan and James P. Wind. Grand Rapids, Mich.: Eerdmans, 1993.

Voskuil, Dennis N. "The Power of the Air: Evangelicals and the Rise of Broadcasting." In *American Evangelicals and the Mass Media,* ed. Quentin J. Schultze. Grand Rapids, Mich.: Academic Books, 1990.

Wuthnow, Robert. *The Restructuring of American Religion.* Princeton, N.J.: Princeton University Press, 1988.

PART 3

RELIGION MADE PUBLIC THROUGH THE MEDIA

We continue our exploration of the public side of the public/private line of demarcation by looking at two case studies of the processes through which the news media come to construct stories about religion. In these cases, there is little debate over the explicitness of the object labeled *Religion*, and little doubt that the media purpose is to understand and project a public version of this object.

John Schmalzbauer takes on these large themes in chapter 7—a look at journalistic conventions in the treatment of religion. As with much of this book, his study is significant not only for what it tells about the conventional routines of professional practice (and potentially about "antireligious bias" and similar issues in the media) but also for what it says about the contemporary cultural status of both religion and the media.

Schmalzbauer's view raises a tantalizingly complex critique of the religion/media nexus. We might wish to argue that religion should not be a difficult topic for the media to cover objectively (for a variety of reasons), but we must at the same time recognize that it is. What emerges here, though, is a recentering of the question: rather than being about objectivity or lack thereof, Schmalzbauer's chapter invites us to consider that the categories of objectivity, morality, and religion may themselves need to be rethought.

Schmaltzbauer's work—like that of other writers in this collection—

intersects with ideas from other fields, and his chapter also dovetails nicely with important work taking place in critical journalism studies. Lurking behind the struggles for definition that Schmalzbauer outlines are unresolved issues along some of our lines of demarcation. For instance, which side of the public/private divide is to be considered the most "legitimate"? How are journalists to conceive of their own relationship to moral claims that are thought to be, at their root, "religious"?

In chapter 8, Mark Borchert presents a specific and focused case of religion coverage: the decades-long political struggle within the Southern Baptist Convention, which in late 2000 again came to prominence with an announcement by former president Carter that he would be leaving the convention for more moderate pastures. Here we see a microcosm of issues raised in other chapters. Schmalzbauer's work on the role of religion in journalism is clearly implied. So are the cases described by Winston and Rosenthal: the Salvation Army and the Protestant establishment can be seen as embodying varying theories on the relationship between Protestantism and public culture and on the lines of demarcation between private and public and between popular and institutional legitimated forms of symbol and meaning. The challenge to authority posed by media coverage both invokes and confirms these views.

Interestingly, the combatants in the Southern Baptist case seem to be on the same side: the approaches of moderates and conservatives represent similar or even parallel sensibilities from within one movement. Borchert's work is particularly helpful for its detailed account of the negotiations that have ensued both within and beyond the movement during this protracted crisis for the denomination.

CHAPTER 7

BETWEEN OBJECTIVITY AND MORAL VISION: CATHOLICS AND EVANGELICALS IN AMERICAN JOURNALISM

John Schmalzbauer

White House reporter Wes Pippert had just written an op-ed piece for the *New York Times* criticizing his colleagues for ignoring what he called the "moral dimension of the news." The piece reflected Pippert's religious convictions as an evangelical Christian, calling for a more ethically engaged approach to daily journalism. The day the article was to appear, a huge snowstorm hit Washington, D.C., making the delivery of the *Times* impossible. At the time, Pippert thought "How lucky!" He was glad that his colleagues in the Washington press corps would not be able to read the article. "I knew this was coming out and I was embarrassed," he recalled, adding, "I didn't want my colleagues to see it, because I just don't wear my heart on my sleeve." That morning, Pippert and a host of White House correspondents flew with President Jimmy Carter to Atlanta on Air Force One. To Pippert's dismay, there was a stack of *New York Times* papers on the tarmac waiting for the presidential entourage. His colleagues would be able to read his op-ed piece after all. "It seemed to me that the first thing they did is to turn to that page and start shaking their heads," Pippert said, recalling his anxiety. Yet, as it turned out, the "reaction was uniformly positive."

This story illustrates some of the basic tensions experienced by religious people in the modern professions. On the one hand, Pippert's op-ed piece for the *Times* reflected a personal desire to relate his religious convictions to the practice of everyday journalism. On the other hand, his anxiety betrayed a fundamental uncertainty about the place of religious values in professional life. Because journalism often draws a boundary between the private values of the reporter and the public world of professional journalism, Pippert's display of religious conviction risked transgressing an invisible line between journalistic objectivity and moral conviction. In a field that places great importance on the distinctions between facts and values, news and opinion, and public and private life, Pippert's article represented a potentially stigmatizing show of personal religious belief. In Pippert's case, his fears of rejection turned out to be ill-founded. Yet a persistent tension between professional and religious identities continues to shape the lives of religious people in American journalism.

In a professional culture that prizes the qualities of objectivity and detachment, what place if any remains for the public display of religious and moral convictions on the part of the reporter? This chapter explores how twenty Catholic and evangelical journalists talk about the relationship between faith and work at the upper levels of New York and Washington journalism. Catholics and evangelicals in American journalism make for an interesting sociological case study because of the seeming contrast between their religious beliefs and the dominant ethos of the modern professional order.

The modern professions (including journalism) are dominated by an ideology that emphasizes detachment, empiricism, and the separation of "facts" from "values."[1] In order to maintain public credibility, professionals are expected to keep their political, moral, and religious convictions confined to the private sphere. Among American journalists, professionalism has long been equated with the goal of "objectivity."[2] Consistent with this emphasis, Herbert Gans's ethnography of the newsrooms of CBS, NBC, *Time,* and *Newsweek* found that reporters practiced "value exclusion," attempting to eliminate "preference statements about nation and society from their copy."[3] By encouraging reporters to keep their values to themselves, U.S. journalism has constructed a "culture of professionalism" that is "largely hostile" to public expressions of political and moral judgments, preferring "cynical detachment to engagement in the public sphere."[4]

As the "quintessentially Enlightenment profession," journalism has tended to privilege empirical "facts" over religious beliefs, leading *Washington Post* columnist (and practicing Roman Catholic) E. J. Dionne to discern "a fundamental conflict between the definition of truth used by journalists and the definition accepted by people of religious faith."[5] While religious communities have seen the world as "God-ordained and ethically oriented," the empiricist mindset of the modern professions has tended to reduce reality to a "causal mechanism."[6] While religion ponders the transcendent, journalism focuses on the mundane flow of daily events.[7]

CATHOLICS AND EVANGELICALS IN AMERICAN JOURNALISM

Given the widespread emphasis on objectivity and detachment in American journalism, it is not difficult to see why Pippert felt awkward discussing his religious beliefs in the presence of professional colleagues. By confessing the "embarrassment" of wearing "my heart on my sleeve," he acknowledged the difficulties of bringing religious identity into a profession committed to "value exclusion." In particular, Pippert's call for greater attention to the "moral dimension" of the news seemed to contradict mainstream journalism's emphasis on the separation of facts and values.

In the face of such obstacles, how do the twenty Roman Catholic and evangelical journalists interviewed for this project talk about the relationship between faith and work? Some scholars argue that people of faith tend to privatize religious identity in professions such as journalism and academia,[8] citing the low levels of religiosity among the media elite.[9] They believe that "to move up in the world of journalism or television, especially on a national level," professionals must abandon "merely regional, ethnic, or denominational views," and develop "a blindness to subtle but important social differences in themselves."[10]

Others have been more critical of such secularization arguments, emphasizing the tendency of people of faith (and Catholics and evangelicals in particular) to "de-privatize" religious convictions, bringing them into the realms of politics, the media, and the workplace.[11] Still others have debunked the myth of the "secular media," noting that mainstream American journalism affirms culturally shared religious values such as altruism and supernatural belief.[12]

Because of the pressures of professionalization, we might expect Roman Catholic and evangelical journalists to downplay the influence of their religious beliefs on their work. Not surprisingly, a small proportion of the journalists contacted for this study do engage in the privatization or bracketing of religious identity, segregating talk about work from talk about faith. At the same time, the vast majority of those interviewed for the project are able to articulate strong connections between their religious convictions and the practice of professional journalism. In particular, Catholic and evangelical journalists translate their religious convictions into professional discourse through what I call *multivocal bridging languages,* which combine vocabularies drawn from both journalism and their religious communities. In forging such bridging languages, respondents draw on "submerged traditions" in American journalism that run counter to the dominant "ideal of objectivity," including the genres of human-interest journalism and advocacy journalism, as well the post-1960s critique of journalistic objectivity.[13]

Despite their willingness to bring their religious convictions into professional life, Catholic and evangelical journalists have not abandoned what I will call the *rhetoric of objectivity.* In the interviews, most express modest support for the ideals of objectivity, balance, and detachment. Paradoxically, respondents are most likely to make use of the rhetoric of objectivity immediately following displays of religious conviction.

The remainder of this chapter describes the three types of strategies Catholic and evangelical journalists use to negotiate the boundary between professional and religious identities. The first section explores the strategies of privatization and bracketing, examining how respondents separate professional and religious identities. The second section describes how Catholic and evangelical journalists use multivocal bridging languages to translate their religious convictions into professional jargon, and vice versa. The third section examines how respondents use the rhetoric of objectivity to separate professional and religious identities.

THE STUDY AND THE SAMPLE

The sample of twenty journalists at the elite level of American national journalism was obtained through snowball sampling. The sample is made up of current or former New York and Washington journalists who have worked at large metropolitan news organizations and national magazines. It is evenly divided between self-identified practicing Roman Catholics and evangelicals.[14]

The interviews consisted of open-ended questions about the journalists' work. The average length of an interview was one hour and fifteen minutes. The journalists were informed of the nonanonymous character of the interview. Journalists could go "off the record" if they wished, but the bulk of each interview was conducted "on the record." Journalists were intentionally asked to speak without guarantee of anonymity in order to simulate a "front-stage" setting: the presentation of self would be hypothetically open to the eyes and ears of their professional colleagues.[15]

The first part of the interview asked individuals about what they found meaningful in their work and for their assessment of the strengths and weaknesses of American journalism. These questions did not mention religion explicitly. This was intentional—a format designed to capture how individuals talk about work generically. The second part of the interview asked more explicit questions about the relationship between faith and work, focusing particularly on the influence of religious identity on the content of journalistic writing.

SEPARATING CULTURAL STRATEGIES: PRIVATIZATION AND BRACKETING

In the survey, both Roman Catholic and evangelical journalists use two styles of boundary management to implicitly or explicitly separate the worlds of professional and religious life. First, some totally privatize their religious identities, categorically refusing to talk about the connections between faith and work or to identify publicly as Catholics or evangelicals. Second, others engage in bracketing, confining religious language to areas of life that, on the surface, have little to do with the *content* of their work, such as individual moral character, spirituality, or personal relationships.

Privatization

In *Stigma: NOTES on the Management of Spoiled Identity*, Erving Goffman describes how individuals engage in "passing" by concealing potentially stigmatizing facts about themselves.[16] In an analogous way, secularization theorists describe how religious people privatize religious convictions in the nonpublic spheres of home, family, and church.[17] Three Catholic and evangelical journalists (roughly 10 percent of those contacted) refused to be included in this study and, consequently, could be seen as engaging in passing or privatization.

Two of the three who refused to be included said they were afraid of harming their professional credibility. One journalist expressed surprise and dismay when I told her that a well-known evangelical foreign correspondent had identified her as a fellow evangelical. She seemed upset that someone had revealed her religious identity. Explaining her preference for keeping faith and work in separate "compartments," she said she feared opening "a copy of *Redbook* someday," and seeing her faith "projected" onto her journalistic work. Another journalist asked to remain anonymous because she said she fears that colleagues will find out her husband works as an attorney in the anti-abortion movement. She cited the example of Linda Greenhouse, the *New York Times* Supreme Court reporter, who was reprimanded for marching in a pro-choice march in Washington, D.C., adding that her publication had circulated several memos cautioning reporters against participation in political demonstrations or movements.

Bracketing

Several other Catholic and evangelical respondents are more open about their religious identities, but they continue to segregate religious faith and profession. Instead of engaging in total privatization, they bracket "God talk" from talk about work, confining faith to areas of their lives that have little to do with the content of their writing. Even when discussing religious topics, they tend to focus on individual moral character and personal salvation rather than public issues.

Bracketing religion and journalism, Don Holt (formerly of *Fortune* and *Newsweek*) talks at length about his professional life without explicitly discussing his religious identity. During the first part of the interview, which asks generic, open-ended questions about work, Holt does not mention his evangelical background, except to say that he attended Wheaton College, an evangelical liberal arts college. When I finally ask Holt about the relationship between faith and work, he questions the premise of the question: "I think it's faith and life. I think, I guess part of me says I don't really see why there should be anything special about a journalist who has a particular faith anymore than there should be about a businessman or a doctor or a lawyer." For Holt, there is no special relationship between his religious identity and his job. In fact, he uses this answer to highlight the exclusion of religious perspectives from his work.

In response to evangelicals who criticize the press for being secular, Holt says: "On the secularity of it, yes absolutely. How could it be otherwise? As I understand the meaning of that term, it's absolutely secular, as are the courts and the legislatures. They need to be free of any kinds of partisan, religious or parochial kinds of concerns. It needs to be able to cover Farrakhan as well as Billy Graham so I don't quite understand that criticism." For Holt, personal faith and professional writing must remain separate.

MULTIVOCAL BRIDGING LANGUAGES: JOURNALISTIC EMPATHY, INTELLECTUAL REFINEMENT, AND JUSTICE AND PEACE

Unlike Don Holt, a large majority of the journalists interviewed for this project do not engage in the privatization or bracketing of religious identity. Rather than separating religious and professional identities into watertight compartments, most respondents are able to translate their religious convictions into professional jargon, and vice versa, forging "multivocal bridging languages." Such combinations of professional and religious vocabularies are called "multivocal" (literally, containing multiple voices) because they incorporate multiple meanings (both professional and religious) that are capable of eliciting more than one interpretation.[18] From one angle they may appear religious. From another they may not. They are called bridging languages because they allow Catholics and evangelicals to bridge the gap between professional and religious identities through modes of public discourse drawn from both American journalism and their religious subcultures. As noted above, these languages draw on "submerged" traditions in U.S. journalism (such as interpretative journalism, advocacy journalism, and intellectual journalism) that go against the dominant emphasis on objectivity. Such genres make more room for the feelings and values of the journalist, making it easier to justify the use of religious language.

This section of the chapter looks at three multivocal bridging languages that Roman Catholics and evangelicals use to fuse the vocabularies of journalism and religion: (1) the language of journalistic empathy; (2)

the language of intellectual refinement; and (3) the language of justice and peace.

The Language of Journalistic Empathy

Three journalists interweave a language of compassion and emotional empathy with discourse about the content of news stories. They describe their reporting as an attempt to help the reader experience the feelings and emotions of individuals who are often the victims of suffering. This language is multivocal because it combines religious and journalistic styles of talking about suffering. As Robert Wuthnow points out, religious people are quite capable of translating religious language about compassion into a form that does not always explicitly invoke the sacred.[19]

For some Catholic and evangelical journalists, talking about emotional empathy in their writing is as much an appropriation of journalism's interpretative and human-interest genres as it is an expression of religious identity. Daniel C. Hallin argues that human tragedies represent a zone of journalistic coverage where values of sympathy and empathy are widely shared.[20] American journalism has a long submerged tradition, dating back to the nineteenth-century muckrakers, that stresses the importance of emotion, color, and vivid storytelling.[21] Human-interest journalism, which came of age in the 1930s and 1940s, stresses the personal side of the news, including the capacity of stories of human suffering or tragedy to evoke the sympathy and interest of readers.[22] Similarly, according to a classic interpretative journalism textbook, so-called impressionistic reporting attempts "to create in the reader the same feeling about an important event as the reporter had as an eyewitness of it."[23] Finally, since the 1960s, the new journalism has experimented with the literary devices of fiction to convey the feelings and experiences of ordinary people.[24]

Foreign correspondent Jack Kelley of *USA Today* is a good example of a journalist who uses the language of journalistic empathy to frame discourse about his writing. He describes his special contribution as "writing with a heart, conveying how people think and feel, giving a voice to the voiceless." If a person "cries during the interview," Kelley tries "to relate that."

Kelley says, "I tend to purposely go after the stories that have a lot of

emotion to them, stories about people being hurt, about people starving."
He invokes similar human-interest stylistic criteria when asked to evaluate
the best work of colleagues, admiring one reporter because she "takes
you inside somebody's life, takes you inside their thought patterns," and
another because he "cares about the people he writes about." When
asked what his most important work has been, he lists his stories on Fil-
ipino rape victims in Kuwait, ailing orphans in Russia, and starving children dying in Somalia. In addition, Kelley talks about his role in contributing to social change, echoing some of the themes of advocacy journalism:
"You write stories about orphans in the former Soviet Union. . . . We had
over ten thousand letters and responses, and we understand that over five
hundred babies were adopted. So it's little things like that. In Somalia, just
a chance to wake people up to realize that you can make a difference, you
can make a change."

When asked directly about the impact of his faith on his writing, Kelley admits there is a connection between his faith and his writing, invok-
ing the judgment of Peter Prichard, former editor of *USA Today* and now
president of the Freedom Forum: "Peter Prichard thinks so. He thinks
that being a Christian gives me a different perspective on things. I certainly hope so, because I pray for which stories I should take, and hopefully that helps."

At another point in the interview, Kelley blends references to divine
providence with a passionate declaration of his commitment to the
"voiceless":

God has been great. God is so awesome because I don't deserve this
job. I wanted to get in because I just love writing about people and I
also wanted to make a change. I want to put my two cents in to write
about people who don't really have a voice. . . . So I see this as an opportunity not only to educate but to influence. . . . I'm not into advocacy. I'm just into telling stories. I hate politics. I think politics is boring
and I think people read politics only because they have to. But if you
can tell somebody's story and in the process relate a political statement
or process of procedure you can change people's lives.

Finally, Kelley attributes his ability to discover important stories to prayer
and divine assistance, arguing that he cannot separate his faith from his
profession:

Prayer is a daily, if not an hourly, part of my job here. In my entire life, I cannot separate my faith from my profession. If I did, I wouldn't be in this profession. I wouldn't have had the success that I've had. I think it's a gift, and I can tell when I'm in tune with the Lord. Circumstances just happen. Stories just fall into my lap. I kid you not. Stories just fall into my lap when I'm in tune with the Lord. That's probably because the Lord knows I'm too dumb to go out and find them myself, because I never find them. It's just unbelievable. You sit back each night, and I feel his pleasure when I write, and there's no greater feeling.

It is instructive to note the strongly emotional language Kelley uses to characterize divine involvement in discovering stories. Identifiably evangelical phrases such as "in tune with the Lord" and "feel his pleasure" reveal an intensely emotional connection between faith and writing. By speaking about emotional empathy for suffering victims in journalistic and religious terms, and by linking religious experience and the jargon of human-interest and advocacy journalism, Kelley brings an implicit, rather than an explicit, religious framework to bear on his journalistic writing.

The Language of Intellectual Refinement

Four Roman Catholic journalists employ a cultural style that could best be described as the language of intellectual refinement. The language of intellectual refinement is multivocal because it interweaves references to religious intellectual figures together with nonreligious references to New York intellectuals and other nodes in the American intellectual elite.[25] Part and parcel of this intellectual mode of self-presentation is a rhetorical style known as "particularizing refinement," a style Steven G. Brint argues is the dominant approach of semi-intellectual magazines such as the *Atlantic Monthly,* the *New Republic,* and the *New York Review of Books.*[26] Instead of emphasizing explicit ideological claims, particularizing refinement focuses on bringing out the nuances and ambiguities of a debate, debunking established interpretations, and dissecting the logic of arguments.

Like the world of the New York intellectuals, liberal Catholic intellectual circles stress the importance of nuanced arguments, ambiguity, and finely grained distinctions, rejecting polarized left/right conceptions of the political order.[27] Since the 1950s, liberal Catholic intellectuals have attempted to distance themselves from, on the one hand, authoritarian forms of Catholicism, and, on the other, aggressively secular versions of liberalism. In the interviews, several Catholic journalists combine public intellectual refinement's emphasis on nuance with liberal Catholicism's principled rejection of the ideological polarities of left and right.

Peter Steinfels of the *New York Times* uses the language of intellectual refinement to bridge professional and religious worlds. Steinfels moved to mainstream journalism from an extended background as a Roman Catholic public intellectual, serving as editor of *Commonweal,* a liberal Catholic weekly, for much of the 1980s. Before moving to the *Times,* he was often quoted in the press as a "liberal Catholic" spokesman. In addition to serving as a columnist and an editor at *Commonweal,* Steinfels worked at the Hastings Center, a medical ethics clearinghouse, and wrote often for journals such as *Dissent* and the *New York Times Book Review.* Steinfels joined the *Times* rich in the cultural capital of public intellectual discourse. He notes that he was hired because the *Times* saw him as "someone with a liberal background" who "could write and interpret religion in terms of the larger world of politics and secular events." According to Steinfels, Arthur Gelb and A. M. Rosenthal wanted someone in the tradition of John Cogley, the famous editor of *Commonweal* who later covered religion for the *Times.*

When asked about his journalistic heroes, Steinfels cites the "historical and moral insight" of what he called "engaged journalists," naming non-Catholic intellectuals such as Albert Camus, George Orwell, Hannah Arendt, and Catholics such as G. K. Chesterton and Cogley. Throughout the interview, Steinfels uses the language of particularizing refinement through appeals to nuance, ambiguity, and a strong focus on interpretive categories and frameworks. He says his major strength as a journalist is the ability to "inform readers of a development in the world of religion . . . with some degree of nuance and complexity," in a "part of our society which is underreported . . . and fit into oversimplified and blatantly inaccurate categories."

Substantively, Steinfels criticizes other journalists for oversimplifying the religious landscape. At a public forum on religion and the media sponsored by *Commonweal,* he faulted journalists for applying the "winners and losers" framework of politics and sports to the world of religion. Instead, reporters need to "spell out the nuances and qualifications attached to almost any religious statement."[28] Likewise, in an essay published in Harvard University's *Nieman Reports,* he criticized the use of "pre-existing plot lines," which too often "ultimately descend from the tension between religious faith and the 18th-Century Enlightenment."[29] It is this polarized tension between enlightenment and religion that Steinfels and other liberal Catholics reject. In the same essay, he called attention to his own attempts to move beyond reified liberal-conservative frameworks: "I . . . wanted to give voice and visibility to those people and positions that get squeezed out when conflicts are reported only in terms of two sides—conservatives and liberals; orthodox and dissenters—rather than the spectrum of perspectives that normally exists."[30]

Significantly, when Steinfels was editor of *Commonweal,* he often used language identical to the kind he uses today, arguing that "a journal which maintains its convictions while respecting complexity and ambiguity has a special role to play amidst today's polarizations."[31] In fact, the rhetoric of nuance characterizes much of liberal Catholic discourse in the postwar era, as when one early 1950s *Commonweal* contributor lamented the fact that "Catholic attitudes have been all black or white, without distinguishing the neutral grays."[32] This metaphorical focus on neutral grays, as opposed to the polarized black and white, highlights liberal Catholicism's own ambiguous position on the religious and political spectrum. While *Commonweal* has often embraced liberal positions on economic and foreign policy issues, it has tended toward cultural conservatism on social issues such as sexuality, the family, and abortion.[33]

When Steinfels, in his position as a *New York Times* reporter, says he seeks to bring "voice and visibility" to the "spectrum of perspectives" between right and left, he is engaging in multivocality, combining particularizing refinement's concern for nuance and ambiguity with liberal Catholicism's ideological centrism. Historian David J. O'Brien argues that liberal Catholics have historically emphasized a pluralistic "balancing act between multiple publics: ecclesiastical, political, and intellectual/cultural."[34] By translating religious language into the terms of the American intellectual elite, journalists such as Steinfels have been able to convert their religious identities into a form of cultural capital at newspapers such as the *Times* and the *Washington Post,* certifying their reputations as both journalists and religious public intellectuals.[35]

The Language of Justice and Peace

A final group of both Catholic and evangelical journalists employ a multi-vocal language of justice and peace, uniting religious and journalistic themes arising out of the 1960s. These journalists are able to articulate a fit between an ethically engaged journalism and the social activism of their religious subcultures. Such a convergence of cultural styles is made possible by the shift of journalism to a more critical and adversarial stance toward the political establishment, combined with heightened Catholic and evangelical emphasis on the themes of peace and social justice.

By the 1960s, many younger journalists grew increasingly impatient with the value-free posture of their profession, faulting conventional journalism for masking the underlying political assumptions of the news underneath the rhetoric of objectivity.[36] In this climate, the genres of "advocacy journalism" and what became known as the New Journalism emphasized the role of the reporter as an advocate for social change.[37] During the same period, parts of the evangelical Protestant and Roman Catholic communities moved to engage issues raised by the social movements of the sixties, embracing the causes of civil rights, social justice, and the antiwar movement.[38]

Four Catholic and evangelical journalists multivocally blend the journalistic critique of U.S. society with religious themes of social justice and peace. Evangelical Wes Pippert, whose story about an op-ed piece opened this chapter, epitomizes this effort to articulate a fit between professional and religious worlds through the language of justice and peace. Throughout the interview, Pippert focuses on what he calls the "moral dimension of public issues."

From 1955 to 1988, Pippert was a reporter for United Press International, and in the 1970s he gradually came to the conclusion that "the pursuit of truth would automatically require a reporter to check out the dimensions of justice and peace in whatever the assignment was." When asked how he came to see his writing this way, Pippert immediately invokes his religious identity: "While I'm a Christian, I didn't know what that meant for sure in terms of my job for a long, long time, and I guess Christians believe that faith should impact on every aspect of your life, and I wasn't certain how it impacted on my job." Pippert says he began to examine how the Bible addressed the concept of truth, which he sees as the central focus of a journalist's work:

The Old Testament is rich in these discussions. I found that in almost every case that truth is discussed, that justice is discussed, and peace at the same time and uprightness. So it seemed to me that there was an organic relationship among truth, peace, and justice and uprightness. And if that's the case, and the job of the journalist is to pursue truth, that's how I came to the conclusion that the pursuit of truth in any story would lead the reporter into issues of justice and peace.

Besides framing his work in the biblical vocabulary of progressive evangelicalism, Pippert is able to articulate his focus on justice and peace in the language of the journalistic profession:

What I'm pleading for is we need to get to the heart of the story. And that will push us into the dimensions of justice and peace. And if you want to say that in a news way, you could say, "Get the lead right." That's all I'm saying, "Get the lead." There's nothing controversial about that. And I think that what I drape my reasoning around may be alien to some people—I mean the idea that this really has its origin in scripture, and the way I flesh it out saying this will compel you to deal with issues of justice and peace. Not everyone may be willing to buy that, but who can disagree with saying that the reporter ought to get to the heart of the story?

By saying that "in a news way," Pippert translates the biblical themes of justice and peace into journalistic verbiage without eliminating their normative focus. The journalists' notions of the "core of the story" or the need to "get the lead right" serve as multivocal phrases. Pippert overlays them with biblical meanings. In this way, Pippert combines advocacy journalism's focus on social change with a progressive evangelical emphasis on the biblical themes of justice and peace.

THE RHETORIC OF OBJECTIVITY AND JOURNALISTIC DETACHMENT

We have seen how Catholic and evangelical journalists use the bridging languages of journalistic empathy, intellectual refinement, and justice and peace to bridge religious and professional worlds. But how do journalists—Catholics and evangelicals—use the rhetoric of objectivity to negotiate the boundary between professional and religious worlds? Asked to define their own attitudes toward professional notions of objectivity, more than half of the journalists in the study draw a boundary between their private views and their professional writing.

Paradoxically, objectivity rhetoric is most passionately mobilized immediately following displays of religious or moral convictions. For example, Jack Kelley uses the rhetoric of objectivity to qualify his repeated use of the language of journalistic empathy. After expressing his desire to "educate" and "influence" readers by writing about the suffering of voiceless victims, Kelley adds, "I'm not into advocacy. I'm just into telling stories." After passionately describing his coverage of Russian orphans and Somali refugees, Kelley shifts gears and talks about his commitment to objectivity:

> But let me backtrack to say I'm not some idealist who's standing up here on some soapbox saying I'm here to make a change. No, I'm here to report the news and report it accurately and fairly and that's one thing that I think is a responsibility for a Christian. You look at the *Washington Post* which is so liberal it's sickening. You look at the *Washington Times* which is so conservative it's sickening, and I think people need to be unbiased and fair, and it's hard to find in journalism. There is no such thing as an objective journalist, but everybody has to try.

Likewise, Peter Steinfels draws sharp symbolic boundaries separating professional and religious life following his use of the bridging language of intellectual refinement. After describing the moral engagement of intellectual heroes such as Arendt and Cogley, Steinfels points out that "there is a difference between what they were doing and what the first responsibility of a reporter is." Asked how his job as religion reporter for the *New York Times* compares to normatively engaged journalism, Steinfels makes a sharp distinction between the evaluative journalism of *Commonweal* and the objective reporting of the *Times:*

> In leaving *Commonweal* and going to the *Times* there really was a certain break with that. . . . My first responsibility, which I was quite happy to insist on, was to try and just report stories. . . . The first objective was to tell people what was happening without making any kind of strong evaluation of whether this development was good or bad. And

that's a certain amount of sacrifice. It certainly cramps your prose style a little bit.

Why do journalists employ the rhetoric of objectivity and detachment? Some interviewees do not talk about objectivity until they are asked about it. For such respondents, objectivity serves as a convenient script for describing the professional role of the journalist. But for Kelley and Steinfels the rhetoric of objectivity does something more: it helps restore the line between professional and religious worlds after this line has become blurred. By immediately shifting from religious language to the rhetoric of objectivity, these journalists indicate they have come close to violating the borders of journalism's professional jurisdiction, and need to pull back from the margins. Gaye Tuchman argues that the use of objectivity language is a credibility enhancing "strategic ritual," used to counter potential threats to journalistic authority.[39] For both Catholic and evangelical journalists in the survey, the rhetoric of objectivity restores the symbolic boundary between news and opinion, facts and values, and between professional and religious spheres.

What is the place of personal religious identity in American journalism? How do Catholics and evangelicals negotiate the boundary between professional and religious worlds? This chapter has described three types of strategies used by journalists to manage the tension between professionalism and religious commitment in New York and Washington journalism: privatization and bracketing, multivocal bridging languages, and the rhetoric of objectivity. Each strategy reveals something important about the relationship between religion and American public life.

The strategies of privatization and bracketing call attention to the potentially stigmatizing nature of public religious identities in the modern professions. Those few respondents who totally or partially conceal their religious identities from professional colleagues say they do so in order to avoid damaging their credibility as objective journalists. For such journalists, the boundary between the public and the private precludes the display of religious convictions in professional life.

By contrast, those respondents (the large majority of the sample) who make use of multivocal bridging languages (such as journalistic empathy, intellectual refinement, and justice and peace), attempt to translate their religious convictions into terms comprehensible to the wider journalistic profession. When Wesley Pippert likens the pursuit of justice and peace to getting to "the heart of the story" and Jack Kelley expresses his Christian compassion through "writing with a heart," they are engaging in multivocality, translating religious terms into professional language, and vice versa. By drawing on journalism's submerged traditions of human-interest, advocacy, and intellectual journalism, they are able to articulate a fit between professional and religious vocabularies.

Finally, the tendency of many respondents to qualify displays of religious conviction with countervailing appeals to the rhetoric of objectivity shows that there are limits to the expression of normative religious language in American journalism. While respondents may translate their religious convictions into professional terms, they must take care to maintain a distinction between their professional and religious identities. The rhetoric of objectivity provides a way of restoring the boundary between professional and religious worlds after it has become blurred.

By analyzing the diverse strategies Catholics and evangelicals use to negotiate the boundary between professional and religious worlds, this study reveals the complex relationship between the public and the private in American society. In *Christianity and Civil Society,* Robert Wuthnow argues that religious people must learn to translate the languages of their subcultures into the broader vocabulary of American civil society in order to gain a wider hearing.[40] My respondents have clearly demonstrated such bilingual sophistication, repeatedly translating their religious convictions into professional terms (including the rhetoric of objectivity). By bridging the spheres of journalism and religion while continuing to insist on their separation, they have illustrated the porous nature of the boundary between the public world of the professions and the world of their religious communities.

NOTES

An earlier version of this chapter appeared in the winter 1999 issue of *Sociology of Religion.* © Association for the Sociology of Religion, Inc.

1. Charles Derber, Yale R. Magrass, and William. A. Schwartz, *Power in the Highest Degree: Professionals and the Rise of a New Mandarin Order* (New York: Oxford University Press, 1990); Magali S. Larson, *The Rise of Professionalism: A Sociological Analy-*

sis (Berkeley: University of California Press, 1977); Alvin.W. Gouldner, "The New Class Project I," *Theory and Society* 6 (1978): 153–204; Eliot Freidson, *Profession of Medicine: A Study of the Sociology of Applied Knowledge* (Chicago: University of Chicago Press, 1988); Talcott Parsons, *Essays in Sociological Theory, Pure and Applied* (Glencoe, Ill.: Free Press, 1949); H. Wilensky, "The Professionalization of Everybody," *American Journal of Sociology* 70 (1964): 137–58.

2. Michael Schudson, *Discovering the News: A Social History of the American Newspaper* (New York: Basic Books, 1978); Gaye Tuchman, "Objectivity as Strategic Ritual: An Examination of Newsman's Notions of Objectivity," *American Sociological Review* 77 (1972): 660–79.

3. Herbert Gans, *Deciding What's News* (New York: Random House, 1979), 182.

4. Daniel C. Hallin, *We Keep America on Top of the World* (New York: Routledge, 1994), 6.

5. E. J. Dionne, "Religion and the Media: Keynote Address," *Commonweal* 122, no. 4 (1995): 26–30, esp. 28.

6. Michael Schudson, *Origins of the Ideal of Objectivity in the Professions: A Study in the History of American Journalism and American Law* (New York: Garland, 1990), 9–10.

7. C. John. Sommerville, *The News Revolution in England: Cultural Dynamics of Daily Information* (New York: Oxford University Press, 1996).

8. Peter L. Berger, "The Worldview of the New Class: Secularity and its Discontents," in *The New Class?* ed. B. Bruce-Briggs (New Brunswick, N.J.: Transaction Books, 1979), 49–56.

9. S. Robert Lichter, Stanley Rothman, and Linda S. Lichter, *The Media Elite* (Bethesda, Md.: Adler & Adler, 1986).

10. Michael Novak, *The Rise of the Unmeltable Ethnics* (New York: Macmillan, 1973), 41, 43.

11. Robert Wuthnow, *The Restructuring of American Religion* (Princeton: Princeton University Press, 1988); Robert Wuthnow, *God and Mammon in America* (New York: Free Press, 1994); David J. O'Brien, *Public Catholicism* (New York: Macmillan, 1989); Jose Casanova, *Public Religions in the Modern World* (Chicago: University of Chicago Press, 1994).

12. Mark Silk, *Unsecular Media: Making News of Religion in America* (Chicago: University of Illinois Press, 1995); John Dart and Jimmie Allen, *Bridging the Gap: Religion and the News Media* (Nashville: Freedom Forum First Amendment Center, 1993).

13. Schudson, *Discovering the News*, 186.

14. Catholic Journalists: E. J. Dionne, Colman McCarthy, Mary McGrory, and Dan Balz *(Washington Post);* Peter Steinfels and Robin Toner *(New York Times);* Kenneth Woodward *(Newsweek);* Brian Healy *(Eye to Eye with Connie Chung);* Donald Wycliff *(Chicago Tribune* and *New York Times);* Cokie Roberts (ABC News/National Public Radio). Evangelical journalists: David Aikman and Richard Ostling *(Time);*

Fred Barnes *(New Republic);* Jack Kelley *(USA Today);* Marianne Kyriakos *(Washington Post);* Don Holt *(Fortune);* Wesley Pippert (formerly United Press International); Jeff Sheler *(US News and World Report);* Cal Thomas (Los Angeles Times Syndicate); Russ Pulliam (editor, *Indianapolis News;* formerly Associated Press, New York). In some cases, the journalists listed are no longer at the publications shown above.

15. Erving Goffman, *The Presentation of Self in Everyday Life* (New York: Anchor Books, 1959).

16. Erving Goffman, *Stigma: Notes on the Management of Spoiled Identity* (New York: Simon & Schuster, 1963).

17. Peter L. Berger, *The Sacred Canopy* (New York: Doubleday, 1967); James D. Hunter, *American Evangelicalism: Conservative Religion and the Quandary of Modernity* (New Brunswick: Rutgers University Press, 1983).

18. W. Griswold, "The Fabrication of Meaning: Literary Interpretation in the United States, Great Britain, and the West Indies," *American Journal of Sociology* 92 (1987): 1077–117.

19. Robert Wuthnow, *Acts of Compassion: Caring for Ourselves and Helping Others* (Princeton: Princeton University Press, 1991).

20. Daniel C. Hallin, *"The Uncensored War": The Media and Vietnam* (New York: Oxford University Press, 1986).

21. Schudson, *Discovering the News.*

22. Robert J. Griffin et al. *Interpreting Public Issues* (Ames: Iowa State University Press, 1991).

23. Curtis D. MacDougall, *Interpretative Reporting* (New York: MacMillan, 1968), 124.

24. Nicolaus Mills, *The New Journalism: A Historical Anthology* (New York: McGraw-Hill, 1974), J. Herbert Altschull, *From Milton to McLuhan: The Ideas behind American Journalism* (Baltimore: Johns Hopkins University Press, 1990).

25. Russell Jacoby, *The Last Intellectuals* (New York: Basic Books, 1987); Charles Kadushin, *The American Intellectual Elite* (New York: Little Brown, 1974).

26. Steven G. Brint, *In an Age of Experts: The Changing Role of Professionals in Politics and Public Life* (Princeton: Princeton University Press, 1994).

27. Garry Wills, *Bare Ruined Choirs: Doubt, Prophecy, and Radical Religion* (New York: Doubleday, 1972); Rodger Van Allen, *The Commonweal and American Catholicism* (Philadelphia, Pa.: Fortress, 1974); Rodger Van Allen, *Being Catholic: Commonweal from the Seventies to the Nineties, the Magazine, the Movement, the Meaning* (Chicago: Loyola University Press, 1994); William Clancy, "Catholicism in America," in *Catholicism in America,* ed. William Clancy (New York: Harcourt, Brace, 1954), 9–24.

28. Peter Steinfels, "Religion and the Media: Keynote Address," *Commonweal* 122 (February 1995), 14–19, esp. 9.

29. Peter Steinfels, "Constraints of the Religion Reporter," *Nieman Reports* 47 (1993): 3–5, 55.

30. Ibid., 55.

31. Steinfels, quoted in Van Allen, *Being Catholic,* 114.

32. J. Kane, "Catholic Separatism," in *Catholicism in America,* ed. William Clancy, (New York: Harcourt, Brace, 1954), 47–57, esp. 56.

33. Van Allen, *Being Catholic.*

34. David J. O'Brien, "Contemporary Reflections: 1985, 1995." *US Catholic Historian* 13 (1995): 53–56, esp. 54.

35. Pierre Bourdieu, *Distinction: A Social Critique of the Judgement of Taste* (Cambridge: Harvard University Press, 1984); M. Lamont, "How to Become a Dominant French Philosopher: The Case of Jacques Derrida," *American Journal of Sociology* 93 (1987): 584–622.

36. Schudson, *Discovering the News;* Peter Novick, *That Noble Dream: The "Objectivity Question" and the American Historical Profession* (Cambridge: Cambridge University Press, 1988).

37. Mills, *New Journalism;* Altschull, *Milton to McLuhan;* David H. Weaver and G. Cleveland Wilhoit, *The American Journalist: A Portrait of U.S. News People and Their Work* (Bloomington: Indiana University Press, 1991).

38. Wills, *Bare Ruined Choirs;* O'Brien, *Public Catholicism;* James T. Fisher, *The Catholic Counterculture in America, 1933–1962* (Chapel Hill: University of North Carolina Press, 1989); Robert B. Fowler, *A New Engagement: Evangelical Political Thought: 1965–1976* (Grand Rapids, Mich.: Eerdmans, 1982); Richard Quebedeaux, *The Young Evangelicals* (New York: Harper & Row, 1974).

39. Tuchman, "Objectivity as Strategic Ritual."

40. Robert Wuthnow, *Christianity and Civil Society: The Contemporary Debate* (Valley Forge, Pa.: Trinity Press International, 1996), 63.

BIBLIOGRAPHY

Abbott, Andrew. *The System of Professions.* Chicago: University of Chicago Press, 1988.

Altschull, J. Herbert. *From Milton to McLuhan: The Ideas behind American Journalism.* Baltimore: Johns Hopkins University Press, 1990.

Berger, Peter L. *The Sacred Canopy.* New York: Doubleday, 1967.

——. "The Worldview of the New Class: Secularity and Its Discontents." In *The New Class?* ed. B. Bruce-Briggs. New Brunswick, N.J.: Transaction Books, 1979.

Brint, Steven G. *In an Age of Experts: The Changing Role of Professionals in Politics and Public Life.* Princeton: Princeton University Press, 1994.

Bourdieu, Pierre. *Distinction: A Social Critique of the Judgement of Taste.* Cambridge: Harvard University Press, 1984.

Bruce-Briggs, B. *The New Class?* New Brunswick, N.J.: Transaction Books, 1979.

Casanova, Jose. *Public Religions in the Modern World.* Chicago: University of Chicago Press, 1994.

Clancy, William. "Catholicism in America." In *Catholicism in America,* ed. William Clancy. New York: Harcourt, Brace, 1954.

Dart, John, and Jimmie Allen. *Bridging the Gap: Religion and the News Media.* Nashville: Freedom Forum First Amendment Center, 1993.

Derber, Charles, Yale R. Magrass, and William.A. Schwartz. *Power in the Highest Degree: Professionals and the Rise of a New Mandarin Order.* New York: Oxford University Press, 1990.

Dionne, E. J. "Religion and the Media: Keynote Address." *Commonweal* 24 (February 1995): 26–30.

Fisher, James T. *The Catholic Counterculture in America: 1933–1962.* Chapel Hill: University of North Carolina Press, 1989.

Fowler, Robert B. *A New Engagement: Evangelical Political Thought: 1965–1976.* Grand Rapids, Mich.: Eerdmans, 1982.

Freidson, Eliot. *Profession of Medicine: A Study of the Sociology of Applied Knowledge.* Chicago: University of Chicago Press, 1988.

Gans, Herbert. *Deciding What's News.* New York: Random House, 1979.

Goffman, Erving. *The Presentation of Self in Everyday Life.* New York: Anchor Books, 1959.

——. *Stigma: Notes on the Management of Spoiled Identity.* New York: Simon & Schuster, 1963.

Gouldner, Alvin W. "The New Class Project I. "*Theory and Society* 6 (1978): 153–204.

Griffin, Robert J., et al. *Interpreting Public Issues.* Ames: Iowa State University Press, 1991.

Griswold, W. "The Fabrication of Meaning: Literary Interpretation in the United States, Great Britain, and the West Indies." *American Journal of Sociology* 92 (1987): 1077–117.

Hallin, Daniel C. *"The Uncensored War": The Media and Vietnam.* New York: Oxford University Press, 1986.

——. *We Keep America on Top of the World.* New York: Routledge, 1994.

Hunter, James D. *American Evangelicalism: Conservative Religion and the Quandary of Modernity.* New Brunswick, N.J.: Rutgers University Press, 1983.

Jacoby, Russell. *The Last Intellectuals.* New York: Basic Books, 1987.

Kadushin, Charles. *The American Intellectual Elite.* New York: Little Brown, 1974.

Kane, J. "Catholic Separatism." In *Catholicism in America,* ed. William Clancy. New York: Harcourt, Brace, 1954.

Lamont, M. "How to Become a Dominant French Philosopher: The Case of Jacques Derrida." *American Journal of Sociology* 93 (1987): 584–622.

Larson, Magali S. *The Rise of Professionalism: A Sociological Analysis.* Berkeley: University of California Press, 1977.

Lichter, S. Robert, Stanley Rothman, and Linda S. Lichter. *The Media Elite.* Bethesda, Md.: Adler & Adler, 1986.

MacDougall, Curtis D. *Interpretative Reporting.* New York: Macmillan, 1968.

Mills, Nicolaus. *The New Journalism: A Historical Anthology.* New York: McGraw-Hill, 1974.

Novak, Michael. *The Rise of the Unmeltable Ethnics.* New York: Macmillan, 1973.

Novick, Peter. *That Noble Dream: The "Objectivity Question" and the American Historical Profession.* Cambridge: Cambridge University Press, 1988.

O'Brien, David J. *Public Catholicism.* New York: Macmillan, 1989.

——. "Contemporary Reflections: 1985, 1995." *US Catholic Historian* 13 (1995): 53–56.

Parsons, Talcott. *Essays in Sociological Theory, Pure and Applied.* Glencoe, Ill.: Free Press, 1949.

Quebedeaux, Richard. *The Young Evangelicals.* New York: Harper & Row, 1974.

Schudson, Michael. *Discovering the News: A Social History of the American Newspaper.* New York: Basic Books, 1978.

——. *Origins of the Ideal of Objectivity in the Professions: A Study in the History of American Journalism and American Law.* New York: Garland, 1990.

Silk, Mark. *Unsecular Media: Making News of Religion in America.* Chicago: University of Illinois Press, 1995.

Sommerville, C. John. *The News Revolution in England: Cultural Dynamics of Daily Information.* New York: Oxford University Press, 1996.

Steinfels, Peter. "Constraints of the Religion Reporter." *Nieman Reports* 47 (1993): 3–5, 55.

——. "Religion and the Media: Keynote Address." *Commonweal* 122 (February 1995), 14–19.

Tuchman, Gaye. "Objectivity as Strategic Ritual: An Examination of Newsman's Notions of Objectivity." *American Sociological Review* 77 (1972): 660–79.

Van Allen, Rodger. *The Commonweal and American Catholicism.* Philadelphia: Fortress, 1974.

——. *Being Catholic: Commonweal from the Seventies to the Nineties: the Magazine, the Movement, the Meaning.* Chicago: Loyola University Press, 1994.

Weaver, David H., and G. Cleveland Wilhoit. *The American Journalist: A Portrait of U.S. News People and Their Work.* Bloomington: Indiana University Press, 1991.

Wilensky, H. "The Professionalization of Everybody." *American Journal of Sociology* 70 (1964): 137–58.

Wills, Garry. *Bare Ruined Choirs: Doubt, Prophecy, and Radical Religion.* New York: Doubleday, 1972.

Wuthnow, Robert. *The Restructuring of American Religion.* Princeton: Princeton University Press, 1988.

——. *Acts of Compassion: Caring for Ourselves and Helping Others.* Princeton: Princeton University Press, 1991.

——. *Christianity and Civil Society: The Contemporary Debate.* Valley Forge, Pa.: Trinity Press International, 1996.

——. *God and Mammon in America.* New York: Free Press, 1994.

CHAPTER 8

THE SOUTHERN BAPTIST
CONTROVERSY AND THE PRESS

Mark G. Borchert

In 1977, Paul Pressler, a Houston judge, and Paige Patterson, the president of Criswell Center for Biblical Studies in Dallas, began an effort to reshape the policies and institutions of the Southern Baptist Convention (SBC), with 13.5 million members the largest Protestant denomination in the United States. Convinced that Southern Baptist colleges, universities, and seminaries had moved toward theological liberalism, Pressler and Patterson devised a plan to establish the SBC as a more conservative denomination and to purge it of what they considered to be heretical influences.[1] The two Texans recognized that the presidency of the denomination, although often considered an honorary position, involved decision making that could alter the board of trustees of every SBC institution. If new leaders were elected, the convention could be guided in a more conservative direction and the threat of "liberalism" could be addressed.[2] By 1979, Pressler and Patterson had gathered enough support to elect the first in a series of fundamentalist presidents.

The efforts to guide the already conservative convention further to the right did not proceed without resistance. Long-time Baptist leaders, denominational officials, seminary professors, and others began to voice their opposition to the rise of fundamentalism. The ensuing controversy quickly became a national news story. By 1980, when a second fundamentalist, Bailey Smith, was elected president, the Religion Newswriters Association selected the denominational battle as one of the top ten religion news stories of the year. The press also began to focus on the controversial statements of the new leadership of the denomination. For instance, Smith, as SBC president, told a rally that God did not hear the prayers of Jews. Later, in an aside during a sermon to his Oklahoma congregation, Smith suggested that Jewish people had "funny-looking noses."[3] Both comments drew national attention and criticism from Baptist, Jewish, and other religious leaders. Although Smith, in partnership with the Anti-Defamation League of B'nai Brith, worked to address these criticisms, for the next two years publications covering stories about the SBC president and the convention continued to refer to the incident.

One SBC official described the reporting of Smith's comments about Jewish people as a "cheap shot" by the media.[4] Many supporters of the new denominational leadership concurred. Fundamentalists in the convention were frustrated by the press's scrutiny of their leaders, as well as the general coverage of their position. There was even quantitative research suggesting journalists had little affinity for conservative religious beliefs, values, and practices.[5] Although this research would be later disputed,[6] fundamentalists affirmed its implications. Secular reporters were viewed as liberal antagonists. In fact, Paul Pressler and a group of partners attempted to buy the *Houston Post* in 1986 in part to correct what they viewed as misrepresentations in reporting on the denomination.

A case can be made, however, for a position that is quite to the contrary. Shaped by the news values and professional practices of journalism, the story of the SBC controversy told by the secular media emphasizes certain aspects of the conflict and ignores others. In this chapter, I argue that while members of the press may not be particularly sympathetic to the far right-wing of the SBC, ironically journalistic accounts often reflect the fundamentalists' understanding of the controversy, rather than alternative accounts. Pressler, Patterson, and others may complain about the antagonism of liberal reporters, but the narratives presented in newspaper articles, news magazines, and wire-service reports on the controversy echo the themes, issues, and agendas of central importance to fundamentalists.

THE VARIETY OF ALTERNATIVE ACCOUNTS

Scholars from a number of disciplines have offered a variety of interpretations of the SBC controversy. For example, J. E. Barnhart, a philosopher of religion, describes it as a battle over understandings of sacred texts.[7] David R. Norsworthy, a sociologist, presents it as an antibureaucratic movement.[8] In a provocative cultural analysis, Ellen Rosenberg links the denominational struggle with the politics of the New Right, describing it as the reassertion of racist and male-dominated patterns of the Old South.[9] Nancy Tatom Ammerman writes, "Dozens of scholars were drawn to the Southern Baptist Convention's controversy."[10] She suggests that they all bring unique perspectives, informed by the questions, methods, and values of their individual disciplines.

In addition to the various scholarly perspectives, U.S. journalism offers its own understanding of the denominational struggle. Just as the conventions of a discipline guide an academician in examining this issue, the values, standards, and practices of professional journalists lead toward a particular interpretation. My analysis of more than five hundred newspaper and magazine articles and wire-service reports written between 1979 and 1986 suggests that journalists across the country approached the SBC conflict in strikingly similar ways. Before examining this story, however, the differing perspectives of the participants in the controversy should be understood.

THE FUNDAMENTALISTS' PERSPECTIVE: PURSUING ORTHODOXY

Beginning with the 1979 election of a conservative pastor from Memphis as SBC president, fundamentalists defined their cause in terms of the defense of the inerrancy of the scriptures. At a conference prior to his election, Adrian Rogers attested to his belief that the Bible was accurate, without error in any respect.[11] For example, Rogers proclaimed the historical reality of Adam and Eve, rejecting "monkey mythology that tells us that man evolved."[12] He argued that Southern Baptists must return to a biblical orthodoxy.

For the fundamentalists, the enemy of orthodoxy was the theological "liberalism" that they believed dominated Southern Baptist academic life.[13] Baptists on the far right, like Rogers, Pressler, and Patterson, rejected the SBC seminaries' teaching of biblical criticism—the analysis of sacred texts using historical, sociological, and literary approaches. They advocated the literal and scientific accuracy of the Bible and opposed any questioning of its miraculous accounts. They evaluated scholarship on the basis of its affirmation of the literal authenticity of the scriptures. In labeling those who raised questions about the Bible as a factual record, they rejected the terms *conservative* and *moderate:* Pressler insisted that such individuals were liberals—because they did not "believe the complete accuracy and complete truth of scripture."[14] To question the integrity of biblical texts was to initiate a process that could unravel the core of the Christian religion.

By 1984, with the right wing of the convention firmly in control of the denominational appointment process, moderates (as they came to be called) formed a united opposition. Leaders like Southern Baptist Seminary President Roy Honeycutt declared the controversy to be a "Holy War." Fundamentalists quickly responded to this opposition. For example, Paige Patterson suggested that, like other liberals, "Honeycutt did not believe all that the Bible says."[15] An attempt in the mid-1980s to resolve the conflict through a "peace committee," with representatives from both sides, met with very little success.

Throughout the 1980s, the new leaders of the SBC focused the attention of the denomination on many theological, social, and political issues; however, the unifying theme in their efforts was inerrancy, or beliefs about the literal accuracy of the Bible. From this position, an end to the ordination of women, the centrality of evangelism, the clear establishment of pastoral authority, and denominational support for conservative political issues and politicians were all merely biblical principles with which any Bible-believing Baptist must agree.[16] In their pursuit of orthodoxy, leaders like Adrian Rogers insisted that although some of the stances taken by the new convention leadership might appear "overtly political," they were in fact "moral and spiritual issues" based on a belief in the Bible.[17]

THE MODERATES' PERSPECTIVE: A QUEST FOR FREEDOM

While fundamentalists framed the conflict in terms of the inerrancy of the scriptures, moderates understood it very differently. Moderates maintained that the dispute had "less to do with defense of the Bible than with the effort of certain persons to set themselves up as the inerrant and infallible interpreters of the Bible and guides to Baptist orthodoxy."[18] Moderates maintained that a central concern for Baptists was not the content of a system of beliefs but the autonomy of the believer. The traditional Baptist principle of *soul competency,* an individual's unique responsibility before God, was for moderates the defining issue of the struggle.

For moderates, fundamentalism contradicted the heritage of their faith. They argued that Baptists traditionally supported the doctrine of the priesthood of all believers, the principle of the separation of church and state, and the independence of the local congregation.[19] All of these beliefs were premised on the notions of religious freedom and individual accountability. "All that we are as Baptists can be summed up in that word—liberty," said a moderate leader in a speech prior to an annual convention.[20] Moderates insisted on the individual's freedom to interpret scripture for one's self. For them, the fundamentalists' demand for the firing of seminary professors who did not accept certain tenets or creeds was anathema to Baptist beliefs.

Although as early as 1979 some denominational leaders openly attacked the ongoing efforts to change the direction of the convention, moderates as a group were relatively slow in formulating and advancing their agenda. Only after a series of defeats in the SBC presidential elections did moderates unite in opposition to the new denominational power brokers. Their first response was to argue that charges of liberalism were unfounded. They also sought to compromise by attempting to incorporate new leaders into the denominational structure. By 1982, frustrated by what they viewed as the dogmatism of the fundamentalists, moderates began to insist on presenting their own definition of the conflict. For them, this controversy indeed had become a Holy War, but they argued that the battleground was not the truth of the Bible: it was a creedalism that undermined the autonomy of the individual believer and disregarded the foundations of Baptist faith.[21] In the 1985 election of a president, moderates united as never before to support a well-known conservative candidate, challenging the fundamentalists' claim that "liberals" were the only critics of the current changes in the SBC, but although they mounted considerable opposition, once again the moderates' candidate was not the winner.

SECULAR NEWS COVERAGE OF THE CONTROVERSY

The media told their own story of the denominational struggle. Beginning in 1979, the year that Pressler and Patterson initiated their plan to guide the denomination in a more conservative direction, a number of the news stories reported on what journalists described as (in the words of one headline) a "Battle over Biblical Truth."[22] During that year, the issue of voting irregularities at the annual convention in Houston also received media attention. The *New York Times*, for instance, recorded that complaints had initiated an investigation of voting procedures in the election of the president.[23] The *Washington Post* related allegations of pastors voting for parishioners and children being registered as messengers.[24] By September, it was reported that 284 illegal votes had been cast for the new, ultraconservative president, Adrian Rogers. On the whole, the treatment of the SBC was muted, at least in comparison with later years.

The following year, the controversy in the convention further captured media interest, and the Religious Newswriters Association ranked the denominational conflict as the year's fifth most significant story about religion. In their discussion of the national convention in Saint Louis and the election of Bailey Smith to presidency, journalists introduced the notion of inerrancy. Some stories described the election of a fundamentalist who argued for the infallibility of the scriptures as a reaffirmation of traditional Southern ways. For example, an article in the *New York Times* described the debate as a conflict over the understanding of the Bible that had regional roots; Southern inerrantists were presented as opposing "Northern biblical scholarship."[25]

Another story, emerging in 1980 and receiving attention for the next two years, focused on Smith's comments concerning Jews and the subsequent responses to those statements. As noted above, the coverage of this issue frustrated and embarrassed fundamentalists; however, it also placed Smith, as well as the agenda that his presidency represented, on the national stage.[26] In covering the story, reporters often linked Smith with Jerry Falwell, and SBC fundamentalism with the wider movement of the Christian Right.[27] Smith became a nationally known religious leader, and his reaction to events associated with the world of religion often entered the headlines.

In the 1981 Los Angeles convention, Bailey Smith was reelected. The denominational conflict continued. Emphasizing the strife at the annual meeting, newspaper reporters sought to explain the battle to their readers. They defined the pivotal issue in the conflict as biblical inerrancy and presented two camps: conservatives who insisted on the literal interpretation of the Bible, and liberals who allowed for a variety of interpretations. During the 1982 convention in New Orleans, resolutions supporting school prayer and condemning the scheduling of NFL football games during times traditionally reserved for religious television programming claimed some media attention. The controversy, defined in the same terms as the prior year, was still center stage, however. Journalists describing the more peaceful 1983 annual meeting of Southern Baptists remained committed to the definition of the debate with which they were familiar.[28] Secular reporters continually told the story as a "Bible Brouhaha."[29]

According to the Religion Newswriters Association, the Kansas City meeting of Baptists in 1984 was among the year's most important religious news developments. A Southern Baptist resolution opposing the ordination of women on the basis of "biblical truth" made headlines across the country. Many reporters covering the conflict continued to focus on inerrancy as defining the players in the struggle, and they framed the debates about women in those terms. Some journalists, however, coupled these explanations with an alternative perspective on the controversy, one that described the fundamentalist movement as a small group using political tactics to gain control of the denomination. David E. Anderson, for instance, discusses the controversy in terms similar to the 1979 coverage of election irregularities, rather than a "battle over the Bible."[30]

In 1985 and 1986, the controversy, often described as a "holy war" in the headlines, continued to have a prominent place in the news. Increasingly, newspaper articles included a description of the controversy as a conflict that was "not theological but political."[31] Articles included what the press defined to be the moderates' position, that the denominational disputes were based on the efforts of a small group of fundamentalists to exercise "raw power."[32] In many stories, however, this viewpoint on the conflict was presented as a secondary consideration, and most often only in the context of the "holy war"—the debate over views on the Bible.

Interestingly, there are surprising similarities between the accounts of the SBC controversy presented by the media and by the fundamentalists. In fact, the story that emerged in the pages of the daily newspapers was one of a battle over the Bible and of a denomination's wrestling with issues of orthodoxy. The two sides consistently were described in relation to their stance on inerrancy. Although reporters raised questions about intradenominational politics associated with the conflict, the terms by which moderates would hope to define the battleground rarely appeared in the press. My analysis of more than five hundred news stories revealed only a few references to the issues of soul competency or the priesthood of all believers.[33] In the newspapers, concerns related to freedom rarely were portrayed as defining issues for Baptists. Fundamentalists might have charged that secular reporters, with their allegiances to liberalism, ignored and misrepresented their position in the news, but it was, in fact, the story of the opposition to fundamentalism that remained untold.

In contemporary society, it is only on rare occasions that government forces directly dictate the editorial policies of mass communicators, and journalists in fact fiercely defend their sense of autonomy. Isaiah Berlin describes this absence of direct interference by the government as "negative liberty."[34] The freedom that reporters and editors share, however, is by no means absolute. In fact, despite libertarian notions to the contrary, many factors shape and restrict the construction of mass-mediated news. In a competitive arena, "institutional imperatives, organizational routines and working exigencies" shape the telling of news stories.[35] Occupational ideologies exist within media institutions, and in this context news is selected and packaged based on preexisting categories of newsworthiness. Paul Hartmann and Charles Husband argue that adversarial situations like events involving conflict, threat, or deviancy make news.[36]

Like a contest, election, or football game, the SBC controversy seen as a "battle over the Bible" was a clear-cut conflict. For both fundamentalists and members of the press, the distinctions between orthodoxy and heresy, between belief and disbelief, defined the two sides in stark opposition. In addition, newspaper reporters latched on to the controversial statements generated by the sharp duality of fundamentalists' worldview. Unlike the moderates' concerns with "soul competency" or the "priesthood of all believers," statements about God's response to Jewish prayers or the eternal damnation of certain groups immediately polarized the issue and generated a clash of opinions. With institutional authority and a propensity for such controversial statements, fundamentalist leaders became focal players in journalistic accounts of the holy war, and their perspectives framed the debate. News stories created clear oppositions and personified the terms of the conflict with the words and images of polemic leaders like Rogers, Smith, and Pressler.

Hartmann and Husband discuss a second major feature of newsworthiness as the ability of a story to be interpreted within familiar media frameworks or through existing stereotypes.[37] For the SBC controversy, alternative explanations of the controversy, like the perspective of the moderates, had no preexisting media framework within which to be understood. This was not the case for the fundamentalists' perspective on the controversy. The clash between the Christian Right and a liberal opposition was a hot topic in the press in the 1980s. Journalists could easily explain the two sides of the SBC by referencing well-known terms from their coverage of the Moral Majority, Jerry Falwell, and the emerging religious Right. In fact, as James Guth notes, the coverage of the politics of the religious Right and of events within the SBC became increasingly linked over time.[38] Thus based not on affinity but on a particular approach to newsworthiness, the press accounts often presented the fundamentalists' perspective on the controversy.

By 1986, fundamentalists had won the battle for control of the largest Protestant denomination in the United States. Arthur Farnsley argues that moderates lost the struggle because of denominational structures;[39] Susan Harding discusses the moderates' combining of orthodoxy and tolerance as preventing their establishment of the moral high moral ground;[40] and Bill Leonard focuses on moderates' failure to unify and articulate an agenda for the convention.[41] This study suggests that an ineffective media strategy by the moderates and the news values of the press contributed to their lack of a public agenda and ultimately to their loss of power.

NOTES

1. Bill J. Leonard, *God's Last and Only Hope* (Grand Rapids, Mich.: Eerdmans, 1990).

2. Nancy Tatom Ammerman, *Baptist Battles: Social Change and Religious Conflict in the Southern Baptist Convention* (New Brunswick, N.J.: Rutgers University Press, 1990).

3. Marjorie Hyer, "Southern Baptist Chief Slips into a New Controversy with Jews," *Washington Post*, 21 November 1980, F11; Kenneth. L. Woodward and Stryker McGuire, "The Evangels and the Jews," *Newsweek*, 10 November 1980, 76–78.

4. Hyer, "Southern Baptist Chief."

5. Robert S. Lichter, Stanley Rothman, and Linda S. Lichter, *The Media Elite* (New York: Adler & Adler, 1986).

6. John Dart and Jimmie Allen, *Bridging the Gap: Religion and the News Media* (Nashville: Freedom Forum First Amendment Center of Vanderbilt University, 1993); Stewart M. Hoover, Shalini Venturelli, and Douglas Wagner, "Religion in Public Discourse: The Role of the Media," MS, Center for Mass Media Research, University of Colorado at Boulder, 1995; Stewart M. Hoover, *Religion in the News: Faith and Journalism in American Public Discourse* (Thousand Oaks, Calif.: Sage, 1998).

7. Joe E. Barnhart, "What's All the Fighting About? Southern Baptists and the Bible," in *Southern Baptists Observed*, ed. Ammerman, 124–43.

8. David Ray Norsworthy, "Rationalization and Reaction among Southern Baptists," in *Southern Baptists Observed*, 71–97.

9. Ellen M. Rosenberg, *The Southern Baptists: A Subculture in Transition* (Knoxville: University of Tennessee Press, 1989).

10. Nancy Tatom Ammerman, introduction to "Observing Southern Baptists," in *Southern Baptists Observed*, ed. Ammerman, 2.

11. Leonard, *God's Last and Only Hope*.

12. Ammerman, *Baptist Battles*, 83.

13. Leonard, *God's Last and Only Hope*.

14. Ammerman, *Baptist Battles*, 84.

15. Leonard, *God's Last and Only Hope*, 140, 142.

16. Arthur Emery Farnsley II, *Southern Baptist Politics: Authority and Power in the Restructuring of an American Denomination* (University Park: Pennsylvania State University Press, 1994).

17. Thomas Edsall, "New Right Finally Gains Control of Huge Southern Baptist Convention," *Washington Post*, 14 June 1986, A4.

18. E. Glenn Hinson, "Baptists and 'Evangelicals': There Is a Difference," in *Are Southern Baptists 'Evangelicals'?* ed. James L. Garrett Jr., E. Glenn Hinson, and James E. Tull (Macon, Ga.: Mercer University Press, 1983), 129–94, esp. 131–32.

19. Ammerman, *Baptist Battles*.

20. Ibid., 112.

21. Leonard, *God's Last and Only Hope*.

22. Marjorie Hyer, "Baptists Battle over Biblical Truth," *Washington Post*, 8 June 1979, C18.

23. Vecsey, George, "Official of Southern Baptists Plans Inquiry on New President," *New York Times*, 16 June 1979, A9.

24. Marjorie Hyer, "Southern Baptists Checking Reports of Some Irregularities in Election," *Washington Post*, 22 June 1979, C21.

25. Robert Blair Kaiser, "Southern Baptists Reaffirm Their Traditional Ways," *New York Times,* 12 June 1980, A20.

26. John Dart, "Ultraconservative Again Heads Southern Baptists," *Los Angeles Times,* 10 June 1981, A1, A21.

27. See, for example, Doug Anderson, "Head of Moral Majority Says God Hears Jewish Prayers," United Press International (UPI), 10 October 1980.

28. See, for example, Katy Buchanan. "Southern Baptists See Quiet Convention," UPI, 13 June 1983.

29. "Bible Brouhaha: A Baptist Power Struggle," *Time,* 22 June 1981, 69.

30. David E. Anderson, "Analysis: Fundamentalist Views Dominate Southern Baptist Convention," UPI, 15 June 1984.

31. John Dart, "Leadership Battle May Draw Record Crowd to Baptist Parley," *Los Angeles Times,* 8 June 1985, B6.

32. See, for example, Joseph Berger, "More Than the Bible at Issue as Southern Baptists Gather," *New York Times,* 9 June 1986, p. A16.

33. David Barron, "Fundamentalists, Moderate Baptists Revive," UPI, 10 June 1985; Paul Taylor, "Baptists Clash over Bible Views: Convention in Dallas to Elect President," *Washington Post,* 11 June 1985, A3.

34. Isaiah Berlin, *Four Essays on Liberty* (New York: Oxford University Press, 1969), 127.

35. Graham Murdock and Peter Golding, "Capitalism, Communication and Class Relations," in *Mass Communication and Society,* ed. James Curran, Michael Gurevitch, and Janet Woollacott (New York: Edward Arnold, 1976), 12–43, esp. 34.

36. Paul Hartmann and Charles Husband, "The Mass Media and Racial Conflict," *Race* 12 (1970): 435–55.

37. Ibid.

38. James L. Guth, "Southern Baptist Clergy: Vanguard of the Christian Right?" in *The New Christian Right: Mobilization and Legitimation,* ed. Robert C. Liebman and Robert Wuthnow (New York: Aldine, 1983), 117–30.

39. Farnsley, *Southern Baptist Politics.*

40. Susan Harding, "Observing the Observers," in *Southern Baptists Observed,* ed. Ammerman, 318–37.

41. Leonard, *God's Last and Only Hope.*

BIBLIOGRAPHY

Ammerman, Nancy Tatom. *Baptist Battles: Social Change and Religious Conflict in the Southern Baptist Convention.* New Brunswick, N.J.: Rutgers University Press, 1990.

——. "Observing Southern Baptists." Introduction to *Southern Baptists Observed*, ed. Ammerman, 2.

Anderson, David E. "Analysis: Fundamentalist Views Dominate Southern Baptist Convention." UPI, 15 June 1984.

Anderson, Doug. "Head of Moral Majority Says God Hears Jewish Prayers." UPI, 10 October 1980.

Barnhart, J. E. "What's All the Fighting About? Southern Baptists and the Bible." In *Southern Baptists Observed*, ed. Ammerman.

Barron, David. "Fundamentalists, Moderate Baptists Revive." UPI, 10 June 1985.

Berger, Joseph. "More Than the Bible at Issue as Southern Baptists Gather," *New York Times*, 9 June 1986, A16.

Berlin, Isaiah. *Four Essays on Liberty*. New York: Oxford University Press, 1969.

"Bible Brouhaha: A Baptist Power Struggle," *Time*, 22 June 1981, 69.

Buchanan, Katy. "Southern Baptists See Quiet Convention." UPI, 13 June 1983.

Dart, John. "Ultraconservative again Heads Southern Baptists," *Los Angeles Times*, 10 June 1981, A1, A21.

——. "Leadership Battle May Draw Record Crowd to Baptist Parley," *Los Angeles Times*, 8 June 1985, B6.

Dart, John, and Jimmie R. Allen. *Bridging the Gap: Religion and the News Media*. Nashville: Freedom Forum First Amendment Center of Vanderbilt University, 1993.

Edsall, Thomas. "New Right Finally Gains Control of Huge Southern Baptist Convention," *Washington Post*, 14 June 1986, A4.

Farnsley II, Arthur E. *Southern Baptist Politics: Authority and Power in the Restructuring of an American Denomination*. University Park: Pennsylvania State University Press, 1994.

Guth, James L. "Southern Baptist Clergy: Vanguard of the Christian Right?" In *The New Christian Right: Mobilization and Legitimation*, ed. Robert C. Liebman and Robert Wuthnow. New York: Aldine, 1983.

Harding, Susan. "Observing the Observers." In *Southern Baptists Observed*, ed. Ammerman.

Hartmann, Paul, and Charles Husband. "The Mass Media and Racial Conflict." *Race* 12 (1970): 435–55.

Hinson, E. Glenn. "Baptists and 'Evangelicals': There Is a Difference." In *Are Southern Baptists "Evangelicals"?* ed. James L. Garrett Jr., E. Glenn Hinson, and James E. Tull. Macon, Ga.: Mercer University Press, 1983.

Hoover, Stewart M. *Religion in the News: Faith and Journalism in American Public Discourse*. Thousand Oaks, Calif.: Sage, 1998.

Hoover, Stewart M., Shalini Venturelli, and Douglas Wagner. "Religion in Public

Discourse: The Role of the Media." Center for Mass Media Research, University of Colorado at Boulder, 1995.

Hyer, Marjorie. "Baptists Battle over Biblical Truth," *Washington Post*, 8 June 1979, C18.

——. "Southern Baptists Checking Reports of Some Irregularities in Election," *Washington Post*, 22 June 1979, C21.

——. "Southern Baptist Chief Slips into a New Controversy with Jews," *Washington Post*, 21 November 1980, F11.

Kaiser, Robert B. "Southern Baptists Reaffirm Their Traditional Ways," *New York Times*, 12 June 1980, A20.

Leonard, Bill J. *God's Last and Only Hope*. Grand Rapids, Mich.: Eerdmans, 1990.

Lichter, S. Robert, Stanley Rothman, and Linda S. Lichter. *The Media Elite*. New York: Adler & Adler, 1986.

Murdock, Graham, and Peter Golding. "Capitalism, Communication, and Class Relations." In *Mass Communication and Society*, ed. James Curran, Michael Gurevitch, and Janet Woollacott. New York: Arnold, 1977.

Norsworthy, David R. "Rationalization and Reaction among Southern Baptists." In *Southern Baptists Observed*, ed. Ammerman.

Rosenberg, Ellen M. *The Southern Baptists: A Subculture in Transition*. Knoxville: University of Tennessee Press, 1989.

Taylor, Paul. "Baptists Clash over Bible Views: Convention in Dallas to Elect President," *Washington Post*, 11 June 1985, A3.

Vecsey, George, "Official of Southern Baptists Plans Inquiry on New President," *New York Times*, 16 June 1979, A9.

Woodward, Kenneth L., and Stryker McGuire. "The Evangels and the Jews," *Newsweek*, 10 November 1980, 76–78.

IMPLICIT RELIGION AND MEDIATED PUBLIC RITUAL

The preceding chapters have represented evidence of the working out in public of the assumed prerogatives, vis-à-vis the media, of explicitly religious institutions; part 4 confronts the assumption that it is only formally constituted religion that can assume such a central role.

The two chapters in this part address the matter of ritual and ask whether the concept of ritual might be helpful in understanding relations between religion and the media. It is a commonplace to think of media behaviors as ritualized, and it is but a small step from there to speculating that such phenomena might be serving implicitly or explicitly religious functions.

Consistent with the overall direction of this book, these chapters look at practice; they also retheorize an understanding of ritual for the media age. In chapter 9, Carolyn Marvin asks us to consider the possibility that in contemporary culture the important rituals are not markedly transformed by the technologies and institutions of media and popular culture. Instead, she argues, fundamental rituals of social, cultural, and national identity revolve around powerful themes of the body and of blood sacrifice. The rise of the media, according to Marvin, has not undermined these essential functions of ritual. Marvin (along the lines we have used earlier to demarcate private and public and implicit and explicit religion) sees a profoundly public place for implicit religion, or at least a kind of implicit civil religion.

Ronald Grimes, an acknowledged scholar of ritual, in chapter 10 explores in some detail the capacities of ritual scholarship to account for media practice, and vice versa. In doing so, he describes a broader field, within which Marvin's project is but one category. Grimes is surely right in cautioning against an easy accommodation between observed media practices and received categories of ritual. Both contexts are more fluid than that, and it is necessary to an honest assessment that we move ahead with some humility.

At the same time, Grimes helps illuminate the range of ways our lines of demarcation are problematic. If we think of ritual as an essential or fundamental category of meaning-making (one that is thus at least potentially "religious"), then a wide range of actions, contexts, artifacts, and practices may qualify. This suggests that we must look beyond the formal markers of practice to be able to come to terms with the essence of the meanings produced by practice.

CHAPTER 9

SCAPEGOATING AND DETERRENCE: CRIMINAL JUSTICE RITUALS IN AMERICAN CIVIL RELIGION

Carolyn Marvin

In a volume devoted to media, religion, and ritual, a chapter on criminal justice may seem a little odd. It will seem less odd if we frame the U.S. criminal justice system as an institution of ritual sacrifice. Placed within the framework of American civil religion, a model of ritual sacrifice may be able to illuminate aspects of both criminal justice and civil religion. As I mean it here, the term *civil religion* does not imply a weak, or faux, religious form. I count nationalism, a less genteel synonym for civil religion, among the powerful living religions of modernity. This view is not widespread. But it is precisely the current and contemporary understanding of the often surprising religious dimensions of modern life in industrial societies that the present volume seeks to expand.

All religion, it could be said, invests in the notion of a transcendent power that commands life and death. Even if God (to take a familiar notion of transcendent power) chooses not to exercise that power, God must have it, in order to be God. The nation that commands the devotion and service of its citizens (in contrast to its imperfect vessel, the nation-state) likewise alone holds the legitimate power to confer life within the community of believers. This condition of being nationally "alive" we call citizenship. The nation also has the power to take the lives of citizens in ritually prescribed ways that include calling on them to offer their lives sacrificially. The dead ancestors who have sacrificed themselves are recalled in a sacred national flag in the same way that the cross calls to mind the sacrificed Christ. The cross signifies a deity that defeats death for believers as the flag signifies the nation that lives on, though its believers die bodily.

Among the ways the nation exercises the power of life and death and demands sacrifice are through criminal justice rituals. The question here is how (and why) U.S. criminal trial proceedings use ritual forms to effect *deterrence,* which legal practitioners and theorists take to be one of the most important practical and moral goals of criminal justice. If ritual structures undergird the civil religious framework of modern nation-states, there should be significant similarities between criminal justice rituals and other important rituals in American society. I will use war, the chief sacrifice ritual of nations, and presidential elections, the most central of American fertility rituals, as reference points for mapping how criminal trial proceedings deploy sacrificial scapegoating. If ritual forms are indeed central to criminal justice and other institutions of American life, their existence supports a larger argument that modern secular life is not "disenchanted," however much we try to convince ourselves it is.

Along with many theorists, I believe the most important purpose of ritual is to create and maintain groups by effecting unity among members. Following René Girard, I stipulate that group unity exists when violence *within* the group is at a (comparatively) low ebb.[2] Deterrence as the goal of criminal justice is consonant with this notion of unity. Emphatically, this is not to say that deterrence or group unity eliminates violence. Rather, they successfully displace and conceal it. Violence is thus channeled to effect group survival. Rituals establish who may be killed and under what conditions. Who is authorized to kill group members has always been a basic religious question. "Why do we die?" restates the sectarian question, "Why does [our] God kill those who are members of our group?" Killing power may be actively and malevolently exercised by transcendent power; it may be expressed as the mysterious will of transcendent power in establishing the moment of death that must come to all men; or transcendent power may simply refuse to interfere with those who kill, though omnipotence requires that it could if it wished.

For Durkheim, the totem is constituted in the practices, beliefs, things, and persons that the group considers sacred and untouchable. Symbolically, the totem is the group itself. In traditional societies and in sectarian religion, obedience to the totem's authority to command life and death is the paramount obligation of believers. In the civil religion of nationalism, the nation is the totem, the flag is the totem emblem, and the nation-state is the agent of totem killing authority. Durkheim operationalizes the totem principle as what the group agrees not to disagree about. He describes this agreement very generally as rules about not eating or killing the totem.[3] Yet, the totem *is* killed or eaten, or both, on designated ritual occasions. Ritually eating or killing the totem rehearses the social fact that group survival depends on sacrifices made by group members, including the most precious and difficult sacrifice of all, their lives. The *totem secret* conceals the disturbing truth that the group from time to time sacrifices its own members. The unity of the group is at risk if the totem secret is revealed. At the least potent end of the continuum of ritual efficacy, this sacrifice is simply dramatized; at the most potent end, it is performed. In modern nation-states, war is the most powerful sacrifice ritual of nationalism.

Ritual sacrifice harnesses the bodies of group members to the survival of the group. It also gathers up scattered individual hostilities and refocuses them collectively on victims whose death at the hands of the group unites its members. Successful sacrifice wipes the slate of social antagonism clean. This is an important feature of ritual sacrifice in (at the very least) Christianity, Judaism, Islam, Hinduism, and ancient Egyptian, Mesopotamian, Mesoamerican, and Andean religions. Ritual sacrifice also structures modern nation-state belonging no less than it structures religion, as we have commonly understood it. In some nation-states, the civic form is coextensive with inherited religious tradition. In others, such as the United States, the nation-state has appropriated the sacrificial authority of inherited religious traditions. These exist under state protection so long as they do not try to usurp the state's sacrificial authority. In organized human groups, sacrificial imperatives are ritualized as group acts in which selected group members are expelled into physical or social death. They become ritually designated goats, one of whom who must die so the group can survive. In Judeo-Christian tradition, the term *scapegoat* is associated with a passage from Leviticus, chapter 16, a document of ritual instruction that describes two ritual scapegoats and their functions, quoted here in the King James Version:

5. And he shall take of the congregation of the children of Israel two kids of the goats for a sin offering. . . .

7. And he shall take the two goats, and present them before the Lord of the door of the tabernacle of the congregation.

8. And Aaron shall cast lots upon the two goats; one lot for the Lord, and the other lot for the scapegoat.

9. And Aaron shall bring the goat upon which the Lord's lot fell, and offer him for a sin offering.

10. But the goat, on which the lot fell to be the scapegoat, shall be presented alive before the Lord, to make an atonement with him, and to let him go for a scapegoat into the wilderness. . . .

15. Then he shall kill the goat of the sin offering, that is for the people, and bring his blood within the vail . . . and sprinkle it upon the mercy seat, and before the mercy seat:

16. And he shall make an atonement for the holy place, because of the uncleanness of the children of Israel, and because of their transgressions in all their sins; and so shall he do for the tabernacle of the congregation, that remaineth among them in the midst of their uncleanness. . . .

18. And he shall go out unto the altar that is before the Lord, and make an atonement for it; and shall take of the blood . . . of the goat, and put it upon the horns of the altar round about.

19. And he shall sprinkle of the blood upon it with his finger seven times, and cleanse it, and hallow it from the uncleanness of the children of Israel.

20. And when he hath made an end of reconciling the holy place, and the tabernacle of the congregation, and the altar, he shall bring the live goat:

21. And Aaron shall lay both his hands upon the head of the live goat, and confess over him all the iniquities of the children of Israel, and all their transgressions in all their sins, putting them upon the head of the goat, and shall send him away by the hand of a fit man into the wilderness:

22. And the goat shall bear upon him all their iniquities unto a land not inhabited: and he shall let go the goat in the wilderness.

One goat is killed outright, its blood displayed for all to see. The other, the scapegoat, is ejected into unsanctified wilderness, or chaos. René Girard calls these sacrificial actors, respectively, ritual and surrogate victims.

Sacrifice rituals are able to unify the group to the extent that they meet the following criteria:

1. The sacrifice must declare himself or herself willing.
2. Victimage must be unanimous. Group members must agree on the rightness and propriety of the sacrifice.
3. The outcome of the ritual must be genuinely uncertain at the time of its undertaking. The outcome must not be capable of being predicted or manipulated.
4. The ritual must have a definite end and beginning.
5. The sacrifice must be valuable. Real group treasure must be offered.

Afterwards:

6. A successful ritual gives rise to commemorative rituals; only new rituals can repair a failed one.

SACRIFICE RITUALS IN THE AMERICAN NATION-STATE

In this section I briefly describe forms of sacrifice in American war and presidential-election ritual and present an illustrative example of scapegoating in the transfer of presidential power. These examples will give me a frame of reference for examining how criminal trials use scapegoating to deter additional violence against group members. Such an achievement would instance a powerful example of ritual efficacy.

War

War allows us to sacrifice our own group members in good conscience without recognizing (thus enabling us to deny) our agency in their deaths. Not all wars are successful sacrifice rituals, but popular wars in which many young Americans die (notably, the Civil War, in which approximately 600,000 died, and World War II, approximately 292,000) and that meet the other conditions noted above have been successful unifying rituals. In war, the role of surrogate victim is projected on the enemy. Our soldiers play the role of ritual victim.[4] Specially selected and ritually prepared for death, they stand in for members of the group with whom we are individually angry, a fact that cannot be acknowledged without great risk to the group and that is concealed by efforts that are always on the brink of unraveling. To reaffirm and renew old bonds in danger of fraying, and from time to time to create new ones, the group must redirect hostilities that endanger group existence and use this energy to unify the group instead. Ritual sacrifice provides that means.

Presidential Elections

Although sacrifice or fertility themes may predominate in particular rituals, neither is ever truly present without the other. In *Blood Sacrifice and the Nation*, David W. Ingle and I examined presidential elections as an important American fertility rite and ritual counterpoint to war. In presidential campaigns, suitors compete for the hand of the electorate. Candidates display their willingness to sacrifice themselves to the cause of group unity by submitting to ordeals of courage and humiliation that guide the electorate in choosing a suitor-candidate with whom to mate. Transformed, the victor ascends to office. Election confers on a duly elected president the totem authority to sacrifice group members. Reciprocally, the president may be sacrificed by the people if ever he is felt not to embody the group idea. Following an election, the defeated incumbent or rival is exiled to the political wilderness. Expelled from the group, he dies politically.

A famous photograph of Richard Nixon, who resigned from the presidency in 1974 following the Watergate scandal, shows him standing on the steps of a helicopter, about to be flown to political exile in California. Nixon's arms are raised skyward, each at approximately an angle of forty-five degrees. The frequency with which this image is reproduced suggests its mythic resonance. Nixon's raised arms model both a dominance gesture common to primates and a crucifixion or sacrificial gesture of submission. Nothing is more characteristic of ritual gestures than this conflation of opposites.

Dominance is a term that describes killing authority. Who displays it has vanquished his rivals. (Recall the 1998 brandishing by New York police officer Justin Volpe of the feces-covered stick with which he had sodomized Abner Louima, a Jamaican immigrant. Eyewitness accounts by fellow officers of this dominance display resulted in Volpe's conviction. He was sacrificed by his own group for ritually improper, dangerously contagious violence that imperiled the cohesiveness of the police as a group by threatening to expose the totem secret.)

Nixon's gesture is also a sign of sacrificial submission deeply familiar to a nation with a majority Christian tradition. Nixon is the embodied killing authority who willingly submits himself for excommunication by the people. As Girard observes, the role of kingship emerges from a divided identity that "bifurcates the function of the victim as founder and savior of the community from the equally necessary destruction of the victim."[5] These warring elements are united in a leader who is sacrificer and sacrifice. In successful ritual, what is forbidden is permitted under highly structured conditions. In successful ritual, confusion becomes order. Irreconcilable opposites are reconciled. Ritual reorders a reality that constantly disintegrates.

The Criminal Justice System

Girard has argued that Christianity unmasks the scapegoat mechanism, rendering it ritually ineffective,[6] while modern democratic legal systems make it unnecessary.[7] Perhaps we should understand the legal system as a potent ritual apparatus in which traditional scapegoat mechanisms are bent to the task of managing conflicts that threaten to unleash disorder. If sacrifice restores peace by restoring difference, as Girard claims, clear and definitive verdicts are ritually crucial. To say, moreover, that every man is equal under the law (that is, killing authority codified) is to define a group member as one who submits to the state's power to sacrifice group members. If this is true for all group members, anyone in the community is a potential sacrifice, meeting the Girardian condition that scapegoats must be arbitrarily chosen.[8] Nor may the outcome of successful ritual trials be predetermined. Such uncertainty has specific ritual merit and likewise underscores the arbitrary status of sacrificial victims. According to some recurring theories of victimization, the very structure of society generates crime. From the pool of criminal agents thus created, some are selected for sacrifice at different levels of visibility and severity. To the extent that both criminals and their victims appear to be arbitrarily chosen, the sacrificial mechanisms of society remain concealed. As McKenna writes:

> Any decision by the courts bearing on a single agent, a single culprit, must emerge as a frame-up, a par-ergon or pseudo-work of truth-seeking justice. The attempt to trace the origin of violence to a single culprit is destined to cover up its complex origin; it is a sacrificial gesture par excellence. It is a matter of finding a scapegoat for a more generalized culpability, a more systemic participation.[9]

With this framework in mind, consider the trial of O. J. Simpson, charged and acquitted of the 1994 murder of his wife Nicole Simpson and a friend. By focusing divisive tensions among blacks and whites, men and women, police and citizens (especially white police and black citizens), the trial became a mythic and sustained media ritual. O. J. Simpson was a beloved American hero, clean-cut in physical appearance and persona, a black man triumphant in a white world partly through making his ethnicity unproblematic for Euro-Americans. He had a rare and graceful athletic talent, had achieved upper-class affluence, played golf, was married to a beautiful Euro-American wife, and had not politically defied the white establishment. He was a spokesman for Hertz Rent A Car, reflecting back to white and black America a flattering image of white racial tolerance and black success. What made him a hero of unquestioned value also made him a marginal man by a number of definitions, especially eligible for sacrificial candidacy.

The two goats of American criminal justice are plaintiff and defendant. As events unfold, group anger may focus on either. One will become a surrogate victim exiled to the wilderness, the other a ritual scapegoat "killed," or socially excommunicated, on the spot. This killing generally means removal from society through imprisonment. It may mean physical death, though the death penalty is a troubled ritual category in U.S. society, skating uncomfortably close to the totem secret.[10] Either plaintiff or defendant may acquire a ritual or surrogate identity, or shift identities back and forth during the trial. By accommodating a variety of circumstances, such flexibility lends ritual strength but also increases the chance of failure by increasing possibilities for group confusion.

In an unsuccessful ritual, the social fates of plaintiff, defendant, and those associated with them as supporters and witnesses may be rendered dangerously ambiguous no matter which party is legally victorious. In an unsuccessful ritual, even a prevailing plaintiff or defendant may be marked as a troublemaker, someone who contributed to his or her misfortune, and so on. And though the verdict must be uncertain at the beginning of a trial, if this uncertainty is not clearly resolved by its conclusion, the ritual will fail.

In the Simpson trial, the plaintiff was the State of California, acting on behalf of the murder victims. Of the two, public interest focused almost entirely on Nicole Simpson. As her former husband's fate was weighed by a jury and a nation, negative assessments of her character and judgment vied with her role as sympathetic victim. Up to a point, this ambivalence reflected appropriate uncertainty in the search for the best scapegoat. Beyond that point was group confusion. The living representations of the dead plaintiffs were the cops on the case, accused by the defense of fraudulently scapegoating Simpson. Formal charges against authorized killing agents always threaten the totem secret. They expose internal hostilities that may exacerbate divisions and imperil group existence. Though the charge of fabricating evidence against Simpson was not proved, it produced a surprise tape recording in which a detective in the case bragged of past racist and abusive police behavior.

The tape reflected either serious ritual violations by police or a key detective's willingness to lie. Partly stemming from these ritual irregularities, Americans were bitterly divided over whether the proper scapegoat was a whitewashed black male polluted by the brutal murder of a white woman or a white cop polluted by his own racial brutality. A majority black jury, refusing to sacrifice one of their own, acquitted. Black citizens favoring the verdict characterized it as payback for white racism, despite Simpson's imperfect fit as a victim of white America. The ritual moment that resolved the defendant's sacrificial fate was nationally broadcast and rebroadcast. White accusations that the verdict was not impartial, and black claims that it was mimetically justified by centuries of persecution, prevented the country from agreeing on a scapegoat. The ritual failed.

There are two relevant questions. One asks how *ritually* suitable our conventionalized model of fair trials is. The other asks how faithfully real-life trials approximate the model they are intended to reproduce. If our model of fair trials matches the model of ideal rituals I am presenting, and if real-life trials are possible on these terms, then the most pressing *ritual* problems of the criminal justice system arise from the tensions between this model and its application to real life. Let us first see how criminal trials relate to the ritual model I have presented:

1. The sacrifice must be willing. The best ritual scapegoat confesses guilt in a demonstrably uncoerced manner. A willing victim helps the group keep the knowledge of its murderous rage from itself.

2. Victimage must be unanimous. The jury must not be divided. Public perception should match the jury's. Trials must be public and not secret so that unanimous victimage can be achieved and observed to be achieved. Ritual demands for unanimous victimage place prosecutors and police under great pressure to produce popular verdicts. Controversial verdicts (and controversial enforcement practices such as racial profiling) signify social unease about which groups ought to supply sacrificial victims and under what conditions. In Philadelphia, a controversial capital murder verdict against an articulate, attractive African American left-wing media personality, Mumia Abu-Jamal, convicted of slaying a policeman, generated sustained protest against the death penalty; a noncontroversial capital conviction against Gary Heidnik—a white loner who chained, starved, raped, and tortured black female victims for weeks, eventually feeding some to others— did not.[11] A cannibal makes a compelling scapegoat. By contrast, Americans as a group are famously uncertain whether African American males are heroes or outlaws.

3. Trials must be perceived as fair and impartial. The verdict must be genuinely uncertain at the outset, incapable of being predicted or manipulated.

4. A trial must have a definite beginning and end and be marked by clear stages and procedures. It must move at a proper pace, speedy enough to be satisfying but not so speedy as to be unfair. The tediously protracted Simpson trial was a signal failure in this respect. The typically drawn-out time frame of appeals while on death row, intended to serve justice, frustrates ritual ends.

5. So far, the attributes of ideal trials seem to match those of ideal rituals. But criminal trials are not ritually well structured along the dimension of sacrificial value *to the group*. Plaintiffs or defendants may be inestimably valuable (or not) to family and friends, but have no

special value at all in a larger social context. (O. J. Simpson was a potential sacrifice of substantial group value whose trial failed to meet other conditions of ritual success.) Ritual attempts to elevate the social value of condemned prisoners facing imminent execution with special last meals, special ritual garments for execution, and the opportunity to say final words are most satisfying when those who are condemned make public and heartfelt pleas for forgiveness. By thus demonstrating willing submission, the sacrificial scapegoat performs his ritual duty of concealing the totem secret.

Viewed from the standpoint of ritual drama, these measures are stripped-down variations on traditional sacrificial forms. Their relative restraint suggests deep-seated ambivalence about the death penalty. So does the actual implementation of the death penalty, which is shielded from public view. This is said to preserve the dignity of the condemned prisoner and his victim and to restrain the community's baser appetites. It may also, however, truncate full ritual resolution. This is not to say that fully public executions would invariably be successful rituals; any specific expression of ritual form may fail. But lack of full public participation in so important and grave an exercise of group killing dictates that execution rituals as they are now practiced in the United States cannot truly unify the community. (Critics of capital punishment may consider this a good thing. They are well advised to consider what other ritual alternatives might repair assaults on the totem secret presented by the most serious and brutal crimes. It is worth noting that the death penalty has been implemented more publicly in societies that embrace their religious commitments more comfortably and explicitly than civilly religious modern nation-states do.)

The word *deterrence* derives from the Latin root for *terror.* It means to restrain or turn aside through fright or intimidation. One observer calls it the "bedrock principle" of the criminal justice system.[12] In Girardian language, deterrence is the means for ending mimetic violence through the memorable and unambiguous assertion of superior force. The term describes both the mode of deterrence and its hoped-for transformation of perpetrators. The term *perpetrator* refers both to criminal perpetrators and the larger group of perpetrators, which is society. We are all perpetrators, either because we submit to and are complicit in the violence of the larger group, or because we exercise violence outside group authority.

Crime is violence that lacks group consent, killing without killing authority. Ritual deterrence describes collective satisfaction with the operation of killing *authority*, which reorganizes violence to restrain its use by private individuals in exchange for its deployment by the state. When deterrence is ritually efficacious, a group that perceives itself to be imperiled by crime-as-wrongful-sacrifice is appeased and unified by reparative sacrifice conducted in its name.[13]

Does deterrence transform individual wrongdoers? No doubt effects are variable. To increase ritual efficacy in *individual* cases, private rituals of restitution between defendants and plaintiffs at the conclusion of a trial have lately become a promising experiment. So long as crimes are framed by law as wrongs to the community that alone possesses the right of punishment, ceremonies of individual redress, spottily administered and with no official standing (that is, lacking group authorization), are likely to have little ritual success. Private remedies are traditionally forbidden in criminal legal doctrine because their capacity for mimetically escalating violence threatens the group. The trick is to find more visible ways to integrate reparative remedies for private parties into group rituals of killing authority.

The ritual minimization of private interest in criminal trials is strikingly different from how such interests are presented in military funerals. I have elsewhere discussed the military funeral as a ceremony that transforms the sacrificed soldier's body into the flag that signifies and contains the eternal life of the group.[14] The family of the deceased soldier is ritually obliged to accept the flag offered in a gesture of reconciliation by the community that has sent their loved one to die. By accepting the flag, the family signals to itself and the community, against which it might otherwise pursue a vendetta, its refusal of vengeance. At the same time, the family embodies the community that has killed this soldier. To accept the flag is also to accept the benefit of sacrifice on behalf of the community. The family demonstrates complicity with the community in their loved one's death and benefits from the sacrificial offering as does the community.

Why are military funerals different in this way from trials? Why do criminal justice rituals resist the reconciliation of individual and community interests that characterizes military ritual? The answer resides in the scapegoat mechanism in general and the totem secret in particular. To admit fully that the group kills its own to survive would risk the group that proper sacrifice works to preserve. By redirecting the rage of group members outward and designating the enemy as responsible for the deaths of group members, war keeps the totem secret. The rituals of criminal justice are far less able to conceal the fact that some of us make war on others of us, particularly when potential scapegoats (plaintiffs and defendants) have scant visible value to the group as a whole. Individual legal rights (the capacity to resist group sacrifice under certain conditions) are powerful for establishing willing sacrifice, but individual justice, as a good in itself of the criminal justice system, is too abstract for group purposes. Rituals will be successful only insofar as bodies and not abstract principles without visible embodiment acquire group aura and resonance. While there may be specific ways to enhance ritual efficacy in criminal trial proceedings, the case by case playing out of the legal system on *bodies in which the group has not been persuaded to have a stake* is a ritual anomaly. Successful war rituals resolve the contradiction of private and public interests. Criminal justice rituals do not, and perhaps never can.

What is the current efficacy of ritual deterrence? The current slaughter of U.S. citizens in the streets constitutes a significant sacrifice that is ritually unorganized and therefore highly disturbing to group members. By one count, there have been 750,000 deaths from guns alone since 1960.[15] In 1995, 35,957 Americans died through use of guns: 18,503 of these deaths were suicides, 15,835 were homicides, 1,225 occurred in unintentional shootings, and in 394 cases the intent was unknown. The numbers for nonfatal gun injuries treated in emergency rooms were approximately three times larger than those for deaths. Such sacrifices may be ritually unifying within a neighborhood or other social unit, and this is not unimportant. But such aggregate numbers, which compete in size with our largest war casualties, suggest a destabilizing, group-wide disturbance in need of ritual ordering. Such numbers also threaten to reveal the totem secret. The public appetite for endless media representations of brutal and sensational murders is further evidence of collective ritual unease. Where ritual executions are not played out and dramatized for the whole group, group members will devise other ways of parading blood sacrifice. These will be unsatisfying to the extent that other ritual conditions are not met.

What alternatives exist? Authoritarian systems have clearer rules for conducting regular ritual sacrifice than democracies and are better able to offer up valuable group treasure in lives and property. By definition, however, authoritarian systems lack the capacity for unanimous victimage and willing sacrifice. In different ways, killing authority in both democratic and authoritarian systems works at cross-purposes with ritual efficacy. The bottom line for ritual efficacy in shaping effective deterrence is this: as a means of temporarily discharging mutual hostilities and deflecting future violence, criminal procedures must operate with clear rules perceived to be fair and freely chosen by those who submit to them. Criminal justice rituals must not threaten the totem secret or raise suspicion that unwilling groups are sacrificed. They must find willing and worthy sacrificial victims. If the totem secret is thus preserved, the group will be able to discharge its hostilities against other members on ritual victims, and group members will be less likely to carry out their own private killing rituals.

NOTES

I wish especially to thank Eliot Lumbard, whose probing questions set in motion the concerns of this chapter. Thanks also to Peter Simonson, Jessica Fishman, and Jen Horner, whose interest and willingness to engage in conversation contributed to the development of several issues raised here. Lynn Schofield Clark was endlessly patient with too many drafts. Finally, thanks to Stewart M. Hoover, whose energy in bringing together scholars of different aspects of media, ritual, and religion has provided a focus and forum.

1. For a full discussion of the ritual dimensions of American nationalism, see Carolyn Marvin and David W. Ingle, *Blood Sacrifice and the Nation* (Cambridge: Cambridge University Press, 1999).

2. René Girard, *Violence and the Sacred,* trans. Patrick Gregory (Baltimore: Johns Hopkins University Press, 1977).

3. Emile Durkheim, *The Elementary Forms of the Religious Life,* trans. Joseph Ward Swain (1915; New York: Free Press, 1965), 154–155, 219.

4. It is with some chagrin that I here reverse the ritual and surrogate victim roles in war that I conceptualized in *Blood Sacrifice and the Nation.* The enemy is the deferred sacrifice, the surrogate. Our own soldiers, the transformed children who are our most valuable group possession, serve as ritual sacrifice. Successful sacrifice requires genuine treasure. The enemy is of no value.

5. René Girard, *Things Hidden since the Foundation of the World,* book 1, trans. Michael Metteer (Stanford: Stanford University Press, 1987), 51ff.

6. See René Girard, *The Scapegoat*, trans. Yvonne Freccero (Baltimore: Johns Hopkins University, 1986), 24–44.

7. René Girard, *Violence and the Sacred*.

8. René Girard, quoted in Andrew J. McKenna, *Violence and Difference: Girard, Derrida, and Deconstruction* (Urbana: University of Illinois Press, 1992), 63.

9. Andrew J. McKenna, *Violence and Difference*, 160.

10. For example, racial bias in populations on death row has been widely documented and publicized. Extended procedural appeals, which some see as necessary to insure justice and others as fruitlessly delaying ritual closure, render ritual outlines unsettling and indefinite. Advances in DNA analysis have exposed a level of error in past convictions that is publicly perceived as alarming. Perhaps the same DNA analysis will make it possible to designate guilty parties with greater precision and justice, which could improve the ritual efficacy of the death penalty.

11. Russell Eshleman Jr., Joseph A. Slobodzian, and Glen Justice, "Torture Killer Heidnik Executed," *Philadelphia Inquirer,* July 7, 1999, A1.

12. Eliot Lumbard, conversation with author.

13. The Simpson trial was frequently portrayed as attempted reparation for another failed sacrifice: the trial of five white Los Angeles policemen accused of wrongfully beating Rodney King, an African American. The failure of that ritual engendered widespread violence and rioting in Los Angeles by black and Latino citizens angered at the perceived ritual leniency of a majority white jury.

14. Marvin and Ingle, *Blood Sacrifice*.

15. Tom Diaz, *Making a Killing—the Business of Guns in America* (New York: Basic Books, 1999). Quoted in Bob Herbert, "America Is Ready," *New York Times,* June 27, 1999, sec. 4, 17.

BIBLIOGRAPHY

Diaz, Tom. *Making a Killing—the Business of Guns in America*. New York: Basic Books, 1999.

Durkheim, Emile. *The Elementary Forms of the Religious Life*. Trans. Joseph Ward Swain. 1915; New York: Free Press, 1965.

Eshleman, Russell, Jr., Joseph A. Slobodzian, and Glen Justice. "Torture Killer Heidnik Executed," *Philadelphia Inquirer,* July 7, 1999, A1.

Girard, René. *Violence and the Sacred*. Trans. Patrick Gregory. Baltimore: Johns Hopkins University Press, 1977.

——. *The Scapegoat*. Trans. Yvonne Freccero. Baltimore: Johns Hopkins University Press, 1986.

——. *Things Hidden since the Foundation of the World,* Book 1, trans. Michael Metteer. Stanford: Stanford University Press, 1987.

Marvin, Carolyn, and David W. Ingle. *Blood Sacrifice and the Nation.* Cambridge: Cambridge University Press, 1999.

McKenna, Andrew J. *Violence and Difference: Girard, Derrida, and Deconstruction.* Urbana: University of Illinois Press, 1992.

CHAPTER 10

RITUAL AND THE MEDIA

Ronald L. Grimes

Media scholars as well as media producers are currently showing considerable interest in both the idea of ritual and the performance of actual rites. But not long ago the terms *ritual* and *media* would have been regarded as labels for separate cultural domains—the one sacred, the other secular; the one term designating a religious activity and the other denoting tools for transferring information. Media not only intruded upon but even profaned many rites. Any attempt to posit a significant connection between ritual and media would have seemed forced since the two were segregated domains.

Today, media often validate rites. The presence of cameras announces, "This is an important event." Today, both notions, ritual and media, are understood quite differently, and the connections between them are remarked upon with growing frequency in scholarly writing. In some accounts, ritual and the media are even equated rather than segregated: the media are ritual in contemporary form. But when a metaphor (media *as* ritual) collapses into a simple identity (media *are* ritual), both terms can become useless. Either strategy—segregating or equating—oversimplifies the complex ways in which media and ritual may be related; hence, it helps to identify some of the many possibilities:[1]

1. The media presentation of a rite. *Example:* Film documentary of a ritual watched by a viewer with little or no connection to the event.
2. A ritual event extended by media. *Example:* TV coverage of a papal mass witnessed by a faithful Catholic viewer.
3. Ritual actions in virtual space. *Example:* Cyberspace weddings resulting in legal marriage.
4. Subjunctive (or "ludic") ritualizing. *Example:* Myth- or fantasy-based games played on the Internet "as if" they were rites.
5. Magical rite with media device as "fetish" (or "icon"). *Example:* Putting a hand on a TV set to receive healing power from an evangelist.
6. Ritualized behavior toward electronic objects. *Example:* The TV set as functional centerpiece of family gatherings; a computer terminal as locus of ultimate concern.
7. A media-delivered ritual object. *Example:* Presentation of a Torafax page on the World Wide Web.
8. A media document as a certificate of ritual act. *Example:* Funeral videos mailed from Toronto to Africa to attest to a death.
9. Ritual use of media device. *Example:* Amplification of Pueblo drumming during a ceremony; worship services built around CD-ROMs produced by the American Bible Society.
10. Mediated ritual fantasy. *Example:* The initiation scene in the film *Emerald Forest.*
11. Media as model for, or butt of, ritual activity. *Example:* Hollywood gestures imitated, consciously or unconsciously, in liturgical space; media-manufactured images as objects of homiletical critique.

We most readily imagine the relation between ritual and media as one in which viewers are on one side of a TV set and ritual is on the other. The rite is elsewhere, and we viewers are here. The media in the middle is doing what it is supposed to do: mediating. Prone as English-speakers are to use container metaphors, we imagine the ritual event, somehow miniaturized, as coming through the TV set, like water through a tube. The electronic device "channels" the action to us. The image on the set is not real, but the actions on the other side of the screen (and the camera) are. We "consume" the images, the virtual realities, but not the rites themselves.

If we, as viewers, are merely curious, just spectating, we take the moving images on the screen to be a kind of visual description (#1 above), a mirror, of reality. We spectate on that reality but are not really part of it. If, on the other hand, our lives are strongly implicated by the events on the other side of the tube, the events on the screen may draw us in. We "participate" in those events (#2), even though we do so at a distance. In such cases, the event is not just described but made present. The rite reaches toward and includes viewers. No longer mere viewers, we are ritualists, participants of sorts.

A different way of conceiving the situation is to imagine that the culminating ceremonial event is not on the other side of the screen and camera but in media space itself. The clearest example is that of a cyberspace wedding (#3). The bride and groom are neither physically in one another's presence nor that of a minister. Instead, all three work from spatially distant terminals. They say—or type—all the right words, in the right circumstances, with the acceptable intentions and proper qualifications. The result is a legal marriage, and the rite did not transpire behind the medium, but within it.

A variation on this mediated wedding ceremony is the sort of virtual ritualizing that happens in myth- or fantasy-inspired games played on the Internet. Like the cyberspace wedding, the ritualized game transpires electronically, but unlike it, the framing of the event is subjunctive (#4). Ritualists participate with playful or fictive intentions—sometimes advertised by the use of pseudonyms. Although the players may be utterly serious, they are also playing a game, so the seriousness is ludic, as-if. As with reading a novel or going to a play, participants in virtual ritualizing can get hurt or angry. Even the virtual or fictive can have real consequences. It is not always easy to separate #3 from #4, especially if participants themselves are unclear about their frames of mind.

Ordinarily, one supposes, middle-class viewers think of the television set as an empty, inert box. When plugged in and turned on, it has power, but that power is understandable, at least by technicians. It is not mystical; it has no will or purpose of its own. The box's power lies solely in mediating the rhetorical and psychological power of performers; their power is to persuade by argument and suggestion. But on occasion, the power mediated by the inert box accrues to the medium itself, transforming it into a ritual object, thus illustrating #5 above. Oral Roberts is praying for us—

no, *with* us—and, following his guidance (as he is following God's), we reach out and touch the set, absorbing its power. Its power is, so to speak, "borrowed" from him, and his, he assures his viewers, is from God.

A slightly different alternative involves ritualization rather than magic.[2] Whereas magical rites assume a causal connection between symbolic manipulation and empirical outcome, ritualization is a tacit form of ritual. Ritualization involves what Erving Goffman called "interaction ritual," ritual-like behavior lacking the social recognition that would earn it recognition as a formal rite.[3] When a family focuses much of its energy and interest on a television set, so much so that its solidarity is maintained and negotiated in the space governed by the screen, the family members have ritualized their behavior around this "icon" (#6). Individuals "iconify" computer screens just as readily as families "enshrine" TV screens. In both cases, the interaction is a ritual substitute, or analog. Among human interactions with media devices might be surfing the Internet as a functional equivalent of drumming rhythm; another example would be sitting in front of a video screen as a form, albeit an unusual one, of sitting meditation.

Ritual objects may be presented electronically on the Web (#7) without any attendant, media-presented actions and without rendering the medium itself iconic. In such instances, ritual actions (e.g., reading and meditating on the Torah) are supplied from the viewer's side, rather than the actor's. In examples like this, an electronic medium presents the *occasion* for ritualizing, not the rite itself.

Asked what video does, we are likely to say that it records, or documents. The documentary is a genre of both film and video, and conventionally understood documentaries are descriptive. If, however, they become suggestive and elliptical, they leap the boundaries of the genre to become art films. The standard documentary states; it declares. However, documentaries can do more; they can *certify* a ritual event (#8). I am told by a Ghanaian friend that Ashantis living in Toronto sometimes send videos of funerals back to their families in Ghana. Inheritance customs may require participation in a funeral, and watching a video can sometimes serve as a witnessing, and therefore certification, of a death.

One can think of the media as containing or mediating (that is, passing on) ritual, but the converse is also true: ritual may "contain" media and media devices. Since it is a cultural convention to think of ritual as old and traditional, and of technology as new and nontraditional, we may be surprised if technological artifacts like amplified drums appear in traditional ceremonies such as Pueblo corn dances (#9).[4] And now that stories from scriptures appear on video and in CD-ROMs, multimedia devices and images are beginning to show up in standard worship services. It may be that the world will witness not just media-assisted liturgy but media-centered liturgy.

For some purposes, the difference between mediated fantasy (#10) and virtual ritualizing (#4) is probably not significant since both are subjunctive. But there is a difference. The latter is overtly interactive—the game player acts in cyberspace—whereas the moviegoer who watches *Emerald Forest* is fundamentally a witness or consumer of initiatory fantasy, not a player in it.

It is conventional in middle-class religious institutions to be critical of the media, to make media the butt of homiletical polemics (# 11). Such polemic is regarded as prophetic critique.[5] But it is just as likely that media also supply models for liturgical leadership, liturgical space, and liturgical imagery. Sometimes the appropriation of media models is witting, sometimes not. Although the influence may be mutual—media modeling rites and rites modeling media—I suspect that in practice mutuality is rare. In religious programming it is certainly sometimes the case that TV programs are modeled after worship services, but such cases are exceptions to the general rule, which I take to be: Influence of the media on liturgy is likely to be more pervasive than liturgical influence on the media.

CURRENT LITERATURE ON RITUAL AND MEDIA

A list of possible ritual/media relations is not itself either a definition or a theory of ritual but only a reminder of the complexity of the relationship, sensitivity to which is often missing in the research and writing on ritual/media relations. In the literature, implied as well as explicit definitions of ritual are often insufficiently nuanced. In *The TV Ritual: Worship at the Video Altar,* Gregor Goethals does not distinguish between explicit rites and tacit ritualization processes.[6] Like her, I have argued that we should attend to the similarities between activities such as TV viewing and ritual, but, unlike Goethals, I find it unnecessarily confusing if we obscure the distinctions. Goethals offers no formal definition of ritual, but she associates it with order, rhythmic patterning, and play, on the one hand, and with things mystical and supernatural, on the other.[7] But it is a mistake to treat all rites as religious by definition.

Bobby Alexander's *Televangelism Reconsidered* mobilizes the theoretical vocabulary of Victor Turner and Richard Schechner, approaches with which I am in considerable sympathy, but Alexander does not carefully or systematically distinguish between ritual and drama. Consideration of ritual and drama as siblings can help us to comprehend both kinds of activity, but equating them, like equating ritual with media, only confuses matters.

Like his theoretical mentors, Alexander also makes ritual by definition a transformative act: "Defined in basic terms, ritual is a performance, planned or improvised, that makes a transition away from the everyday world to an alternative context, within which the everyday is transformed. . . . Ritual is transformative of everyday experience, especially everyday human encounters."[8] Such a view is idealized. Not all rites transform, even those that are intended to. Vincent Crapanzano has provided the most compelling argument against the ideology of transformation.[9] He studies Moroccan circumcision rites. Although the ceremonial rhetoric speaks of young boys as men, the ritual behavior, both during and after the rite, returns the boys to the domain of women. In short, we need to question the received assumptions about ritual transformation, challenge the easy equation of patterned behavior with rites, and resist too ready an identification of all ritual with religion.

Probably because of his influence in media studies, James Carey's few remarks on ritual in *Media, Myths, and Narratives* are widely cited. But his use of the notion of ritual is light-handed and undeveloped. For this reason it has little theoretical utility. Carey employs ritual only as an analogue, and phrases such as "ritual view of communication" make it unclear whether ritual is an activity in its own right or merely a point of view taken in studying something else.[10]

In Vivian Sobchack's treatment of genre film, myth is cast as content, ritual cast as form.[11] The function of the form ritual is that of disguising conflict or avoiding contradictions. Her characterization of ritual—in my view, a distillation of popular attitudes toward it—identifies it with everything that is culturally conservative and antiintellectual:

Ritual is, of course, repetitive. Its power is also cumulative, action building serially upon action, gathering emotional weight as it grows.

Ritual is symbolic and employs various simple objects to evoke complex associations. It celebrates tradition and the status quo. It is oriented toward the past, and what has been done before that ought to be done again: it is nostalgic. Ritual is simple, too, acting through patterns that are easily recognizable and often dualistic. . . . Most comforting, ritual is predictable. . . . It provides its audience with a respite from social anxiety, with a sense of belonging to a group that suffers the same conflicts and has homogenous goals.[12]

At the very least, authors who express views like this should say why they revert to an unchastened Durkheimian view of ritual, and why they reject the Turnerian claim that ritual either is, or can be, transformative.

Robert Abelman distinguishes among ritualized, instrumental, and reactionary television viewers.[13] He claims that 65 percent of the religious televiewing audience is of the ritualized sort. The portrait he paints of ritualized viewers is not complimentary. As with Sobchack's characterization, ritual is defined in a way that would likely inspire the scholars writing about it to avoid practicing it. For Abelman, ritualized viewers are habitual, likely to be church members, conservative in attitude, high consumers of television, "demographically downscale," older, poorer, less educated, blue-collar, and allured by the personality of televangelists. According to Abelman, highly ritualized viewers provide 95 percent of all financial contributions to television evangelism, and they were among those least shaken by the scandal surrounding Jim and Tammy Baker. According to Abelman, viewing does not evangelize or challenge ritualized viewers. It merely confirms the beliefs and attitudes they already hold. By contrast, instrumental viewers are more educated, less religious, and, by implication, more analytical. They seek information rather than confirmation, and the Baker scandal typically caused them to stop viewing.

Abelman's ritualized/instrumental distinction is prejudicial. Not only does the rhetoric of his discussion make it plain that he himself does not identify with the category *ritualized viewer*, it prevents his seeing the ritual dimensions of the other two types of viewers. His understanding of ritual is a tacitly "Protestant" view of it; it is not only value-laden, but also negatively valued. In this view, ritual amounts to habituated, unthinking action. Abelman feels no obligation to show that ritualized viewers display any of the qualities we normally associate with ritual. For instance, he does not show that they engage in stylized or symbolic behavior. Nor does he demonstrate that instrumental viewers do *not* engage in such behavior. He seems to assume that his readers will not question the implied definition of ritual that equates it with mindlessness.

A more provocative, less biased attempt to think about the ritual dimensions of media is found in Michael Schudson's reflections in *The Uneasy Persuasion* on advertising as capitalist realism. His discussion of ritual is not fully developed. But in viewing advertising as hyperritualization and drawing on the theories of Erving Goffman, he grasps the similarities between ritual and advertising; namely, their manipulation of ideals. He emphasizes their dependence on hypertactile surfaces, their manipulation of typifications, and their capacity to shape attitudes without having to inspire beliefs.[14]

The association between ritual and the media has begun to seem so obvious to some cultural observers that they posit an identity between the two. Quentin Schultze, for instance, declares flatly, "Television is ritual."[15] In a similar fashion, other writers declare that TV watching is ritual, negotiating cyberspace on the Internet is ritual, and attending genre films is ritual. The impulse to label media as ritualistic is sometimes motivated by a conviction that their impact affects fundamental values, therefore they are religious in function. The implication is that ritual is by definition religious. Ron Burnett, for instance, says, "This theological impulse continues to exercise great influence, but now the gatekeeper is the media. Power resides yet again in a place beyond the control of those who are proposed as its victims."[16] By *theological,* he seems to mean religious. But calling the media ritualistic when all one means is that it is religious is, I think, a mistake. Ritual is not necessarily religious. We need to distinguish the general category ritual from specific types or dimensions of it.

The equating strategy (media = ritual) has limited utility. It turns heads, it attracts attention, but the shock value is short-lived. If the two notions are not differentiated as well as connected, conversation between ritual studies and media studies is hardly worth pursuing.[17] If in the long run there is nothing more to say than "Media activity is ritual activity," each idea loses its capacity to provoke interesting perspectives on the other, because there is insufficient tension between them. "Media *as* ritual," unlike "Media *are* ritual," reminds us that the claim is metaphoric, requiring a simultaneous predication of identity and difference: media *are* ritual; media are *not* ritual. Metaphors provoke their users into noticing identity and difference simultaneously.

If media studies are to increase the level of their sophistication, the understanding of ritual must become more nuanced. For example, scholars need to ask not just whether some aspect of media *is* ritual, but *in what respect* it is ritual. Do we treat something as ritualistic because it is formulaic? Because it is repetitive? Because it is religious? In short, what definition of ritual do we imply by our claims? Further, we need to ask not just *whether* something is ritual or ritual-like, but *what kind* of ritual it is like. Is it like pilgrimage? Like celebration? Like a rite of passage? Just as there are many different kinds of media, there are different kinds of ritual, and the differences among them are important. And to ensure that we refrain from overstatement and overextension of our metaphors, we need also to ask in what respects media are not ritual.

There is a tendency, perhaps best exemplified by Quentin J. Schultze, to multiply metaphors. Television is not only "ritual," it is also "religion," "theology," "sacred text," "mythopoesis," "storytelling," "liturgy," "morality play," "soap opera," and "drama."[18] Like the equating strategy, the multiplication of metaphors soon discourages the critical thinking necessary for theory construction. However important metaphor may be to storytelling and poetry, if it takes over and consumes analytical prose, it discourages readers from taking it seriously.

DEFINING RITUAL FOR USE IN MEDIA RESEARCH

The fruitfulness of considering media's relations to ritual depends largely on the understanding of ritual that animates the discussion. Too often the word *ritual* is an empty trope, a mere analogy or weak metaphor that is then mixed or overextended. Metaphors should be chosen with care, and be developed, rather than multiplied. The word *ritual* functions too much like a badge of membership in the Current Discourse Club. It flags an author's intention of taking a broadly "cultural" approach, but it adds little or nothing to the analysis.

In media discussions, authors who make ritual a key concept rarely present clear definitions of what they mean by the word. On the few occasions when explicit definitions of ritual are used in media research, they can be as prejudicial as the older uses of *magic* were. Largely prejudicial or merely celebratory usages do nothing to enhance our understanding. Neither do conceptions that reduce ritual to one kind of ritual, liturgy, or ritualization behavior. On the one hand, ritual is used as a synonym for religion and the sacred; on the other, it is identified with anything routine, patterned, or stylized. Defined too narrowly, its relation to ordinary life is obscured. Defined too broadly, its difference from ordinary interaction is occluded.

Like rites themselves, definitions of ritual have a history. In the late nineteenth century, the idea of ritual was at the center of an *origin* question. In that era's evolutionary framework, religion was construed as primal, a cultural activity located at the beginning (metaphorically, the bottom) of the evolutionary scale. Ritual was taken to be religion's primary mode of expression: primal religion was acted, not thought. The essence of religion was ritual, not theology, myth, or ethics. In some versions of this account, ritual was *the* primal cultural phenomenon, prior even to speech. Imagined in this way, ritual was the great undifferentiated action from which other cultural activities originally emerged and from which they differentiated themselves. Art, law, economic exchange, ecology, dance, drama, storytelling, and even the building of cities were descendants of the primal parent, ritual.

Scholars of ritual studies no longer believe they can know the origins of either religion or ritual. However, there is still afoot a vague sense that the religiosity of preindustrial societies may be more deeply ritualistic than that of postindustrial societies. It is commonplace for anthropologists to maintain that rites of passage, for instance, have their proper home in small-scale, preindustrial societies.

Claims about the origin or primacy of ritual amount to scholarly myth making, a kind of abstract storytelling that can be provocative but that is in principle unverifiable. Its usefulness is in reminding us how complex rites are, how many kinds of cultural activity may flow into their planning and enactment, and how much latter-day North Americans of the new millennium long to participate in some synthesizing, whole-making activity. Such myth making also reminds us that the media are not only electronic, printed, or spoken, but also enacted. Ritual, like television, is a medium of communication, an enacted one. Without resorting to origin myths, one can still say that ritual is a multimedium, a synthesis of drama, storytelling, dance, and art. There are definitions of ritual that take this fact into explicit account. M.E. Combs-Schilling, for instance, defines ritual as "a circumscribed, out of the ordinary, multiple media event—recognized by insiders and outsiders as distinctively beyond the

mundane—in which prescribed words and actions are repeated and crucial dilemmas of humanity are evoked and brought to systematic resolution."[19]

In the early twentieth century, the ritual question became largely one
of function. No longer did scholars ask, "Where does ritual come from?"
or "Which came first, myth or ritual?" Instead, they wanted to know,
"What do rites do?" The widespread, assumed answer was, "They provide
social cohesion and personal consolation." The first, and dominant, part
of the answer was borrowed from Durkheim, the second, from Freud.
These two assumed answers to the function question remained intact until the late 1960s.

The mid-twentieth century witnessed a dramatic shift in ritual's scholarly and public image. No longer conservatively republican in its sensibilities, ritual became creative and potentially subversive. Inspired by Victor
Turner, students of ritual articulated a new, or unrecognized, function to
ritual's repertoire: that of social transformation. Turner did not deny that
ritual could engender solidarity or that it could bring about consolation,
but he insisted that these were only part of a rite's real work. The other
power of ritual was that of temporarily dissolving social hierarchies, re-
making personal identity, and engendering cultural creativity. Communitas and liminality were the great forges, the formative social processes,
utilized by ritual in exercising its transformative energies.

Presently, at the beginning of a new millennium, the ritual question is
being conceived as a boundary issue. Theorists are engaged in debating
the boundaries of ritual. Both ritual and the definition of ritual are understood to be acts of marking-off. For some, boundary maintenance is a
way of protecting a preserve; for others, it is a way of bridging, of making connections between cultural or cognitive domains. Jonathan Z.
Smith claims that ritual is "a means of performing the way things ought
to be in such a way that this ritualized perfection is recollected in the ordinary, uncontrolled, course of things."[20] Ritual, as he characterizes it, is an
idealized, controlled "space," making it different from the uncontrollable
messiness characteristic of the extraritualistic arenas of human interaction. Recollection is the bridge between the "ought to be" of ritual and
the "is" of ordinary behavior.

Meaningful ritual-and-media discussion becomes possible when the
two domains are neither equated nor segregated but rather differentiated
and conceived as sharing a common boundary. In my view, performance-

oriented theories offer the most provocative approaches to the interface of ritual and media. If performance is, as Richard Schechner describes it, the "showing of a doing" or "twice-behaved behavior,"[21] ritual and media are species of performance having much to do with one another.

The notion of performance can be almost as slippery as that of ritual. There is the ever-present equating tendency: Ritual is performance; performance is ritual. And there is a reductionist tendency, which would make ritual a function of something more primary (performance, for instance). In performance studies, a discipline located at the intersection of drama and anthropology, the tendency is to make performance a superordinate category and ritual a subordinate one. In this view, both ritual and theater are kinds of performance, the difference being that ritual aims at efficaciousness and theater at entertainment, or that ritual arises from belief and theater from play or make-believe. Such claims, of course, provoke debates, but so far the ritual/theater debate has been more sophisticated than the ritual/media discussion. This is not the place to initiate a full-blown critique and reformulation of performance-oriented theories of ritual, but I will suggest that performance theories of ritual are the most useful beginning points. The list at the beginning of this chapter was generated by asking performance-oriented questions: Who are the actors? What constitutes on-stage and off-stage? Where is the audience? What scripts dictate the performance? If nothing else, performance theories keep us from forgetting the obvious. They call attention to the surfaces upon which we humans inscribe meaning and on the basis of which we act.

NOTES

1. A similar list, based on literature rather than media, is in my *Reading, Writing, Ritualizing* (Washington, D.C.: Pastoral Press, 1993).

2. The distinctions among rite, ritualization, and magic are worked out in my *Ritual Criticism: Case Studies in Its Practice, Essays on Its Theory* (Columbia: University of South Carolina Press, 1990), 9, and *Beginnings in Ritual Studies*, 2nd ed. (Columbia: University of South Carolina Press, 1995), chap. 3. See also Ronald L. Grimes, ed., *Readings in Ritual Studies* (Upper Saddle River, N.J.: Prentice-Hall, 1996).

3. Erving Goffman, *Interaction Ritual* (Garden City, N.Y.: Doubleday, 1967).

4. Pueblos themselves do not think of these as "corn" dances; the designation is an "Anglo" one.

5. *Prophetic* here obviously does not mean predictive, but socially critical.

6. Gregor Goethals, *The TV Ritual: Worship at the Video Altar* (Boston: Beacon Press, 1981). In *Birth as an American Rite of Passage* (Berkeley: University of California Press, 1992). Robbie E. Davis-Floyd assumes the same strategy. I develop a critique of this position in Ronald L. Grimes, *Deeply into the Bone: Re-Inventing Rites of Passage* (Berkeley: University of California Press, 2000).

7. Peck's discussion of ritual and television depends on Goethals for her understanding of ritual: Janice Peck, *The Gods of Televangelism* (Cresskill, N.J.: Hampton, 1993).

8. Bobbie Alexander, *Televangelism Reconsidered: Ritual in the Search for Human Community* (Atlanta, Ga.: Scholars Press, 1994), 4; Victor Turner, *The Forest of Symbols* (Ithaca, N.Y.: Cornell University Press, 1967); Victor Turner, *The Ritual Process* (Chicago: Aldine, 1969); Richard Schechner, *Essays in Performance Theory, 1970–1976* (New York: Drama Book Specialists, 1977); Richard Schechner, *Between Theater and Anthropology* (Philadelphia: University of Pennsylvania Press, 1985).

9. Vincent Crapanzano, "Rite of Return: Circumcision in Morocco," in *The Psychoanalytic Study of Society,* ed. Werner Muensterberger (New Haven: Yale University Press, 1980), 9: 15–36.

10. James Carey, ed., *Media, Myths, and Narratives: Television and the Press* (Newbury Park, Calif.: Sage, 1989). See also James W. Carey, "A Cultural Approach to Communication," in *Communication as Culture: Essays on Media and Society,* ed. James W. Carey (Boston: Unwin Hyman, 1989).

11. Vivian Sobchack, "Genre Film: Myth, Ritual, and Sociodrama," in *Film/ Culture: Explorations of Cinema in Its Social Context,* ed. Sari Thomas (Metuchen, N.J.: Scarecrow, 1982). Sobchack's understanding of ritual is borrowed from Roger Grainger, *The Language of the Rite* (London: Dartan, Longman, & Todd, 1974).

12. Sobchack, "Genre Film," 163.

13. Robert Abelman, "Who's Watching, for What Reasons?" in *Religious Television: Controversies and Conclusions,* ed. Robert Abelman and Stewart M. Hoover (Norwood, N.J.: Ablex, 1990). Abelman borrows the distinction between ritualized and instrumental viewing from A. M. Rubin, "Ritualized and Instrumental Television Viewing," *Journal of Communication* 34, no. 3 (1984): 67–77.

14. Michael Schudson, *Advertising, the Uneasy Persuasion: Its Dubious Impact on American Society* (New York: Basic, 1984), 209–33, esp. 214, 228. See also Goffman, *Interaction Ritual.*

15. Quentin J. Schultze, "Television Dramas as Sacred Text," in *Channels of Belief: Religion and American Commercial Television,* ed. John P. Ferre (Ames: Iowa State University Press, 1990), 3–27, esp. 20.

16. Ron Burnett, *Cultures of Vision: Images, Media, and the Imaginary* (Blooming-

ton: Indiana University Press, 1995). I use the term *liturgy* when speaking of specifically religious ritual (Grimes, *Beginnings in Ritual Studies*, 51ff.).

17. Fortes warns, "It is a short step from the notion of ritual as communication to the non-existence of ritual *per se*": Myers Fortes, "Religious Premises and Logical Technique in Divinatory Ritual,"*Philosophical Transactions of the Royal Society of London* 251 (1966): 409–22.

18. Schultze, "Television Dramas;" Quentin J. Schultze, "The Lure of Drama," in *Televangelism and American Culture: The Business of Popular Religion*, ed. Quentin J. Schultze (Grand Rapids, Mich.: Baker Book House, 1991), 97–124. Stewart M. Hoover's strategy is more strained. For him, television is "armchair pilgrimage, " see "Television, Myth, and Ritual," in *Media, Myths, and Narratives: Television and the Press*, ed. James W. Carey, (Newbury Park, Calif.: Sage, 1988), 171.

19. M. E. Combs-Schilling, *Sacred Performances: Islam, Sexuality, and Sacrifice* (New York: Columbia University Press, 1989), 29. Another definition similar in its emphasis on the multimedia nature of ritual is offered by Kapferer: it is, he says, "a multimodal symbolic form, the practice of which is marked off (usually spatially and temporally) from, or within, the routine of everyday life, and which has specified, in advance of its enactment, a particular sequential ordering of acts, utterances and events, which are essential to the recognition of the ritual by cultural members as being representative of a specific cultural type": Bruce Kapferer, *A Celebration of Demons: Exorcisms and the Aesthetics of Healing in Sri Lanka* (Bloomington: Indiana University Press, 1983), 2.

20. Jonathan Z. Smith, *Imagining Religion* (Chicago: University of Chicago Press, 1982), 63. A critique of Smith's theory can be found in Ronald L. Grimes, "Jonathan Z. Smith's Theory of Ritual Space," *Religion* 29 (1999): 261–73.

21. Schechner, *Between Theater and Anthropology*.

BIBLIOGRAPHY

Abelman, Robert. "Who's Watching, for What Reasons?" In *Religious Television: Controversies and Conclusions*, ed. Robert Abelman and Stewart M. Hoover. Norwood, N.J.: Ablex, 1990.

Alexander, Bobbie. *Televangelism Reconsidered: Ritual in the Search for Human Community*. Atlanta, Ga.: Scholars Press, 1994.

Burnett, Ron. *Cultures of Vision: Images, Media, and the Imaginary*. Bloomington: Indiana University Press, 1995.

Carey, James W. "A Cultural Approach to Communication." In *Communication as Culture: Essays on Media and Society*, ed. James W. Carey. Boston: Unwin Hyman, 1989.

Carey, James W., ed. *Media, Myths, and Narratives: Television and the Press.* Newbury Park, Calif.: Sage, 1989.

Combs-Schilling, M. E. *Sacred Performances: Islam, Sexuality, and Sacrifice.* New York: Columbia University Press, 1989.

Crapanzano, Vincent. "Rite of Return: Circumcision in Morocco." In *The Psychoanalytic Study of Society,* ed. Werner Muensterberger. New Haven: Yale University Press, 1980.

Davis-Floyd, Robbie E. *Birth as an American Rite of Passage.* Berkeley: University of California Press, 1992.

Fortes, Myers. "Religious Premises and Logical Technique in Divinatory Ritual." *Philosophical Transactions of the Royal Society of London* 251 (1966): 409–22.

Goethals, Gregor. *The TV Ritual: Worship at the Video Altar.* Boston: Beacon Press, 1981.

Goffman, Erving. *Interaction Ritual.* Garden City, N.Y.: Doubleday, 1967.

Grainger, Roger. *The Language of the Rite.* London: Dartan, Longman, & Todd, 1974.

Grimes, Ronald L. *Ritual Criticism: Case Studies in Its Practice, Essays on Its Theory.* Columbia: University of South Carolina Press, 1990.

——. *Reading, Writing, Ritualizing.* Washington, D.C.: Pastoral Press, 1993.

——. *Beginnings in Ritual Studies,* 2nd ed. Columbia: University of South Carolina Press, 1995.

——. "Jonathan Z. Smith's Theory of Ritual Space." *Religion* 29 (1999): 261–73.

——. *Deeply into the Bone: Re-Inventing Rites of Passage.* Berkeley: University of California Press, 2000.

Grimes, Ronald L., ed. *Readings in Ritual Studies.* Upper Saddle River, N.J.: Prentice-Hall, 1996.

Hoover, Stewart M. "Television, Myth, and Ritual." In *Media, Myths, and Narratives: Television and the Press,* ed. James W. Carey. Newbury Park, Calif.: Sage, 1988.

Kapferer, Bruce. *A Celebration of Demons: Exorcisms and the Aesthetics of Healing in Sri Lanka.* Bloomington: Indiana University Press, 1983.

Peck, Janice. *The Gods of Televangelism.* Cresskill, N.J.: Hampton, 1993.

Rubin, A. M. "Ritualized and Instrumental Television Viewing." *Journal of Communication* 34, no. 3 (1984): 67–77.

Schechner, Richard. *Essays in Performance Theory, 1970–1976.* New York: Drama Book Specialists, 1977.

——. *Between Theater and Anthropology.* Philadelphia: University of Pennsylvania Press, 1985.

Schudson, Michael. *Advertising, the Uneasy Persuasion: Its Dubious Impact on American Society.* New York: Basic, 1984.

Schultze, Quentin J. "Television Dramas as Sacred Text." In *Channels of Belief: Religion and American Commercial Television,* ed. John P. Ferre. Ames: Iowa State University Press, 1990.

——. "The Lure of Drama." In *Televangelism and American Culture: The Business of Popular Religion,* ed. Quentin J. Schultze. Grand Rapids, Mich.: Baker Book House, 1991.

Smith, Jonathan Z. *Imagining Religion.* Chicago: University of Chicago Press, 1982.

Sobchack, Vivian. "Genre Film: Myth, Ritual, and Sociodrama." In *Film/Culture: Explorations of Cinema in Its Social Context,* ed. Sari Thomas. Metuchen, N.J.: Scarecrow, 1982.

Turner, Victor. *The Forest of Symbols.* Ithaca, N.Y.: Cornell University Press, 1967.

——. *The Ritual Process.* Chicago: Aldine, 1969.

EXPLICIT AND PUBLIC EXPRESSION IN NEW MEDIA CONTEXTS

The essential meanings we hoped for in part 4 are easier to see in the work that follows. The chapters of part 5 have a common concern with marginal, as opposed to mainstream, forms. They describe situations where the marginal is also "popular," in the sense that these expressions attract the attention of practitioners who reject the legitimating power of dominant, mainstream religions and who do so in novel and inventive ways. In each of these accounts, we also see how arguments, meanings, rituals, and symbols are made and reformulated for new media contexts.

In chapter 11, Bruce Lawrence addresses a faith tradition of rising importance in the West: Islam, and the emergent presence of Islam on the Internet. As is the case with other "alternative" or "new" religions (as they tend to be seen in the context of the developed West) Muslims—that is, *some* Muslims—have begun to find a place on-line. Lawrence's purpose is not to provide a formal or systematic analysis, but to describe evolving practices and expressions of grounded religious sensibility. These uses, we learn, are not Islam in any formal or essential sense, but are the result of a negotiation between Islam and the broader cultural context within which the religion finds itself. More precisely, these negotiations represent the capture of this new technology by some Muslim contemporaries, and in this sense we have a "popular" expression.

Jan Fernback, in chapter 12, explores the extent to which the emergence of the Internet and the so-called Internet community provides the capacity for authentic rituals of resistance and difference. Fernback investigates the practices of neopagans who migrate to the Internet in order to craft ways of being and belonging that are refused them "in real life." The chapter does not claim more for neopaganism than what it can be seen to be—a religious movement with contemporary currency; however, that the movement sees openness in this new context does raise questions about both the capacities of the movement and of the technology.

In chapter 13, David Nash traces the constructive and reconstructive actions of contemporary practitioners of Internet religion, and sees historical parallels in them. This raises an issue seen in earlier chapters—that there may be something inherent in the capacities of mediated religious contexts that makes them prone to antiinstitutional, popular, marginal discourses. What Nash perceives in the Internet can also be seen in earlier religious and media eras: the new medium can be a ready context for the working out of new, alternative, and organically diverse ways of seeing the project of religion.

These chapters raise an intriguing possibility. It may be that, in the media age, capacities for religious meaning are more present in forms that are specific and particular—that are, in a way, local. The salience of Islam, paganism, and freethought cultures on the net may be more related to their particularity and their ways of finding particular audiences of affinity than to their presence, through the net, in the broader culture.

CHAPTER II

ALLAH ON-LINE:
THE PRACTICE OF GLOBAL ISLAM
IN THE INFORMATION AGE

Bruce B. Lawrence

What is authority in Islam? It is scriptural, since it upholds the Holy
Qur'an as divine revelation. It is charismatic, since it invokes hadith,
which depicts the exemplary life and words of the prophet Muhammad. It
is also juridical, since it relies on a practical code, the shari'a, and also on
the custodians of shari'a, the ulama, who are seen to be faithful guides to
Muslim norms and values.

All three nodes—the scriptural, the charismatic, and the juridical—
project a specifically Islamic authority, and all three have ample narratives.
Yet they are also contested narratives. The Qur'an stands as the linchpin
of Muslim belief and practice. It affirms the one God of creation and
judgment, both in this world and the next world. Yet who interprets the
Qur'an, and what makes one interpretation more valid than another?

Muslims differ among themselves in their answers to these questions.
Similarly, Muhammad is uncontestable as a source of authority: he stands
next to the Qur'an as the source of all legitimacy from a Muslim perspective. It was, after all, this seventh-century, middle-aged Arab merchant
who was chosen by God to be the perfect medium. Muhammad ibn Ab-
dullah was the final prophet for God's complete revelation, the Holy
Qur'an. Muhammad is affirmed as the human signifier of the most basic
Muslim creed: There is no god but God, and Muhammad is the apostle of
God. Yet Muslims disagree about the profile of Muhammad. After all,

how can anyone know, several centuries removed, what was the shape and the intention of his life as God's emissary to the Arabs, and, beyond them, to all humankind?

Finally, beyond scriptural authority and prophetic authority, we have juridical authority. We are faced with the custodians of the shari'a, the ulama. It was not until the end of the ninth century, more than two hundred years after the introduction of Islam into Arabia, that schools of law, both Sunni and Shi'i, became fully elaborated. They were given institutional force within Muslim polities, and hence preserve the double authority of both the Qur'an and Muhammad; yet the ulama continue to differ among themselves about the precise nature of that twin authority.

In other words, to say that there is authority in Islam, and to specify that authority as threefold—scriptural, charismatic, and juridical—does not end the question of what counts as true Islam or who are the real Muslims. Rather, the question itself has to be pushed to another level of inquiry, at once more speculative and more precise.

The benefits of Islam—its clear revelation, its exemplary messenger, its juridical custodians—are also its deficit, at least for some. It has no final, rubber-stamp authority. There is no papal equivalent. Islam lacks a single canonical authority or a fixed story that holds together all the elements of a religion such as Christianity and imparts to them legitimacy. Without a pope or a papal narrative, Islam also does not have a Luther or a counternarrative that defines a movement such as the Reformation, or makes possible the proliferation of alternate groups, claiming authority other than that of the pope and the Church of Rome.

So dominant is the Christian frame for telling a religious narrative that one must be cautious about telling the Muslim story as if it were "just another religion." How can we tell the Muslim story in order to foreground what is distinctive about the practices of Islam in contemporary culture?

The usual way of telling the Muslim story is to frame Islam as a religion that is also a polity. The most politically powerful are also deemed to be the custodians of orthodoxy, but power is shared, at least from the mid-eighth century on, so that over the last thousand years and more we do not find a single or orthodox Islam, but multiple Islams, all of which are shaped by the political, or dynastic, history of the premodern Muslim world. There is much of value to this approach, coupling religion and politics as two parts of a seamless whole called Islam, and in its most sophisticated version it offers to students of world history an understanding of Islam as a civilization that stands over against the triumphalist notions of the West as the Best or the East as the Least.[1]

There is another way of telling the Muslim story, however. One does not have to privilege religious/political or church/state categories as the key dyads or sets of key double terms that define Islamic authority. Instead of talking about Muslim deficits, one can simply highlight the Islamic difference. That difference is, above all, etched in diversity: one can tell, and retell, the Muslim story and explore Islamic authority by looking at diversity. There is diversity not only within Islam but also beyond Islam—diversity not only between the dominant Sunni and the minority Shi'i branches, but also between both of them and a third, yet smaller, group called the Khariji;[2] and at the same time there is diversity between Muslim norms and values and other civilizational forces that share with Islam the stage of world history.[3]

In this chapter I opt for the second way of telling the Muslim story, and stress external rather than internal elements of Islam-specific diversity. Such an approach allows one to think of the multiple experiences of Muslim individuals and groups within the emergent time frame now called the information age. This is an age defined by media—print (newspapers), auditory (radio and telephone), auditory-visual (television and movies), and print-auditory-visual-tactile (the Web). There could be no World Wide Web without antecedent technological breakthroughs, but the Web represents the culmination of a process the further consequences of which no one yet knows, except perhaps Manuel Castells.

Manuel Castells is the Berkeley-based metasociologist who has argued that the network society will become the dominant edge of global exchange during the next two decades. Although many chapters in this volume address the role of media in defining, or redefining, religion and culture, we might briefly look at Castells's prediction: the period from 1980 to 2020 will become the first discrete phase of the information age augured by the Information Technology Revolution (ITR). In Castells's view, the ITR will be the biggest revolution experienced by humankind since the invention of the Greek alphabet in 700 B.C.E., and even in its initial phase it will begin to affect all cultures and all religions as well as the societies, economies, and polities of the current global order.[4]

What will be the consequence of the ITR for Islam in this forty-year period? This question will occupy me for the remainder of the chapter. I accept Castells's grand vision, but I believe it has to be qualified on three points. First, the boundaries of religious knowledge are not so easily or so swiftly changed. Second, as Peter Mandaville has noted, "the encounter between Islam and the transnational technologies of communication will be as multifaceted as the religion itself."[5] And third, information technologies, like religious traditions, remain inherently conservative: as Saskia Sassen has argued, they tend to reinforce global structures and asymmetries rather than bode a new era for civil society and transformative justice.[6]

THE BOUNDARIES OF DIGITAL ISLAM

One of the most fertile and recurrent metaphors from the Muslim imaginary is the Straight Path. It is first introduced in the opening chapter of the Qur'an, and all Muslims, every day and every time they engage in canonical prayer or salat, ask of Allah: "Guide us on the Straight Path." The Straight Path, and only the Straight Path, leads to Peace, to Truth, to Certainty, in this world and the next.

In looking at Islam in cyberspace or digital Islam, we should not be surprised to find this image occurring there, too, as a central element. As the on-line world of computer networks transforms more and more believers into cyber-Muslims, it is increasingly important to define what is and what is not acceptable as Muslim discourse. The bedrock criterion remains the Straight Path, and what deviates from, blocks, or undermines that path and its goal. Thus, the boundaries of digital Islam are defined by the scriptural, creedal, and historical boundaries of Islamic thinking before the information age. There is no Islam without limits or without guideposts. One cannot have a Straight Path without knowing what is beyond or outside or against the Straight Path. Cyberspace, like social space, to be effectively Muslim, must be monitored.

Yet the very testing of authority that the Internet provokes makes the boundaries of digital Islam more porous and more subject to change than those of its predecessors. There are still the same guideposts: the scripture (the Qur'an), the person (the Prophet) and the law (shari'a, and with it, the custodians of Muslim standards, the ulama), but each—the book, the prophet, the moral custodian—has to be defined or redefined in cyberspace. And since not all Muslims have equal power or equal access to the

Web, there is already a preselection, a filtering, of Muslim perspectives on the Net.

Nevertheless, even the most novice surfer will find staggering diversity, a diversity within Islam, in cyberspace, and if we are to understand the practice of global Islam in the information age we must account for Muslim internal diversity. The first stage of diversity is the global distribution of Muslims themselves. Muslims total between one-quarter and one third of the world's population. There are more Asian Muslims than African, and more African Muslims than Arab. South Asia and South-east Asia are the most populous regions in the Muslim world. South Asia—Pakistan, India, and Bangladesh, which until 1947 formed a single administrative unit under British rule—today is home to more than 300 million Muslim inhabitants. To the east, Indonesia, with more than thirteen thousand islands and a population exceeding 170 million, is, and will remain for some time, the largest Muslim country in the world: 150 million Indonesians profess faith in Allah and his prophet Muhammad.

The second stage of diversity comes from the relocation of many Asian Muslims, and some African, to Europe and North America. A major comparative study by the French political sociologist Gilles Kepel looks at common characteristics of Muslim immigrant communities in France and the United Kingdom, then compares them with the African American Muslim community in the United States.[7] In the United States there is, however, in addition to the African Americans, also an immigrant Asian, largely South Asian, Muslim community,[8] and it, like its counterparts in Europe, is increasingly represented on the Net. Which brings us to a large question: Who shapes whom? Does the homeland have a greater impact on immigrants abroad than immigrants have on expectations and circuits of power within the homeland? The question has not been answered, but however it will be answered in the future, the new media—the World Wide Web in particular—will be part of the answer.

It is too easy to assume that the expansive technology of the Web makes it as democratic in access as it is global in scope. Only certain groups of Asian—or Arab or Iranian—Muslims get their views projected on Web pages in cyberspace. While no catalog can be exhaustive, we will look at three different players in digital Islam. They roughly correspond to the three complementary vectors of contemporary religion identified by Stewart Hoover and Shalini Venturelli in their path-breaking article on religion and the contemporary media.[9] One vector is institutional, and it revolves around independent cultural associations and their portrayal of Muslim norms and practices. Another is public, and it relates to polities, major Muslim governments who project their view of Islam. A third is private, and it derives from individuals who have neither the institutional nor political clout of the other two vectors but are also committed to projecting Islam on the Net.

INDEPENDENT CULTURAL ASSOCIATIONS

It is not easy to thread one's way through all the groups who claim to speak on behalf of all Muslims. There is a huge overlap. The following sites stand out, although others that compete with them also project a strong Muslim presence on the Web.

IslamiCity in Cyberspace

www.islam.org   www.islamic.org   www.islamicity.org

Yes, this one megasite for links to other Islamic resources on the Net has itself garnered three domain names, so the chances are that wherever Net surfers go in a keyword search they will come to this omnibus site. In keeping with its "city" metaphor, this site will take the Web user to the virtual mosque on Mecca Street, where there are links to the Qur'an, to hadith, to Islamic history, and much, much more. The Web user can also go to the virtual market for links to Islamic commercial groups on the Web or visit the CyberPort to travel to other Web links. For surfers with an issue in mind there is also a chat platform, and for those who want to hear Islamic sounds, there is Radio Al-Islam; the audio files there rank with the best on the Net.

With 57 million hits by 1998, a year or so after starting operation, this would seem to be the Mother of all Muslim Web sites, and a user might assume that it represents all Muslims. But in fact, IslamiCity in Cyberspace is itself an offshoot of HADI—Human Assistance and Development International. In Arabic, the acronymn HADI conveniently spells out the word for guide, or leader; it also relates to the phrase from the Qur'an cited above: "Guide us on the Straight Path." In this case, although HADI is based in Culver City, California, the straight path guides the Muslim cybernaut toward norms and values that reflect its overseas Saudi sponsorship.

Muslim Student Association (MSA) at University of Michigan

www.ais.org/~islam/

There are many individual home pages for Muslim student associations at universities throughout North America and West Europe. They can be visited through any search engine, but Net users will not find many as complete as this one at the University of Michigan, Ann Arbor. The Islamic interlink for the University of Michigan Computer Club, it has links to an array of other Muslim Web sites.

Again, however, this is not merely a student initiative—one without external assistance or attention. The MSA national leadership and many local MSA chapters relate to the Islamic Society of North America (ISNA), funded by Saudi sources. One of the major links for ISNA is IslamiCity. It can be found at www.isna.net.

International Institute of Islamic Thought

www.iiit.org/introduction.htm

Like IslamiCity and MSA Web sites, this site appears to have independent institutional status in the public sphere. But this think tank based in Herndon, Virginia, has global links to England, Morocco, Egypt, India, Bangladesh, and Malaysia, where it has sister institutes. The collective goal is to project a multidimensional intellectual and cultural approach to issues underlying the plight of the contemporary Muslim world. Above all, IIIT wants to *Islamize knowledge*—a technical phrase that means to integrate all contemporary sciences, from biology to economics, within the framework of revealed knowledge; in this case, stated more specifically, it means the knowledge revealed by Allah through Muhammad in the Qur'an. Not every Muslim would agree with the soundness of this approach, but it does have substantial backing, and most of it comes from the Arabian Peninsula, particularly Saudi Arabia.

GOVERNMENTS

It will by now be evident that the Muslim world is no longer an empty quarter when it comes to projecting an Islamic presence in cyberspace. Many Muslim countries, from Malaysia to Saudi Arabia, a kingdom, and Iran, an Islamic republic, are fully wired. Saudi Arabia leads the charge, not only to project a Muslim presence on the Net but also to have its version of Islamic norms and values dominant in cyberspace. However, other countries are not so wired, and in some of them there is careful monitoring of what kinds of Internet access is provided to individuals.

Saudi Arabia

www.arab.net/saudi/saudi_contents.html

A click on this site reveals how one of the most important players in the Arab Muslim world understates its role on the Net. While all of the above institutions are strongly linked to a Saudi perspective, the actual governmental view of the ruling elites in Riyadh is downplayed. For example, let us say that one has a special interest in religion. You click the culture button on the left side of the home page. That takes you to the official Saudi view of the Islamic faith, for which its ruler is the custodian of the holiest sites, Mecca and Medina, the major cities for the faithful to visit on *hajj,* or the pilgrimage.

Egypt

www.arab.net/egypt/egypt_contents.html

Suppose that Egypt is one's favorite Arab Muslim country: the Net user who clicks on this site is given a bird's eye view of the history of Egypt, ancient, medieval, and modern. The site also has a button for religion—conveniently located in the same spot, on the left, as the button for religion at the Saudi Arabia site.

Iran

www.al-Islam.org

Travelers on the information superhighway may be disheartened to discover that no one domain maps all of Islamic diversity. Despite the visual
and manual wizardry of Islamicity.org, it does not eliminate a major
countervailing force: Shi'i Islam. The Shi'i are a minority of Muslims—
little more than 10 percent. The real difference between Sunnis (who
comprise almost 90 percent of Muslims) and the Shi'i goes back to
seventh-century Arabia—to the origins of Islam as a religious polity. After
Muhammad's death, those who became Sunni Muslims accepted the succession that passed through his close followers (first Abu Bakr, then Umar,
then Uthman), not through his blood relatives. For those who later became Shi'i Muslims, the succession should have been limited to close
blood relatives. Muhammad had no son who lived to maturity, which
meant that his first cousin Ali (who happened also to be his son-in-law)
should, under such a system, have been his first successor. Ali did become
a successor to Muhammad for Sunnis, but only after Uthman. For Shi'i
Muslims, Ali is first, not third, and Ali's descendants (beginning with his
two sons Hasan and Husain, but especially Husain) became very important figures for Shi'i Muslims. They were called imams, were thought to
be spiritually perfect, and had ritual as well as legal authority for the Shi'i.

Digital Islam gives space to both Shi'i and Sunni interpretations of Islamic authority. At www.al-Islam.org is the most sophisticated Shi'i view
of the world. It is sponsored by a group with close links to the Iranian
worldview, if not to the Iranian government. It includes a button on the
Infallibles, another name for the imams venerated in Shi'ism but unac-
knowledged by the Sunni.

Malaysia

www.iiu.edu.my

It would have been difficult to guess, five years ago, that tiny Malaysia, located in South-east Asia, with a mere 20 million population, would be one
of the brightest cybersites for digital Islam. The site www.iiu.edu.my
takes one to the home page for the International Islamic University (IIU),
Malaysia (it is not, strictly speaking, a government site, but the university
has ties to government). For many, it is the best university site in the entire Muslim world. It includes a beautifully simple but evocative home
page, offering an array of Islamic resources as well as literature on differ-

ent departments and faculty within the IIU. It tries to do what the Saudi-funded International Institute of Islamic Thought holds out as its goal: to integrate revealed knowledge with the social sciences in a thoroughly modern university setting, but it is much more low key and eclectic in its approach. A click on its links page brings up hyperlinks to all the major Muslim topics, including a Muslim sisters' page.

PRIVATE INDIVIDUALS AND SMALLER GROUPS

Beyond cultural associations, governments, and universities with government ties there are many sites run by Muslim individuals and smaller groups. These sites, although for Muslims, also have keen interest in projecting Muslim norms and values in cyberspace. They include the voices of Muslim women, the views of Sufi groups, and the aspirations of minorities looking for a niche in digital Islam.

Muslim Women

There are tens of hundreds and perhaps thousands of pages by and about Muslim women in cyberspace. I offer a sampling of those found to be outstanding:

Islam: the Eternal Path to Jannah

www.jannah.org

One of the best sites comes from a cybersavvy Muslim software engineer, Huma Ahmad. Not a single-issue site, it is, rather, a kind of megasite, or subject directory on Muslim women. A user surfing through the nine buttons on the index of the home page finds, first in the list, a button for Sisters. A click then brings up everything from general articles about Muslim women to tips on getting married to advice about dress codes. It is all done with a tongue-in-cheek sense of humor that tempers the seriousness of the enterprise. Equally extensive and impressive is the second button, labeled Mama's List (sometimes referred to on other sites as Huma's

Mama's List). The site is even better than the rhymes that invite you to try it. It has buttons arrayed alphabetically by title; click to find the resources for looking into data about Muslim women on the Web. Under the letter *W*, for instance, are more than a dozen articles or alternative sites with information on Muslim women.

Iman al-Mu'minah's Home page

www.geocities.com/Wellesley/3565/

Billed as an e-zine for sisters following the path of Islam, this Muslim woman's home page is attractively laid out, with a beautiful background tapestry and color-coded topics that range from the familiar Qur'an and hadith to the less-expected Adaab and Sisterhood.

Like www.jannah.org, this site projects a sense of Muslim women's empowerment to be who they want to be within the boundaries of acceptable but also flexible Islamic norms. It also takes on FAQs (Frequently Asked Questions) and answers them with consistent humor and scriptural authority.

Ummawalid's Home page

www.geocities.com/Heartland/Meadows/5621/[10]

This page is much more schematic and predictably laid out than the preceding two. It does, however, have a wealth of information, with cross-links to various sites, including ones with practical items on women's clothes and two that refute the legitimacy of the Nation of Islam as a representative Muslim organization.

Sufi Surfing

The organized brotherhoods, also known as Sufi societies, are one of the major Muslim groups that have been subjected to misunderstanding. For many devout Muslims, they are an integral part of the Muslim outlook and way of life. Their aesthetic and mystical pursuits have also attracted non-Muslims who do not otherwise identify with or pursue the goals of mainstream Muslims. A subject of controversy, they are for that reason as well as the "Netaphysical" cyber wisdom of many practitioners, they are well represented on the Web. For lack of space, I list only three of the many outstanding Sufi Web sites:

Islamic Sufi Orders on the World Wide Web

homepages.haqq.com.au/salam/sufilinks/

There is no more complete index to all the Sufi orders and their current representation in cyberspace than this site. Maintained by Faridudien Rice, it offers a classic example of how to communicate religious views on the Web. A survey of its links would suffice for an introduction to both the historical background and modern-day legacy of institutional Sufism.

Alan Godlas's Home Page—Sufi Links

www.arches.uga.edu/~godlas/Sufism.html

A personal home page, this one is subject to the usual limitations on permanence and updating; its creator, however, is a university professor with deep commitment to Sufism and also experience as a Webmaster. The site is constantly invoked as one of the best places to review the vast literature of Sufism and to find links to other Sufi sites.

Hazrat Inayat Khan

www.cheraglibrary.org/library.htm

This home page was created by Hamid Cecil Touchon, a cherag, or ordained minister, based in Cuernavaca, Mexico. Touchon is in the Chishti-derived tradition of Hazrat Inayat Khan, a North Indian Sufi master of the early twentieth century. It offers a broad appeal to many spiritual paths, all under the canopy of a universal perspective of Sufism.

Other Minority Groups

Nearly all the groups cited above are cybersavvy because they represent socioeconomic elites who have the education, residence, and professional status to pursue topics of interest on the Net. They happen to be Muslim, but they share other characteristics of class, outlook, and opportunity with non-Muslims. The minority groups cited next do not have the same traits or options in their worldview (it is difficult to describe the first generation of Muslim cybernauts without replicating the asymmetries characteristic of the world order in general). Some are very wealthy, but they are not privileged to be linked with dominant Muslim groups.

Agha Khanis

www.ismaili.net

This site explores one of the most dynamic and socially active Islamic groups in the world. Advertised as the First Ismaili Electronic Library Database (FIELD), it is a boon to Muslims and non-Muslims alike. Its drawback is a limited array of information about Ismaili lay activities, and no links to other non-Ismaili groups.

Ahmadis

www.ahmadiyya.org

The scourge of Orthodox Sunni Muslims, the Ahmadis have long suffered isolation, and worse, for their view of a nineteenth-century North Indian reformer as a prophet to modern-day Muslims. Muhammad being held to be the *last* prophet, the suggestion of a latter-day supplement or successor has not been well received. The site gives some suggestion as to the beleaguered outlook of Ahmadis, a.k.a. Qadyanis, after their place of origin in North India.

Queer Jihad

www.geocities.com/queerjihad

The subtitle to this group's Web site says it all: The queer Muslim struggle for acceptance. It has had 91,000 visitors since 1997.

REDEFINING THE DOMINANT BY THE MARGINAL

The above catalog of sites has been split into three main categories. Neither of the first two, independent cultural associations and governments, are marginal; they represent the dominant vectors of power in the global Muslim community—social, economic, political, and now digital. Only the third category, private individuals and small groups, opens up a space for some marginal actors. But there are still others we must consider—minorities that are seen not to walk the Straight Path however broad and fluid that path may be. These are the polemicists standing outside the fold of Islam for whom the Straight Path is the path to hell, not heaven—the promulgators of a Protestant Christian evangelical assault on Islam. Several Web sites witness to this assault's now occurring through cyberspace. Two are listed here.

Welcome to the-Good-Way.Com

www.the-good-way.com

This looks like a Muslim site but it is actually a Christian evangelical group trying to convert Muslims to Protestant Christianity.

Answering Islam

answering-islam.org.uk

Based in England, this site gets a lot of global attention through the Net. An evangelical group, it attempts to show contradictions in the Muslim worldview in order to convert Muslims to the "true" faith.
There is now a Muslim site with a counterpolemic:

The Wisdom Fund

www.twf.org

This site attempts to set the record straight about the truth of Islam. Though it often sounds overly combative, it is probably the best counteroffensive to the Islamophobic sites.

DIGITAL DREAMS AND DIGITAL DRAMAS AMONG MUSLIM CYBERNAUTS

It may be still the early days of the information age, but two things stand out: techgnosis misses the real drama that is taking place in cyberspace, and the conflict between different Muslim groups in cyberspace broadens the appeal of Islam. The print media can echo but not predict or influence how Muslim cybernauts chart their future.

Manuel Castells has performed a brilliant service, showing how an emergent electronic globalism will impact almost all levels of cosmopolitan culture. It is a roseate view of a network society. However, ground-level realities remain fractious, with different groups being committed to contesting the truth, or the authority, of religious tradition—in this case, Islam. We should learn to expect the unexpected: digital dreams will have their counterparts in digital dramas, and those outcomes no seer will dare predict. This much, however, is certain: Muslim cybernauts will be pivotal players in the information revolution: women, men, Sufis, Shi'is, and Sunnis will all play their distinctive, if not equivalent, roles.

NOTES

1. To rethink Islamic civilization without a performed Western or Orientalist bias is a persistent and crucial challenge. In the information age, we now have *Britannica Online,* the version of *Encyclopaedia Britannica* to which anyone has immediate access given a computer with sufficient memory. Check out http://www.eb-.com:180/bol/topic?artcl=106443 for a masterful overview of Islamic civilization written more than a decade ago by an accomplished historian of premodern Afro-Asian Islam, Marilyn Waldman. Waldman builds on the work of the most inventive world historian to write on Islamic civilization, Marshall G. S. Hodgson. Instead of accepting the anti-Muslim bias that, alas, still informs much scholarly as well as popular assessment of Islam, Waldman, like Hodgson, tries to make sense of the actual stages of shift within Islamic civilization.

2. The best example of this unpacking of early Islamic notions of political/religious authority is provided by Hamid Dabashi, *Authority in Islam: From the Rise of Muhammad to the Establishment of the Ummayads* (New Brunswick, N.J.: Transaction, 1989). Dabashi traces three tendencies or frames of reference from seventh-century Arabia: pre-Islamic Arab patrimony, Muhammadan charismatic authority, and post-Muhammadan egalitarianism. Not pure ideal types in the Weberian sense, each of

these tendencies is reflected, transmitted, and attenuated in the historical divisions of Islamic civilization labeled Sunni, Shi'i, and Khariji.

3. There are many exponents of Islam within the complex of world historical patterns or global civilizational developments. The benchmark of insightful, imaginative, but sympathetic assessment of Islam as a world historical force remains Marshall G. S. Hodgson, *The Venture of Islam: Conscience and History in a World Civilization* (Chicago: University of Chicago Press, 1974), 3 vols., now to be supplemented with his *Rethinking World History: Essays on Europe, Islam, and World History* (Cambridge: Cambridge University Press, 1993). A magnificent effort to compress and retell Hodgson's (and also Waldman's) multiply nuanced version of Islamic civilization is Richard M. Eaton, "Islamic History as Global History," in *Islamic and European Expansion: The Forging of a Global Order,* ed. Michael Adas (Philadelphia, Pa.: Temple University Press, 1993), 1–36.

4. Manuel Castells, *The Information Age: Economy, Society, and Culture,* (Cambridge, Mass.: Blackwell, 1996–97). I am indebted to James Piscatori for reference to Castells's work during a stimulating conversation at Oxford in November 1998. I have also streamlined and revised some of Castells's subtle but complex arguments, esp. those in vol. 1, *The Rise of the Network Society.*

5. Peter Mandaville, "Digital Islam: Information Technology and the Changing Boundaries of Religious Knowledge," *ISIM* (International institute for the Study of Islam in the Modern World) *Newsletter #2* (March 1999): 23. I benefited from hearing the initial presentation of this talk at the 1998 MESA annual meeting in Chicago and also from subsequent e-mail exchange with Mandaville, a political scientist teaching at the University of Kent in Canterbury.

6. Saskia Sassen, *Globalization and Its Discontents* (New York: New Press, 1998), esp. 177–94.

7. Gilles Kepel, *Allah in the West: Islamic Movements in America and Europe,* trans. Susan Milner (Stanford: Stanford University Press, 1997).

8. The only study to appear to date on the South Asian Muslim community in the United States appears as a subset of the study of all South Asian immigrants to this country. See Karen I. Leonard, *The South Asian Americans* (Westport, Conn.: Greenwood, 1997).

9. Stewart M. Hoover and Shalini S. Venturelli, "The Category of the Religious: The Blindspot of Contemporary Media Theory?" *Critical Studies in Mass Communication* 13 (1996): 260.

10. At the time this site was originally researched, the description given in this section applied. However, in the ever-changing nature of cyberspace, the site is now home to a related, but not identical, issue. For a site similar to the one described, see the Muslim Women's League at www.mwlusa.org.

BIBLIOGRAPHY

Castells, Manuel. *The Information Age: Economy, Society, and Culture* [3 vols.], vol. 1: *The Rise of the Network Society*. Cambridge, Mass.: Blackwell, 1996–97.

Dabashi, Hamid. *Authority in Islam: From the Rise of Muhammad to the Establishment of the Ummayads*. New Brunswick, N.J.: Transaction, 1989.

Eaton, Richard M. "Islamic History as Global History." In *Islamic and European Expansion: The Forging of a Global Order*, ed. Michael Adas. Philadelphia, Penn.: Temple University Press, 1993.

Hodgson, Marshall G. S. *The Venture of Islam: Conscience and History in a World Civilization*. 3 vols. Chicago: University of Chicago Press, 1974.

——. *Rethinking World History: Essays on Europe, Islam, and World History*. Cambridge: Cambridge University Press, 1993.

Hoover, Stewart M., and Shalini S. Venturelli, "The Category of the Religious: The Blindspot of Contemporary Media Theory?" *Critical Studies in Mass Communication* 13 (1996): 260.

Kepel, Gilles. *Allah in the West: Islamic Movements in America and Europe*. Trans. Susan Milne. Stanford: Stanford University Press, 1997.

Leonard, Karen I. *The South Asian Americans*. Westport, Conn.: Greenwood, 1997.

Mandaville, Peter. "Digital Islam: Information Technology and the Changing Boundaries of Religious Knowledge," *ISIM* (International Institute for the Study of Islam in the Modern World) *Newsletter # 2* (March 1999): 23.

Sassen, Saskia. *Globalization and Its Discontents*. New York: New Press, 1998.

Waldman, Marilyn. *http://www.eb.co_Hlt472329149m_Hlt472329149:180/bol/topic? artcl=1 06443q,Britannica Online*. Overview of Islamic civilization.

CHAPTER 12

INTERNET RITUAL:
A CASE STUDY OF THE CONSTRUCTION OF COMPUTER-
MEDIATED NEOPAGAN RELIGIOUS MEANING

Jan Fernback

As computer-mediated communication (CMC) technologies attain wide-spread use throughout the world, media scholars are examining these technologies as new forms of media and as extended cultural environments. Although some scholars criticize the use of CMC as an atomizing force that promotes ersatz social bonding,[1] others hail its use as the progenitor of new sites of community and social action.[2] This chapter follows a tradition of interpretive approaches to communication phenomena by examining the realm of cyberspace as a site for the construction of cultural practice for a religious group. Specifically, I explore the ritual processes and meanings evident in the discursive communities formed around various neopagan-oriented computer bulletin boards. After giving some brief background on neopaganism and ritual theory, I take a case-study approach to investigate ritual within a computer-mediated communicative environment and its significance with regard to the relationship between religion and technology.

A VIRTUAL CASE STUDY

This analysis of the ritual attributes of the textual exchanges within pagan-oriented virtual groups stems from the observation of three discus-

sion groups (alt.pagan and alt.magick on Usenet, and Paganism and
Wicca on OneNet), the Compuserve New Age Forum, and the Cyber
Samhain World Wide Web site, in addition to several virtual interviews
with participants in these discussion groups.

Methodologically, the analysis follows the tradition of ethnography; I
did not act as a participant-observer in the public discussion groups, I
merely "lurked." However, I clearly stated my intentions and objectives to
the subjects I interviewed. I monitored the discussion groups for several
months and downloaded hundreds of pages of conversations.

NEOPAGANISM AS A RELIGIOUS MOVEMENT

While neopaganism is often regarded as a so-called New Age religious
movement in the contemporary United States, it has roots in the ancient,
pre-Christian, polytheistic religions. Current estimates put the number of
neopagans in the United States at 83,000 to 333,000.[3] Margot Adler, in her
definitive history of the contemporary pagan movement in the United
States, articulates the essence of the neopagan belief system as nature
centered.[4]

Most neopagans tend to view technological progress as a force alienat-
ing humans from nature. Moreover, neopagans believe in the divine as
God and Goddess and that there is no distinction between the sacred and
the secular or the spiritual and the material. This rejection of dualistic
thinking, prevalent throughout pagan belief, is reminiscent of Eastern
philosophies and religions, and clearly rejects Durkheim's distinction of
the sacred and the profane. Neopagans find spirituality in the earth, in nature, in people, and in the everyday world. They reject Judeo-Christian
notions of divine judgment, original sin, an omnipotent patriarchal deity,
vicarious atonement, and even eschatology; rather, they espouse a philosophy of harmony with nature, divinity within humans and nature,
karma, and a humane universe.

A long tradition of misunderstanding and persecution (referred to as
the Burning Times) surrounds the practice of Wicca and other forms of
paganism, however.[5] As many as one-quarter of American neopagans,
fearful of being mischaracterized as "devil worshippers" or satanists, do
not reveal their religious identities to others.[6] This desire for secrecy
makes it difficult for neopagans to create a community that might serve

to educate people about their beliefs,[7] although neopagans still consider themselves to be a spiritual community.[8] Danny L. Jorgenson and Scott E. Russell, researchers studying the demographics of neopagans, report that they are "ordinary Americans" except for their rejection of other religions, and characterize neopagan tenets as "innovative," "alternative" and new, despite the fact that pagan traditions predate Christianity.[9]

In recent years, the neopagan movement has inspired a subcultural offshoot of young people who have fused neopagan ideals with an acceptance of high technology (particularly computer technology). Called zippies (Zen-inspired professional pagans, or Zen-inspired pronoia pagans, or Zen-inspired pronoia professionals), they embrace a version of neopaganism that works to balance the spontaneous, intuitive right side of the brain with the rational, pragmatic left side. Zippies, according to "shamanic zippie spokesperson" Fraser Clark, have a faith in a technology-based spiritualism.[10] A zippie is a blend of hippie philosophy and computer-hack practicality to create a weltanschauung that is balanced between the spiritual and the technological. Because the zippie movement is so new, there is some confusion regarding its degree of religiosity. J. Marshall and P. J. Huffstutter both note that zippies have a sense of Zen spirituality, but zippies seem to be a culturally, if not ideologically, diverse lot.[11]

Zippie festivals (mostly raves and similarly music- and dance-oriented gatherings) generally do coincide with neopagan holidays—solstices, equinoxes, Samhain (October 31), Oimelc (February 1), Beltane (May 1), and Lughnasadh (August 1). And zippies do cohere around a technology-based spiritualism that emphasizes unity and affinity with others. This spirituality is evident in this statement by a twenty-six-year-old male zippie:

> I grew up going to church and believing what I was told. But as I got older, I felt like I couldn't go to church anymore because it just didn't make sense. . . . I still consider myself a fairly religious person and I pray every day. Instead of kneeling down in front of an altar, I sit down in front of a computer screen. Out there (on the Internet) is a sense of peace, of community, of working together, of sharing ideas. That, to me, is true spirituality.[12]

Technology, then, offers zippies a chance to explore religious themes through the use of computers to log on to the Internet, mix their own music, or publish their own magazines in a quest for personal spirituality. And while syncretism is a facet of zippie religious construction, the zippie community seems closely unified in terms of its spiritual nature.[13]

THE APPLICATION OF RITUAL THEORY

Although James W. Carey's "ritual" view of communication is frequently invoked by media scholars interested in applying interpretive approaches to communication study, Carey's use of ritual is more metaphorical than practical.[14] Carey emphasizes a somewhat Durkheimian approach to the notion of ritual in that he links communication to fellowship, social unity, and the preservation of shared meanings, but he does not examine ritual as a process. I will use a more anthropological notion of ritual theory to argue that members of neopagan virtual discursive communities indeed participate in rituals of a certain kind.

Ritual theory has provided fertile terrain for the interpretation of cultural practice and meaning construction. Ronald L. Grimes notes that approaches to the study of ritual encompass many different theoretical vantage points, including functionalism, phenomenology, and semiotics.[15] Emile Durkheim's notions of ritual are embedded in his concept of religion as belief and practice associated with the sacred as juxtaposed against the profane or everyday.[16] He emphasizes the collective identity fostered by ritual as a functionally unifying practice. In a similarly functionalist vein, Victor Turner acknowledges that ritual's performative aspect affords an opportunity for social critique and resistance, in addition to functioning as a mechanism for building social solidarity.[17] Yet the corpus of Turner's work on ritual focuses more on the notions of *liminality* and *communitas,* where, through ritual, one experiences a "liminal" threshold moment of transition from an everyday, profane, structured world (societas) to a substantive, sacred, antistructural world of communitas.[18] Here, Turner acknowledges that ritual is not necessarily a conservative mechanism for social reinforcement; it can be creative, speculative, and contrary. Turner's work on the liminal is derived from Arnold VanGennep's notion that ritual has three phases: separation, transition (the liminal), and incorporation.[19]

Roy Rappaport's notion of ritual incorporates a secular dimension to ritual studies. He defines ritual as "the performance of more or less invariant sequences of formal acts and utterances not encoded by the performers."[20] Thus Rappaport sees performance as central to ritual, although he considers ritual to be the embodiment of the social contract, granting it status as "the fundamental social act upon which society is founded."[21] Hence, Rappaport theorizes that ritual is not necessarily purposive; it can be rather rote. Catherine M. Bell takes a similar stance on the performative aspects of ritual, although she argues that ritual is inherently purposive.[22] Bell uses the term *ritualization* to refer to ritual as a distinction between the sacred and the profane, but she notes that the strategies of ritualization are rooted in the body and in the body's dynamic connection with a symbolically delineated temporal and spatial realm.

Taking a similar stance, Bobby Alexander also emphasizes the performative aspect of ritual, but he claims that ritual serves to maintain Turner's notion of communitas.[23] Participants, according to Alexander, reflect idealized notions of community by acting them out through ritual. The liminal experience of the collective ritual creates a shared sense of everyday reality and spiritual community. Thus, Alexander argues that ritual is a response to gesellschaft and alienation in an attempt to transcend the almost contractual nature of the social structure (Turner's societas) to create a more organic sense of communitas.

Clifford Geertz's view of religious ritual is similar to Alexander's with regard to his perspective on both religion and ritual.[24] Geertz argues that the religious domain contemplates the commonplace by transcending it, not through scientific method but through encountering reality in wider, more open terms. Ritual helps in that encounter; it is through ritual that religious "truth" is established symbolically and in practice. It reinforces the concreteness of religious conviction so that the character and the conceptual nature of religious existence cohere.

Stressing the more quotidian nature of ritual, Robert Wuthnow asserts that ritual is structured to evoke meaning; thus it is communicative and symbolic.[25] He argues that ritual should not be bracketed from other types of social activity—because, he says, it is a dimension of all social activity. Ritual then is concerned with more than particular aspects of human expression; it informs all symbolic behavior.

This brief review of ritual theory indicates a lack of agreement regarding the nature of ritual as thought or action, sacred or profane, and embodied or not embodied. Most scholars of ritual do, however, acknowledge that ritual may provide a shared referent for a culture yet allow the expression of different values, and that some rituals can be disruptive rather than unifying. I accept the notion that ritual may be profane, may comprise thought and belief, and that the performative aspect of ritual is not central to understanding ritual as a process. In the following section, I assert that logging on to and participating in neopagan discussion groups is a form of ritual behavior. In addition, I use Grimes's six modes, or phases, of ritual action to interpret my findings: ritualization, decorum, ceremony, liturgy, magic, and celebration.[26]

But first, a brief (and hence reductive) explication of each mode: Ritualization is gesturing and posturing. Decorum is a system of expectations within social occasions. Ceremony is large group action or social drama involving civil religion. Liturgy is any ritual action with an ultimate frame of reference and cosmological significance. Magic is any element of pragmatic ritual work. Celebration is ritual with a sense of playfulness.

COMPUTER-MEDIATED COMMUNICATION AND RITUAL

Ritual as a social practice involving the body in physical space is, necessarily, impossible within a body-less medium, although some work has been done on ritual involving the mass media. Because the nature of community within computer-mediated communicative environments is essentially discursive in nature, ritual must be examined with regard to these limitations.

Television can serve as a ritual experience since mass-mediated forms of entertainment contain the performative and dramaturgical elements of ritual practice that Victor Turner elucidated.[27] James Ettema argues that media ritual can encompass Turner's performative notion of ritual in which both social solidarity and conflict are expressed.[28] Using press coverage of Chicago mayoral politics as an example, he asserts that press coverage serves a ritual function if it not only tells a story but interacts with political institutions and individuals as well. This interaction provides the dramaturgical and performative context for media ritual. Similarly, Elihu Katz and Daniel Dayan use significant live televised events (e.g., the funeral of a national leader) to claim that television is liminoid—it transports the viewer symbolically between structure and antistructure.[29] In addition, Stewart Hoover argues that religious broadcasting serves a ritual function of liminality for viewers based on their awareness that they are transcending societas and experiencing communitas—that they are sus-pending their consciousness of the profane and encountering the sacred.[30]

Logging on to a discussion group, real-time chat service, or multiuser dungeon (MUD) is itself a ritual practice. Participation in these on-line fo-rums is a ritual embrace of Internet technology; it is expressive, perfor-mative, and dramaturgical. The exchange of textual messages that argue religious philosophy, strategize political protests, discuss parenting tech-niques, lament the death of a public figure, or simulate sexual activity can have great salience for cyberspace inhabitants. Users position themselves ideologically against other users; they argue, console one another, ostra-cize one another, and form face-to-face friendships with each other. The CMC environment is the site for this contemporary, technological ritual where users seek a communal experience in the placeless realm of cyber-space. Indeed, logging on and participating in on-line culture is a liminal experience; the user is suspended "betwixt and between" the structure of the everyday societas and the antistructure of the autocracy, boundless possibility and the communitas of the CMC environment. This liminality encourages expressivity, reflexivity, and a celebration of belief. The user is of course sitting at a computer and ostensibly participating in the ritual alone, but, Robert Wuthnow notes, private ritual can be just as significant as public ritual. He claims that private ritual communicates valuable con-ceptualizations of the individual within the larger collectivity since "the individual has internalized a conception of that collectivity."[31]

The secular ritual quality of participating in these groups notwith-standing, logging on to religious discussion groups is a ritual activity that has a sacred dimension that cannot exist when participating in a discus-sion group based on hobbies or intellectual concerns. Participants in reli-giously oriented CMC groups engage in serious dialogue about ontology, cosmology, metaphysics, and epistemology. These discussions revolve around faith and spirituality and have apparent religious salience for users. They exhibit fervor and investment in these discussions, and this guaran-tees a sacred, meaningful character to these virtual exchanges. On alt .pagan, for example, where participants intelligently discuss the tenets of neopaganism, they embrace these conversations with a personal invest-ment and faith that extends beyond the intellectual exercise. Moreover, the repetitive nature of this ritual increases its meaningfulness and sub-stance.

In the example of a series of exchanges on alt.pagan given below, this sense of investment is apparent. One user is responding to the comments of two other users about participating in a neopagan ritual involving sexual contact. The participants' names have been changed, but the text is unedited unless indicated.[32]

Date: 31 Mar 1995
From: "Skyhawk"
["Tinne" wrote in part; much snipped:]
Recently during some rites and celebrations I've noticed the use of drugs. I have a strong belief in staying away from drugs but am feeling pressured by a few others to accept drugs and maybe do some. This has become something of an issue for me with regard to my position in my coven.

[Response from "Skyhawk":]

This is exactly the sort of issue I hoped to address in my proposal of "Rules of the Circle," a starting point for individuals to draw up their own agreements of what they would and would not do as group activities; I think the first two "rules" apply in your scenario.

RULES OF THE CIRCLE

The Rules of Informed Consent

1. Tell everyone participating what to expect, before the circle is closed or anything else begins.
2. Give everyone participating the chance to say *no* and to withdraw, before the circle is closed or anything else begins—and then respect that decision.
3. Be open, honest, and fair: spring no surprises, trip no traps; *never* use what you learn or do in circle to manipulate or compel any other person, or diminish anyone's dignity and free will. [post edited]

This exchange, focused on the rules of participation in a neopagan ritual, has an additional, deeper significance. "Skyhawk," while exhibiting concern for "Tinne's" well-being, is simultaneously using the situation to reinforce his own beliefs about the integrity and benevolence of the circle's religion. Using Grimes's schema, this exchange demonstrates ritualization (posturing), decorum (system of expectations), and liturgy (it is contemplative and mystical).[33]

Because an aura of misunderstanding shrouds the mainstream notions of neopaganism and other polytheistic religions, participants on alt.pagan, alt.magick, and Paganism and Wicca must endure periodic ideological attacks from Christians and satanists. These attacks necessitate a defensive response. The following series of exchanges again illustrates the unifying character of ritual participation in these groups. First there is an attack by a Christian who believes neopagans are satanic; this is followed by response from an alt-pagan group member.

Subject: Re: *babykillers!*
Date: Thursday, 23 Mar 1995
[TR wrote:]
You Satanists think that it is just fine and dandy to go around performing your little sacrifices and whatnot are fine and dandy, but I'll tell you what—
You can keep up with all your self-righteous bullshit about how different people can have different moralities, but I know for a fact that sacrificing babies is wrong and I know that you people are responsible for doing it.
I don't care what your beliefs are, or what you think your mission or job in life is, murder is a sin, and if I ever meet one of you people, I'll gun you down so fast you won't even know what hit you.
TR

[Response from "Drew":]
Some people have a very strong propensity for swallowing every line of propaganda that comes their way. Above is an average example.
To: sysadmin root@news.gac.edu
Mr. TR has, in this article, uttered slander and threatened murder. Would you be so kind as to give Mr. TR a few pointers on netiquette and law, and advise him that if his feelings regarding non-christians are so strong, he would perhaps be better off not subscribing to any of the listed groups, where non-christian religions have a strong presence or indeed are the dominant theme. If he insists on involving himself in

these groups, at the very least he can be called upon to stay legal, if not polite.
"Drew"

In response to such attacks, one user proposed the following serious yet satirical strategy.

Subject: Re: Burn in Hell
Date: 25 Apr 1995
["Cathy" wrote in part:]
You know people, we get this kinda stuff all the time. I have a solution to end all turmoil and allow people to get on with more constructive topics. Forgive me if this is already done or if it's been suggested.
Why not create a general response to these kind of posts and tape it to them each time they come on. Wouldn't that save time? We could even cut and paste some info from the FAQ perhaps.

Then came a response from "Will":

An alt.pagan Epistle to Christian Proselytizers
First of all . . . if you are under the delusion that *anyone* [on this list] has not heard "The Word," from any number of denominations, you should run, not walk, to your nearest psychiatric institution and commit yourself, since you are so far out of touch with reality that you might as well be a cartoon character.
Furthermore, even in the *highly* unlikely chance we had *not* heard it before, we get people like yourself every month or two who tries [sic] again. Whatever you have to say, therefore, has been said before, and almost certainly said better than you can say it. . . .
Third, if such phrases as "circular logic," "argument by authority," "argument by antiquity," or "ad hominem argument" mean nothing to you, you should go read the argument FAQ posted in news.answers regularly, if you expect to be treated in a manner other than a drunken bum yelling about Jeezuz, standing on a streetcorner, with a breath strong enough to light with a match, can expect to be treated.
Finally, if you have not read the alt.pagan FAQ (which says in section 18, that witnessing is *not* acceptable), or do not have a clear understand-

ing of what it is that many of us believe, or think we are "Satanists" (as defined by funnymentalist preachers) and devil-worshippers, then not only will you be laughed at, flamed, or ignored, but your net access provider will probably be complained to that you are violating the charter of the newsgroup, and, if you are at an academic or work site, you will stand a good chance of losing your net access if that provider gets enough complaints.

And if it *still* isn't clear to you, let's try it in words of few syllables: Anything you have to say was said better by someone else. Recently. Either Shut Up, until you learn manners and gain some knowledge or Go Away.

— "Will"

funny FAQ, 9 Aug. 1994

There is of course a theological underpinning to these exchanges. These users are defending their belief, both intellectually and emotionally, in the tenets of neopaganism. This type of ritual defense and affirmation seems to unite the community of users on alt.pagan in solidarity. This group sustains itself through the regular participation of a core group of users.[34]

A similar group exists on OneNet's Paganism and Wicca forum, and the ritual process of affirmation is evident in this post addressing the difference between atheism and paganism. "Donna" writes about the tenets of neopaganism while also addressing the "positive" aspects of her faith. She asserts both to the group and to herself who they are and what they believe.

Thursday, March 23, 1995

From: "Donna"

Subject: Re: Pagan vs. Atheist

Paganism is not synonymous with atheism, but neither is it synonymous with Wicca. The dictionary definition of a pagan is anyone who follows a religion other than Christianity, Judaism or Islam. In common usage, it tends to be defined a little more specifically, usually referring to someone who worships nature and/or the Old Gods of the various pre-Christian religions in some form.

Wicca is one form of paganism, which centres on a God and Goddess who are seen as the male and female sides of divinity, with all the gods and goddesses of mythology seen as aspects of these Two. A few other defining characteristics of Wicca are an emphasis on the four elements (air, fire, water and earth), a belief in reincarnation and karma (usually, an ethic of "an it harm none, do as ye will,") and the practise of folk magic in many forms. . . . .

I believe that everything occurs in everyones [sic] life for a reason—it is a stepping stone to the next moment and the next realization. If you invalidate the stepping stones then you remove from the path you are the ability to get to the next stepping stone. You can always create your life to be the way you desire it to be—and when you allow events to be there for a reason this will allow you to extract from scenarios what will most assist you in that creating. You lack nothing and have all the tools and abilities you require at any given moment to be anything you are willing and bold enough to believe you can be.

Blessed be,

Donna

The realm of cyberspace functions not only as a ritual site for these neo-pagans but also as what Stewart Hoover refers to as a site for "parachurch religiosity."[35] This is an opportunity for individuals to have religious experiences outside of church or other communal avenues of worship—to participate in nondenominational institutional activities. Mass media, and by extension CMC, may serve as the parachurch. Several participants in alt.pagan and Paganism and Wicca elaborated on their feelings of religiosity and community and experiences of religious meaning through the discussion groups. "Flamedancer," a participant on Paganism and Wicca for a year and a half, states, "It's nice to have at least a tenuous connection to pagans through the conference because I have no real-world pagan connections (i.e., no coven) since I moved to [name of state] in 1993." "Jerry," an atheist who participates regularly on alt.pagan, expresses a similar feeling:

> I'm an atheist with a lot of pagan friends; I don't *believe* what they believe, but we think the same way. Linear, logical discussion is easy to find on any topic, but my creative side lives in patterns and symbols and echoes, like a poet, and pagans are the only ones I know who speak that language regularly. I find it a very useful discussion group for this, and useful also in keeping everyone from getting too narrow-minded about their own way of doing things.

"Tinne," a participant on alt.pagan for sixteen months, argues that, while her sense of communal feeling with other neopagans is increased by her participation on a local bulletin board devoted to pagan issues, alt.pagan especially provides her with a sense of meaning, saying that her participation "had caused me to think in deeper detail about concepts I have held for years, sometimes clarifying problems I have with them." These types of "clarifying" discussions take place frequently on the Usenet neopagan groups. Users affirm their sense of faith and meaning through these educational exchanges. For example, in a number of discussion threads on alt.magick, participants offer their positions on the origin and significance of the pentagram in paganism and Christianity.

Thus we see that while cyberspace is a ritual site of religiosity, it can also serve as a site for the reconstruction of embodied rituals in a textual mode. Even a quasi-religious affiliation through ritual participation in discussion groups may manifest itself in the practice of on-line ritual within these groups. For example, according to Elizabeth Reid virtual marriages and public shaming rituals are performed within multiuser dungeons (MUDs).[36] MUD marriages are performed when two people (regardless of gender) agree to participate in the ritual. A third MUD member marries the couple by typing out the text of the wedding ceremony, other players serve as witnesses, and textual descriptions of rings or other tokens accompany the exchange of vows. Similarly, players in MUDs who harass or insult other players or repeatedly violate the sanctity of the MUD environment by posting threatening or antisocial messages may be subject to rituals of public humiliation. These rituals entail the ostracism of the offending player through the recreation (by the MUD's system operator) of the player's character into something socially undesirable. The player's character is moved into a public area where other players humiliate and chastise the offender. Reid notes that this ostracism ritual generally results in the player being banished from the MUD.

Several forums exist where neopagan religious rituals are performed in either a real-time mode or in a discussion format in which one participant administers the virtual ritual and others offer feedback following the ritual "performance." A number of neopagan rituals posted on Compuserve even make specific reference to cyberspace as the ritual site. These real-time rituals in cyberspace probably have an even greater sacred salience for users than do the discussion groups. They are a pastiche of other mythical and ritual elements—cosmological myths, religious symbolism,

the element of pilgrimage, celebration, and even the mythos of democratic participation in public discussion. Sacred pagan myths are retold in
these forums, and sacred symbology is evident in the character names of
the participants, original poetry they post to the group, and even in the
art they construct in their signature files.

All of Ronald Grimes's phases of ritual are evident in these cyber
rituals: ritualization, decorum, ceremony, liturgy, magic, and celebration
combine to reinforce users' cosmological outlook and to create meaning.
Clearly, these participants are not merely performing the profane, instrumental ritual of logging on to these forums; the discursive community
that forms around these groups directly addresses the legitimacy of religious poignancy derived from their ritual participation. I do not say that
participants in these cyberfora necessarily receive their primary religious
experience from this ritual (although some may, fearing the potential consequences of being openly neopagan), but that they do attain some level
of religiosity through this technological ritual practice.

RELIGION AND TECHNOLOGY

Given the somewhat antagonistic, suspicious relationship that has historically existed between technology and religion, it may seem odd to assert
that the technological realm can be a site of religiosity. But, as televangelism has sacralized television, CMC is certainly worthy of exploration in
this vein.

According to Jacques Ellul, Christianity was an obstacle to technological development prior to the Reformation because it judged technological
and scientific advancements according to their righteousness before God,
measuring their worth against criteria other than technological ones.[37]
The technological impetus of Western civilization arose from a society
that had isolated itself from the dominant influence of Christianity. Traditionally, the tenets of Christianity held that the natural must not be tam-
pered with and that technology was subject to all forms of moral judgment. Clearly, this is no longer the prevailing view; a Newtonian revolt
against nature paved the way for a technologically advanced society, and
Ellul is pessimistic about that society. Referring to technological development as a "technical invasion," he claims that it results in the collapse of
traditional value systems, including religious ones. Moreover, those reli-

gious values are transforming into a type of civil religion that worships technology, and technology is responsible for the moral and social dissolution of communal, organic culture.

Other prognosticators, particularly Lewis Mumford, argue that technology has supplanted religion as the arbiter of truth, has introduced and popularized secular forms of knowledge, and has demystified religious symbolic epistemology.[38] Mumford claims that sacred ritual created social order in the past; but now we rely on technology to create that order. The expression of our humanity is directed toward technology (Mumford's "machine"), and the scientific mind rejects the components of this past order that made us human, such as ritual, magic, and religion. Further, Mumford asserts that widescale religious conversion is the only salvation for a humanity doomed to destruction at the hands of the machines and computers it so dearly worships.

In a less apocalyptic vision, Bruce Mazlish notes that humans are compelled to create machine technology because they fear death, and technology represents eternal life; we loathe the body, and technology will perform bodily functions for us; we desire to be error-free and moral, and technology is neutral and infallible; we desire to master nature, and technology is the ultimate expression of this desire.[39] Technology, then, according to Mazlish, is a type of human prosthesis, and the computer is an extension of the brain of humanity. Religious fundamentalists seem to adhere to this philosophy, regarding computers as a tool for spreading the gospel.

Ian G. Barbour identifies ways in which science/technology and religion are related in popular conceptions of the dichotomous tension that exists between these two worldviews.[40] One of these ways sees major disruption between science/technology and religious beliefs (this model purports that science and religion both make unequivocal, mutually exclusive claims about the same ontological turf). Another way identified by Barbour views science/technology and religion as completely autonomous to one another, such that, epistemologically and ontologically, they do not address the same domain(science is based on empiricism and reason, while religion is based on divine revelation). Yet another way holds that a synthesis is possible between the content of both religion and science (nature informs science, or scientific theories may impact theological reformulations—such as the creation myth).

Clearly, the tension between technology and religion seems to be easing somewhat among the more progressive religious thinkers. Science-fiction novelists and even scholars such as Ethiel de Sola Pool, Michael Goldhaber, and Alvin Toffler have more utopian visions of society's embrace of the technological. Technology has been associated with the sacred in these utopian fantasies of social (and perhaps spiritual) growth and enlightenment that accompany the cultural embrace of the technological world. While Margot Adler notes that an earth-based religion such as the neopagan might seem to disapprove of the proliferation of technological development, she found that pagans tend to be more open-minded about the social benefits of technology; they seem to espouse Barbour's thinking.[41] Many neopagans embraced scientific inquiry and high technology in an organic, or alternative, vein, agreeing with Buckminster Fuller's theories and solar-energy development. Some neopagans argue that technology is used to diminish human sensory experience, but that this is the result of a less spiritual, more materialistic focus on life. Adler found that many neopagans worked in the computer industry, and that attitudes about computer technology are rather progressive. Jon Bloch's research similarly found that neopagans were enamored of technology when it aids in spiritual development.[42] Neopagans, and in particular zippies, argue that technology can be spiritual if it does not attempt to dominate nature but rather works *with* nature and demonstrates respect for the ecosystem.

But, while neopagans are influenced by the past, they seem not to want to return to it. Many feel that convenient technologies have created more leisure time so that people can develop philosophical pursuits. They argue that technology is not inherently good or evil, but that it is subject to misuse. Technology is useful; problems occur only when science and technology are idolized. By extension, CMC technology can increase the scope of the neopagan community by fostering face-to-face gatherings among discussion-group participants. Indeed, messages providing details of gatherings are fairly common on these forums.

The ritualistic behavior of using CMC technology to participate in these meaningful religious discussions could be indicative of the search for communal experience within what some social forecasters perceive as an increasingly atomistic world. Yet, this ritual has an even greater importance for neopagans who are often "closeted" in a country that is increasingly conservatively religious. Religion involves emotion, morality, contemplation, and fulfillment. Technology is not generally associated with these ontological aspects of life, but these religious goals can be realized through a form of ritual in which technology aids in the process of discovery. While neopagans and zippies may recognize that a Beltane ritual on the Internet is a sort of postmodern simulacrum, this realization does not seem to detract from the individual and collective meaning it holds for them. Their religion is important to them, and insofar as the Internet ritual constitutes parachurch religiosity for them, it is an authentic, legitimate experience.

Stephen O'Leary and Brenda Brasher point out that cyberspace is the modern public forum, and in that forum all types of religious practices, from prayer to ritual to proselytizing, are prospering.[43] An example of the burgeoning myths and lore of cyberspace illustrates their point: the Cyberpunk's Prayer is an homage to the divinity of the system operator and the spirituality of the virtual realm.[44] Their research, like this research, purports that ritualized behavior in cyberspace can enhance and even transform the nature of faith and the practices of believers. And while some on-line groups, particularly Usenet groups like alt.pagan and alt.magick, can be raucous places of strident disagreement and flaming, the members return habitually, just as those who attend church regularly do, to affirm and participate in their faith.

Just as, in 1988, Carey advocated a reexamination of the transmission view of mass communication to incorporate his ritual metaphor,[45] computer-mediated communication is now ripe for this type of analysis. The amount of attention cyberspace and virtual community have received in the popular press indicates that CMC is already being considered in terms of its potential for new modes of communicative interaction and new types of cultural structures and forms. The "information superhighway" metaphor is incomplete; CMC is an environment, a placeless realm where meaningful individual and collective experiences happen among the invested members. To the extent that some of these experiences are liminal, religious consciousness is sustained, new cultural possibilities are unveiled, and a profound sense of communitas is cultivated.

NOTES

1. Jim McClellan, "Netsurfers' Paradise," *Observer* (London), 13 February 1994, magazine section, 8.

2. Howard Rheingold, *The Virtual Community: Homesteading on the Electronic Frontier* (New York: Addison-Wesley, 1993); Elizabeth Reid, "Cultural Formations in Text-Based Virtual Realities" (master's thesis, University of Melbourne, Australia, 1994).

3. Jon P. Bloch, *New Spirituality, Self, and Belonging: How New Agers and Neo-Pagans Talk about Themselves* (Westport, Conn.: Praeger, 1998); Aidan A. Kelly, "An Update on Neopagan Witchcraft in America," in *Perspectives on the New Age*, ed. James R. Lewis and Gordon Melton, (Albany: State University of New York Press, 1992), 136–51.

4. Margot Adler, *Drawing Down the Moon: Witches, Druids, Goddess-Worshippers, and Other Pagans in America Today* (Boston: Beacon Press, 1986), 4.

5. Maryann Povey, "What Is Wicca and Who Do Wiccans Worship?" electronic MS: www.lullabypit.com/spirit/paganism.html.

6. Adler, *Drawing Down the Moon*.

7. Gordon J. Melton and Isotta Poggi, *Magic, Witchcraft, and Paganism in America: A Bibliography*, 2nd ed. (New York: Garland, 1992).

8. Bloch, *New Spirituality, Self, and Belonging*.

9. Danny L. Jorgensen and Scott E. Russell, "American Neopaganism: The Participants' Social Identities," *Journal for the Scientific Study of Religion* 38, no. 3 (1999): 325–38.

10. J. Marshall, "Zippies," *Wired* (May 1994): 75–84, 130–31.

11. P. J. Huffstutter, "We're Not in Woodstock Anymore: Crank Up the Music, Spread Peace and Love, but This Isn't the 60s So Plug into the Internet and Meet the Zippies, a Cyber-rave, Altered-states Kind of Movement," *Los Angeles Times*, 7 August 1994, 5f.

12. Ibid.

13. Marshall, "Zippies."

14. James W. Carey, *Communication as Culture* (Boston: Unwin Hyman, 1988).

15. Ronald L. Grimes, *Beginnings in Ritual Studies* (Washington, D.C.: University Press of America, 1982).

16. Emile Durkheim, *Elementary Forms of the Religious Life*, trans. Joseph Ward Swain (New York: Free Press, 1965).

17. Victor Turner, *Dramas, Fields, and Metaphors: Symbolic Action in Human Society* (Ithaca, N.Y.: Cornell University Press, 1974).

18. Victor Turner, *The Ritual Process: Structure and Anti-Structure* (Chicago: Aldine, 1969).

19. Arnold VanGennep, *The Rites of Passage* (Chicago: University of Chicago Press, 1960).

20. Roy Rappaport, "Ritual," in *Folklore, Cultural Performances, and Popular Entertainments*, ed. R. Bauman, (New York: Oxford University Press, 1992), 249–60. esp. 249.

21. Ibid., 254.

22. Catherine M. Bell, *Ritual Theory, Ritual Practice* (New York: Oxford University Press, 1992).

23. Bobby Alexander, *Victor Turner Revisited: Ritual as Social Change* (Atlanta: Scholars Press, 1991), 24.

24. Clifford Geertz, *The Interpretation of Cultures* (New York: Basic Books, 1993).

25. Robert Wuthnow, *Meaning and Moral Order* (Berkeley: University of California Press, 1987), 101.

26. Grimes, *Beginnings in Ritual Studies*.

27. *Communication Research Trends* 8, no. 1 (1987). Special issue on television myth and ritual (London: Center for the Study of Communication and Culture).

28. James Ettema, "Press Rites and Race Relations: A Study of Mass-mediated Ritual," *Critical Studies in Mass Communication* 7, no. 4 (1990): 309–31.

29. Elihu Katz and Daniel Dayan, "Media Events: On the Experience of Not Being There," *Religion* 15 (1985): 305–14.

30. Stewart M. Hoover, "Television Myth and Ritual: The Meaning of Substantive Meaning and Spatiality," in *Media, Myths, and Narratives: Television and the Press,* ed. James Carey (Newbury Park, Calif.: Sage, 1988), 161–78.

31. Wuthnow, *Meaning and Moral Order,* 104.

32. I have given new craft names to participants who post their craft, or pagan, names; similarly, I have substituted new given names for posted given names.

33. Grimes, *Beginnings in Ritual Studies*.

34. During the period of observation, one user was asked to leave alt.pagan after making a series of posts that the group deemed to be inappropriate. That user appears to have left without hesitation.

35. Hoover, "Television Myth and Ritual," 169.

36. Reid, "Cultural Formations."

37. Jacques Ellul, *The Technological Society,* trans. John Wilkinson (New York: Alfred A. Knopf, 1964).

38. Lewis Mumford, *The Myth of the Machine,* 2 vols. (New York: Harcourt, Brace & World, 1967, 1970).

39. Bruce Mazlish, *The Fourth Discontinuity: The Co-Evolution of Humans and Machines* (New Haven: Yale University Press, 1993).

40. Ian G. Barbour, *Religion in an Age of Science* (New York: Harper Collins, 1990).

41. Adler, *Drawing Down the Moon*.

42. Bloch, *New Spirituality*.

43. Stephen D. O'Leary and Brenda E. Brasher, "The Unknown God of the Internet: Religious Communication from the Ancient Agora to the Virtual Forum," in *Philosophical Perspectives on Computer-Mediated Communication,* ed. Charles Ess (Albany: State University of New York Press, 1996), 233–69.

44.

The Cyberpunk's Prayer

Our Sysop
Who art On-Line
High be thy clearance level.
Thy System up,
Thy Program executed
Off-line as it is on-line.
Give us this logon our database,
And allow our rants,
As we allow those who flame against us.
And do not access us to garbage,
But deliver us from outage.
For thine is the System and the Software
and the Password forever.

Cited from O'Leary and Brasher, "Unknown God of the Internet," 233–69. A footnote says the prayer is quoted with permission from author Bill Scarborough and that Scarborough claims the prayer is not copyrighted and that anyone is free to print it.

45. Carey, *Communication as Culture.*

BIBLIOGRAPHY

Adler, Margot. *Drawing Down the Moon: Witches, Druids, Goddess-Worshippers, and Other Pagans in America Today.* Boston: Beacon Press, 1986.

Alexander, Bobby. *Victor Turner Revisited: Ritual as Social Change.* Atlanta: Scholars Press, 1991.

Barbour, Ian G. *Religion in an Age of Science.* New York: Harper Collins, 1990.

Bell, Catherine M. *Ritual Theory, Ritual Practice.* New York: Oxford University Press, 1992.

Bloch, Jon P. *New Spirituality, Self, and Belonging: How New Agers and Neo-Pagans Talk about Themselves.* Westport, Conn.: Praeger, 1998.

Carey, James W. *Communication as Culture.* Boston: Unwin Hyman, 1988.

Communication Research Trends. Special issue (8, no. 1 [1987]) on television myth and ritual. London: Center for the Study of Communication and Culture.

Durkheim, Emile. *Elementary Forms of the Religious Life.* Trans. Joseph Ward Swain. New York: Free Press, 1965.

Ellul, Jacques. *The Technological Society.* Trans. John Wilkinson. New York: Alfred A. Knopf, 1964.

Ettema, James. "Press Rites and Race Relations: A Study of Mass-mediated Ritual." *Critical Studies in Mass Communication* 7, no. 4 (1990): 309–31.

Geertz, Clifford. *The Interpretation of Cultures.* New York: Basic Books, 1993.

Grimes, Ronald L. *Beginnings in Ritual Studies.* Washington, D.C.: University Press of America, 1982.

Hoover, Stewart M. "Television Myth and Ritual: The Meaning of Substantive Meaning and Spatiality." In *Media, Myths, and Narratives: Television and the Press,* ed. James W. Carey (Newbury Park, Calif.: Sage, 1988).

Huffstutter, P. J. "We're Not in Woodstock Anymore: Crank Up the Music, Spread Peace and Love, but This Isn't the 60s So Plug into the Internet and Meet the Zippies, a Cyber-rave, Altered-states Kind of Movement." *Los Angeles Times,* 7 August 1994, 5f.

Jorgensen, Danny L., and Scott E. Russell. "American Neopaganism: The Participants' Social Identities." *Journal for the Scientific Study of Religion* 38 (1999): 325–38.

Katz, Elihu, and Daniel Dayan. "Media Events: On the Experience of Not Being There." *Religion* 15 (1985): 305–14.

Kelly, Aidan A. "An Update on Neopagan Witchcraft in America." In *Perspectives on the New Age,* ed. James R. Lewis and Gordon Melton. Albany: State University of New York Press, 1992.

Marshall, J. "Zippies." *Wired* (May 1994): 75–84, 130–31.

Mazlish, Bruce. *The Fourth Discontinuity: The Co-Evolution of Humans and Machines.* New Haven: Yale University Press, 1993.

McClellan, Jim. "Netsurfers' Paradise." *Observer* (London), 13 February 1994, magazine section, 8.

Melton, Gordon J., and Isotta Poggi. *Magic, Witchcraft, and Paganism in America: A BIBLIOGRAPHY.* 2nd ed. New York: Garland, 1992.

Mumford, Lewis. *The Myth of the Machine.* 2 vols. New York: Harcourt, Brace & World, 1967, 1970.

O'Leary, Stephen D., and Brenda E. Brasher. "The Unknown God of the Internet: Religious Communication from the Ancient Agora to the Virtual Forum." In *Philosophical Perspectives on Computer-Mediated Communication,* ed. Charles Ess, 233–69. Albany: State University of New York Press, 1996.

Povey, Maryann. "What Is Wicca and Who Do Wiccans Worship?" Electronic MS, 1994: www.lullabypit.com/spirit/paganism.html.

Rappaport, Roy. "Ritual." In *Folklore, Cultural Performances, and Popular Entertainments,* ed. R. Bauman. New York: Oxford University Press, 1992.

Reid, Elizabeth. "Cultural Formations in Text-based Virtual Realities." Master's thesis, University of Melbourne, Australia, 1994.

Rheingold, Howard. *The Virtual Community: Homesteading on the Electronic Frontier.* New York: Addison-Wesley, 1993.

Turner, Victor. *The Ritual Process: Structure and Anti-Structure.* Chicago: Aldine, 1969.

——. *Dramas, Fields, and Metaphors: Symbolic Action in Human Society.* Ithaca, N.Y.: Cornell University Press, 1974.

VanGennep, Arnold. *The Rites of Passage.* Chicago: University of Chicago Press, 1960.

Wuthnow, Robert. *Meaning and Moral Order.* Berkeley: University of California Press, 1987.

CHAPTER 13

RELIGIOUS SENSIBILITES IN THE AGE OF THE INTERNET: FREETHOUGHT CULTURE AND THE HISTORICAL CONTEXT OF COMMUNICATION MEDIA

David Nash

Religious messages have been a fundamental form of cultural communi-cation and cultural cohesion for at least two millennia. Throughout, such messages and their promoters have perpetually interested themselves in the methods and media that new technological developments regularly put at their disposal. Investigators of this phenomenon should thus re-member that revolutions in communication have occurred on many occa-sions during the last two thousand years. Thus we need not be perplexed and without analytical methods when we are confronted by the growth of new forms of media and their use in the sphere of religious communica-tion. This chapter aims to demonstrate that the technique of comparing new developments with parallels from a past age constitutes a very useful tool of analysis. Taking as its example the parallels between the adoption and use of the Internet among American freethinkers and the similar adoption of print culture among their nineteenth-century forebears in Britain, a range of similar (and different) experiences and strategies can be demonstrated.[1]

The Internet as an information and communication resource is often described as organic. From the consumer's point of view, this guarantees that all individual tastes and outlooks are catered to and new ones can be actively developed. Commentators often describe the power now available on the average desktop as the dramatic consequence of an "information revolution" and the creation of a so-called global village. Two issues glossed over in hyperbolic descriptions of this "revolution" are that much of the information content of this revolution is neither new nor innovative. We should remember that the speed, convenience, and interaction provided by the Internet is not the first "information revolution." And some particular ideologically motivated groups—the worldview that encompasses atheism, agnosticism, secularism, and freethought—historically have been adept at harnessing the opportunities offered by the arrival of new information media as a central part of their mission.[2]

Atheists and freethinkers have a visible presence in the United States. Many encounter them first through seeing a Darwin's Fish bumper sticker on a car. While not all owners of this bumper sticker are professed atheists, the symbol signifies the freethinker's penchant for the presentation of an alternative belief system alongside subtle (and often not so subtle) parody as a form of cultural criticism. Attacks upon accessible forms of Christian communication such as the fish symbol are also regularly mirrored by slogans and critiques of a more transitory kind (one bumper sticker popular during 1999 had the slogan "Come the Rapture can I have your car?")

A visit to the Secular Web's Web site at infidels.org/, run by the self-styled Internet Infidels, provides confirmation of both these emphases. A range of interrogatable resources are available from this site, with pages covering contemporary religious/nonreligious issues in U.S. society related to church-and-state issues and the conflict between religion and science. In addition a section in the virtual library seeks to make classic "nontheistic" texts available. These include works from Charles Bradlaugh,[3] Charles Darwin, David Hume, and Thomas Paine (*The Age of Reason*), as well as Ernest Renan's *The Life of Jesus* and works by American authors such as Robert Ingersoll. The texts are supplemented by links to freethought periodicals and magazines on both sides of the Atlantic (e.g., in the United States, *Free Inquiry* and *Atheist Nation,* and in Britain, the *Freethinker*). The renewed and accelerating interest in the paranormal[4] and the foreboding that this inspires in rationalists is also reflected in a number of links to CISCOP (Committee for the Scientific Investigation of Claims of the Paranormal) and periodicals such as the *Skeptical Inquirer*.

THE BACKGROUND: BRITISH FREETHINKERS
AND THEIR COMMUNICATION STRATEGIES

In Britain, the history of secularist and antireligious outlooks sprang from Enlightenment thinking and the writings of isolated individuals like the deists Peter Annet and John Toland.[5] Perhaps the twin exemplars of this tradition of freethinking in solitude were Thomas Paine and Richard Carlile, the fusion of whose thoughts have been considered by historians to comprise an intellectual and ideological tradition for nineteenth-century freethinkers.[6] Thomas Paine's crusade for natural-rights ideology was accomplished through the medium of a literary style that was accessible for at least two generations of radicals.[7] His participation in two revolutions on either side of the Atlantic and his endless exposition of natural-rights theory perhaps marks him as the first practitioner of the "global village" concept. Arguably Paine was the first to transport and translate a single Enlightenment-inspired idea across cultures, continents, and communities with dramatic effects. Thus it is significant to see how quickly his works have appeared in electronic form.

Paine's influence was supplemented in the 1820s by the work of Richard Carlile in radical newspapers such as the *Lion,* the *Prompter,* and the *Republican,* which were frequently considered blasphemous and seditious.[8] Carlile's agitation was closely related to the campaign for a free, unstamped press.[9] One ideology that effectively took the mantle of Carlile and provided a focus for the unreligious was the rational philosophy of Robert Owen, which eventually spawned communitarian experiments in both Britain and the United States.[10] A strategy adopted by the Owenites was the disputation of the truth or otherwise of religion upon public platforms—a tactic that met with some success but also much hostility. With the collapse of Owenism in Britain, a less confrontational movement, secularism, offered a more defensive strategy.[11] This movement espoused a form of agnosticism that, rather than openly attacking supernatural explanations of the universe, denied knowledge of them. In this way, secularists hoped to display the confrontational attitude of Christianity to themselves as unjust. This movement flourished in provincial England as a vibrant subculture supported by a prolific publishing output and well-organized lecture circuit. The secular movement in Britain was, however, riddled with personality clashes, leadership and financial squabbles, and ideological conflicts that conspired ultimately to limit its effectiveness.

Despite this, one indispensable feature of the rise and prominence of secularism and freethought was the pivotal role played by the press that serviced this community. Papers in Britain like the *Secular Review, National Reformer,* and the *Freethinker* did much to link the secularist community together.[12] For many individuals, the secularist press represented their only contact with secularism and the only method they had of discovering fully the nature of their belief (or unbelief). This press reached out to the geographically isolated and (although some secularists did campaign for the occasional cause celebre) was read secretly by people otherwise forced into a life of outward conformity. The secularist culture, which emphasized the social value of knowledge as a force for promoting rationalist views of the universe, remained important. The decline of this culture in Britain has been largely attributed to the diminishing importance of religion as well as the rapid expansion of mass university, college, and adult education, which have undermined the organic conception of knowledge and its acquisition.

THE UNITED STATES AND MODERN PARALLELS

The rapid rise of the Internet raises important questions for freethinkers about how opinions are to be informed and generated and how the culture conveyed by this new medium is to be selected and portrayed. Moreover, freethinkers' Internet resources are a graphic demonstration that the arrival of new media presents both problems and opportunities—ones that were addressed earlier with the arrival of specific forms of print culture.

Freethinking Internet resources exist because Christian resources, too, exist. This, while obvious, is more than a simple tautology. Historically, secularists have refuted the suggestion that the Judeo-Christian worldview is in any sense a given constant, and they have presented constant challenges to it in areas of public space varying from Web pages to car bumpers. This has sought to counterbalance the picture of Christianity and its attendant morality as in some sense a norm. As one Internet infidel declared:

Maybe the most important aspect of the secularist presence on the Internet is in its public relations value. These days, somehow people assume everyone is religious. The more visible we are, the harder this assumption becomes. This is why my own personal Web page has pointers to the Secular Web and the other resources. It doesn't preach: it lets people know that folks who are perfectly "normal" and share common interests, don't necessarily share their religious beliefs.

Historians have frequently observed this phenomenon, noting that the provision of religious material has been quick to adapt to the arrival of new forms of communication.

One historian has seen religious provision as a "supermarket" model— one that contains elements of competition, pricing, and marketing policy as well as response to changing patterns of demand.[13] However, the religious landscape of Western societies at the beginning of the twenty-first century indicates that there are competing religious ideas that go beyond a simple theistic/nontheistic dichotomy. Several Internet freethinkers mentioned periods in which they investigated forms of Buddhism, New Age paganism, and Wiccan Rede as alternatives to the conventional Christian/atheist dichotomy.

Nonetheless, the supermarket analogy is historically informative since the "competition" for British freethinkers represented from the 1880s onwards by the Salvation Army was ridiculed in press articles, pamphlets, and cartoons, and secularists were also not above providing missions and street-corner celebrations of their own ideologies. Thus, as one prominent British freethinker has recently confided, the proliferation of Christian computer and Internet resources has been seen within secularist circles as a perceived "threat that must be countered."

In the same vein, observers of contemporary Christianity have noticed that alongside defensive strategies to counter a "postmodern situation," proactive strategies are tabled that seek to enhance religion's profile in the postmodern world.[14] Unlike the religious practitioners of previous generations, who in the main saw social and cultural change as occurring inevitably for the worse, the devotees of contemporary Christianity are actively exploring uses of such new media as film, television, video, and the Internet in conducting religious services and as a tool for evangelism.

A very important function of atheist and freethinking Internet resources, once again analogous to the nineteenth-century British press, is as an important antidote to feelings of isolation or anger that holding such opinions can engender. One respondent suggested: "I am now much more open regarding my atheism. Two things brought me out of my apathy: (1) The arrogant conservative-Christian atmosphere in the US, and (2) The presence of activist atheists on the Internet."

The pressure to accept Christian sentiments at public occasions was also mentioned (one respondent identified an uncomfortably religious graduation ceremony as a confirmatory experience). Moreover, the simple geographical isolation of some communities in the United States makes the pervasiveness of religious culture more obvious. As one respondent outlined his struggle:

> I began to ask questions during study of the Bible and I was not looked upon as a disciplined individual any longer. I received detentions and punishments instead of answers. I sat in detention for most of my senior year of high school. Thus began my thirst for knowledge about what the hell was really going on. I began to get this idea that this whole religion thing was a big scam.

Another respondent said:

> Most of the churches, including mine, were very political, with the older ladies running the show and looking down their noses at the other less Christian Christians. Also, I hate hypocrisy, and try to avoid it in my life. I saw a lot of it in church, where a man would sit with his family on Sunday being a good churchgoer, then drink or run around on his wife during the week.

Undoubtedly, the discovery of the Internet infidels, the Secular Web, or the various atheist and freethought newsgroups has done much to remove the sense of isolation felt by many with antireligious opinions:

> For no matter how unusual you think you are, you're going to be able to find hundreds of like-minded individuals on the Net. This is tremendously important with American atheists in particular, who find use of the Net very liberating after being brought up with a heavy diet of

strict theism. The sub-text in all these difficult groups (atheists are just one example, another obvious example are the homosexual groups) is that it's ok to be different, because you're with friends.

Another Internet infidel drew an analogy to suggest that the isolation felt by the antireligious and the support network that secularist Web sites provided had even more significant historical parallels:

> One of the primary services rendered by this neocommunity is the outgrowth of supportive resources relating to atheism. The vast majority of information relating to atheism on the net, from the USENET FAQ for alt.atheism to the ever-expanding web sites dedicated to secular issues, is compiled by volunteers, often working in concert with one another. I am reminded of the way that pioneer families would help one another to raise houses for their neighbors, only our "houses" are intellectual constructs meant to provide us with mental shelter.

From this first contact, one respondent felt that the discovery of such resources could become a viable alternative to religious ideas and an essentially "theism-free space," rather than a means of proactively combating theistic ideas:

> One thing that strikes me is the very large degree of voluntary 'segregation' that exists between secularists and the religious, on the net. . . . By weeding out (or at least providing areas in which they keep quiet) theists from specific areas by self-segregation, the net provides forums "unlike" our actual physical neighborhoods and work places, in which we can discuss the broader issues of life, death, etc. without the poisonous undercurrent of theism tainting the entire conversation.

The opportunity for this space to take on new functions due to its blend of intimacy and distance also holds out tantalizing prospects for altering the way discussions about theism, Christianity, atheism, and freethought could actually take place. One respondent stated: "You can imagine a progression from 'lurking' in atheist-related newsgroups, to posting and debating in them, on to using the Web for research to back up your claims, and then running an atheism resource or two as I have done."

Such use of the Internet by American freethinkers reenacts a stage of

British freethought, when public disputation of the perceived truth of the Bible or revealed religion was seen as an essential tactic, taking freethought into a new public arena. The lecturers of the nineteenth century disputed the moral power of Christianity with religious apologists on the public platforms of provincial Britain; a recent posting on the freethought Web distinctly echoed the tactic. The Web page challenged Christians to provide documentary evidence to verify biblical miracles and offered a "reward": if the evidence was forthcoming, the freethinker promised to put in three months of church attendance or read three books of the Christian correspondent's choice.

Another respondent noted that Christians and Muslims alike felt it incumbent upon themselves to undertake discussion on the alt.atheism electronic discussion list. The quality of the input varied greatly, however, ranging from the erudite and coherent to the "YOU WILL BURN IN HELL" variety. In spite of such messages, another respondent echoed the view that public disputation and the creation of new public spheres (modes such as the discussion group) were of value, and said they would prove more satisfactory than having recourse to print culture. This suggests that the "real-time" face-to-face interaction of platform debate that characterized the early British freethought movement is now, on the Web, augmenting and supplanting the print culture of which it was originally a victim. The Internet is thus being seen as a more organic, interactive, method of sharing information. In some respects, such a movement—away from print culture and toward interactive media—echoes the optimism of Marshall McLuhan. In the words of one respondent:

> I hope the Web might go some way towards doing away with the standard way in which issues and social discussions take place within the rigid confines of the print media, and back towards more traditional forms of discourse in which ideas and knowledge were exchanged directly between many individual people. In some sense society was defined by the collective body of myth that defined reality.

Access to the Internet for secularists does not simply provide a support network for themselves and their sympathizers. The question of what constitutes the culture worthy of presentation to the population is one that has been continually addressed by secularists, and the explosion of the Internet has only made such questions more urgent and important.

The Internet, like cheap mass publishing before it, is a potential means of redefining a culture through forms of selection and portrayal. Secularists have historically taken a leading role in contributing to such technological changes. This is first because, like purveyors of any religious message, they seek to exploit the potential of new technology to enhance their role within the wider information community; and second because any construction of new information communities and storage/access media entails an inevitable redefinition of cultural and information canons. A secularist concern, identified in all ages, is that, without vigilance, such a canon will inevitably be by default masculine, white, Western, and Judeo-Christian in orientation, reestablishing such "norms" at the expense of diversity.

Secularists thus celebrate the range of philosophical points of view while simultaneously presenting an alternative cultural canon. The former supplies information while the latter genuinely attempts to counteract what are seen as dangerous elisions of the truth. Such elisions can occur almost imperceptibly—the masthead title of the premier repository of electronically stored text-based culture—"Project Gutenberg"—seems innocuous to a society steeped in the legacy of text- and book-based education. However, to secularists it presents a certain version of the truth that associates learning and intellectual development with the Bible and late-medieval Christianity, which to many secularists is a misleading, even distasteful, assumption. Some secularists, like their forbears, believe that such Victorian notions as free trade and "natural selection" should equally apply to the realm of ideas, allowing the socially useless ones to wither away rather than be accorded special protection in new cultural forms.

Alongside the composition of this new culture, the issue of access to this information is equally important. Secularists and freethinkers have always been particularly conscious of the distinction between "information rich" and "information poor." Nineteenth-century England witnessed secularists as active in the struggle for the social-utilitarian belief that knowledge is power. The leading unstamped paper of the 1830s, the *Poor Man's Guardian*, run by the atheist radical Henry Hetherington, carried this "Knowledge is power" legend surrounding a picture of a small printing press, which as an icon of print culture acted as a radical counterpoint to the official stamp that appeared on mainstream newspapers.[15] Moreover, it was a rationalist expression of the power of technology to transform society and social relations. This stands in stark contrast to some

Weberian versions of technological innovation, which posit a special role for Christianity—Protestantism, in particular—in the rise and triumph of the machine.[16]

A part of the nineteenth-century secularists' mission has also been to demystify man. They believed that Christianity restricted certain knowledge, placing a moral perimeter around its dissemination and use, and the numerous prohibitions upon the publication of birth-control literature, which have been a part and parcel of Western societies since 1800, have been an important factor in convincing secularists of this.[17] Thus for modern Internet Infidels, the provision of a virtual library is an essential source of explanations to justify and sustain diverse versions of the universe for compatriots and opponents alike.

Some survey respondents used the Web sites to fortify themselves against religious arguments and also to strengthen their own convictions. Many respondents equally took pleasure from humorous entries (one respondent noted that the funnies were the most "blasphemous" posts of all). Another respondent saw the freedom of the Internet as undermining existing legislation that limited print culture, not to mention potentially "hidden" sanctions against unpopular religious opinions that are often wielded by nervous advertisers.

A most important liberating feature of the Net is that it is uncensorable—that it appears "the truth will out," contrary to a lot of "real world" experience. In this context, it is interesting that, while attempts to limit "blasphemy" on the Internet are at present ineffective, some Internet infidels feel the need to undertake and enjoy what they themselves consider to be blasphemy. Many sites contain explicit disclaimer screens that seek to prevent the potentially offended from proceeding further. This perhaps indicates that perceptions of blasphemy are in fact components of secularist culture, rather than blasphemy being purely an attack upon the prevailing religious culture—a culture that itself has responded through producing cyberprayer Web sites explicitly asking for deliverance from blasphemy.

From this point it is possible to speculate about the role that humor plays in modern secularist culture, as it did for nineteenth-century adherents. Just as the British Victorian periodicals the *Freethinker* and the *Jerusalem Star* contained cartoons and satirical attacks upon the sacred doctrines of the Bible, the sheer visibility of evangelicalism in the United States makes the abrasive and abusive the currency of criticism. Cartoons and parodies of religious forms vie with satire and material aimed to undermine the ideas and icons of Christianity, some self-styling atheism as a conspiracy. All flourish under First Amendment protection—but how far they may come to be threatened by communications legislation is another matter. Other sites that blend the sacrilegious with the pornographic may in time constitute the occasion for action against all.

Nonetheless, the Internet's relative uncensorability gives late-twentieth-century atheists and freethinkers distinct advantages in the arena of publishing that were not enjoyed by their forebears. A loose confederation of Internet resources give today's atheists the power and organic interaction enjoyed by their nineteenth-century compatriots but without the personality clashes and problems caused by "official" forms of organization. Atheists coexist on Web pages with agnostics, humanists, and pagans, while the perpetual problems faced by fringe groups of managing and administering "membership" of "official" forms of organization are completely avoided. Moreover, the transmission of opinion to the "lurker," or casual observer, is an active, self-regulating, empowering process, with infinitely more variety, thus avoiding the off-the-shelf ideological package of newspapers that have specific editorial stances. This in itself is an even bigger advantage for a group whose ideas and beliefs can be guaranteed to be considerably more eclectic than most.

Historically, Christian societies have taken a dim view of the world of secularist print publishing.[18] However, the normal strategies and procedures for denying access to and prosecuting published material considered to be offensive, blasphemous, or immoral are not (currently) at the disposal of authorities or individuals where the Internet is concerned. In some respects, the whole issue asks important questions about tolerance as an in-built assumption among those in the wider Internet community. This is particularly important when we consider that the issue of causing offense in a religious context can no longer be relied upon to wither away, as the positivist devotees of secularization theory once presumed it would. Given that an innate attraction of the Internet is its "incorruptibility" and its organic attitude to administration, it effectively becomes difficult to police and ultimately to superimpose a "norm" worldview over one considered unorthodox.

Since the U.S. Constitution makes blasphemy prosecutions more unlikely, those seeking to limit the dissemination of secularist and atheist opinions must explore other less obvious avenues in their quest.[19] A particular application of copyright laws to prevent the discussion of religious sects by name showed that the seizure of equipment, papers, and files can result from pursuit by an injured part (this incident led to the coining of the shuddering phrase *electronic book burning*).

Of perhaps even deeper concern is the wave of moral panic that afflicts governments that seek to oversee the growth of new communication idioms and media. Yet again history repeats itself, so that events such as the secularist adoption of tabloid journalism in the 1880s, the use of public mass meetings during the Edwardian period, and the issue of atheist access to radio in the 1930s have all caused concern among Western governments. Thus it is no surprise that attempts at legislation to control telecommunications can cause such alarm, particularly when opponents argue that public money has been used to support networks responsible for transmitting this material. One Internet provider declared, "You know, if the Internet makes democracy this accessible to the average citizen, is it any wonder Congress wants to censor it?" This again brings us to the question of how long the Internet can remain an organic, unpoliced, autonomous "commons," rather than an area where information is artificially "enclosed."

Thus we can see that an examination of the growth and development of one worldview's relationship to a new communications media can be successfully explored through a historical comparison with this view's ideological ancestors. What is striking is that many of the problems and speculations about the new possibilities are replicated in both. Similarly, the concerns about how the new media empower individuals and the nature of new information canons and who shapes them are clearly the rehearsal of much older arguments.

NOTES

Much of this chapter is based on a survey of those users and service providers who placed their e-mail address on the Secular Web Web site under the title "The Internet Infidels." A brief inquiry letter, e-mailed to all those listed, asked deliberately general questions about secular resources on the Internet but also requested respondents to mention any life and religious experiences they felt had been important. The response was overwhelming and provided a wealth of interesting material—far too much to include in this chapter. This indeed provides articulate testimony to the speed and vitality of at least one branch of Internet culture.

While respondents were assured that all information received would be treated anonymously, all those who replied were forthright about their beliefs; many in fact said they felt it would be an honor to be associated with their beliefs in print. Full citation of the authors is not possible due to space constraints, but I would like to thank all those who replied. They did so with wit, wisdom, honesty, and eloquence.

1. Others who have done similar work in other areas are Carolyn Marvin, *When Old Technologies Were New: Thinking about Electric Communication in the Late Nineteenth Century* (New York: Oxford University Press, 1988), and Thomas Streeter, *Selling the Air: A Critique of the Policy of Commercial Broadcasting in the United States* (Chicago: University of Chicago Press, 1996).

2. Susan Budd, *Varieties of Unbelief: Atheists and Agnostics in English Society, 1850–1960* (London: Heinemann, 1977); Jim Herrick, *Vision and Realism: A Hundred Years of the Freethinker* (London: G. W. Foote, 1982); David S. Nash, *Secularism, Art, and Freedom* (London: Leicester University Press, 1992); Edward Royle, *Victorian Infidels* (Manchester: Manchester University Press, 1974); Edward Royle, *Radicals, Secularists, and Republicans: Popular Freethought in Britain, 1866–1915* (Manchester: Manchester University Press, 1980); David Tribe, *One Hundred Years of Freethought* (London: Elek, 1967).

3. Walter L. Arnstein, *The Bradlaugh Case: A Study in Late Victorian Opinion and Politics* (Oxford: Clarendon Press, 1965); David Tribe, *President Charles Bradlaugh, M.P.* (Hamden, Conn.: Archon Books, 1971).

4. "Paranormal" calls up more than one hundred books published since 1995 in the WorldCat library database and more than four hundred thousand items in the AltaVista search engine on the Internet.

5. Royle, *Victorian Infidels.*

6. Guy Alfred Aldred, *Richard Carlile, Agitator: His Life and Times,* 3rd ed. (Glasgow: Strickland Press, 1941); Richard Carlile, *The Life of Thomas Paine, Written Purposely to Bind with His Writings* (London: 1821); H. T. Dickinson, "Thomas Paine's Rights of Man 1791–2: A Bi-centenary Assessment," 32 *Historian* (1991): 18–21; Ian Dyck, ed., *Citizen of the World: Essays on Thomas Paine* (New York: St. Martin's, 1988); Patricia Hollis, *The Pauper Press: A Study in Working Class Radicalism of the 1830s* (Oxford: Oxford University Press, 1970); Iain. D. McCalman, "Popular Radicalism and Free-Thought in Early Nineteenth Century England: A Study of Richard Carlile and His Followers, 1815–32" (master's thesis, Australian National University, 1975); Joel H. Wiener, *Radicalism and Freethought in Nineteenth-Century Britain: The Life of Richard Carlile* (Westport, Conn.: Greenwood Press, 1983).

7. Dyck, *Citizen of the World.*

8. Iain D. McCalman, *Radical Underworld: Prophets, Revolutionaries, and Pornogra-*

phers in London, 1795–1840 (Cambridge: Cambridge University Press, 1993), 148–49, 181–231; Wiener, *Radicalism and Freethought.*

9. Hollis, *Pauper Press;* Joel Wiener, *The War of the Unstamped* (Ithaca, N.Y.: Cornell University Press, 1969); Wiener, *Radicalism and Freethought.*

10. J. F. C. Harrison, *Robert Owen and the Owenites in Britain and America: The Quest for the New Moral World* (London: RKP, 1969).

11. Nash, *Secularism, Art, and Freedom,* 14–20; Royle, *Victorian Infidels.*

12. David S. Nash, " 'Unfettered Investigation'—The Secularist Press and the Creation of Audience in Victorian England," *Victorian Periodicals Review* 28 (summer 1995): 123.

13. S. Yeo, *Religion and Voluntary Organizations in Crisis* (London: Croom Helm, 1976).

14. Gilles Kepel, *The Revenge of God* (Cambridge: Polity Press, 1994), 56–59.

15. Hollis, *Pauper Press.*

16. David Lyon, *The Information Society: Issues and Illusions* (Oxford. Polity Press, 1988), 145.

17. Joseph A. Banks, *Victorian Values: Secularism and the Size of Families* (Boston: Routledge & Kegan Paul, 1981).

18. David Lawton, *Blasphemy* (London: Harvester Wheatsheaf, 1993); Leonard W. Levy, *Blasphemy: Verbal Offense against the Sacred from Moses to Salman Rushdie* (New York: Knopf, 1993); David S. Nash, *Blasphemy in Modern Britain, 1789–Present* (London: Ashgate Press, 1999); Nicholas Walter, *Blasphemy Ancient and Modern* (London: Rationalist Press Association, 1990); Richard Webster, *A Brief History of Blasphemy: Liberalism, Censorship, and 'The Satanic Verses'* (Southwold, Suffolk: Orwell Press, 1990).

19. Levy, *Blasphemy.*

BIBLIOGRAPHY

Aldred, Guy Alfred. *Richard Carlile, Agitator: His Life and Times.* 3rd ed. Glasgow: Strickland Press, 1941.

Arnstein, W. L. *The Bradlaugh Case: A Study in Late Victorian Opinion and Politics.* Oxford: Clarendon Press, 1965.

Banks, Joseph A. *Victorian Values: Secularism and the Size of Families.* Boston: Routledge & Kegan Paul, 1981.

Budd, Susan. *Varieties of Unbelief: Atheists and Agnostics in English Society, 1850–1960.* London: Heinemann, 1977.

Carlile, Richard. *The Life of Thomas Paine, Written Purposely to Bind with His Writings.* London: 1821.

Dickinson, H. T. "Thomas Paine's Rights of Man 1791–2: A Bi-centenary Assessment." 32 *Historian* (1991): 18–21.

Dyck, Ian, ed., *Citizen of the World: Essays on Thomas Paine.* New York: St. Martin's, 1988.

Harrison, J. F. C. *Robert Owen and the Owenites in Britain and America: The Quest for the New Moral World.* London: RKP, 1969.

Herrick, Jim. *Vision and Realism: A Hundred Years of the Freethinker.* London: G. W. Foote, 1982.

Hollis, Patricia. *The Pauper Press. A Study in Working Class Radicalism of the 1830s.* Oxford: Oxford University Press, 1970.

Kepel, Gilles. *The Revenge of God.* Cambridge: Polity Press, 1994.

Lawton, David. *Blasphemy.* London: Harvester Wheatsheaf, 1993.

Levy, Leonard W. *Blasphemy: Verbal Offense against the Sacred from Moses to Salman Rushdie.* New York: Knopf, 1993.

Lyon, David. *The Information Society: Issues and Illusions.* Oxford. Polity Press, 1988.

McCalman, Iain. D. "Popular Radicalism and Free-Thought in Early Nineteenth Century England: A Study of Richard Carlile and His Followers, 1815–32." Master's thesis, Australian National University, 1975.

McCalman, Iain D. *Radical Underworld: Prophets, Revolutionaries, and Pornographers in London, 1795–1840.* Cambridge: Cambridge University Press, 1993.

Nash, David S. *Secularism, Art, and Freedom.* London: Leicester University Press, 1992.

——. " 'Unfettered Investigation'—the Secularist Press and the Creation of Audience in Victorian England." *Victorian Periodicals Review* 28 (summer 1995): 123.

——. *Blasphemy in Modern Britain, 1789–Present.* London: Ashgate Press, 1999.

Royle, Edward. *Victorian Infidels.* Manchester: Manchester University Press, 1974.

Royle, Edward. *Radicals, Secularists, and Republicans: Popular Freethought in Britain, 1866–1915.* Manchester: Manchester University Press, 1980.

Streeter, Thomas. *Selling the Air: A Critique of the Policy of Commercial Broadcasting in the United States.* Chicago: University of Chicago Press, 1996.

Tribe, David. *One Hundred Years of Freethought.* London: Elek, 1967.

Tribe, David. *President Charles Bradlaugh, M.P.* Hamden, Conn.: Archon Books, 1971.

Walter, Nicholas. *Blasphemy Ancient and Modern.* London: Rationalist Press Association, 1990.

Webster, Richard. *A Brief History of Blasphemy: Liberalism, Censorship, and 'The Satanic Verses.'* Southwold, Suffolk: Orwell Press, 1990.

Wiener, Joel. *The War of the Unstamped.* Ithica, N.Y.: Cornell University Press, 1969.

Wiener, Joel H. *Radicalism and Freethought in Nineteenth-Century Britain: The Life of Richard Carlile.* Westport, Conn.: Greenwood Press, 1983.

Yeo, S. *Religion and Voluntary Organizations in Crisis.* London: Croom Helm, 1976.

PART 6

SPECIFIC RELIGIONS AND SPECIFIC MEDIA IN NATIONAL AND ETHNIC CONTEXTS

Finally, we turn to a series of chapters dealing with specifics of a different kind: specific national and ethnic contexts. In contrast to part 5, where the concern was more with the practices whereby specific mediated contexts and appeals are authored, here we look at specific contexts of reception or consumption. We see the complexity of the negotiations through which meanings are made at the consumption end of things. These chapters (like Lawrence's chapter 11) also raise the North/South line of demarcation. All of them deal with phenomena and contexts where self-consciousness of ethnic or national difference is an important marker of negotiated meaning.

Alf Linderman (chap. 14) gives a careful account of the way audiences in a particular national context come to receive and interpret television with explicitly religious content. Linderman has specialized in laying out the place of religion within culturalist media analysis. His approach challenges the received notion that the process of interpretation or meaning-making is transparent to audiences. As will be obvious from many other chapters, the media do constitute a new context and a new set of practices for the doing and knowing of religion. The media are not transparent conveyors of religious meaning.

When thinking about the media and meaning, we often teeter on the brink of causal inference; that is, we quickly want to move from observed practice to speculation that something in the system clearly caused something else: we impute causal power to a source or message. Linderman shows that we must look elsewhere for causation—that the capacities of the system of practice whereby viewers encounter and interact with religious television locate causation in a complex and subtle interplay between experience, history, structure, identity, symbol, and meaning.

In what amounts to a case study of the semiological theory laid out by Linderman, Michael Berkowitz in chapter 15 looks at the symbolic formation of themes and values of leadership and social authority in Judaism in the early twentieth century. Consistent with other chapters here, he holds that such negotiations and constructions must be seen with reference to the emergent mediated public of the period. Whatever might have provided the currency of social power and movement prominence before the late nineteenth century, by the turn of the twentieth things had changed radically: entirely new conditions and contexts of authority had emerged. Specifically, Berkowitz looks at questions of the authenticity of symbolism and iconography as important factors. Reminiscent of earlier chapters by Winston and Morgan, he sees the emergence of Jewish identity as taking place in the larger context of public culture, and sees them deriving some of their logic from that context.

In chapter 16, Knut Lundby takes us to a very specific place and time. His investigations into the interplay between religion, media, modernity, identity, localism, and globalism find fertile ground in a small "growth point" in Zimbabwe. Lundby, an expert in the rarefied world of the new media, sees in this village and in the negotiations of religious meaning in specific religious settings there a lesson in the extent to which much of the material that this book has studied is small, specific, and focused. The images, symbols, and claims that are being remade into religious meaning and identity around the world today make particular sense when seen in such places and practices. Tsanzaguru raises important challenges to the easy and facile way we have chosen to understand globalism, the global context, and modernity. The question is not so simple as the "authentic" local versus the "inauthentic" or "imposed" translocal or foreign. Out of both of these meaning systems, new meanings are made in Tsanzaguru.

The book ends end with a fascinating and unique perspective on the phenomenon that first stimulated scholarly and public interest in these issues: televangelism. Keyan Tomaselli and Arnold Shepperson, media scholars from South Africa, take a theoretically based look at its place and potential. Their view is not specific to Southern Africa, but it draws much of its force from a Southern African perspective. Televangelism has long been criticized for being culturally imperialistic. Even in the hands of "local" or "national" producers, the form of televangelism has long been thought to undermine its authenticity.

Tomaselli and Shepperson demonstrate that this thinking is too narrow. For both pragmatic and theoretical reasons, they argue, we must attempt to understand televangelism (and indeed, any meaning-centered communication) with reference to its authenticity for specific communities and places of reception or articulation.

CHAPTER 14

RELIGIOUS TELEVISION IN SWEDEN: TOWARD A MORE BALANCED VIEW OF ITS RECEPTION

Alf Linderman

While research within the social sciences and media studies once relied primarily on quantitative methods, today qualitative methods are often applied when studying phenomena like television reception. Studies in media now look toward how meanings are constructed,[1] making possible connections with the branch of religious studies that focuses on the role of media in the development of values, conceptions of the world, and religious identity.[2] In this chapter I compare the findings of earlier quantitative studies with more recent studies of the reception of religious television. The more recent studies have been founded on a theoretical framework called social semeiology, and a qualitative approach has been the primary method of data collection and analysis. I try to show here that while there is a fair amount of continuity and coherence between the studies, the qualitative approach also reveals information missed by the earlier studies. The nuance and complexity of additional insights of the recent qualitative studies is such that it seems fair to assume that the differences, at least in part, are determined by the change of methodology.

THE SWEDISH CASE

Sweden is a Lutheran country where the Lutheran Church of Sweden was the state church until church and state were separated on January 1,

2000. Public broadcasting has been under the control of the state, and commercial television did not become a significant part of the Swedish media market until the late 1980s. The state-owned Swedish Broadcasting Corporation broadcasts church services almost every week, over both radio and television. Thus, there are many differences between the development of religious broadcasting in Sweden and in the United States. For this very reason, it is interesting in the context of this book to briefly explore media practices and the reception of religious television in the Swedish context.

The development of religious broadcasting in Sweden has been the subject of several scholarly works.[3] However, there has not been much scholarly attention devoted to how religious broadcasting in Sweden works in the lives of its audiences. The most significant studies of the reception of religious television in Sweden were conducted by Thorleif Pettersson in the early 1980s. From a perspective of uses and gratification, and relying on a general mass-communication theory model that explores media consumption as a functional alternative to other activities in the social world,[4] Pettersson studied the role of religious television in the lives of the audience using quantitative research methods.[5] Given Pettersson's theoretical framework, the primary objective was to explore the level of religious gratification associated with religious television viewing.

Pettersson found that for people intending to take part in religious services, but who were unable to do so due to such factors as health, mobility, or distance, religious television services were functionally similar to "real" religious services in terms of religious gratification. For regular service attenders, on the other hand, frequent viewing of television services was primarily associated with nonreligious gratification. For occasional service attenders, frequent viewing was primarily associated with religious gratification, similar to the situation for those who were unable to attend.

On the basis of these findings, Pettersson drew the conclusion that television services "might be said to foster nonreligious, 'secularized' service experiences" for regular church service attenders. For occasional service attenders, television services might be said to have a "privatizing" effect, since there was no evidence that the religious gratification they received from broadcasts would lead to increased service attendance.[6]

For obvious reasons, Pettersson's results were perhaps not good news to those in the Swedish Christian community who were involved in the production of religious television. Only those who wanted to go to church, but were unable to do so, used televised religion as a functional alternative to regular church services, the programs' presumed actual objective. For other viewers, watching these television programs brought primarily something other than religious experience, "privatized" or not. As these results constituted an interesting challenge to the Christian community, further research explored whether there was more to this than Pettersson unveiled in his studies.

In 1996 the religion department at the Swedish Broadcasting Corporation started to try out a new model for their weekly broadcasting of religious television services (which are, with few exceptions, Christian services). Instead of broadcasting services from new places each week, they selected eight churches, each of which was responsible for four services distributed over the year. Four churches from the Church of Sweden, three so-called "free" churches (two Swedish Covenant churches and one Pentecostal church) and one Roman Catholic church were included in the project. The goal was to increase the sense of community and togetherness among those who watch these programs. However, another motive coincided with this goal: it is less expensive to produce church services from a restricted number of locations, since this saves on physical costs of scouting and staging new sites and clergy and others become more and more familiar with the television production process.

A QUALITATIVE APPROACH

In a qualitative study of how these productions were perceived by the audience, some forty individuals were selected for repeated interviews about their experiences with them. They were interviewed not only about their direct experiences of religious television, but also about their life in general and about their religious and media practices. Included in the study were individuals who regularly attend religious services as well as those who only occasionally attended religious services in traditional church settings, allowing for further explorations of Pettersson's categories and results.

The study was rooted in social semeiology, a theoretical framework in which the practice of meaning making is the focus.[7] The theoretical foundation for social semeiology can be found in three traditions: the semiology of F. de Saussure, the semiotics of C. S. Peirce, and symbolic interactionism, primarily in the tradition of George Herbert Mead. Foundational to all is the semiological idea that conventional sign systems are the basis of human communication. Each act of communication is related to one or more socially established signification systems. Any "text" resulting from an act of communication will signal its belonging to a signification system in that its elements will be organized according to rules and conventions within this particular system. This relation to a signification system constitutes a constraint on the individual construction of meaning. However, this does not at the same time mean that the process of meaning construction is completely determined. Divergent "readings" are possible since each reader has a variety of ways of relating a text to different signification systems, and of combining elements from different signification systems.

In the semiotic tradition associated with C. S. Peirce, a more process-oriented perspective on the individual construction of meaning has been developed. The emphasis is on the individual (mental) process of meaning construction and reconstruction. This extension is foundational to the "social" semiological approach introduced here.

These foci on the social level and on the individual level can be interrelated in a model inspired by Mead's interactionism. Mead asserted that the dynamic process on the individual level is directly related to the dynamic process on the social level, where social signification systems are created, maintained, and recreated. Through the individual's previous experiences in social interaction, he or she has acquired knowledge about how certain signs are used; that is, what meaning certain signs are "supposed" to carry in a certain situation. The process by which the individual acquires this knowledge consists of the engagement in common activities and social interactions with others. In this interaction, various signs are used as individuals act and express themselves. As the individual develops a certain meaning out of certain signs, there will be an inclination to act in a certain way linked to this meaning. Thus, the individually actualized meaning can result in verbal or physical action by this individual that expresses how he or she processed the meaning in certain signs.

In this phase, when meaning is expressed, there is a potential for this meaning to become something more than just individually actualized meaning. Once expressed on the social arena, it can influence discourses and social conventions. It is through this continuous use of signs in social interaction that socially established signification systems can undergo continuous change and development. As we interview people about their media practices and related meaning making, we are thus on the individual level studying something that is rooted in the social context and something that in the situation of the interview again becomes part of the social context. The interview itself therefore becomes part of the practice it sets out to study. This does not, however, make the interview invalid as a method for data collection in empirical research. The construction of meaning is social by nature. Thus, the interview actually reflects meaning making in a realistic way as it generates interaction and meaning making in a social context.

We can now move to a few observations as we compare the quantitative and qualitative studies of the reception of religious television in Sweden. These will relate the qualitative study to a few key findings presented by Pettersson. Thus the actual complexity of the qualitative material will not be fully reflected. But for a few categories that through Pettersson's quantitative studies have been pointed out as relatively significant, I hope to demonstrate that the qualitative study of meaning making represents a fruitful and illuminating contribution.

A MORE BALANCED VIEW OF RECEPTION

Preliminary findings in the qualitative social semeiology-based research in many ways correspond with Pettersson's results. For those regularly attending church services in a traditional setting, it was found in the qualitative study that viewing of religious services on television indeed nurtured a more detached attitude toward the religious services. Watching a service on television could be combined with various activities; for example, making and drinking coffee, preparing food, making phone calls, talking with others (both about the service and other things). The religious service to some degree becomes like anything else that is flowing out of the television set and can be dealt with accordingly. As one interviewee—who preferred watching the televised service to visiting a church on Sundays in which many young families with noisy children were present—expressed it: "Television is so good because when there is something you don't like you can just turn it off" (a response that it is more difficult to make in the church setting). This relates to what Pettersson refers to as the secularizing "effect" of religious television: viewers can deal with religion as they deal with other kinds of media stories. Neither did viewers seem to get much in the way of social connectedness from these programs. The effort to create more continuity by screening several services from the same churches did not seem to make any difference. In comparison with watching the same news anchor several hundred times in one year, it did not seem to make any difference to viewers if there were a couple of services from the same place. What made the difference was if they thought the service was good or bad, and each program seemed to be evaluated individually.

The watching of religious television services among those who are regular churchgoers seemed also to contradict the notion that media play a role in secularization. First, it was expressed that television actually had the potential to become more personal than the church experience. The individual story and witness could turn out to be even more intimate when watched on television in the security and comfort of the home. Second, when audience members watched how people in other places celebrate religious services, they experienced themselves as being part of something beyond their own local horizon. To this experience is added the particular social and cultural significance attributed to television, and consequently the confirmation of religious identity that stems from seeing religion per se being represented on the television screen. For several individuals included in the qualitative study, this experience of religious presence on television was seen to be contradicted by the circumstance that services might be broadcast from churches related to religious traditions other than the viewers' own affiliations. Even though some viewers felt that their negative feelings toward others were reinforced as they watched services from other denominations, others felt that these services could dissolve rather than reinforce negative preconceptions about other denominations. As one interviewee expressed it: "It is important that we in the different denominations try to find something to help each other with, and try to promote the Christian message and the gospel."

The above were views among those in the qualitative study that regularly attended church. For those who are not regular churchgoers, however, there were at least three different types of cases present in the qualitative material. There were those who explored Christianity via television within the private sphere of the home, but with little reference to, or experience in, "real" religion. Their use of televised services correspond to what Pettersson referred to as "privatizing" effects of religious television.

However, there were also those in the group participating in the qualitative study who had experienced various types of social tensions and problems with direct involvement in religious settings. For them, televised services were a way of "keeping up" with religious interest without being physically present. This, of course, could be seen as making religion a private affair, but it is distinctly different from previous cases. This watching of television services was, in fact, one way for these individuals to add at least some sort of social dimension to their religious lives.

Finally, there were those among the respondents who for various reasons could not attend church services, even though they might wish to. Among these, there were those who tried to follow and "participate" in the services. They followed hymns and took part in the ritual activities reflected on the television screen. This category was the one for which Pettersson found that the televised service was functionally similar to the real thing. However, two things should be noted in the qualitative study. First, many interviewees made it very clear that televised services were good primarily because they were "better than nothing." Second, it seems clear that positive experiences are based on a construction of meaning that comes from previous experiences in the traditional religious community. One person had bread and juice ready for the purpose of being able to take part in the communion when this was part of the televised service. Even if this for that particular person could be perceived as a very private way of acting out religious conviction, it seemed to be experienced as social by virtue of being interpreted as reflecting previous social experiences.

There is, of course, a great deal of differentiation in the qualitative material, which is not accounted for in this discussion. The purpose here is not to give a comprehensive account of either the qualitative study or the quantitative studies to which it relates; it is, rather, to show that if we want to understand religious (media) practices we should combine different approaches. By the employment of qualitative methods in the study of the reception of religious television, Pettersson's categories gain in depth and complexity. Taken together, the quantitative and qualitative studies here address a wider spectrum of dimensions related to the viewing of religious television than any one of the approaches could render on its own.

However, the refinement achieved by broadening the methodological repertoire not only relates to the results of previous research, it also confronts previous research on the level of theory. Pettersson discussed his findings in relation to theories of secularization and privatization of religion. Findings from the qualitative study suggest that the framework of secularization theory, which takes institutional religion as its point of reference, is in need of refinement. Even though the qualitative study primarily focused on Christian television services, the way in which the audience appropriates elements in these television programs becomes interesting and indicative. Religious television services, other television programs, traditional church services, and various other types of social and cultural experiences seem to constitute an inventory of symbols and discourses, all of which can be put to use for religious meaning making. Most likely, this has always been the case. What we have observed in the way of recent movement of audiences toward these other sources and away from institutional religion is perhaps primarily the inability within institutionalized religion to guide such processes of appropriation authoritatively.

These privatizing and secularizing tendencies discussed by Pettersson are perhaps best understood as characteristics of a larger cultural development where religious attitudes are being formed and conceived in new ways. Consequently, we need to develop further our categories, methods, and conceptual frameworks to be able to describe and discuss the religious practices of today and tomorrow.

NOTES

This chapter draws on research conducted within a research project funded by the Swedish Council for Research in the Humanities and Social Sciences (ref. no.: F636/95).

1. Klaus B. Jensen, "The Qualitative Turn," introduction to *A Handbook of Qualitative Methodologies for Mass Communication Research,* ed. Klaus B. Jensen and Nicholas W. Jankowski (New York: Routledge, 1991).

2. Lynn Schofield Clark and Stewart M. Hoover, "At the Intersection of Media,

Culture, and Religion.: A Bibliographic Essay," in *Rethinking Media, Religion, and Culture*, ed. Stewart M. Hoover and Knut Lundby (Thousand Oaks, Calif.: Sage, 1997).

3. See, for example, J. A. Hellström, *Samfund och Radio* (Vällingby: Harriers Förlag, 1979); E. Svala, *Tro på TV: Prästmätesavhandling för Göteborgs Stift* (Uppsala: Bokförlaget Pro Veritate, 1981); L. Hedman, *Närradion—innehållet, Medlemmarna och Invandrarna* (Stockholm: Utbildningsdepartementet, 1982); Thorleif Pettersson, "Television eller Religion? Om Tittarnas Användning av TV Gudstjänster" (Religionssociologiska Institutet, Stockholm, Forskningsrapport, 1985), 187–88; C. Dahlgren, "Sverige," in *Religiös Förändring i Norden 1930–1980*, ed. G. Gustafsson, 196–237 (Malmä: Liber Förlag, 1985); R. Larsson, *Religion i Radio och TV under Sextio år* (Stockholm: Almquist and Wiksell International, 1988); Alf Linderman, *Religious Broadcasting in the United States and Sweden: A Comparative Analysis of the History of Religious Broadcasting with Emphasis on Religious Television* (Lund Research Papers in Media and Communication Studies, Report No. 10, 1993).

4. K. E. Rosengren and S. Windahl, "Mass Media Consumption as a Functional Alternative," in *Sociology of Mass Communication*, ed. Denis McQuail, 166–94 (Harmondsworth, U.K.: Penguin Books, 1972).

5. Pettersson, "Television eller Religion?"; Thorleif Pettersson, "Religion som Underhållning," (Religionssociologiska Institutet, Stockholm, Forskningsrapport 189, 1985); Thorleif Pettersson, "The Audiences' Uses and Gratifications of TV Worship Services," *Journal for the Scientific Study of Religion* 25, no. 4 (1986).

6. Pettersson, "Audiences' Uses and Gratifications," 403–4.

7. See Alf Linderman, *The Reception of Religious Television. Social Semeiology Applied to an Empirical Case Study*, Acta Universitatis Upsaliensis, Psychologia et Sociologia Religionum, 12 (Stockholm: Almqvist & Wiksell International, 1996); Alf Linderman, "Making Sense of Religion in Television," in *Rethinking Media, Religion, and Culture*, ed. Stewart M. Hoover and Knut Lundby (Thousand Oaks, Calif.: Sage, 1997); also Klaus B. Jensen, *The Social Semiotics of Mass Communication* (Thousand Oaks, Calif.: Sage, 1995).

BIBLIOGRAPHY

Clark, Lynn S. and Stewart M. Hoover. "At the Intersection of Media, Culture, and Religion. A Bibliographic Essay." In *Rethinking Media, Religion, and Culture*, ed. Stewart M. Hoover and Knut Lundby. Thousand Oaks, Calif.: Sage, 1997.

Dahlgren, C. "Sverige." In *Religiös Förändring i Norden 1930–1980*, ed. G. Gustafsson. Malmö: Liber Förlag, 1985.

Hedman, L. "Närradion—Innehållet, Medlemmarna och Invandrarna." Stockholm: Utbildningsdepartementet, 1982.

Hellström, J. A. *Samfund och Radio*. Vällingby: Harriers förlag, 1979.

Jensen, Klaus B. "Introduction: the Qualitative Turn." In *A Handbook of Qualitative Methodologies for Mass Communication Research*, ed. Klaus B. Jensen and Nicholas. W. Jankowski. New York: Routledge, 1991.

——. *The Social Semiotics of Mass Communication*. Thousand Oaks, Calif.: Sage, 1995.

Larsson, R. *Religion i Radio och TV under Sextio år*. Stockholm: Almquist & Wiksell International, 1988.

Linderman, Alf. "Religious Broadcasting in the United States and Sweden: A Comparative Analysis of the History of Religious Broadcasting with Emphasis on Religious Television." Lund Research Papers in Media and Communication Studies, Report No. 10, 1993.

——. "The Reception of Religious Television: Social Semeiology Applied to an Empirical Case Study." *Acta Universitatis Upsaliensis, Psychologia et Sociologia Religionum*, 12. Stockholm: Almqvist & Wiksell International, 1996.

——. "Making Sense of Religion in Television." In *Rethinking Media, Religion, and Culture*, ed. Stewart M. Hoover and Knut Lundby. Thousand Oaks, Calif.: Sage, 1997.

Pettersson, Thorleif. "Television eller Religion? Om Tittarnas Användning av TV Gudstjänster." Religionssociologiska Institutet, Stockholm, Forskningsrapport, 1985.

——. "Religion som Underhållning." Religionssociologiska Institutet, Stockholm, Forskningsrapport, 1985.

——. "The Audiences' Uses and Gratifications of TV Worship Services." *Journal for the Scientific Study of Religion*, 25(4) 1986.

Rosengren, K. E., and S. Windahl. "Mass Media Consumption as a Functional Alternative." In *Sociology of Mass Communication*, ed. Denis McQuail. Harmondsworth, U.K.: Penguin Books, 1972.

Svala, E. *Tro På TV: Prästmötesavhandling för Göteborgs Stift*. Uppsala: Bokförlaget Pro Veritate, 1981.

CHAPTER 15

RELIGIOUS TO ETHNIC-NATIONAL IDENTITIES: POLITICAL MOBILIZATION THROUGH JEWISH IMAGES IN THE UNITED STATES AND BRITAIN, 1881–1939

Michael Berkowitz

As we begin the twenty-first century, Jews in North America and the United Kingdom are recognized for achieving an astounding measure of organizational success. To many it seems "natural" that Jews adapted well to changing circumstances and managed to protect and assert their communal interests. But the historical question remains: How did modern, largely secular, Jewish-oriented identities for Western Jews come into being from the age of mass immigration to the mid-twentieth century? How were Jews mobilized, as an ethnic-national, religious minority, in an age when acculturation seemed to be the overwhelming historical imperative? As a partial answer, I will examine Jewish iconography, especially pertaining to the Jewish experience with political movements in the United States and Britain from 1881 to 1939. In contrast to most works relating Jews and images, my emphasis is not on anti-Semitism.[1] I have attempted to look over the shoulder of previous generations of Western Jewry in order to appreciate Jews' representations of themselves.

This is not, formally speaking, a study in "Jewish art" or "Jewish photography,"[2] but rather an interpretation of applications of graphics and photography, over time, that accompanied and fostered Jewish politics in the realm of popular culture. To be sure, the teachings of the Frankfurt school and the resurgence of interest in Walter Benjamin have underscored the antihumanist and anti-Semitic consequences of mass culture for commercial and explicitly political purposes.³ Yet in the decades before the Holocaust, organized segments of Western Jews enthusiastically used modern media in order to exert a greater control of their lives as well as to more fully realize their humanity. It is hoped that this brief glimpse into how Jews visualized themselves is suggestive for exploring how religious identities become secularized, and to question the relationships between the secular and religious, and everyday life and ideology. It also addresses the function of images, and the mediation of images, with regard to identity formation and ethnic politics.⁴

EARLY PHOTOGRAPHIC IMAGES OF IMMIGRANT COMMUNITIES

As much as Americans have become accustomed to idealizing the work of Jacob Riis as uniquely capturing "the immigrant experience," it is crucial to affirm that his pictures did not necessarily reflect the self-perceptions of his subjects.⁵ Most of the photo-journalistic "social reformers" of early-twentieth-century England and the United States reinforced derogatory stereotypes of Jews that ascribed the wretchedness of their material circumstances to hereditary proclivities, inner-Jewish exploitation, and collective stubbornness. "The Jewish quarter of New York," wrote Hutchins Hapgood in 1902, is thought "to be a place of poverty, dirt, ignorance and immorality—the seat of the sweat-shop, the tenement house, and where 'red-lights' sparkle at night, where people are queer and repulsive."⁶ Wherever Jews were found to live in densely packed blocks, and the ranks of those moving out replenished by immigrants from Eastern Europe, it is not difficult to find roughly interchangeable descriptions. Adolf Hitler's haunting line about the caftan-Jew in Vienna would not have been out of place in treatments of urban centers from Central Europe to the Midwestern United States.

Among Westernized Jews themselves there was no dearth of critics, and contempt toward their Russian and Polish brethren, however ambivalent, was palpable.⁷ Surely some of the anti-Semitic and even racist rhetoric was internalized. Jewish immigrants were, in photographic treatments of life and labor, occasionally dealt with sympathetically, or at least benignly, such as in the street scenes and individual portraits of Lewis W. Hine.⁸ But there is little evidence that Hine's pictures, or the more famous scenes of Jacob Riis from *How the Other Half Lives,* had much resonance in the Jewish street. The dominant renderings of Jewry by both anti-Semites and well-intentioned reformers bore little relation to the self-image in Jews' own inner eye.

It has been stated as a historical axiom that "all cultures require icons,"[9] but the icons of Jewry at the end of the nineteenth century and the first half of the twentieth century have barely been recovered, let alone interpreted. It is mainly in Eastern Europe and Palestine that Jews have been recognized for trying to mold their political identity; here, though, I explore the West, to look against the current of a supposedly overwhelming rush to acculturation.[10] Although Zionism, Yiddishism, Jewish socialism, territorialism, trade unionism, religious parties, and other movements did not uniformly succeed in mastering the fate of their imagined constituencies, scholars need not be blind to their efforts to carve out Jewish public spaces.

THE JEWISH LEADER AS "HANDSOME" MAN

In the terms of nationalism scholar Anthony Smith, the representations evoked by these causes provide a kind of ethnic "map" that rarely has been consulted.[11] Within the contemporaneous Jewish communities themselves, it is clear that such images contained various "codes" of understanding Jewish politics and peoplehood.[12] Long before "Black is beautiful" became the watchword for African American pride, Jews among themselves often spoke of the handsomeness of their leaders. The kind of good looks they praised as appropriate for their heroes was no simple aping of the Gentiles; the modern Jewish knight-errant could be unapologetically dark, wiry-haired, and wearing spectacles—as was the case with Baruch Charney Vladeck when he entered the United States in 1908 (see fig. 15.1). This was "a real man."[13] Melech Epstein, a commentator who was not prone to generosity, prefaced his profile of Chaim Zhitlovsky by asserting that "Zhitlowksy was a handsome man with sparkling blue eyes and thick blond hair and beard. His appearance, plus his poise and academic bearing, made him an impressive figure."[14] Similar sentiments were echoed by a picture caption in a publication of the Arbeter-Ring (Workmen's Circle): "Dr. H. Zhitlovsky, socialist, revolutionary and preeminent Yiddish writer."[15] Hence the physiognomy, stature, and mind were conceived in total; a rhetoric of virility, of spawning ardent followers, seemed a natural consequence of the leaders' appearance, intellectual labor, and charisma.

FIGURE 15.1

Baruch Charney Vladeck and his brother, the poet Shmuel Niger, in Baruch Charney
Vladeck, *B. Vladeck in leben un shafen,* ed. Yefim Yeshurin (New York: Forverts
asosiayshon, 1935). (Courtesy of the Forward Association.)

FIGURE 15.2
Mass-produced postcard of Louis Brandeis.

FIGURE 15.3
Mass-produced portrait of Chaim Weizmann.
(Courtesy Central Zionist Archives, Jerusalem.)

ZIONISM AND ITS DEPICTIONS

It may be argued that the aspect of Jewish politics that sought most deliberately to use the visual to its advantage was the Zionist movement, which beginning in 1897 released hundreds of multiply reproduced images. Although Zionism did not gain a significant following in the United States and Britain until World War I, there is evidence that portraits of Theodor Herzl and scenes of national-Jewish life burgeoning in Palestine were already starting to shape Jewish public consciousness. Therefore, by the time Chaim Weizmann in England and Louis Brandeis entered the mainstream of Jewish politics through Zionism, the ground was well prepared for seeing them as leading a viable movement. During most of the interwar years, Weizmann was dominant in Zionism while Brandeis represented the opposition to Weizmann's regime. Nevertheless, both of them were seen, in their respective American and British contexts, as proudly embodying Jewish politics as the demands of the movement were increasingly pressed (see figs. 15.2 and 15.3).

But several others besides Weizmann and Brandeis played significant roles. Among women Zionists in Britain, for instance, the fact that Rebecca Sieff was seen as "brilliant and handsome" contributed to her ability to ignite "the imagination of the rank and file of Jewish women";[16] another memoirist writes that "she became a legend in her own day for her regal beauty and personal charm; but it was her fiery spirit . . . that won for her a place in history."[17] The terms *fiery* and *restless,*[18] almost always inferring positive traits, appears with great frequency no matter what the brand of Jewish politics. Assertiveness was not off-putting, although there was room for those who exemplified a more reticent dignity like the anarchist S. Janowsky, and like Hermann Lilliput, a labor editor of the *Jewish Daily Forward*—another character who was well-remembered in three dimensions: "Lilliput, who stood over six feet and had a crown of red hair, was known throughout the movement as a gentle warrior. He was capable of weeping over the injuries of a dog; but when he was arrested in Czarist Russia for revolutionary work, he attacked a police guard for abusing some of the weaker prisoners, and he fought until he was beaten into insensibility."[19] This visual sensibility was embraced, as well, by the International Ladies' Garment Workers' Union. Although it was not an expressly "Jewish" organization, its heads were sensitive to the fact that it was perceived as Jewish. Therefore they wanted to positively picture the "national 'types'" in its ranks.[20] In the literature both supportive of and hostile to the trade union movement, an underlying assumption is that organized garment workers are mostly Jews and that their leadership is Jewish. In one anti-Semitic and anti–trade union tirade of 1909, the stereotype of Jews as leaders and sympathizers of unionism and socialism is conflated with the (hyperinflated) accusation that Jews possessed the monopoly on "White Slavery," the international traffic in coerced prostitutes.[21] There could be no doubt that antiunionism of a certain sort was anti-Semitic, and a prounionism of a certain sort was a positive affirmation of Jewishness in the secular realm. In contrast to myriad unflattering allegations against self-organized Jewry, one of the most prominent shared features of Jewish politics was that Jews representing autonomously Jewish movements were morally upright, respectable, and supremely dignified.

FEMALE SPECTATORS OF THE JEWISH POLITICAL IMAGE

It also is important to consider that "viewers are active participants in determining meaning."[22] Women's roles take on a heightened importance from the perspective of "spectatorship." It is interesting that Miriam Hansen begins her study of *Spectatorship in American Silent Film* with the 1897 premiere of *The Corbett-Fitzsimmons Fight*, noting that women made up a substantial share of the audience. "Unlike live prizefights with their all-male clientele," Hansen writes, the film "gave women access to a spectacle from which they traditionally had been excluded."[23] Although I do not wish to exaggerate the overwrought analogy between sports and politics-as-a-game, it does not seem accidental that women became notable "spectators" in Jewish politics, particularly Zionism and Bundism, beginning in 1897.[24]

The notion of Zionist and Jewish trade union leaders having a seductive quality was not totally hidden in accounts of the movement, in which notions of eroticism and messianism were intertwined.[25] Above all this was true of Theodor Herzl, the founder of "political" Zionism (fig. 15.4). But the early Jewish labor movement in New York also boasted an "unselfish and courageous" champion possessing a strikingly handsome Semitic countenance: Joseph Barondess. In the novel *Zalmonah*, Edward King's fictionalized account of the life of Cloak-maker Union leader

Theodor Herzl

Herausgegeben vom Keren Kajemeth Lejisrael zum 25. Todestag Theodor Herzls.

FIGURE 15.4
Theodor Herzl overlooking the Rhine Bridge in Basel.
(Photo by E. M. Lilien. Courtesy Central Zionist Archives.)

Barondess, Zalmonah (Barondess) is a veritable heartthrob: tall and allur-
ing, with "blue fearless eyes" and a brow "marked with power," he was a
magnet to beautiful women.[26] In union meetings he was "worshipped by
the mothers and wives who recognized in him the deliverer, leading their
sons and husbands up out of the land of Egypt."[27] It is not surprising that
both Barondess and Herzl had theatrical aspirations, Herzl as a playwright
and Barondess as an actor.[28] Rose Schneiderman made sure, in a reminis-
cence about the diverse attributes of Sidney Hillman that contributed to
his effective leadership—including *yiches* (prestigious, notably learned
forebears), Talmudic acumen, and broad humanism—to include his at-
tractiveness to women:[29]

> I first met Sidney in 1913 . . . at a beach picnic on Staten Island orga-
> nized by mutual friends and, from that time on, we were good friends.
> Sidney was quite a charmer and several of the girls there were prepared
> to fall in love with him but he was already engaged to Bessie
> Abramowitz. . . . Sidney was a slender young man, then in his middle
> twenties. He was entirely wrapped up in trade unionism, as we all
> were. That was all we talked about in those days and that's what we
> talked about that Sunday on Staten Island. And, of course, the future of
> mankind. I remember how very gay and witty Sidney was and I knew
> even then that he had the ability to get along with people. . . . Sidney
> was a Talmudic scholar, a descendant of a long line of learned rabbis,
> but he had rebelled against his father's choice of a career for him as a
> respectable rabbi. Coming to this country by way of England, he
> stopped first in New York, but after a short time moved on to Chicago
> where he learned to be a cutter at the Hart Schaffner & Marx factory
> and where he continued his intense interest in the plight of the worker
> which had first been aroused in his native land.[30]

Despite the fact that neither Zionism nor Jewish trade unionism was
genuinely welcoming to women, spectatorship evolved into recruitment.
Throughout the interwar years, the largest single segment of United
States' Zionists was Hadassah, the Women's Zionist Organization of
America, and the International Ladies Garment Workers' Union became a
mainstay of the labor movement. *Recruitment* also was often synonymous
with the cultivation of fundraising subscriptions and membership fees,[31]
without which few of these organizations could have hoped to survive.

The point may indeed be argued that prominent women and women's organizations existed in the Jewish public realm to a greater degree than scholars have suggested. For example, one finds no women included in the authoritative works on Zionism by Arthur Hertzberg and Shlomo Avineri,[32] or in older, collective portraits of the Lower East Side of New York, such as *Profiles of Eleven* by Melech Epstein, and *Des shpigel fun der ist seyd* [The mirrors of the East Side], by Jacob Magidoff. Despite the title of his magnum opus that infers the contrary—*World of Our Fathers*—Irving Howe shows that Jewish women did play substantial roles, on many levels, in the Lower East Side.[33] In Zionism during the interwar years, Henrietta Szold was a dominant, if embattled, leader. Before her ascendance to the head of Hadassah she was an important, if undervalued, shaper of the program and products of the Jewish Publication Society of America.[34] Certainly Lillian Wald and Rose Schneiderman deserve mention for their influence among the masses in the Lower East Side. Wald, "the nurse who founded the Henry Street Settlement, grew within her lifetime into a figure of legend, known and adored on every street."[35] Schneiderman was among the most critical interlocutors bringing the concerns of Jewish labor to the door of the Roosevelt White House, receiving a fair hearing, and ultimately a sincere embrace. The history of movements such as Zionism and trade unionism, although clearly male-dominated, appear very different from the normative narratives when the history of women is deliberately and consistently interwoven.[36]

THE INRAGING OF PROGRESSIVE, RADICAL, AND ANTI-ZIONIST FIGURES

Along with images related to the Zionist movement and Jewish workers' and trade union activities, "Jewish" socialism and communism, territorialism, the political dimension of "progressive" religious sects, and Orthodox and ultra-Orthodox parties may be included among visually attuned Jewish political strands. Beginning with the more explicitly radical orientation, one of the most forgotten movers (*machers*) was the chief icon of the far Left, M. Olgin (fig. 15.5). Olgin was, in fact, one of the most ardent advocates of Yiddish, who saw in the creation of the Soviet Union the best chance for the flourishing of a distinctive, Yiddish-based national Jewish culture.

The kingmaker of the Jewish street for more than half a century, how-

FIGURE 15.5
M. Olgin, cover of Aaron Kurtz, *Moshe Olgin* (Cleveland: shtot-komitet
fun yidisher sektsie AAO fun Cleveland, 1940). (Courtesy of
Ohio State University Photographic Services.)

ever, was the editor of the *Forward*, Abraham Cahan.[37] Cahan is a quintes-
sential figure in this brief study, because his likeness could be used to promote politics from a specifically Jewish-leftist militancy, to Zionism, to
"assimilationism." Hutchins Hapgood wrote that "the great passion of
the intellectual quarter results in the consciously held and warmly felt

principle that literature should be a transcript from life. Cahan represents this feeling in its purest aspect; and he therefore is highly interesting not only as a man *but as a type.*"[38] Cahan shows that the lines between journalism and politics, and even poetry and politics, were almost always obscured in this period (232).

Although Cahan was in a class of his own as the personification of a newspaper (in his case, the *Forward*), other papers, as well, were closely identified with their guiding spirits. Part of this is due to the fact that most newspapers were forced to have public fundraising events in order to carry on, and their editors and featured writers were the main speakers. Even the anarchists were pressed into this: "The weekly Anarchistic paper, the *Fraye arbeter-shtimme,* prints about 7,000 copies. Of this circulation, with the assistance of balls, entertainments, and benefits at the theatres, the paper is able to exist. It pays a salary to only one man, the editor S. Janowsky, who receives the sum of $13 a week" (192–93).

Like so many of the figures of Jewish politics who wrote in different languages and advocated different programs at various stages of their lives, the writer David Pinsky and poets Abraham Reisen, Abraham Liesin, and Morris Winchevsky also were "transitional" figures. Pinsky, notes Hapgood, "a writer for the *Abendblatt,* is very interesting not only as a writer of short sketches of literary value . . . but also as a dramatic critic and as one of the more wide-awake and distinctively modern of the young men of Yiddish New York" (198). Morris Winchevsky, like many of the others, "is a Socialist, a man who has edited more than one Yiddish publication with success, of uncommon learning and cultivation" (196). Both Shalom Aleichem and Chaim Zhitlowsky are remembered mostly for their contributions to Yiddish literature and the advocacy of a public space for Yiddishism, respectively; these men embodied what are generally considered contradictory aspects of Jewish-national politics at different times. The point I wish to stress, though, is that the Jewish element tended to overwhelm the specific political program of the sect or individual.

The pantheon of Jewish politicos featured those aligned with socialism and trade unionism, such as Manny Shinwell and Harold Laski, in Britain, and, familiar to the Jewish masses of New York's Lower East Side, Meyer London, Rose Schneiderman, and Morris Hillquit. Baruch Charney Vladeck, identified with the *Forward,* the Arbeter-Ring, and the United

FIGURE 15.6
Albert Einstein, portrait with dedication to Zionist leader Arthur Ruppin.
(Courtesy of Central Zionist Archives.)

Hebrew Trades also belongs with the affirmatively-Jewish cohort of the period before World War II. The great scholar-agitator on the Lower East Side was Isaac Hourwich; more than any other individual, he helped Jewish immigrants to understand their supremely productive role in the economy. Along with the personalities, organizations such as the Arbeter Ring, the United Hebrew Trades, and the Jewish Section of the Socialist Labor Party became well defined, vibrant elements of Jewish political life. Yet, compared with the Zionist movement, which helped its constituents visualize a total Jewish society in Palestine, the purview of the occupation-based organizations was more circumscribed: the workmen's organizations mainly heralded their efforts at caring for members in sickness, duress, and death.[39]

Contrary to the popular belief that ultra-Orthodox Jewry abhorred any type of "graven image,"[40] anti-Zionist orthodox parties—particularly Agudas Yisroel—had their own lionized leaders; for example, Nathan Birnbaum, R. Moshe Blau, R. Yosef Haim Sonnenfeld, and Jacob Israel De Haan. These icons carried profound significance in Jewish circles that are often seen as being hostile to the instruments of mass politics; this was not simply a matter of glorifying great rabbis.[41] De Haan, as the first victim of a Zionist "political murder" in 1924, became a uniquely significant visage whose legacy continues to burn brightly in the world of the Haredim, or ultra-ultra-Orthodox. There also were progressive Jewish religious leaders, such as Moses Gaster and Stephen S. Wise, whose poses embodied expressly political, courageous stances.[42] But no celebrity, Jewish or non-Jewish, had the cachet of Albert Einstein, whose value to Jewish pride and Zionism was beyond compare (fig. 15.6).

THE ROLE OF IMAGES IN THE FORMATION OF A POLITICALLY MOBILIZED JEWISH IDENTITY

It may be argued that iconography became a means of entry to modern political movements and institutions, as well as a means to preserve, adapt, and enchant forms of Jewish distinctiveness. A leftist stalwart in London asserted that the spirit of the old anarchist and trade unionist comrades was "poured into the new movement which has established the State of Israel."[43] One of the striking examples of this confluence may be found in the 1928 jubilee volume of the Gewerkshaften (United Hebrew

Trades): Despite the fact that he was the living exponent of "Hebrew" labor, and therefore assumed to be a staunch advocate of Hebrew over and above Yiddish, David Ben Gurion conveyed his greetings, in Yiddish, to the union's rank and file.[44] The official history of the United Hebrew Trades ten years later would call the Histadruth, the federation of Zionist unions in Palestine, one of its "kindred movements abroad," and it would increasingly dedicate itself to "refugee aid work" and "the development of Palestine as a homeland."[45]

Although I do not mean to minimize the galvanizing force of the Holocaust and the birth of the State of Israel, I contend that Jews were already "politically mobilized" in the West by the outbreak of World War II and the Holocaust. As they were becoming less working-class and Yiddish-speaking, Zionism was left as one of the more viable alternatives for an affirmatively Jewish form of self-identification. And it was a phenomenon that Jews had been trained to "see." Regarding the United States in the 1930s, Warren Sussman has written that photography, radio, and film "created a special community of all Americans (possibly an international community) unthinkable previously. The shift to a culture of sight and sound was of profound importance; it increased our self-awareness as a culture; it helped create a unity of response and action not previously possible; it made us more susceptible than ever to those who would mold culture and thought."[46]

Within the dominant, macrocultures of the Americans and British resided a variety of Jewish microcultures that simultaneously resisted and absorbed the larger trends, and built up worlds of their own. A critic of the visual arts writes that "the more fragile our identity, the more we need to reinforce it. To show that we exist."[47] Beyond asserting the mere existence of Jewry as a whole and its corporate bodies, the men and women behind these images fervently sought the transformation of themselves and their world into something greater. "We know," wrote Walter Benjamin at the conclusion of his "Theses on the Philosophy of History" (XVIII B),

> that the Jews were prohibited from investigating the future. The Torah and the prayers instruct them in remembrance, however. This stripped the future of its magic, to which all those succumb who turn to soothsayers for enlightenment. This does not imply, however, that for the

Jews the future turned into homogeneous, empty time. For every second of time was the strait gate through which the Messiah might enter.[48]

Messianism, for Western Jews in the early twentieth century, would assume any number of guises; its pace and form depended on the particular strains of Jewish politics with which one identified. Such hopes were stirred not only from discreet religious traditions and ideologies, but through the engagement of specific Jewish countenances.

NOTES

This chapter is an adapted excerpt from Michael Berkowitz, *The Jewish Self-Image* (London: Reaktion; New York: New York University Press, 2000). Dedicated to my colleagues Moses and Ruth Rischin.

1. Among the notable exceptions are Jack Kugelmass, "Jewish Icons: Envisioning the Self in Images of the Other," in *Jews and Other Differences: The New Jewish Cultural Studies,* ed. Jonathan Boyarin and Daniel Boyarin (Minneapolis: University of Minnesota Press, 1997), 30–53; Michael P. Steinberg, "Aby Warburg's Kruezlingen Lecture: A Reading," an interpretive essay following *Images from the Region of the Pueblo Indians of North America,* by Aby M. Warburg, trans. Michael P. Steinberg (Ithaca: Cornell University Press, 1995), 59–114; see also Richard I. Cohen, "Jewish Art in the Modern Era," in *The Modern Jewish Experience: A Reader's Guide,* ed. Jack Wertheimer (New York: New York University Press, 1993), 228–41.

2. Richard I. Cohen, *Jewish Icons: Art and Society in Modern Europe* (Berkeley: University of California Press, 1998); Norman L. Kleeblatt, ed., *Too Jewish? Challenging Traditional Identities* (New York: Jewish Museum; New Brunswick, N.J.: Rutgers University Press, 1996).

3. Walter Benjamin, "The Work of Art in the Age of Mechanical Reproduction," in *Illuminations,* ed. Hannah Arendt, trans. Harry Zohn (New York: Schocken, 1968), 217–51.

4. A great stride in this direction has been achieved in Linda Nochlin and Tamar Garb, eds., *The Jew in the Text: Modernity and the Construction of Identity* (London: Thames & Hudson, 1995); see also Matthew Frye Jacobson, *Special Sorrows: The Diasporic Imagination of Irish, Polish, and Jewish immigrants in the United States* (Cambridge: Harvard University Press, 1995) and Jacobson, *Whiteness of a Different Color:*

European Immigrants and the Alchemy of Race (Cambridge: Harvard University Press, 1998), 171–99.

5. Jacob A. Riis, *How the Other Half Lives: Studies among the Tenements of New York* (New York: Dover, 1971).

6. Hutchins Hapgood, *The Spirit of the Ghetto,* ed. Moses Rischin (1902; repr., Cambridge: Harvard University Press, 1967), 5.

7. Eugene Black, *The Social Politics of Anglo-Jewry, 1880–1920* (New York: Basil Blackwell, 1988); Moses Rischin, *The Promised City: New York's Jews, 1870–1914* (Cambridge: Harvard University Press, 1977), 95–111; Irving Howe, *World of Our Fathers: The Journey of the East European Jews to America and the Life They Found and Made* (New York: Harcourt Brace Jovanovich, 1976); Ronald Sanders, *The Downtown Jews: Portraits of an Immigrant Generation* (New York: Harper & Row, 1969); Jonathan Frankel, *Prophecy and Politics: Socialism, Nationalism, and the Russian Jews, 1862–1917* (Cambridge: Cambridge University Press, 1981), 453–551; Lloyd Gartner, *The Jewish Immigrant in England, 1870–1914* (London: Allen & Unwin, 1960); William J. Fishman, *East End Jewish Radicals, 1875–1914* (London: Duckworth, 1995).

8. See *Lewis Hine: Passionate Journey: Photographs 1905–1937,* ed. Karl Steinorth (Rochester, N.Y.: Edition Stemmle, in association with International Museum of Photography, George Eastman House, Rochester, 1996) see "Armenian Jew, Ellis Island Immigrant, New York ca. 1926" (40), and "Street Scene, New York, ca. 1910" (66); in Judith Mara Gutman, *Lewis W. Hine, 1874–1940: Two Perspectives* (New York: Grossman, 1974), see "Young Russian Jew, Ellis Island, 1905" (11), and "Elderly Jewish Immigrant, Ellis Island, 1905" (13).

9. Lawrence W. Levine, "The Historian and the Icon: Photography and the History of American People in the 1930s and 1940s," in *Modern Art and Society: An Anthology of Social and Multicultural Readings,* ed. Maurice Berger (New York: Harper, 1994), 194.

10. Paula Hyman, "Was There a 'Jewish Politics' in Western and Central Europe?" in *The Quest for Utopia: Jewish Political Ideas and Institutions through the Ages,* ed. Zvi Gitelman (Armonk, N.Y.: M. E. Sharpe, 1992), 105–17.

11. Anthony D. Smith, *The Ethnic Origins of Nations* (Oxford, U.K.: Blackwell, 1993), 5.

12. See Gunther Kress and Theo van Leeuwen, *Reading Images: The Grammar of Visual Design* (London: Routledge, 1996), 32–33; see Roland Barthes, "Rhetoric of the Image" in *Image-Music-Text,* trans. Stephen Heath (New York: Hill & Wang, 1977), 36, 42–46.

13. Testimonial of Edward F. McGrath, in Ephim H. Jeshurin, *B. C. Vladeck: Fifty Years of Life and Labor* (New York: Forward Association, 1936), 7, 14.

14. Melech Epstein, *Profiles of Eleven: Profiles of Eleven Men Who Guided the Destiny of an Immigrant Society and Stimulated Social Consciousness among the American People*

(Detroit: Wayne State University Press, 1965), 298; David H. Weinberg, *Between Tradition and Modernity: Haim Zhitlowski, Simon Dubnow, Ahad Ha-Am, and the Shaping of Modern Jewish Identity* (New York: Holmes & Meier, 1996), 83–144; Jonathan Frankel, *Prophecy and Politics*, 258–87.

15. Y. S. Hertz, *Fuftsik yor arbeter-ring in yidishn lebn* (New York: National Executive Committee of the Workmen's Circle, 1950): picture section, n.p.

16. Rosalie Gassman-Sherr, *The Story of the Federation of Women Zionists of Great Britain and Ireland, 1918–1968* (London: Federation of Women Zionists, 1968), 8.

17. Rebecca Sieff, *Who's Who in WIZO, 1966–1970* (Tel Aviv: Dept. of Organisation & Education, Women's International Zionist Organisation, 1970), 1.

18. Testimonials of Daniel W. Hoan and David Dubinsky, in Jeshurin, *B. C. Vladeck*, 7, 14.

19. "In Memoriam," in *Gewerkschaften: Jubilee Book*, ed. Harry Lang and Morris Feinstone (New York: United Hebrew Trades, 1938), 62.

20. *Handbook of Trade Union Methods with Special Reference to the Garment Trades* (New York: Education Department, International Ladies' Garment Workers' Union, 1937), 54.

21. Wiley Britton, *The White Slavery: A Study of the Present Trade Union System* (Akron, Ohio: Werner, 1909).

22. Richard Leppert, *Art and the Committed Eye: The Cultural Functions of Imagery* (Boulder, Colo.: Westview Press, 1996), 6; see also W. J. T. Mitchell, *Picture Theory: Essays on Verbal and Visual Representation* (Chicago: University of Chicago Press, 1994), 324; Martin Jay, "Vision in Context: Reflections and Refractions," in *Vision in Context: Historical and Contemporary Perspectives on Sight*, ed. Teresa Brennan and Martin Jay (New York: Routledge, 1996), 7; David Freedberg, *The Power of Images: Studies in the History and Theory of Response* (Chicago: University of Chicago Press, 1991), 440.

23. Miriam Hansen, *Babel and Babylon: Spectatorship and American Silent Film* (Cambridge: Harvard University Press, 1991), 1.

24. *Die Welt*, 3 September 1897, 12.

25. Irma Lindheim, *The Immortal Adventure* (New York: Macaulay, 1928), 22–23.

26. Edward Smith King, *Joseph Zalmonah* (Boston: Lee & Sheperd, 1893), 11, 32, 260, 335; Joseph Barondess, drawing by S. Raskin, from *Des shpigl fun der East Side* (New York: published privately, 1923).

27. King, *Joseph Zalmonah*, 244.

28. Melech Epstein, *Profiles of Eleven*, 115.

29. "Sidney Hillman in 1908," in George Soulde, *Sidney Hillman: Labor Statesman* (New York: Macmillan, 1939), facing 12, published for and presented to the membership of the Amalgamated Clothing Workers of America; reproduction through the British Library; photo of Sidney Hillman in Y. S. Hertz, *Foftzig Yor*.

30. Rose Schneiderman, *All for One* (New York: P. S. Eriksson, 1967), 241–42.

31. Gassman-Sherr, *Story of the Federation*, 8–9.

32. Arthur Hertzberg, ed., *The Zionist Idea* (New York: Atheneum, 1986); Shlomo Avineri, *The Making of Modern Zionism* (New York: Basic, 1982).

33. Howe, *World of Our Fathers*.

34. Jonathan Sarna, *JPS: The Americanization of Jewish Culture, 1888–1988* (Philadelphia: Jewish Publication Society of America, 1989), 47–94.

35. Howe, *World of Our Fathers*, 90.

36. On Zionism, see Michael Berkowitz, *Western Jewry and the Zionist Project, 1914–1933* (Cambridge: Cambridge University Press, 1997).

37. Abraham Cahan, in Y. S. Hertz, *Foftzig Yor.*

38. Hapgood, *Spirit of the Ghetto*, 235. Emphasis is mine.

39. J. S. Hertz; see pictures of Arbeyter-ring cemetery in New York and the Arbeyter-ring sanatorium in Liberty, New York; Maximillian Hurwitz, *The Workman's Circle: Its History, Ideals, Organization, and Institutions* (New York: Workmen's Circle, 1936), 108–9; Morris C. Feinstone, "A Brief History of the United Hebrew Trades," in *Gewerkschaften*, ed. Lang and Feinstone, 27.

40. Lionel Kochan, *Beyond the Graven Image: A Jewish View* (London: Macmillan, 1997).

41. See Richard Cohen, *Jewish Icons*, 151–53.

42. Untitled article with photo of Moses Gaster in *Die Welt*, November 19, 1897, 8.

43. Joseph Leftwich, introduction to Rudolf Rocker, *The London Years*, trans. Joseph Leftwich (London: Robert Anscombe, 1956), 31.

44. Lang and Feinstone, *Gewerkschaften*, 31.

45. Feinstone, "Brief History," 24.

46. Warren Sussman, *Culture as History: The Transformation of American Society in the Twentieth Century* (New York: Pantheon, 1984), 160; quoted in Lawrence W. Levine, "The Historian and the Icon," 197.

47. Halla Beloff, *Camera Culture*, 22, quoted in Kugelmass, "Jewish Icons," 30.

48. Walter Benjamin, "Theses on the Philosophy of History," in *Illuminations*, ed. Hannah Arendt, trans. Harry Zohn (New York: Schocken, 1968), 264.

BIBLIOGRAPHY

Avineri, Shlomo. *The Making of Modern Zionism*. New York: Basic, 1982.

Barthes, Roland. "Rhetoric of the Image." In *Image-Music-Text*, trans. Stephen Heath. New York: Hill & Wang, 1977.

Benjamin, Walter. "The Work of Art in the Age of Mechanical Reproduction." In *Illuminations*, ed. Hannah Arendt, trans. Harry Zohn. New York: Schocken, 1968.

——. "Theses on the Philosophy of History." In *Illuminations*, ed. Hannah Arendt, trans. Harry Zohn. New York: Schocken, 1968.

Berkowitz, Michael. *Zionist Culture and West European Jewry before the First World War*. Cambridge: Cambridge University Press, 1993.

——. *Western Jewry and the Zionist Project, 1914–1933*. Cambridge: Cambridge University Press, 1997.

Black, Eugene. *The Social Politics of Anglo-Jewry, 1880–1920*. New York: Basil Blackwell, 1988.

Britton, Wiley. *The White Slavery: A Study of the Present Trade Union System*. Akron, Ohio: Werner, 1909.

Cohen, Richard I. "Jewish Art in the Modern Era." In *The Modern Jewish Experience: A Reader's Guide*, ed. Jack Wertheimer. New York: New York University Press, 1993.

——. *Jewish Icons: Art and Society in Modern Europe*. Berkeley: University of California Press, 1998.

Epstein, Melech. *Profiles of Eleven: Profiles of Eleven Men Who Guided the Destiny of an Immigrant Society and Stimulated Social Consciousness among the American People*. Detroit: Wayne State University Press, 1965.

Feinstone, Morris C. "A Brief History of the United Hebrew Trades." In *Gewerkschaften: Jubilee Book*, ed. Harry Lang and Morris Feinstone. New York: United Hebrew Trades, 1938.

Fishman, William J. *East End Jewish Radicals, 1875–1914*. London: Duckworth, 1995.

Frankel, Jonathan. *Prophecy and Politics: Socialism, Nationalism, and the Russian Jews, 1862–1917*. Cambridge: Cambridge University Press, 1981.

Freedberg, David. *The Power of Images: Studies in the History and Theory of Response*. Chicago: University of Chicago Press, 1991.

Gartner, Lloyd. *The Jewish Immigrant in England, 1870–1914*. London: Allen & Unwin, 1960.

Gassman-Sherr, Rosalie. *The Story of the Federation of Women Zionists of Great Britain and Ireland, 1918–1968*. London: Federation of Women Zionists, 1968.

Gutman, Judith Mara. *Lewis W. Hine, 1874–1940: Two Perspectives*. New York: Grossman, 1974.

Handbook of Trade Union Methods with Special Reference to the Garment Trades. New York: Education Department, International Ladies' Garment Workers' Union, 1937.

Hansen, Miriam. *Babel and Babylon: Spectatorship and American Silent Film*. Cambridge: Harvard University Press, 1991.

Hapgood, Hutchins. *The Spirit of the Ghetto,* ed. Moses Rischin. 1902. Rpr. Cambridge: Harvard University Press, 1967.

Hertz, Y. S. *Fuftsik Yor Arbeter-ring in Yidishn Lebn.* Picture section. New York: National Executive Committee of the Workmen's Circle, 1950.

Hertzberg, Arthur, ed. *The Zionist Idea.* New York: Atheneum, 1986.

Howe, Irving. *World of Our Fathers: The Journey of the East European Jews to America and the Life They Found and Made.* New York: Harcourt Brace Jovanovich, 1976.

Hurwitz, Maximillian. *The Workman's Circle: Its History, Ideals, Organization and Institutions.* New York: Workmen's Circle, 1936.

Hyman, Paula. "Was There a 'Jewish Politics' in Western and Central Europe?" In *The Quest for Utopia: Jewish Political Ideas and Institutions through the Ages,* ed. Zvi Gitelman. Armonk, New York: M. E. Sharpe, 1992.

Jacobson, Matthew Frye. *Special Sorrows: The Diasporic Imagination of Irish, Polish, and Jewish Immigrants in the United States.* Cambridge: Harvard University Press, 1995.

——. *Whiteness of a Different Color: European Immigrants and the Alchemy of Race.* Cambridge: Harvard University Press, 1998.

Jay, Martin. "Vision in Context: Reflections and Refractions." In *Vision in Context: Historical and Contemporary Perspectives on Sight,* ed. Teresa Brennan and Martin Jay. New York: Routledge, 1996.

Jeshurin, Ephim H. *B. C. Vladeck: Fifty Years of Life and Labor.* New York: Forward Association, 1936.

King, Edward Smith. *Joseph Zalmonah.* Boston: Lee & Sheperd, 1893.

Kleeblatt, Norman L., ed. *Too Jewish? Challenging Traditional Identities.* New York: Jewish Museum; New Brunswick, N.J.: Rutgers University Press, 1996.

Kochan, Lionel. *Beyond the Graven Image: A Jewish View.* London: Macmillan, 1997.

Kress, Gunther, and Theo van Leeuwen. *Reading Images: The Grammar of Visual Design.* London: Routledge, 1996.

Kugelmass, Jack. "Jewish Icons: Envisioning the Self in Images of the Other." In *Jews and Other Differences: The New Jewish Cultural Studies,* ed. Jonathan Boyarin and Daniel Boyarin. Minneapolis: University of Minnesota Press, 1997.

Lang, Harry, and Morris Feinstone, eds. *Gewerkschaften: Jubilee Book.* New York: United Hebrew Trades, 1938.

Leftwich, Joseph. Introduction to Rudolf Rocker, *The London Years,* trans. Joseph Leftwich. London: Robert Anscombe, 1956.

Leppert, Richard. *Art and the Committed Eye: The Cultural Functions of Imagery.* Boulder, Colo.: Westview Press, 1996.

Levine, Lawrence W. "The Historian and the Icon: Photography and the History of American People in the 1930s and 1940s." In *Modern Art and Society: An An-*

thology of Social and Multicultural Readings, ed. Maurice Berger. New York: Harper, 1994.

Lindheim, Irma. *The Immortal Adventure.* New York: Macaulay, 1928.

Mitchell, W. J. T. *Picture Theory: Essays on Verbal and Visual Representation.* Chicago: University of Chicago Press, 1994.

Nochlin, Linda, and Tamar Garb, eds. *The Jew in the Text: Modernity and the Construction of Identity.* London: Thames & Hudson, 1995.

Riis, Jacob A. *How the Other Half Lives: Studies among the Tenements of New York.* New York: Dover, 1971.

Rischin, Moses. *The Promised City: New York's Jews, 1870–1914.* Cambridge: Harvard University Press, 1977.

Sanders, Ronald. *The Downtown Jews: Portraits of an Immigrant Generation.* New York: Harper & Row, 1969.

Sarna, Jonathan. *JPS: The Americanization of Jewish Culture, 1888–1988.* Philadelphia: Jewish Publication Society of America, 1989.

Schneiderman, Rose. *All for One.* New York: P. S. Eriksson, 1967.

Smith, Anthony D. *The Ethnic Origins of Nations.* Oxford, U.K.: Blackwell, 1993.

Soulde, George. *Sidney Hillman: Labor Statesman.* New York: Macmillan, 1939.

Steinberg, Michael P. "Aby Warburg's Kruezlingen Lecture: A Reading." Interpretive essay following *Images from the Region of the Pueblo Indians of North America,* by Aby M. Warburg, trans. Michael P. Steinberg. Ithaca: Cornell University Press, 1995.

Steinorth, Karl, ed. *Lewis Hine: Passionate Journey: Photographs 1905–1937.* Rochester, N.Y.: Edition Stemmle, in association with International Museum of Photography, George Eastman House, Rochester, 1996.

Sussman, Warren. *Culture as History: The Transformation of American Society in the Twentieth Century.* New York: Pantheon, 1984.

Weinberg, David H. *Between Tradition and Modernity: Haim Zhitlowski, Simon Dubnow, Ahad Ha-Am, and the Shaping of Modern Jewish Identity.* New York: Holmes & Meier, 1996.

Who's Who in WIZO, 1966–1970. Tel Aviv: Dept. of Organisation and Education, Women's International Zionist Organisation, 1970.

BETWEEN AMERICAN TELEVANGELISM AND AFRICAN ANGLICANISM

Knut Lundby

Against global cultural flows, people may redefine their personal projects and thus their identities. This is usually done in the context of groups that they belong to or relate to. Identities are then regarded as sources of meaning, constructed by social actors within group settings. Group-like relations might be established at a distance, through the media, or by means of identifications with people one would like to refer to. Group interactions, either face-to-face or by communication technology, strengthen such identification. Symbolism in global media might be used as a resource in the shaping of identity within local groups.

The relationship between media, religion, and culture is a patchwork reproduced throughout various communities around the globe.[1] Even restricting oneself to the Christian sphere, as is the case here, the variety in local expressions is wide. Still, we can see three recognizable threads across countries and across continents.

First, within organized Christianity, one thread comes from the history of church mission projects, today extended by cooperation through a network of independent, if not equally influential, churches of various denominations. Second, there is a thread that crosses boundaries of denominations: the charismatic movement, which stresses spiritual expression in contrast to sacraments and church hierarchies. The charismatic movement further links up with a third force, networks of electronic churches that—like religious multinationals—introduce themselves into religious life in the local settings where people actually live.

The threefold globalized structure of church organizations, charismatic movements, and media ministries can be found on all continents, although appropriated locally in different patterns and ways.

In Africa, organized Christianity is growing. And, in modern Africa, local congregations must be studied with reference to the transnational influence of these former colonial church structures, the charismatic movement, and American electronic-church "televangelism."

In this chapter I ask how these transnational threads work out within small-scale patterns of media, religion, and culture practice in a specific community setting. How do people involved in a local congregation understand and shape cultural identities and patterns of belonging through the networks of church organizations, charismatic movements, and televangelism they link up with?

IN THE MIDDLE OF TRANSFORMATION

Of all the group settings around the globe where people are watching American televangelism, I happened to meet a small congregation of Anglicans in the southern part of Africa.[2] Through cooperation between two universities,[3] I had the opportunity to access a "growth point"—a locality in the middle of transformation.[4]

In Tsanzaguru in Eastern Zimbabwe, some three thousand citizens live together trying to cope with modernity in a community constructed anew some twenty years ago. This semiurban location was established in a rural area as an alternative to migration into cities. Tsanzaguru is a "high-density suburb," as the former black townships came to be known after Zimbabwean independence in 1980.

An American visitor to Tsanzaguru might expect a "Small Town," as described by Arthur J. Vidich and Joseph Bensman.[5] However, compared with Springdale of the 1950s or 1960s, Tsanzaguru of the 1990s seems more modern and more pluralistic. In both cases an emerging middle class is important.[6] As a suburb, Tsanzaguru supplies the neighboring town and the growth point itself with civil servants working in modern sectors of the society: health services, schools, administration. A higher level of education distinguishes most of the growth-point dwellers from their rural neighbors. In Tsanzaguru the citizens live close together in fairly small, but modern, brick houses, neatly lined up along dusty streets. This locality has modern facilities like well-run schools, shops, a restaurant, a beer hall, a clinic, and an office for the local administration. But at the outskirts of the growth point, cows and goats from the neighboring villages might be seen grazing. Tsanzaguru is located at an intersection between urban and rural, between traditional and modern.

The specific group here provides insights of wider relevance: the social and cultural processes in this case can be seen in a number of other communities and settings. Although, strictly speaking, the validity of this study is limited to those interviewed in Tsanzaguru, people can be found in a similar context elsewhere, and insights from the various groups of Anglicans in Tsanzaguru may inform our understanding of similar cases. Analysis of this single case might be of relevance to our more general understanding. At a certain level of social and cultural abstraction, some of the dynamics between Anglicans in Tsanzaguru might even be identified in other settings.

I chose the local group of Anglicans as an entry into the so-called growth point of Tsanzaguru because they invite questions of identity in relation to an indigenous cultural form linked to a colonial past.[7] Within this Anglican congregation there is a considerable charismatic subgroup entangled into and partly acting in opposition to the traditional church. Conventional and charismatic Anglicans alike sit down Sunday after Sunday to watch the international version of the "700 Club" from the U.S. televangelism enterprise of Pat Robertson and his Christian Broadcasting Network. The identity negotiations of the selected Zimbabweans could then be analyzed in relation to all the three transnational influences under study.[8]

The small group of Anglicans in Tsanzaguru (no more than some seventy persons, including children) relate to the three globalizing influences of religion within a wider identity-formation project of what it is to be an African with a specific ethnic background in the new nation of Zimbabwe.

The Mediascape

A wider "mediascape" opens into the landscape of Tsanzaguru, carrying images of the world created by the media.[9] Compared with the multichannel environment in most urban areas of the world, the mediascape available in Tsanzaguru is still a fairly limited and controlled one. However, as a growth point where they do have electricity, people in Tsanzaguru can buy several newspapers and receive four different radio stations and the main national television channel of the Zimbabwe Broadcasting Corporation (ZBC).

Television is regarded the most important medium by those with a set, which is usually equipped for black-and-white reception, with a small screen. Others have access through neighbors. A pilot study in Tsanzaguru showed that the 8:00 P.M. news is the most watched program.[10] The news is usually part of the two- or three-hour prime-time evening diet. Some watch breakfast TV. Drama, especially Zimbabwean drama, is popular; American series are more numerous, however. Music attracts viewers, as do some documentaries. Female viewers in the pilot sample found pleasure in wrestling, but also preferred watching cookery programs. One twenty-nine-year-old woman listed her favorites throughout the week: *Flying Doctors, Family Matters, Santa Barbara, Wrestling, Neighbors,* musicals, talk shows, cookery, and features. A man, thirty-one years old, reported his favorite programs as documentaries, news, sports, features, and foreign film from CNN on the national channel.

Television penetration throughout Zimbabwe is limited. Most television programs are in English. Local productions are rare. U.S. made series make up a considerable amount of the schedule.[11]

There is religious freedom in Zimbabwe, nurturing a market of mostly Christian denominations and sects. Some 60 percent of the population are churchgoers, and the number is rising, especially in the charismatic groups. Their growth is attributed partly to economic hardship.[12]

In Zimbabwe, the churches are important participants in civil society, locally as well as nationally.[13] There are a variety of Zimbabwean churches or denominations of missionary descent. One of these, the Anglican Church, came with the British colonizers in the late 1800s.[14] Today this denomination is an independent African church, though links to the Anglican church in England are maintained. The Anglican Church in Zimbabwe is part of the Central African Archdiocese, whose archbishop is based in Gaborone, Botswana.

The growing charismatic movement in Zimbabwe is visible within a variety of pentecostal "Apostolic," or so-called independent, African churches, or sects. Charismatic groups are strong within established churches as well, like the Anglican.[15] The charismatic strand within the Anglican church in Zimbabwe is particularly strong in the province of Manicaland, which is the context for this study.

Tsanzaguru as a local religious market is a microcosm of the national one. However, when Christianity was brought to this part of Africa, alongside the colonizers, there was not much choice. The various European denominations settled in different parts of the country, with the African population expected to relate to the mission in their area. Even so, the loyalty to the denomination is strong, even though there may be interest in moving outside it. It might be easier to explore alternatives from within the tradition, as when the Anglicans listen to charismatic voices within their own congregation or sit down at home to watch a U.S. televangelism program.

IDENTITIES OF THE INTERVIEWEES

Interviewees selected for this case study were ones for whom religion matters. We carried out in-depth interviews with twenty of the Anglicans in Tsanzaguru. The sample represents nearly one-third of the youth and adult members in the locality, ten men and ten women, from fifteen to sixty-eight years old, representing a span from those who have undertaken advanced studies to those less used to books and writing.

For these Anglicans, to be African means to have roots in the land of their forefathers and to share that cultural heritage. This sense of belonging is a composite of land, customs, and skin color. Most basically, these Anglicans think of themselves as African because of a sense of belonging to the continent. In their relationship to the country of Zimbabwe, modern attitudes of citizenship are predominant. Still, half of the interviewees stress a less-rational sense of belonging to the nation. To be a Zimbabwean means "I am unique, I have got an identity. It is important. I know where I belong," as a teacher said. Their identity as Africans is thus expressed through Zimbabwe.

Most interviewees say their ethnic background is of moderate importance to them. A few of the young were not at all sure which ethnic relations they were born into. However, their ethnic group is regarded a part of their group identity within the nation. Still, ethnic background could be mobilized in a national conflict.

All Zimbabweans learn English at school, and English is the official language of administration in the country. The interviewees speak English only when they have to; they prefer their indigenous language. But they are happy to know an international language, to learn and to be able to communicate through it.

Anglican Identity

Anglicanism is in a similar way used as a currency of exchange in the interviewees' relation to modernity. They are able to appropriate European Anglican roots into a truly African church. A certain "Anglicanness" seems to inform the identities of the interviewees. This obviously comes out of socialization processes through generations of Anglican presence in the country. Most interviewees were members of the Anglican Church from birth, when they were baptized.

In reply to the question "What does it mean to you to be an Anglican?" most interviewees in Tsanzaguru indicated that the meaning of being an Anglican is in the belonging to the church as a tradition, a set of norms, or as a ritual community. To me, the concept of cultural belonging goes back to socialization, where one stops asking questions about the social bond. It is simply there, to be experienced as "natural." Such a sense of belonging of course is an important part of a person's identity, taken as an understanding or definition of self in relation to others.

For interviewees, belonging to the Anglican Church in Zimbabwe is not experienced as in conflict with being African. However, the basic cultural and social anchoring of the two is in the sense of belonging to the continent. This is, after all, even less a matter of choice than being an Anglican. Still the traditional African beliefs are there. Some of the interviewees think beliefs in spirit mediums and ancestral spirits could go hand in hand with being an Anglican. Others strongly oppose traditional African religiosity.

In the forefront of those who reject spirit mediums are the active cadres in the charismatic movement. The charismatics under study in Tsanzaguru operate within the Anglican Church. They reject spirit mediums and ancestral spirits because they believe only in the Holy Spirit, "in God only." However, they perform strong, similar spiritual acts themselves, like healing, in the name of the Holy Spirit.[16]

Becoming an active charismatic Christian requires a decision about religious identity, a deliberate stand, against the somewhat culturally duller belonging to the traditional Anglican Church. One-fourth of the interviewed Anglicans are active in what could be termed a charismatic opposition within the local Anglican congregation in Tsanzaguru: they gather for their own midweek worship in a private home, as well as for separate prayer meetings several evenings during the week. On Sunday mornings, when the Tsanzaguru congregation meets for worship in a classroom at the school, most of the charismatic opposition go into the rural area—a fifteen-minute walk or so, to an old Anglican church building, where they are able to influence the service according to their liking. The charismatic attraction invites exploration: some of those who stick to the traditional congregation on Sunday attend prayer meetings or midweek worships with the Anglican charismatics.

This even applies to some people on the committee of the "formal" church. More than half of the interviewees are involved with the charismatics.

Charismatics within the Anglican church develop a modern alternative. They need neither the mediation of church clergy nor of spirit mediums, not the collectivity of an established congregation nor the traditional rites of extended families. Through the charismatic experience, they are empowered as individuals.[17] This empowerment certainly takes place in a group setting, but it is basically a relationship between the "born again" and God—a response to rapid societal transformations that is suited to a more mobile, modern life.

Belonging and Identity

Despite the expanding mobility of modern life, all the interviewees felt a sense of belonging to a specific locality. For a majority of them, this was belonging to their immediate living place. However, for these Africans a modern growth point like Tsanzaguru is "home" only in a limited sense, even if they have stayed there a long time. The real "home" is the rural home, the place of origin for the family, the burial place of their forefathers.

A sense of belonging is maintained through social and cultural participation in collectivities or groups usually developed over generations. Together with such social interaction come identifications with people, symbols, and material structures carrying these collectivities. Hence, social belonging always encompasses a cultural identity.

A few of the interviewees in Tsanzaguru had no understanding of the word *identity*, even after translation into their first language. They were among the least-educated and were unemployed. They were all women, most of them older women. They did not think in terms of identity, but they did have a sense of belonging to Africa as well as to their living place, Tsanzaguru. Their ethnic background was of great importance to them. However, most interviewees in Tsanzaguru did reflect on their cultural identity, or identities, positioned in a pattern of belonging. For some of them, belonging and identity were explicitly linked, as for a young man who explained: "Identity means identifying your group, your category, where you exactly belong."

AMERICAN RELIGION ON AFRICAN TELEVISION

Identity is negotiated; social belonging is not. Globalized challenges to identity negotiations reach Anglicans in Tsanzaguru through television as one of the available media. Not all interviewees had a working television set in their home, but all of them had access to the medium. Eight of these twenty Anglicans said they watch television simply for the pleasure of watching, while five watch with a perspective that is primarily moralistic—that is to say, on guard against programs that are regarded as destructive. The remaining seven, although they condemn some programs, enjoy television and watch less guardedly.

The International 700 Club has appeared as a religious program on ZBC Television for many years.[18] It appears on Zimbabwean screens every Sunday in the early afternoon, after church time. Compared with *The 700 Club*, the program shown in the United States, the international version is reedited to play down controversial and political statements. Reports of current events are left out to make the program less constrained by space and time. The magazine format—the talk show—is kept. The programs, which present testimony and success stories, "become a metaphor for the 'wealth and prosperity gospel' in their combination of a verbal message of redemption and conversion, with the visual imagery of a successful and prosperous way of life."[19] This product of the American televangelism industry is popular among the Anglicans in Tsanzaguru. After church, whether they go to worship or not, half of the interviewees sit down at home to watch *The International 700 Club.*

Active charismatics are more numerous among those watching the show than among those who do not, though there is no simple pattern. *The International 700 Club* associates with the Born Again movement, and charismatic African viewers find support for their socio-spiritual project in this American production. However, a significant number of viewers distance themselves from the charismatic movement. This group searches actively for the goods and values of modernity in business or cultural expression. In the life stories portrayed by *The International 700 Club,* such viewers seem to find role models handling the contradictions of life in modernity. An adult woman reported, "It helps me in the way I interact with people from different parts of life, makes me able to communicate with them." She finds the programs "very real." After viewing and listening, she has "that experience of peace. I also learnt about other people's lives. And how to pray on my own." An older woman in this category of modern-oriented Anglicans explains the relevance as, "I just feel they preach what happens in life, whether in Tsanzaguru, in town, or [elsewhere]. . . . They preach the reality of life—problems and how to overcome them."

The International 700 Club addresses the viewer as an individual.[20] These two modernity-oriented women express a sense of belonging to Zimbabwe and Africa, but their orientation to modern life is explicated through a further understanding of identity. They both think of themselves as "individuals" (as do several of the active charismatics). One of these women said about the difference between identity and tradition, "Tradition has to do with the things that I value in culture. Identity has to do with me as an individual living in Tsanzaguru." These two women, without themselves joining the charismatics, appreciate the religious solutions to problems in modern life pointed out in *The International 700 Club.*

The charismatics, for their part, also negotiate modernity through watching *The International 700 Club.* The charismatic movement could be regarded a response to the ambivalences of modernity. They seek strong, partly fundamentalistic answers to the complications and contradictions of modern life, expressed in a religious language without too many nuances. But both charismatic and noncharismatic Anglican viewers of *The International 700 Club* in Tsanzaguru fit the implied profile of viewers of this televangelism product. According to Hilde Arntsen, such viewers are "positioned as sick, lonely and in dire need of *The International 700 Club*. This is primarily achieved by the mode of verbal address and the mode of visual portrayal. At the verbal level this takes place through a discourse based on personal address, in which the implied reader is positioned as one in need of social and spiritual fulfillment."[21]

Most of the interviewees who watch *The International 700 Club* have the sense of belonging to Africa that is typical of these Anglicans. In general, they are fairly heavy television users; they are used to television. They tend to be young, rather than old, and there are more men than women, they are well educated, and very few have a strong sense of belonging to Tsanzaguru. Their bonds of belonging are rather to the nation than to the locality. In the context of globalization, they are the cosmopolitans of modern Zimbabwe, whereas the nonviewers are strongly "local."[22]

How Critical a Reception?

In her study of how Zimbabweans interpret *The International 700 Club*, Arntsen found a greater variety of critical reading than she anticipated. The students and employees at the University of Zimbabwe who made up her focus groups showed cultural resistance in their negotiation with the program. However, in this "battle of the mind" there were considerable differences in negotiation practices—differences according to religious involvement and knowledge of television genres.[23]

However, in Tsanzaguru I met people who, while giving the impression of making an independent evaluation of the colonial influence, did not make a similar critical reading of American televangelism. Those of my interviewees who watched *The International 700 Club* were probably as well educated and used to television as those whom Arntsen met at the University of Zimbabwe. However, the Anglicans in Tsanzaguru watching *The International 700 Club* leaned toward the Born Again or prosperity option portrayed in the program. They were thus probably too close to be critical.

The Anglicans who rely on *The International 700 Club* in their negotiation of modernity seem not to consider the implicit political messages of the programs, even though the producers of this media ministry seem to intend political linkage to the New Religious Right. Our informants, however, seem not to bother about the inherent ideology of the programs.[24]

Geir Magnus Nyborg, working among Quechua Indians in Bolivia who watched *The International 700 Club,* found the same: the Quechua did not perceive the political aspects of the Robertson program. The program "is seen as a clearly religious television text which reinforces and renews their Christian heritage. The program works in this Latin American context as a call to identification, a testimony of God's work in people's life."[25]

Anglicans in Tsanzaguru who follow *The International 700 Club* are, after all, embedded in a pattern of social and cultural belonging. Such bonds offer a feeling of ontological security, but also exert social control. In public, people may act individually, but cultural belonging has to be nurtured in collectivities. By watching *The International 700 Club,* Anglicans in Tsanzaguru enter a global public. When they experience that their problems in handling modern life are somewhat similar to those portrayed in the program, these Zimbabweans have moments of identification that create new bonds. For them, these are bonds of fluent identity, not of fixed belonging. This is contrary to the experience of American viewers of the *700 Club* who were analyzed by Stewart Hoover: in their attention to the *700 Club,* the U.S. viewers pursued a quest for a lost sense of belonging.[26] The Anglicans in Tsanzaguru encounter *The International 700 Club* as an offering of global interconnectedness, or "global ecumene."[27] Ecumenicalism was also perceived in the sense of fellowship between different churches. The interviewees regarded *The International 700 Club* as being "above" denominationalism, seeing it as focused on life problems, rather than churchly discussions. They were less conscious of the specific theological and ideological position behind the television narratives.

CULTURAL IDENTITY UNDER GLOBALIZING INFLUENCES

During the colonial period, Africans were forced into distorting identities. Colonialism forced Africans into an early experience with cultural hybridization.[28] This gives a background to our understanding of today's globalizing influences. The Anglicans in Tsanzaguru to a large extent approach and negotiate the globalizing aspects of religion analyzed here from a base in their cultural belonging to land, place, and people. Being African is basic. These Zimbabweans subsume relations to nation and ethnic group under the sense of belonging to Africa. However, in relation to the basic cultural identity and belonging to Africa, the three globalized structures of organized Christianity are negotiated in different ways.

To be an Anglican is a kind of belonging. Even if there is a choice of denominational identity, most Zimbabwean Anglicans have been Anglican from birth. As the Anglican Church was closely associated with colonial power, identifying with the Anglican tradition might be seen as a move toward modernization. However, the former colonial-based missionary church has been Africanized. In independent Zimbabwe, being an active member of the established Anglican Church has become part of being an African—which implies a certain association with traditional African beliefs. This gives the Anglican Church a base in African traditional culture; however, these traditions are under pressure from globalizing modernity. Africans linking their cultural identity with the established Anglican Church will feel the challenges of negotiating these modernizing influences. Some will appropriate the messages of modernity into their everyday lives;[29] others will withdraw from the perceived globalizing threats of modernity. The two groups live in the same locality, some looking inwards, some outwards.

The active charismatic opponents within the African Anglican framework make a deliberate choice based in a search for moral and religious values that they believe they do not find in established church and traditional culture. This is in itself a response to modernity—a kind of withdrawal from the secularizing dilemmas of the modern life into a spiritual discourse. However, the charismatic response is in itself modern, because it makes the relation to God an individual matter through direct spiritual communication. This cultural identity fits into a modernizing African society as an alternative spirituality, where mobility and dispersion of extended families make it difficult to meet for rites according to the traditional African religion.

Strikingly, the alternative cultural identities of African Anglicans who relate to church organization, as opposed to the charismatic movement, negotiate with *The International 700 Club* as a part of the available mediascape. Those who are locally oriented watch selectively, leaving the U.S.-made program behind, as they choose to involve themselves in voluntary negotiations to a limited extent. Active charismatics and cosmopolitan church members, on the other hand, seek out, use, and interpret this product of televangelism in negotiating their various modernizing projects. For the charismatic Anglicans, the links to a program like *The International 700 Club* are easy to trace, through the focus on spiritual power in a modernized world.

The traditional, or conventional, Anglicans could build on their church's century-long experience of adapting to modernity. Today, the church is truly indigenous, and in a growth point like Tsanzaguru, these well-educated, conventional Anglicans combine global outlook with local roots; theirs is a basically modern project in a place where a religious worldview still is strong. Even from such a base, appropriation of globalized modernity under U.S. hegemony, as in televangelism, is quite possible.

This case study gives insights into the duality of identity confronted with globalized modernity. Religion is a basis for communality (in the traditional congregation) as well as for countercultural definitions (the charismatics within the same Anglican Church). Both are negotiated positions that relate to globalizing influences, and each base has its own defined relationship to modernity. The mediascape is being used to strengthen both of these cultural identities.

NOTES

In writing this chapter I had research assistance from Winston Mano and Tawana Kupe and learned a lot in discussions with them. The responsibility for the text is nevertheless mine. Mano also took part in interviewing and fieldwork in Tsanzaguru.

1. Stewart M. Hoover and Knut Lundby, eds., *Rethinking Media, Religion, and Culture* (Thousand Oaks, Calif.: Sage, 1997).

2. The indigenous U.S. variant is the Protestant Episcopal Church. There are, of course, Anglican congregations in the United States.

3. Cooperation between the University of Zimbabwe and the University of Oslo. My work with Mano and Kupe was in this context.

4. Tsanzaguru was selected due to availability: one of the Zimbabwean research assistants—a media student involved in the university cooperation—hailing from there, was able to introduce me to the locality.

5. Arthur J. Vidich and Joseph Bensman, *Small Town in Mass Society: Class, Power, and Religion in a Rural Community*, rev. ed. (Princeton, N.J.: Princeton University Press, 1968).

6. However, today the modern society would not be a "mass society" in Vidich

and Bensman terms in *Small Town*. Modernity makes more complicated structures than those created when conceptualizing "small" communities relating to big urban centers and institutions.

7. The Anglican tradition is close to my Lutheran background, and the selection of an Anglican congregation was in part also because it gave me a greater chance of understanding across the differences between Europe and Africa. Since I did not intend to do fieldwork over a long period, I had to minimize the distance to my own cultural background.

8. Knut Lundby, *Longing and Belonging: Media and the Identity of Anglicans in a Zimbabwean Growth Point* (report no. 34, Department of Media and Communication, University of Oslo, 1998).

9. Arjun Appadurai, "Disjuncture and Difference in the Global Cultural Economy," in *Global Culture, Nationalism, Globalization and Modernity*, ed. M. Featherstone (London: Sage, 1990); Arjun Appadurai, *Modernity at Large: Cultural Dimensions of Globalization* (Minneapolis: University of Minnesota Press, 1966).

10. Knut Lundby, "Media, Religion, and Democratic Participation: Community Communication in Zimbabwe and Norway," *Media, Culture, and Society* 19 (1997): 29–45.

11. Michael Bruun Andersen, "The Janus Face of Television in Small Countries: The Case of Zimbabwe," in *Perspectives on Media, Culture, and Democracy in Zimbabwe*, ed. Ragnar Waldahl (report no. 33, Department of Media and Communication, University of Oslo, 1998); Winston Mano, "The Plight of Public Service Television: Television Programming in Zimbabwe" (master's thesis, Department of Media and Communication, University of Oslo, 1997).

12. IPS news bulletin (Inter Press Service), November 13, 1995.

13. David J. Maxwell, "The Church and Democratisation in Africa: The Case of Zimbabwe," in *The Christian Churches and the Democratisation of Africa*, ed. P. Gifford (Leiden: Brill, 1995).

14. John Weller and Jane Linden, *Mainstream Christianity to 1980 in Malawi, Zambia, and Zimbabwe* (Gweru: Mambo Press, 1984), 65.

15. See Maxwell, "Church and Democratisation"; David J. Maxwell, *Christians and Chiefs in Zimbabwe: A Social History of the Hwesa People, c. 1890s–1990* (Edinburgh: Edinburgh University Press, 1999); M. L. Daneel, *Quest for Belonging: Introduction to a Study of African Independent Churches* (Gweru: Mambo Press, 1987); M. L. Daneel, *Fambidzano: Ecumenical Movement of Zimbabwean Independent Churches* (Gweru: Mambo Press, 1989); Terence Ranger, *Peasant Consciousness and Guerilla War in Zimbabwe: A Comparative Study* (London: James Currey, 1985); Terence Ranger, "Religion, Development, and African Christian Identity," in *Religion, Development, and African Identity*, ed. K. H. Petersen (Uppsala: Scandinavian Institute of African Studies, 1987).

16. Maxwell, *Christians and Chiefs*, 215–16, maintains that Pentecostalism in Zimbabwe has a close connection to traditional spirit possession.

17. Meredith B. McGuire, *Pentecostal Catholics. Power, Charisma, and Order in a Religious Movement* (Philadelphia: Temple University Press, 1982), 45.

18. Hilde Arntsen, *The Battle of the Mind: International Media Elements of the New Religious Political Right in Zimbabwe* (report no. 26, Department of Media and Communication, University of Oslo, 1997).

19. Arntsen, *Battle of the Mind*, 114–15.

20. Ibid., 113.

21. Ibid., 112.

22. Robert K. Merton, "Patterns of Influence: Local and Cosmopolitan Influentials," in *Social Theory and Social Structure*, ed. Robert K. Merton (New York: Free Press, 1968); Ulf Hannerz, "Cosmopolitans and Locals in World Culture," in *Global Culture, Nationalism, Globalization, and Modernity*, ed. M. Featherstone (London: Sage, 1990).

23. Arntsen, *Battle of the Mind*, 148.

24. The difference might be due to different methods. Arntsen showed and discussed the program in focus groups, while I asked about use and interpretation of the program during individual interviews. Still, the difference might be significant.

25. Geir Magnus Nyborg, "Conquest, Dominance, or Spiritual Reformation? Bolivian Quechua Families Watching U.S. Televangelism" (Ph.D. diss., Department of Media Studies, University of Bergen, 1997), 287–88.

26. Stewart M. Hoover, *Mass Media Religion: The Social Sources of the Electronic Church* (Newbury Park, Calif.: Sage, 1988), 206.

27. Ulf Hannerz, *Transnational Connections: Culture, People, Places* (London: Routledge, 1996), 7.

28. Terence Ranger, "Colonial and Postcolonial Identities," postscript in *Postcolonial Identities in Africa,* ed. Richard Werbner and Terence Ranger (London: Zed Books, 1996), 273–74.

29. John B. Thompson, *The Media and Modernity: A Social Theory of the Media* (Oxford: Polity Press, 1995), 42.

BIBLIOGRAPHY

Andersen, Michael Bruun. "The Janus Face of Television in Small Countries: The Case of Zimbabwe." In *Perspectives on Media, Culture, and Democracy in Zimbabwe,* ed. Ragnar Waldahl. Report no. 33, Department of Media and Communication, University of Oslo, 1998.

Appadurai, Arjun. *Modernity at Large: Cultural Dimensions of Globalization.* Minneapolis: University of Minnesota Press, 1966.

——. "Disjuncture and Difference in the Global Cultural Economy." In *Global Culture, Nationalism, Globalization, and Modernity,* ed. M. Featherstone. London: Sage, 1990.

Arntsen, Hilde. *The Battle of the Mind: International Media Elements of the New Religious Political Right in Zimbabwe.* University of Oslo, report no. 26, Department of Media and Communication, 1997.

Daneel, M. L. *Quest for Belonging: Introduction to a Study of African Independent Churches.* Gweru: Mambo Press, 1987.

——. *Fambidzano: Ecumenical Movement of Zimbabwean Independent Church.* Gweru: Mambo Press, 1989.

Hannerz, Ulf. "Cosmopolitans and Locals in World Culture." In *Global Culture, Nationalism, Globalization, and Modernity,* ed. M. Featherstone. London: Sage, 1990.

——. *Transnational Connections: Culture, People, Places.* London: Routledge, 1996.

Hoover, Stewart M. *Mass Media Religion: The Social Sources of the Electronic Church.* Newbury Park, Calif.: Sage, 1988.

Hoover, Stewart M., and Knut Lundby, eds. *Rethinking Media, Religion, and Culture.* Thousand Oaks, Calif.: Sage, 1997.

Lundby, Knut. "Media, Religion, and Democratic Participation: Community Communication in Zimbabwe and Norway," *Media, Culture, and Society* 19 (1997): 29–45.

——. *Longing and Belonging: Media and the Identity of Anglicans in a Zimbabwean Growth Point.* Report no. 34. Department of Media and Communication, University of Oslo, 1998.

Mano, Winston. "The Plight of Public Service Television: Television Programming in Zimbabwe." Master's thesis, Department of Media and Communication, University of Oslo, 1997.

Maxwell, David J. "The Church and Democratisation in Africa: The Case of Zimbabwe." In *The Christian Churches and the Democratisation of Africa,* ed. P. Gifford. Leiden: Brill, 1995.

——. *Christians and Chiefs in Zimbabwe: A Social History of the Hwesa People, c. 1890s–1990.* Edinburgh: Edinburgh University Press, 1999.

McGuire, Meredith B. *Pentecostal Catholics: Power, Charisma, and Order in a Religious Movement.* Philadelphia: Temple University Press, 1982.

Merton, Robert K. "Patterns of Influence: Local and Cosmopolitan Influentials." In *Social Theory and Social Structure,* ed. Robert K. Merton. New York: Free Press, 1968.

Nyborg, Geir Magnus. "Conquest, Dominance, or Spiritual Reformation? Bolivian Quechua Families Watching U.S. Televangelism." Ph.D. diss., Department of Media Studies, University of Bergen, 1997.

Ranger, Terence. *Peasant Consciousness and Guerilla War in Zimbabwe: A Comparative Study*. London: James Currey, 1985.

——. "Religion, Development, and African Christian Identity." In *Religion, Development, and African Identity*, ed. K. H. Petersen. Uppsala: Scandinavian Institute of African Studies, 1987.

——. "Colonial and Postcolonial Identities." Postscript in *Postcolonial Identities in Africa*, ed. Richard Werbner and Terence Ranger. London: Zed Books, 1996.

Thompson, John B. *The Media and Modernity: A Social Theory of the Media*. Oxford: Polity Press, 1995.

Vidich, Arthur J., and Joseph Bensman, *Small Town in Mass Society: Class, Power, and Religion in a Rural Community*. Rev. ed. Princeton, N.J.: Princeton University Press, 1968.

Weller, John, and Jane Linden. *Mainstream Christianity to 1980 in Malawi, Zambia, and Zimbabwe*. Gweru: Mambo Press, 1984.

CHAPTER 17

"SPEAKING IN TONGUES, WRITING IN VISION": ORALITY AND LITERACY IN TELEVANGELISTIC COMMUNICATIONS

Keyan G. Tomaselli and Arnold Shepperson

This chapter examines the electronic church's primary use of the rhetorical power of oral codes in the production of messages for a visual medium. We suggest, following the work of Walter Ong,[1] that such codes recuperate the rituals and language structures of preliterate forms of expression. The chapter analyzes a semiotic aspect of the relationship between televangelistic oratory (which uses primary orality) and the secondary electronic orality codes of TV, with a view to understanding teleministries in industrial and postindustrial societies. This relates to issues of community (or solidarity) and the recovery of the religious imagination in a secular world.

Televangelists connect with their audiences by offering some kind of intelligibility to people for whom *local* and familiar ways of going-on have begun to break down. The form and content of these offerings are, as we will expand below, contradictory; however, the oral style and local organization of the electronic churches assist in making people's habitual activities consonant with experience once more. This recuperation of local intelligibility by televangelists is characterized by their steady colonization of country stations and the use of local communications (telephones, faxes) to both elicit and follow up on responses to their broadcasts.

We examine this phenomenon in terms of the local television model developed by Eric Michaels,[2] with variations we have elaborated to account for the orality/literacy thesis. Our elaboration of Michaels's diagrams is based on an interpretation of the original, taking into account the actual entertainment, media, and journalism practices used in the commercial models upon which televangelism bases its approach. In this we go a step further than Michaels, in that we try to accommodate the essentially top-down communications ethics we identify in the broader context of televangelism's growing reach. We conclude that the reach and success of televangelism, and the models that explain this, are a valuable resource for practitioners in nontelevangelistic community broadcast media.[3]

ORALITY AND TELEVANGELISM

The introduction of writing and printing has contributed to thinking of words as objects—objectifying speech—rather than as happenings, and as parts of processes.[4] This shift has had a fundamental impact on how industrialized societies make sense of their worlds. It helps to explain why conflicts of meaning arise between oral (local) and literary (general) ways of understanding. Each context generates quite different ideas of what the world is, how it works, and how individuals and groups relate to it.

Because literacy tends to separate individuals from the local dimension of their contexts, evangelism and televangelism as primary and secondary oral codes are able to penetrate the consciousness of individuals in industrial societies. Televangelistic recovery of oral residues embedded in the collective memory means that the spoken word (of God) is not objectified by these readers/listeners. Televangelists use the expressive techniques of orality to recuperate the suppressed or compartmentalized religious sense of meaning and life into an all-embracing reconnection of subject and object. The socially atomized individual participating in the electronic church experiences an organic reconnection into a spiritual center of authority that stands above the alienation of everyday life—but not necessarily of material life.

This "reconnection" primarily occurs at the level of the local. Oral culture can be conceived only in local terms. In the world of established modernity, however, there are codes of meaning and conduct that make it possible for individuals not to remain in any one locality all their lives. One outcome of the rise of general literacy, therefore, has been the development of ways of making meaning in a mobile world. Certainly in the United States and Europe, institutions and communications are structured for mobile individuals. Indeed, one of the features of the colonial experience outside the metropolitan nations has been the imposition of socioeconomic systems that enforce some kind of mobility (usually in the form of migrant labor) on indigenous populations accustomed to settled agrarian ways of life.

Even in developed modern society, however, communities consisting of more than one generation develop. For example, a whole town or region can become "home" to several generations of workers in a large manufacturing concern. Around this, a similar generational stability will develop in service and supply businesses associated with the central business enterprise. As those belonging to generations born in this locality grow up into the possible ways of living offered by the economy of the town, so "dynasties" of workers come into being: the offspring of original workers marry, go to work in the factory, office, or distribution arms of the main enterprise. Others enter the associated service and supply enterprises. Within very few decades, three or more generations will be present in this locality, ranging from preschoolers to retired persons.

Events or conditions that threaten the stability of the generations present in such communities challenge the accepted local "cosmos" within which those present have lived together. Such crises of experience cannot readily be explained as part of some intellectually coherent social process, like the "economy," "postindustrial production," "the forces of supply and demand," and so on. These are forces beyond local experience, and the community or individual crisis of experience (joblessness, a collapse in commodity prices, and so on) is usually described as insignificant in relation to these "forces" and "processes."

Televangelism, with its oral presence on the screens of TV watchers experiencing these crises, provides answers to these questions in a familiar voice and style. The oral mannerisms, or codes, of the studio preacher are those of village-green rhetoric or the union local meeting, with messages related both to the causes of the crisis of experience and to its solutions. Both the content and style of the message draw on a comprehensible source, the word of God, to offer explanations for people's feelings and frustrations. The appeal of televangelism therefore also works through the reconnection of experience and intelligibility to those whose worlds have not been forged on a need for expert intellectual literacy.

LOCAL KNOWLEDGE, ORALITY, AND SIGNIFICANCE

Individuals begin their encounter with the world in an oral local environment, and consciousness retains this primary orality as the basic quality against which the individual experiences and makes sense of the world. Even in industrial society this is the case, because people simply are not *born* literate: they *become* more or less literate as they develop their endowments into talents through education. This property of the becomingness of literary experience provides the starting point for our reading of televangelistic communication: the nondualistic philosophy of Charles S. Peirce.

Peirce's monistic philosophy was developed in conscious opposition to Descartes's mental/material dualism. It possesses three categorical dimensions. Linked in an evolutionary logic, the three categories are: (a) Firstness, which we call the *Encounter:* the concrete qualitative being-there in the cosmos of a signifying organism; (b) Secondness, which we call *Experience:* this evolves from firstness as quantity evolves out of quality; the signifying organism develops an active or conscious directedness toward the local and particular; (c) Thirdness, or *Intelligibility:* this evolves as the relations between organism and cosmos develop into new forms of first and second; thirdness, as Peirce puts it, grows as new ways of doing things lead to old terms taking on new meanings.[5]

The vehicle through which this intelligibility is achieved is the *sign,* which acts in the signifying subject in the form of *interpretants.* There are many different kinds of interpretants,[6] but the evolution of the triad of dynamical interpretants is important here. First, the emotional interpretant appears. This effect is that of the feeling of recognition that accompanies a sign. Because they are so general, emotional interpretants "can range from the first feeling of comprehension of linguistic signs to the feeling that is generated by listening to a musical composition."[7]

Next, the energetic interpretant develops out of the emotional. This evolution involves some form of mental labor: there is always some kind of work done at this level of interpretation.[8] Consequently, it involves the time-bound activity of recognizing this sign as opposed to all others. Finally, the logical, or ultimate, interpretant comes about as both the feeling and work of the other interpretants become representation. Peirce recognized that any given sign could become rationally applicable across different situations because the activity of signification leads to a logical interpretant that is in itself a sign. These interpretants relate to the sign as law, intelligibility, or potentiality, and contain the possibility of future interpretations of the sign.[9] At the local level, signs attain meaning as they are realized in the form of habits and habit change.[10]

There are two key ways in which televangelism acts through interpretants so that communities make sense of their conditions:

1. Emotional and energetic interpretants are experienced under conditions brought about by the Enlightenment collapse of the bodily into the material universe. Emotions and habits, being essentially bodily in nature, are made subject to explanation in terms of the natural or life sciences.

2. Voluntary aspects of action and other mental or logical-discursive spheres of human existence have been idealized. As such, they became subject to other (psychological) kinds of explanation.

These conditions are not necessarily obvious for those not privy to the arcane analysis and convoluted jargon of intellectual professions. Everyday people get on with life as they encounter it, draw on their experience as a basis for getting along, and make it all intelligible by virtue of the fact that what they do *works for them*.[11]

In situations brought on by influences beyond ordinary people's control, familiar things can begin to work differently. Conditions elicit different kinds of emotional interpretant for habitual energetic and logical interpretants. Things become unfamiliar; consequences follow differently to the way they did before. In cultural terms, customary activity and responses fail. What once were traditional explanations for the consequences of people's everyday conduct become strange and lack justificatory power. The lure of televangelism, then, can be seen in the way its practitioners offer to reconnect a community in crisis with its vision of what has always worked.

TELEMINISTRIES AND COMMUNICATION

Televangelists proceed from the position that individuals are subjected to the necessities of specific logics of punishment (eschatology) or salvation (soteriology), and that these necessities are realized in confessional organi-

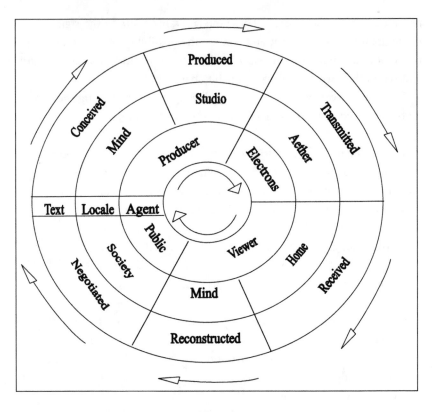

FIGURE 17.1

Eris Michaels's original "Systems Conceptualization of Television as a
Socially Organized Message Transmission System" (*Continuum* 3, no. 2).

zation. People, in this view, are caused to be eternally saved or damned by
virtue of rules and norms that are perhaps of their own choosing, but not
subject to interpretation or discussion: the rules and norms are given by
authority. Such subjection to authority is indistinguishable from subjection to laws of nature, and sometimes can be analyzed in terms of
the kind of stimulus/response communications theories so beloved of the
"sociological mass communications" industry.

In this model, illustrated here in Eric Michaels's "cycle" diagram
(fig. 17.1), there is supposed to be some ideal system of transmission, reception, and feedback in terms of which outcomes can be predicated for
commercial media production.[12] Briefly, Michaels uses a variation on the
early transmission theories of communication that derived from Claude
Shannon and Warren Weaver's mathematical model.[13] Michaels extends
their model by adding two levels of "text" to the original conception of

"message." Thus the new model considers what happens at the production, transmission, and reception stages of the older model in terms of three different, but parallel, levels of interpretation—the texts themselves, the locale in which that text is active, and the agent that manipulates the message, story, or narrative.

In effect, we read the diagram as an attempt to trace three different kinds of production, transmission, and reception with their associated feedback loops. The top half of the circle basically reproduces the production and transmission black boxes of the basic transmission model. The bottom half reproduces the reception and feedback stages. In one important respect, Michaels simultaneously challenges and reinforces transmission theories. The idea of a *public text* challenges the conventional notion of feedback by introducing a hermeneutic element, but also reinforces the notion in particular, instead of general, terms:

> The *Public Text* . . . returns the message back to the producer, whether the impoverished readings of a Morgan, Gallup or Nielson rating or the richer ones provided by literary critics or by recent cultural studies theorizing. But these "official" readings are only one example. Audiences themselves recognize their power to varying degrees and lobbying and interest groups have arisen over the years, notably with regard to children's TV, but also fundamentalist Christians, sports enthusiasts, anti-smoking, anti-drinking, violence lobbies and so forth. These groups develop particular readings of the media and may develop ingenious ways to privilege these in the eyes of producers.[14]

Although Michaels does succeed in challenging the mass-media conception of transmission theories, he still sees these variegated public texts as versions of a form of feedback within a media loop.

To compare the original textual loop with what we believe is actual communications modeling in mass media, we have therefore reconceived the standard linear representations in Michaels's cyclic form. In figure 17.2 we use Michaels's template to restructure the received modeling categories as texts, in Michaels's sense. However, this way of representing the common linear stimulus/response or message/effects analysis shows that figures 17.1 and 17.2 essentially refer to the same thing, but from within different frames of reference. All that differs are the actual categories of knowledge "encoded" in the texts. On the one hand, Michaels's local

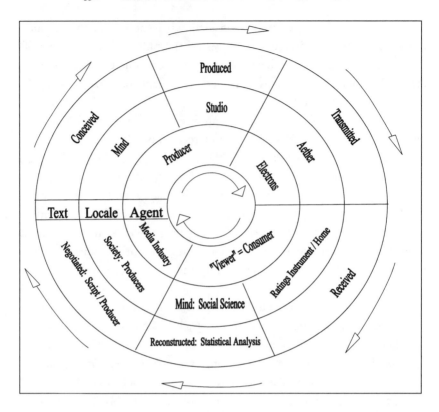

FIGURE 17.2
Michaels's model reconceptualized around actual media practice, taking account
of professional systems of viewership "measurement" and evaluation.

model indicates that smaller media have a less amorphous feedback text. On the other hand, the mass media employ more precise (and therefore more expensive and quantitative) methods to assess their larger and more variegated public.

In figure 17.3, we reconstruct the basic model of transmission from the point of view of the viewer, whether of national mass media or of a local televangelism station. Viewers develop a textual relation with their world(s), which they interpret individually within their neighborhoods. This habitual text forms the grid against which, as everyday agents, they encounter messages on the screen. In interpreting the received text, their readings are therefore not confined to a place (a living room or public recreation area), but take place within the local experiences these places confirm in everyday life. Whatever reconstructions they carry out as viewers are thus performed in the context of their own interpretive habits that

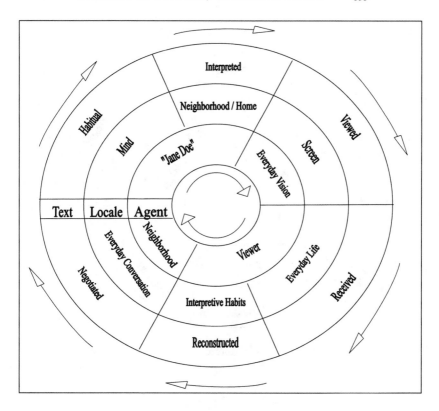

FIGURE 17.3

A reconstruction of the communications relationships of an
average everyday television viewing situation.

work for them in their homes, workplaces, and gatherings. As such, these
reconstructions become the basis upon which viewers in their everyday
conversation negotiate a meaning.

In figure 17.4 we combine the analyses represented in figures 17.2 and
17.3 in order to incorporate within Michaels's framework one possible way
to model the textual character of community-based television in general.
Although we do not claim that this model exhausts the analytic resources
offered by the televisual relation between the local and the global, it does
draw on the success of televangelism and the relevance of Michaels to offer one level of strategic planning for community media policies. Princi-
pally, we offer the proposal as a means of developing critical approaches
to the mass-mediated "moral panics" that place so much emphasis on the
dire intentions that violent or sexually explicit representations are supposed to stimulate in audiences.

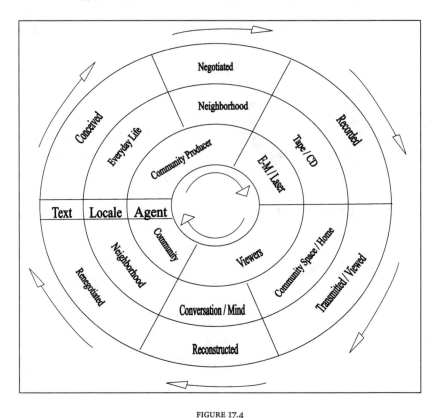

FIGURE 17.4

Combination of figures 17.2 and 17.3 into a tentative model for community-produced television, incorporating Michael's elaboration of the Yuendumu video project.

THE POLITICS OF MEDIA, MESSAGE, AND EVERYDAY LIFE

As we have seen with the plethora of studies into the links between media violence and actual violent behavior, such links simply do not exist, or, if they exist at all, they do not do so in the forms postulated by the theories. We suggest that the texts Michaels calls reconstructed and negotiated do indeed occur in the experience of a local (oral) televangelistic encounter. The phenomenon we should therefore be looking at is the failure at the local social level of a national politics that draws on the techniques of local electronic churches.

To get a better understanding of the local and oral effectiveness of televangelists, we have therefore developed Michaels's diagram in three ways. First, as shown in figure 17.3, practitioners "plug into" the habitual concerns they pick up from the viewers' context. In a sense, they fathom the "mind text" exhibited through neighborhood conversations. From this they can then develop conceived texts (fig. 17.1) that people view through their "everyday vision" texts, and that they then negotiate in terms of those interpretive habit texts with which they are familiar in their everyday conversation(s).

In the realm of U.S. national politics, the "new Republican" wave built on the effectiveness of local televangelistic congregations to disseminate the generally reactionary agenda that garnered so many votes in the congressional elections of 1994. Yet the Congress so constituted rapidly fragmented into something less than monolithic as soon as local interests and ideologies began to dominate actual policy debates. This largely has to do with the fact that the attempt to create a nationally based textual loop (in terms of figure 17.2) resulted in the emergence of something that contradicts the experiences embodied in the *multiplicity of independent loops centered on local televangelistic congregations* (fig. 17.3). The arcane language and concerns of congressional debate are as disconnected from the local as are the reasons given by intellectuals for the collapse of local economies.

A politician elected on the basis of televangelistic support cannot escape the glee with which the media report on the politician's financial peccadilloes. Newt Gingrich was as immune from such local understanding as was Bill Clinton. People in communities of crisis understood the financial hanky-panky of the former in exactly the way they understood the latter's dalliances with a club dancer and a White House intern: these moral panics did nothing to lessen the economic and community disasters that globalization and downsizing entailed. It is expected that the collapse of the dot.com stock bubble, with its knock-on effects on millions of working people's 401(k) pension investments, will in time have its responses from the televangelists, irrespective of their close ties to the administration of President George W. Bush.

What this seems to indicate is that the standard approaches to media miss the implications of certain assumptions in philosophical anthropology. The logics of damnation and salvation that drive televangelism are oral replications of the assumptions that underpin the two visions—one romantic, the other Hobbesian—behind the liberal and conservative paradigms, respectively: that humankind is either born free or is intrinsically fallen. These paradigms are as arcane in their own right as any other intellectual discipline and are readily refuted by experience in a local and oral environment.

If the idea of communication has some connection to the ideas of "community" and the essential link to mutual public responsibility implied by this (from the Latin root *munus*), then we need to find the items of significance in the televangelistic experience upon which it might be possible to recreate the democratic project. We conclude by rebuilding on this analysis a Peircean vision of how the local and oral can be reintegrated into wider concerns without the apparent contradictions of contemporary political and media practice.

MEDIA FOR MORTALS

The concept of local and oral telecommunications techniques has taken off in recent times. "Community access" is one example of the kind of label created to intellectualize what is essentially an emotional and practical business. The success of the electronic churches lies precisely in their ability to engender strong emotional interpretants in their congregants. The strongest emotion readily experienced by anyone is fear, and the fear of death that underpins eschatological and soteriological anthropologies has a powerful appeal when introduced into communities that have undergone some major crisis of experience.

For Peirce,[15] energetic interpretants are related to the "normative science" of ethics, and local democratic media approaches can thus emphasize the practicalities of "development of endowments into talents."[16] This does not exclude many concerns traditionally associated with economics and politics; instead, we see that the local is a richer environment of individual experience than the national or global. Many more talents are available locally than the general ones of making money and maneuvering between institutions associated with Enlightenment programs of economics and politics (i.e., political economy).[17] This practical focus introduces the dimension of the final or logical interpretant of democratic local media. The habits into which new generations are being raised can be changed, as can those of present-day generations.

Recent examples of movements and events that indicate different possibilities in the United States include the prominence of the conservative Promise Keepers and the Nation of Islam's Million Man March. Each of these is an emblematic attempt to change general habits. Whether the *local* effectiveness of the Nation of Islam's demonstration will have nationwide effect is open to question, and by a similar token it is open to doubt whether a *national* movement like Promise Keepers will have a uniform effect in local communities of stress. The point is not that such action or organization necessarily lead to effective local change, but that they represent outcomes within a plurality of effective local organizing drives.

For the media to have broad general effect, however, cognizance has to be taken of the plurality of habitual textual loops. These are both actual (as already exist in televangelistic congregations) and potential (as demonstrated by the response of women to the Million Man initiative). In general, the media have a place in creating new democratic meanings by "narrowcasting" at a local level, eliciting new habits or changes to existing habits in the context of actual conditions people encounter in everyday life.

The lesson of televangelism is that the media are most effective in a system comprised of local interpretive communities. In a democratic environment, however, these cannot be seen as absolute contexts of meaning and interpretation, but as locations between which individuals can both express and develop their uniqueness. In other words, where the electronic churches recreate community through an anthropology of identity in faith, democratic local media need to advance the potential of people as individuals and groups to realize the plurality of habits that encompass the self and its relations.

NOTES

This chapter is developed from Keyan G. Tomaselli and Fr. Nhlanhla Nkosi, "Political Economy of Televangelism: Ecumenical Broadcasting vs. Teleministries," *Communicare* (1995). We are indebted to Robert White, Fr. Nhlanhla Nkosi, Stewart M. Hoover, Ruth Teer-Tomaselli, and Eric Louw for their helpful critiques and advice. Travel funding facilitating the study was provided by the Department of Theology, University of Uppsala, Sweden, the World Council for Christian Communication, London, and the Natal University Research Fund.

1. Walter Ong, *Orality and Literacy: The Technologizing of the Word* (London: Methuen, 1982); J. Bartz, "The Many Words of Walter Ong," *Universitas: The Alumni Magazine of St. Louis University* (1988).

2. Eric Michaels, "A Model of Teleported Texts," *Continuum* 3, no. 2 (1990): 8–31.

3. Keyan G. Tomaselli and Arnold Shepperson," Resistance through Mediated Orality," in *Rethinking Media, Religion, and Culture*, ed. Stewart M. Hoover and Knut Lundby (Thousand Oaks, Calif.: Sage, 1997), 209–23.

4. Bartz, "Many Words," 25; Jack Goody, *Literacy in Traditional Societies* (Cambridge: Cambridge University Press, 1968).

5. Charles S. Peirce, *Collected Papers*, 2:302.

6. See John J. Fitzgerald, *Peirce's Theory of Signs as Foundation for Pragmatism* (The Hague: Mouton: 1966).

7. Fitzgerald, *Peirce's Theory*, 79.

8. Peirce, *Collected Papers*, 5:475.

9. Ibid., 8:184.

10. Ibid., 5:476.

11. Arnold Shepperson, "On the Social Interpretation of Cultural Experience: Reflections on Raymond Williams's Early Cultural Writing, 1958–63" (master's thesis, University of Natal, Durban, 1995), 70.

12. Michaels, "A Model of Teleported Texts," 13. It is noteworthy that Michaels began his research career with his Ph.D dissertation, an ethnographic examination of a Texas televangelist's congregation (1982).

13. Claude Shannon and Warren Weaver, *Mathematical Theory of Communication* (Urbana: University of Illinois Press: 1949).

14. Michaels, "Model of Teleported Texts," 20.

15. Peirce, *Collected Papers*, 36.

16. Agnes Heller, *Beyond Justice* (Oxford: Basil Blackwell, 1987), 302–15; Agnes Heller and Ferenc Fehér, *The Postmodern Political Condition* (Cambridge: Polity Press, 1988).

17. Ibid.

BIBLIOGRAPHY

Bartz, J. "The Many Words of Walter Ong." *Universitas: The Alumni Magazine of St. Louis University*. Saint Louis, Mo., 1988.

Budlender, D. "The Debate over Household Headship." Pretoria: Statistics South Africa (http://www.statssa.gov.za/debating/debating.htm).

Fitzgerald, John J. *Peirce's Theory of Signs as Foundation for Pragmatism*. The Hague: Mouton, 1966.

Goody, Jack. *Literacy in Traditional Societies*. Cambridge: Cambridge University Press, 1968.

Heller, Agnes. *Beyond Justice*. Oxford: Basil Blackwell, 1987.

Heller, Agnes, and Ferenc Fehér. *The Postmodern Political Condition*. Cambridge: Polity Press, 1988.

Hoover, Stewart M. *Mass Media Religion: The Social Sources of the Electronic Church*. New York: Sage, 1988.

Michaels, Eric. "A Model of Teleported Texts." *Continuum* 3, no. 2 (1990): 8–31.

Ong, W. *Orality and Literacy: The Technologizing of the Word*. London: Methuen, 1982.

Peirce, Charles Sanders. *The Collected Papers of Charles Sanders Peirce*. Vols. 1–6, ed. Charles Harteshorne and Paul Weiss. Cambridge: Harvard University Press, 1965. Vols. 7–8, ed. Arthur W. Burks. Cambridge, Harvard University Press, 1966.

Shepperson, Arnold. *On the Social Interpretation of Cultural Experience: Reflections on Raymond Williams's Early Cultural Writing, 1958–63*. Master's thesis, Durban: University of Natal, 1995.

Tomaselli, Keyan G., and Arnold Shepperson. "Popularising Semiotics." *Communication Research Trends* 11, no. 2 (1991): 1–20.

——. "Resistance through Mediated Orality." In *Rethinking Media, Religion, and Culture*, ed. Stewart M. Hoover and Knut Lundby. Thousand Oaks, Calif.: Sage, 1977.

World Association for Christian Communication. "Communication versus Alienation: Latin American Challenge of WACC." *Media Development* 31, no. 1 (1984).

White, Robert A. "Community Radio as an Alternative to Traditional Broadcasting." *Media Development* 30, no 3 (1983).

White, Robert A. "Networking and Change in Grassroots Communication." *Group Media Journal* (June 1989).

CONTRIBUTORS

Michael Berkowitz is reader in modern Jewish history at University College London (University of London). He is author of *The Jewish Self-image: American and British Perspectives* (New York University Press, 2000), *Western Jewry and the Zionist Project, 1914–1933* (Cambridge University Press, 1997), and *Zionist Culture and West European Jewry Before the First World War* (Cambridge University Press, 1993). His current work is on perceptions of Jews and criminality.

Mark Borchert is assistant professor in the Communication Studies Department of Christopher Newport University. His research examines the interconnections between media content, communication policy, and new communication technologies. In "The Challenge of Cyberspace," a chapter in *Cyberghetto or Cybertopia: Race, Class and Gender on the Internet* (Greenwood Publishing, 1998), he examines the development of the Internet as it relates to persons with disabilities.

Lynn Schofield Clark is assistant research professor at the School of Journalism and Mass Communication at the University of Colorado. She is author of *From Angels to Aliens: Teens, the Media, and Beliefs in the Supernatural* (Oxford University Press, forthcoming) and co-author of *Accounting for the Media: The Making of Family Identity* (forthcoming). She has published several articles and book chapters in the areas of new media, media and religion, and qualitative methodology. She is currently researching new media technology issues among underserved communities.

Erika Doss is professor of art history at the University of Colorado, Boulder, where she also directs the American Studies Program. She is the author of numerous articles and books, including *Benton, Pollock, and the Politics of Modernism: From Regionalism to Abstract Expressionism* (University of Chicago Press, 1991), *Spirit Poles and Flying Pigs: Public Art and Cultural Democracy in American Communities* (Smithsonian Institution Press, 1995), *Elvis Culture: Fans, Faith, and Image* (University of Kansas Press, 1999), *Looking at Life Magazine* (2001), and the forthcoming *Twentieth-Century American Art* (Oxford University Press, in press).

Jan Fernback is assistant professor in the Department of Broadcasting, Telecommunications and Mass Media at Temple University. Her dissertation, *The Wired Community* (University of Colorado, 1998), examined the meaning of virtual community in contemporary culture. Fernback has published several book chapters on the nature of cybercommunity and serves as a consultant on various Web-related projects. She is presently working on a project on the theory of cyberdemocracy.

Ronald L. Grimes is professor of religion and culture at Wilfrid Laurier University in Waterloo, Ontario, Canada. He is author of several books on ritual, including *Ritual Criticism* (University of South Carolina Press, 1990); *Reading, Writing, and Ritualizing* (Pastoral Press, 1993), *Marrying & Burying: Rites of Passage in a Man's Life* (Westview, 1995), *Readings in Ritual Studies* (Prentice-Hall, 1996), and *Deeply into the Bone: Re-inventing Rites of Passage* (University of California, 2000). He was a founding editor of the *Journal of Ritual Studies* and a frequent consultant in the area. Currently, he is working on a documentary film series on ritual as well as a book on ritual studies and performance theory.

Stewart M. Hoover is professor of media studies at the School of Journalism and Mass Communication and professor adjoint in religious studies and American studies, all at the University of Colorado. He is the author of *Religion in the News: Faith and Journalism in American Public Discourse* (Sage, 1998) *Mass Media Religion* (Sage, 1988), and co-author of *Accounting for the Media: The Making of Family Identity* (forthcoming). He is co-editor of *Rethinking Media, Religion, and Culture* (Sage, 1997) and of *Religious Television: Controversies and Conclusions* (Ablex, 1990). An internationally known researcher in religion and media, Hoover was the founding chair of the International Study Commission on Media, Religion, and

Culture and directed the first major public conference on media, religion, and culture. His current research interests are in the areas of media and religious identity.

J. Shawn Landres is a doctoral candidate in religious studies at the University of California, Santa Barbara, and a research student in social anthropology at Lincoln College, Oxford. Most recently he was a member of the faculty of the Institute of Social and Cultural Studies, Matej Bel University, Banská Bystrica, Slovakia. He has published several articles on Generation X and religion, as well as sociological and anthropological studies in ritual, identity, and civil society in East-Central Europe and the United States. He has done fieldwork in the Slovak Republic and the United States.

Bruce B. Lawrence is professor of Islamic studies, Nancy and Jeffrey Marcus Professor of Religion, and chair of the Department of Religion at Duke University. He is the author of several books, including *Defenders of God* (Harper, 1989), *Shattering the Myth* (Princeton, 1998), and most recently, *Beyond Turk and Hindu* (with David Gilmartin) (University Press of Florida, 2000). He is also author of the only comparative religion guide to the Internet: *The Complete Idiot's Guide to Religions Online* (Macmillan, 2000). In addition to his research interests in the use, and misuse, of cyberspace, he studies both premodern and modern institutional Islam (especially in South and Southeast Asia), Indo-Persian Sufism in all periods, the comparative study of religious movements, religion as ideology, ideology as religion in the twenty-first century, and the relationship of religion and violence.

Alf Linderman is the director of studies at the faculty of theology at Uppsala University. He is the author of *The Reception of Religious Television: Social Semiology Applied to an Empirical Case Study* (Almqvist and Wikell Internation, 1996) and has published several articles on media, religion, and culture. Linderman is currently involved in research projects focused on computer-mediated communication and religion, on religion in television, and on the mediation of interreligious dialogue and attitudes.

Knut Lundby is professor of media studies at the University of Oslo, Norway. He has published book chapters and articles on the relationship between "Media–religion–culture" in Norway as well as in Zimbabwe. He is co-editor of *Rethinking Media, Religion, and Culture* (Sage, 1997) and *Media and Communication: Readings in Methodology, History and Culture* (Scandinavian University Press/Oxford University Press, 1991). Lundby is currently director of intermedia, University of Oslo, an interdisciplinary center working on new media and Net-based learning.

Carolyn Marvin is associate professor of communication at the Annenberg School for Communication at the Universtiy of Pennsylvania. She is the author of *When Old Technologies Were New: Thinking About Communication in the Late Nineteenth Century* (Oxford University Press, 1988) and coauthor of *Blood Sacrifice and the Nation: Totem Rituals and the American Flag* (Cambridge University Press, 1999). She is currently working on a book about the way in which mediated events repeat and transform traditional collective ritual events.

David Morgan is Duesenberg Professor in Christianity and the Arts at Valparaiso University. He is author of *Visual Piety: A History and Theory of Popular Religious Images* (University of California Press, 1998) and *Protestants and Pictures: Religion, Visual Culture, and the Age of American Mass Production* (Oxford University Press, 1999), and editor (with Sally M. Promey) of *The Visual Culture of American Religions* (University of California Press, 2001). He is chair of the International Study Commission on Media, Religion, and Culture. Morgan was awarded a 2001–2002 fellowship by the National Endowment for the Humanities in support of his next book project, *A History of the Religious Tract in America*.

David Nash is senior lecturer in history at Oxford Brookes University and has written widely on aspects of religion, secularism, and republicanism in nineteenth- and twentieth-century Britain. His most recent monograph was *Blasphemy in Modern Britain 1789—Present* (Ashgate, 1999).

Michele Rosenthal is an instructor in the Department of Communication at the University of Haifa. Her dissertation was titled *TV: Satan or Savior?: Protestant Responses to Television in the 1950s* (University of Chicago Press, 1999). Her research interests include the reception and use of new technologies by religious communities, history of religion, and media.

John Schmalzbauer is assistant professor and E.B. Williams Fellow at the College of the Holy Cross in Worcester, Massachusetts. From 1996 to 1998 he was a postdoctoral fellow at the Center for the Study of Religion and American Culture. He has published articles in such publications as the *Journal for the Scientific Study of Religion, Sociology of Religion,* and *Poetics.* During the 1999–2000 academic year he served as a co-evaluator of the Lilly Endowment's ten-year initiative on religion and higher education. He is currently completing a book on the experiences of Catholics and evangelicals in the academic and media elite.

Arnold Shepperson is research asistant and doctoral candidate in the Graduate Center in Cultural and Media Studies at the University of Natal in Durban, South Africa. He is co-author with Keyan Tomaselli of numerous articles and book chapters on communication, semiotics, and visual anthropology. His principal research interests are the pragmatic approach to social research, and the logic of social change.

Keyan G Tomaselli is professor and director of the graduate program in Cultural and Media Studies, University of Natal, Durban. His books include *Appropriating Images: The Semiotics of Visual Representation* and *The Cinema of Apartheid*. He is editor of *Critical Arts: A Journal of South-North Cultural and Media Studies*.

Diane Winston is program officer in religion at the Pew Charitable Trusts. She is the author of *Red Hot and Righteous: The Urban Religion of the Salvation Army* (Harvard University Press, 1999). Her research interests include American evangelicalism, religion and media, urban religion, women and religion, and religion, and philanthropy.

INDEX